THE WINES OF THE RHÔNE VALLEY AND PROVENCE

ROBERT M. PARKER, JR.
Author and Publisher of *The Wine Advocate*

Drawings by
CHRISTOPHER WORMELL

Simon and Schuster
New York • London • Toronto
Sydney • Tokyo

Published by Simon and Schuster
A Division of Simon & Schuster, Inc.
Simon & Schuster Building
Rockefeller Center
1230 Avenue of the Americas
New York, NY 10020
SIMON AND SCHUSTER and colophon are registered trademarks of
Simon & Schuster, Inc.

Designed by Levavi & Levavi
Maps by Jeanyee Wong

Manufactured in the United States of America

10 9 8 7 6 5 4 3 2 1

Library of Congress Cataloging-in-Publication Data

Parker, Robert M.
  The wines of the Rhône Valley and Provence/Robert M. Parker, Jr.;
  drawings by Christopher Wormell.
     p.   cm.
  Bibliography: p.
  Includes index.
  ISBN 0-671-63379-1
  1. Wine and wine making—Rhône River Valley (Switzerland and
France) 2. Wine and wine making—France—Provence.   I. Title.
TP559.R48P37   1987
641.2′22′094458—dc 19   87-17912
                    CIP

ACKNOWLEDGMENTS

To Pat—My best friend, spouse, and lover as well as constant companion, thank you for showing me the joy of wine, teaching me French, and giving me such pleasure.

To my Mother and Father and Sarah—I thank you for your love, patience, and most importantly, for always being there when I needed.

To Bob Lescher—My dear friend, skilled representative, patient counselor, and unwavering Rhône wine enthusiast, saying thank you will never fully convey the many things, both tangible and intangible, you have so graciously provided.

To Paul Evans—Dear friend and confidante and unselfish wine enthusiast, your guidance, company, and advice will always be cherished.

To Frank Polk—Thanks for writing that article in the *Washingtonian* magazine years ago—it influenced me more than you will ever imagine.

To Jay Miller—My assistant and friend, thanks for always listening.

To Carole Lalli—This book would never have seen the light of day without your support and encouragement. Thank you for believing.

To Jill Norman—Thank you for having the courage of your convictions that an American could make a contribution in the wine-writing capital of the world—England.

To Joan Passman—Thanks for everything.

In addition, many growers and producers in the Rhône Valley and Provence were remarkably generous with their time and their wines. From the north to the south, I would like to thank Robert Jasmin, Albert

Dervieux, the Guigal family, the Chapoutier family, the Jaboulet family, the Chave family, the Clape family, the Perrin families, the Brunier family, the growers and members of the two Châteauneuf-du-Pape associations, Les Reflets and Prestige et Tradition, Jean Abeille, Paul Avril, Jérome Quiot, André Roux, Eloi Durrbach, Marcel Ott, and the Peyraud family.

Also, I would like to acknowledge the following people who have either written about or represented these marvelous wines long before they became fashionable. To John Livingstone-Learmonth and Melvyn Master, authors of the book *The Wines of the Rhône;* to Kermit Lynch, the Berkeley, California, wine merchant; to Robin and Judith Yapp, Wiltshire, England, wine merchants; and to Mark Williamson of Willi's Wine Bar in Paris; thanks for leading the way.

Finally, it is always hard for me to write about wine without being touched by the thoughts of the late Martin Bamford. His encouragement, support, and belief in this writer at the very beginning of a career will never be forgotten.

This book is dedicated to Pat, my Mother,
Father, Sarah, the late Captain David Etzel,
and to the subscribers of The Wine Advocate,
without whom none of this
would have been possible.

CONTENTS

CONTENTS

Do not search in a wine for the reflection of an exact science! The formulas of scientific oenology are only a thin competition which does not know how to respect the mysteries of eternal creation.

—THE LATE JACQUES PERRIN
Château Beaucastel
Châteauneuf-du-Pape

It is sad that few people understand naturally made, individual wines. Technology has progressed to the point that far too many wines lack the taste of their place of origin and resemble one another.

—GÉRARD CHAVE
Domaine J. L. Chave
Hermitage

The only way of guaranteeing quality is to take a small quantity from the vineyard.

—JACQUES REYNAUD
Château Rayas
Châteauneuf-du-Pape

The search for something new, for the best that man can achieve without compromise, has brought me here.

—ELOI DURRBACH
Domaine Trévallon
Coteaux d'Aix-en-Provence

For the last thirty-five years I have fought for this appellation's wines, for lower yields, for the Mourvèdre grape, for the highest quality . . . I have lived to realize my dreams.

—LUCIEN PEYRAUD
Domaine Tempier
Bandol

INTRODUCTION

After numerous trips to the Rhône Valley and Provence, the thousands of wines tasted, the hundreds of vineyards, cellars, and growers visited, and having completed the text of this book, I was still not sure how, in several short paragraphs, I could convincingly summarize two regions so vast, not only with wine riches, but with centuries of history and spectacular natural beauty and resources. Pictures could convince anyone with an eye for beauty or adventure to visit these areas. A multitude of books have documented their remarkable history. But how could I convey to you the splendor, the majesty, the value, and the sheer pleasure of these wines? I knew the only absolute way of doing this was to hand you a glass filled with this wondrous liquid. That of course I am only able to do indirectly, through the written word, and I realize that no matter how inspired, articulate, precise, enthusiastic, or vivid I may attempt to be, this prose, by any standard of measure, is wholly inadequate in portraying the magic and experience of a Guigal Côte Rôtie, a Vernay Condrieu, a Jaboulet or Chave Hermitage, a Clape Cornas, a Châteauneuf-du-Pape from Beaucastel, a Gigondas from Les Pallières, a Coteaux des Baux from the Domaine Trévallon, or a Bandol from the Domaine Tempier, to name just a few of the extraordinary wines that transcend normal wine vocabulary and establish new tasting parameters for even the most advanced wine enthusiast.

But try I will, because these are exhilarating as well as compelling wines. For many of them, their golden age was 2,000 years ago and it coincided with the Roman conquest of France (or Gaul, as it was then known). They are the products of France's oldest vineyards and have endured centuries of being ignored, misunderstood, undervalued, and, of course, unappreciated. Yet remarkably high standards of wine-making were maintained and the decade of the eighties has brought the renewed interest, praise, respect, and recognition that so many of these wonderful wines merit. While the wines of Provence remain largely uncharted territory, the wines of the Rhône are the very heart and soul of France. Despite the grandeur many of them may possess, there is nothing pretentious about their prices or their proprietors.

They represent France's and the world's most underrated great wines, and this is their story, from the humble generic Côtes du Rhônes, to the bold, innovative new vineyards of Provence, to the most sublime and celestial wines of Côte Rôtie, Hermitage, Condrieu, and Château-neuf-du-Pape. The wines, the producers, their personalities, the vintages, their successes and failures are covered in detail. This is a comprehensive close-up look at the Rhône Valley, one of France's and the world's most compelling and fascinating wine-producing regions, and Provence, one of France's most promising viticultural areas. I hope I have done them justice.

An Overview of the Appellations
of the Côtes du Rhône and Provence

APPELLATION	WHITE WINE	RED WINE	ROSÉ WINE	SPARKLING	FORTIFIED SWEET WINE
Northern Rhône					
Côte Rôtie		X			
Condrieu	X				
Château Grillet	X				
St.-Joseph	X	X			
Cornas		X			
Hermitage	X	X			
Crozes-Hermitage	X	X			
St.-Péray				X	
Southern Rhône					
Côtes du Rhône	X	X	X		
Côtes du Rhône-Villages	X	X	X		
Châteauneuf-du-Pape	X	X			
Gigondas		X	X		
Tavel			X		
Lirac	X	X	X		
Rasteau					X
Beaumes-de-Venise					X
Côtes du Ventoux	X	X	X		
Coteaux du Tricastin	X	X	X		
Provence					
Bandol	X	X	X		
Bellet	X	X			
Cassis	X	X	X		
Coteaux d'Aix-en-Provence	X	X	X		
Côtes de Provence	X	X	X		
Palette	X	X	X		
Côtes du Lubéron	X	X	X		

HOW TO USE
THIS BOOK

T he commentaries and evaluations of the growers and producers of the wines of the Rhône Valley and Provence presented in this
book are extremely comprehensive and extensive. They are a product
of a love affair with these wines that started on my first visit to that
region in 1970. Since then I have followed the producers and their wines
very closely, and in the course of the last three years I have spent a
considerable amount of time visiting the Rhône and Provence to see in
person as many of the producers as possible. These visits, together with
the numerous tastings held both in my office and at the properties of
the producers, have given me an insight and an appreciation of these
wines far greater than I ever imagined.

It goes without saying that in evaluating wines professionally, proper
glasses and correct serving temperature of the wine must be prerequi-
sites to any objective and meaningful tasting. Traditionally, the best
glasses for critical tasting have been those approved by the Interna-

tional Standards Organization. Called the ISO glass, it is tulip-shaped and has been designed for tasting. However, in my office I have begun to use a new glass developed in France several years ago. Called "L'Impitoyable" (the pitiless), this is without question the finest tasting glass ever designed. Much larger than the ISO glass, the Impitoyable glasses exaggerate the wine's bouquet, making flaws or defects much easier to spot. They are not good glasses to drink from in normal situations because their opening is so narrow, but for critical evaluation they have no peers. As for the temperature of the wine, 60°F to 65°F is best for both reds and whites. Too warm a temperature and the bouquet becomes diffuse and the taste flat. Too cold, and there is no discernible bouquet and the flavors are completely locked in by the chilling effect on the wine.

When I examine a wine critically, there is both a visual and physical examination. Against a white background the wine is first given a visual exam for its brilliance, richness, and intensity of color. For Rhône red wines, color is extremely important. Virtually all the great vintages have shared a very deep, rich, dark ruby color when young, whereas the poorer vintages often have weaker, less rich-looking colors because of poor weather and rain. So a young Rhône wine that is light in color, hazy or cloudy, or both, has serious problems. Certainly, in 1967, 1970, 1978, and 1985 the general color of the red wines was very dark. In 1980 and 1981, it was dark but generally not nearly as deep in color as these four vintages. In 1977 and 1982, the color was rather light.

In looking at an older wine, the rim of the wine next to the glass should be examined for amber, orange, rusty, or brown colors. These are normal signs of maturity, but when they appear in a good vintage of a serious wine under six or seven years old something is awry. For example, young wines that have been sloppily made and exposed to unclean barrels or air will mature at an accelerated rate and take on the look of old wines when in fact they are still relatively young in years.

In addition to looking at the color of the wines, I examine the "legs" of the wine, which are the tears or residue of the wine that run down the inside of the glass. Rich vintages tend to have "good legs" because the grapes are rich in glycerols and sugar-producing alcohol, giving the wine a viscosity that causes this "tearing" effect. Examples of vintages which produced wines with good to excellent "legs" would be 1985, 1981, 1978, and 1967.

After the visual examination is completed, the actual physical examination of the wine takes place. The physical exam is composed of two parts, the smell of the wine, which depends on the olfactory senses, and the taste of the wine, which is tested on the palate. After swirling a wine, the nose must be placed into the glass (not the wine) to smell the aromas that the wine is giving off. This is an extremely critical step because the aroma and odor of the wine will tell the examiner the ripeness and richness of the underlying fruit, the state of maturity, and whether there is anything unclean or otherwise suspicious about the wine. The smell of a wine, young or old, will tell a great deal about its quality, and no responsible professional taster understates the significance of a wine's odors and aromas, often called the nose or bouquet. Emile Peynaud, in his classic book on wine tasting, *Le Goût du Vin* (Bordas, 1983), states nine principal categories of wine aromas. They are:

1. animal odors: smells of game, beef, venison
2. balsamic odors: smells of pine trees, resin, vanilla
3. woody odors: smells of new wood of oak barrels
4. chemical odors: smells of acetone, mercaptan, yeasts, hydrogen sulfide, lactic and fermentation odor
5. spicy odors: smells of pepper, cloves, cinnamon, nutmeg, ginger, truffles, anise, mint
6. empyreumatic odors: smells of crème brûlée, smoke, toast, leather, coffee
7. floral odors: smells of flowers, violets, roses, lilacs, jasmine
8. fruity odors: smells of blackcurrants, raspberries, cherries, plums, apricots, peaches, figs
9. vegetal odors: smells of herbs, tea, mushrooms, vegetables

The presence or absence of some or all of these aromas, their intensity, their complexity, their persistence, all serve to create the bouquet or nose of a wine that can be said to be distinguished and interesting, or flawed and simple.

Once the wine's aroma or bouquet has been examined thoroughly, the wine is tasted, slushed, or chewed around on the palate while also inhaling to release the wine's aromas. The weight, richness, depth, balance, and length of a wine are apparent from the tactile impression the wine leaves on the palate. Sweetness is experienced on the tip of the tongue, saltiness just behind the tongue's tip, acidity on the sides, and bitterness at the back. Most professional tasters will spit the wine out, although a bit of wine is swallowed. The finish or length of a wine, its ability to give off aromas and flavors even though it is no longer on the palate, is the major difference between a good young wine and a great young wine. When the flavor and the aroma of the wine seem to last and last on the palate, it is usually a great, rich wine that has just been tasted. The great wines and great vintages are always characterized by the purity, opulence, richness, depth, and ripeness of the fruit from which the wines are made. When the wines have sufficient tannin and acidity, the balance is struck. It is these traits that separate many a great 1985, 1978, or 1967 from a good 1983 or 1981.

RATING THE PRODUCERS/GROWERS

Who's who in the world of wine becomes readily apparent after years of tasting and visiting the vineyards and wine cellars of the world's producers and growers. Great producers are, unfortunately, still quite rare, but certainly more growers and producers today are making better wine, with better technology and more knowledge than ever before. The charts that follow rate the producers on a five-star system, awarding five stars and an "outstanding" rating to those producers deemed to be the very best, four stars to those who are "excellent," three stars to "good" producers, and two stars or one star to "average" and "below average" producers. Since the aim of the book is to provide the names of the very best producers, the content is dominated by the top producers rather than the less successful ones.

The few growers/producers who have received five-star ratings are indeed among those who make the world's finest wines. They have been selected for this rating for two reasons: they make the greatest wine of their particular appellation and they are remarkably consistent and reliable even in mediocre and poor vintages. Any ratings, whether specific numerical ratings of individual wines or classifications of growers, are likely to create controversy among not only the growers but wine tasters themselves. But if done impartially, with a global viewpoint and at first hand, on the premises ("sur place"), and with some knowledge of the wines, the producers, and the type and quality of the winemaking, such ratings can be reliable and powerfully informative. The important thing for readers to remember is that those growers/producers who receive either a four-star or five-star rating are producers to search out; I suspect few consumers will ever be disappointed with their wines. The three-star rated growers/producers are less consistent, but can be expected to make fine wines in the very good to excellent vintages. Their weaknesses come either from the fact that their vineyards are not so strategically placed, or because for financial or other reasons they are unable to make the severe selections year after year that are necessary to make only the finest quality wine. In short, purchasing their wines in the less than spectacular vintages is fraught with greater risk.

Rating the growers/producers is one of this book's most significant features and its importance cannot be underestimated. Years of wine tasting have taught me many things, but the more one tastes and assimilates knowledge, the more one begins to isolate the handful of truly world-class growers and producers who seem to rise above the crowd in great as well as mediocre vintages. I always admonish consumers against blind faith in one grower or producer, or one specific vintage, but the producers and growers rated "outstanding" and "excellent" are as close to a guarantee of high quality as you are likely to find.

TASTING NOTES AND RATINGS

For each appellation, the growers/producer are listed alphabetically and their current wines are reviewed, scored, and commented upon. In this instance, great attention has been given to trying to provide an overview of the style and quality level of the producer/grower. Such factors as whether the producer is steadily improving the wine's quality, resting on its allegedly superior reputation, or slipping in quality because of mismanagement, replanting, or simple negligence are issues that I deem extremely important to bring to the attention of readers. Related matters regarding the size of the estate, vinification methods, choice of grape varieties, and insights into the personality of the producer are also provided.

All of my tastings were done in peer-group, single-blind conditions, if possible (meaning that the same type of wines are tasted against one another and the producers' names are not known), either in my tasting room or in the cellars of the producers. The ratings reflect an independent, critical look at the wines. Neither the wine's price nor the reputation of the producer/grower affect the rating in any manner. I spend three months of every year tasting in vineyards. During the other months, six- and sometimes seven-day work weeks are devoted solely to tasting and writing. I do not participate in wine judgings or trade tastings for many reasons, but principal among these are the following: (1) I prefer to taste from an entire bottle of wine, (2) I find it essential to have properly sized and cleaned professional tasting glasses, (3) the temperature of the wine must be correct, and (4) I alone will determine the time allocated to the number of wines to be critiqued.

The numerical rating given is a guide to what I think of the wine vis-à-vis its peer group. Certainly, wines rated above 85 are very good to excellent, and any wine rated 90 or above will be outstanding for its particular type. Although some have suggested that scoring is unfair to a beverage that has been so romantically extolled for centuries, the fact of the matter is that wine is no different than any other product being sold to the consumer—there are specific standards of quality that full-time wine professionals recognize, and there are benchmark wines against which all others can be judged. I know of no one with three or four different glasses of wine in front of him, regardless of how good or bad the wines might be, who cannot say "I prefer this one to that one." Scoring wines is simply taking a professional's informed opinion and applying some sort of numerical system to it on a consistent basis. Scoring permits rapid communication of information to expert and novice alike.

The rating system I employ in my wine journal, *The Wine Advocate*, is the one I have utilized in this book. It is a 100-point scale, the most repugnant of all wines meriting 50 since that is the meaningful starting point of the scale, and any rating below it not worth calculating; the most glorious, perfect gustatory experience commands 100. I prefer my system to the more widely quoted 20-point scale called the Davis Scale (of the University of California at Davis) because it permits much more flexibility in scoring. It is also easier to understand because it corresponds to the American grading system most of us have experienced in school, and it avoids the compression of scores from which the Davis Scale suffers. It is not without its own problems, though, because readers will often wonder what difference there is between an 86 and an 87, both very good wines. The only answer I can give is a simple one, that when tasted side by side I thought the 87-point wine slightly better than the 86-point wine.

The score given for a specific wine reflects the quality of the wine at its best. I often tell people that evaluating a wine and assigning a score to a beverage that will change and evolve in many cases for up to ten or more years is analogous to taking a photograph of a marathon runner. Much can be ascertained, but the wine will continue to evolve and change—it is a work in progress. If I happen to taste from an obviously badly corked or defective bottle, I will try another, since a wine from such a single bad bottle does not indicate an entirely spoiled batch. Many of the wines reviewed here have been tasted many times, and the score represents a sort of cumulative average of the wine's performance in tastings to date. Scores, however, do not tell the entire story about a wine. You may find that the commentary that accompanies the ratings offers more information regarding the wine's style and personality, its relative quality level vis-à-vis its peers, and its relative value and aging potential than any score could ever possibly indicate. The easiest way for the reader to understand my scoring system is to remember the grades received in school.

Here then is a general guide to interpreting the numerical ratings: 90–100 is equivalent to an A and it should be given for an outstanding or excellent special effort. Wines in this category are the very best produced for their type and, like a three-star Michelin restaurant, worth a special effort to find and try. There is a big difference between a 90 and a 99, but both are top marks. As you will note throughout the text, there are few wines that actually make it into this top category, simply because there just are not many truly great wines.

80–89 is equivalent to a B in school and such a wine, particularly in the 85–89 range, is very, very good; many of the wines that fall into this range often are great values as well. I would not hesitate to have any of these wines in my own personal collection.

70–79 represents a C, or average mark, but obviously 79 is a much more desirable score than 70. Wines that receive scores between 75 and 79 are generally pleasant, straightforward wines that just lack complexity, character, or depth. If inexpensive, they may be ideal for uncritical quaffing.

Below 70 is a D or an F, depending on where you went to school; for wine too it is a sign of an unbalanced, flawed, or terribly dull or diluted wine that will be of little interest to the smart wine consumer.

In terms of awarding points, my scoring system gives a wine 50 points to start. The wine's general color and appearance merit up to 5 points. Since most wines today have been well made thanks to modern technology and the increased participation of professional oenologists, most tend to receive at least 4, often 5 points. The aroma and bouquet merit up to 15 points. Obviously, the intensity level and extract of the aroma and bouquet are important, as well as the wine's cleanliness (i.e., it is free of any chemical or foul smells). The flavor and finish merit up to 20 points, and again, intensity of flavor, balance, cleanliness, and depth and length on the palate are all important considerations when giving out points. Finally, the overall quality level or potential for further evolution and improvement (aging) merits up to 10 points.

Scores are important for the reader to gauge a professional critic's overall qualitative placement of a wine vis-à-vis its peers. But don't ignore the description of the wine's style, personality, and potential, which are just as important. No scoring system is perfect, but a system that provides for flexibility in scores, if applied without prejudice and fairly, can quantify different levels of wine quality and impart a professional's judgment quickly and decisively to the reader. If implemented properly, then, this book will lead you to the finest wines as well as the very finest wine values from the Rhône Valley and Provence. But no scoring system could ever convey the hedonistic experience of wine that arises from the ambience, gorgeous setting, excellent food, and fine company that may accompany it.

ABOUT THE BOOK'S ORGANIZATION

This book is broken down into three major parts: Part I, The Wines of the Northern Rhône; Part II, The Wines of the Southern Rhône; and Part III, The Wines of Provence.

Within each of these parts, the sections are organized by appellation, followed by a small box of facts summarizing the wines of that area, introductory text about the appellation, a chart evaluating the growers and producers, and general comments about the recent vintages for that specific appellation. Afterwards, the best and best-known growers and producers are listed alphabetically and their wines and winemaking styles are analyzed in detail. In short, each appellation is set up as follows:

1. the name of the appellation
2. an easy-to-access "facts box" summarizing in brief the salient points of that appellation
3. introductory text on that appellation
4. a quick reference chart to that appellation's best producers and growers
5. a summary of recent vintages
6. an alphabetical listing of the producers with commentary, tasting notes, and evaluations of their wines

I

THE

NORTHERN

RHÔNE

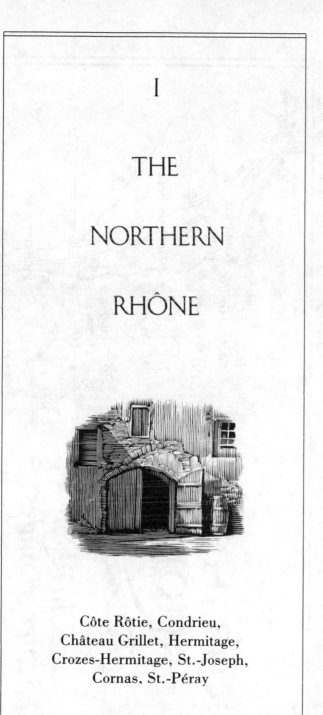

Côte Rôtie, Condrieu,
Château Grillet, Hermitage,
Crozes-Hermitage, St.-Joseph,
Cornas, St.-Péray

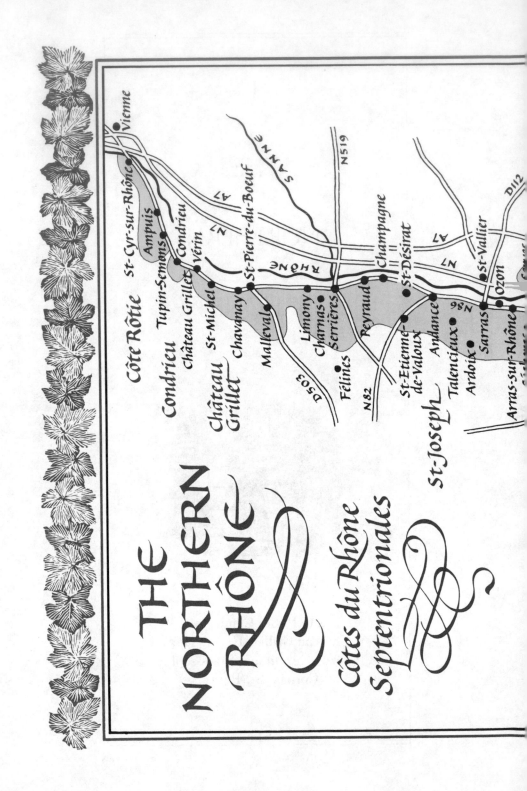

THE
NORTHERN
RHÔNE

Côtes du Rhône
Septentrionales

Côte Rôtie

Condrieu

Château
Grillet

St-Joseph

Vienne

St-Cyr-sur-Rhône

Ampuis

Tupin-Semons

Condrieu

Château Grillet

Vérin

St-Michel

St-Pierre-du-Boeuf

Chavanay

Malleval

Limony

Charnas

Serrières

Félines

Peyraud

Champagne

St-Désirat

St-Vallier

Ozon

St-Etienne-
de-Valoux

Andance

Talencieux

Ardoix

Sarras

Arras-sur-Rhône

SAÔNE

RHÔNE

N 519

N 7

A 7

N 86

N 82

D 503

D 112

A 7

N 7

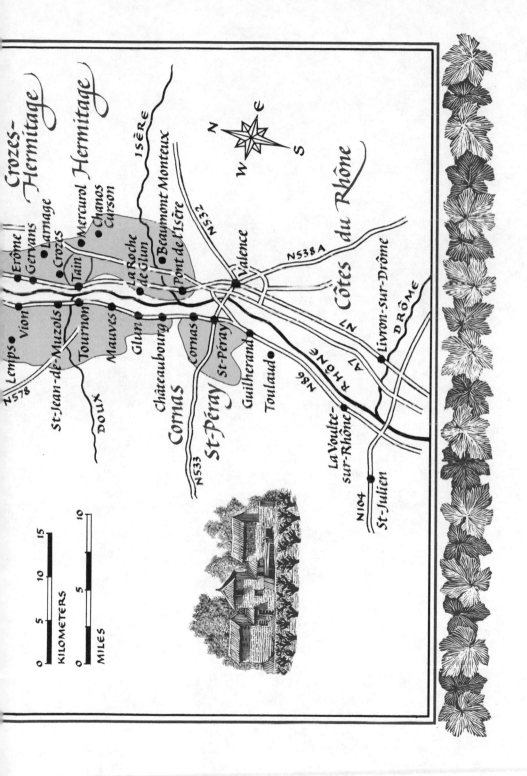

Crozes-Hermitage

Mercurol *Hermitage*

Érôme
Gervans
Larnage
Crozes
Chanos Curson
Tain
Beaumont Monteux
La Roche de Glun
Pont de l'Isère
ISÈRE
N532
N538A
Valence
Côtes du Rhône
Livron-sur-Drôme
DRÔME
Lemps
Vion
St-Jean-de-Muzols
Tournon
Mauves
Glun
Châteaubourg
Cornas
St-Péray
DOUX
Cornas
St-Péray
Guilherand
Toulaud
N578
N533
N86
N7
A7
RHÔNE
La Voulte-sur-Rhône
St-Julien
N104

N
E
W
S

KILOMETERS
0   5   10   15
MILES
0   5   10

INTRODUCTION

The Rhône River starts as a trickle of water in the icy depths of Switzerland and passes in view of some of that country's best vineyards before it enters France 44 miles west of Geneva. It flows quickly through the gorges of the Jura Mountains in eastern France and then southwesterly until it intersects and absorbs the waters of another river, the Saône, at Lyons, France's second largest city as well as a great gastronomic and commercial center. The northern viticultural region of the Rhône begins just 20 miles south of Lyons at Ampuis where the turbulent river surges southward through steep hillsides. It is there that the wines of Côte Rôtie are made on the western bank. One hundred twenty-five miles later, at Valence, the vineyards of the northern Rhône terminate. In between there are eight major appellations and one simple Côtes du Rhône appellation. The two appellations of Hermitage and Crozes-Hermitage are the only wine zones to sit on the eastern bank of the Rhône. The others, Côte Rôtie, Condrieu, Château Grillet, St.-Joseph, Cornas, and St.-Péray, all sit on the western bank. Côte Rôtie and Cornas make only red wine. Condrieu, Château Grillet, and St.-Péray make white wine exclusively. Hermitage, St.-Joseph, and Crozes-Hermitage produce both red and white wine, with the great majority being red. Interestingly, there is no rosé made in the northern Rhône, except from the few areas entitled only to the generic Côtes du Rhône designation, although no important generic Côtes du Rhônes have been produced in the northern Rhône.

The apparent geological characteristics of the northern Rhône are the steep hillside vineyards planted on granite soil. All of the best vineyards overlook the swift-moving, dangerously deep and swirling Rhône River.

The range and style of wines made here are considerable. At Côte Rôtie and Hermitage there are red wines that undoubtedly have the complexity and richness of the finest classified-growth Bordeaux or Grand Cru burgundies. At Condrieu there are stunningly fragrant, exotic wines that are among the most pleasurable as well as rarest on the face of the earth. At Cornas the world's most massive and densest dry red table wine is produced. At the other appellations are wines of considerable value, but also boring, dull, lifeless wines. Yet all of them share one similarity—they have suffered virtual anonymity through most of this century, something that appears incomprehensible given their quality and the fact that they are made from the oldest vineyards in France as well as being produced in and around towns that have witnessed some of the most exciting history of France.

The geography, the climate, and of course the wines of the northern Rhône are very different from those of the southern Rhône. In the south, the wines can be the product of over a dozen different grape varieties, and in most cases at least three different grapes are used for making red wine and two to three for white wine. In the north, there are only four grape varieties permitted in the eight principal appellations. In actuality, there are only three grapes employed with any regularity. For red wine, the Syrah is the only accepted red varietal. For white wine, the fickle, rare Viognier is planted exclusively in Condrieu and at Château Grillet, as well as in Côte Rôtie. At St.-Joseph, Crozes-Hermitage, Hermitage, and St.-Péray, the white varietal in favor is the Marsanne, although tiny amounts of Roussanne are also seen. While all of these grapes are grown in the southern Rhône, they do not play major roles in the winemaking there, but instead are supporting cast members, for it is the Grenache which holds center stage in the south.

The following sections will take you through the northern Rhône appellations starting in the north with Côte Rôtie and then proceeding south until terminating at St.-Péray, the final appellation of the northern Rhône. The quality of the wines, their characteristics, aging potential, as well as the quality of the growers and producers are analyzed in detail. Tasting notes of recent and older vintages are provided for all the leading producers. The northern Rhône produces three of the greatest wines in the world—the white wines of Condrieu and red wines of Côte Rôtie and Hermitage. The latter two are also remarkably long-lived. Most of my wine education started with the great classics of Bordeaux. It is these wines, from both humble and grand châteaux, that have given me such great satisfaction and pleasure in the past, and continue to do so today. However, the most exhilarating moments I have had have been not with a glass of Margaux or Pétrus in front of me, but with a mature, top Côte Rôtie or Hermitage. I believe anyone who gives these remarkable wines a chance will partake of a momentous gustatory experience.

CÔTE RÔTIE

One of France's Greatest Red Wines

CÔTE RÔTIE AT A GLANCE

Type of wine produced:	Red wine only
Grape varieties planted:	Syrah and a tiny quantity of Viognier (up to 20% can be added)
Acres currently under vine:	320
Quality level:	Exceptional, among the finest red wine in the world
Aging potential:	5–30 years
General characteristics:	Fleshy, rich, very fragrant, smoky, full-bodied, stunning wines
Greatest recent vintages:	1985, 1983, 1978, 1976, 1969
Price range:	$12–$50

Côte Rôties have become the most fashionable and most demanded wines of the Rhône Valley. Whether it is the extraordinary, sometimes explosive perfume—often consisting of cassis, raspberries, smoky or roasted aromas—or its cascade of velvety, berry-flavored fruit flavors, Côte Rôtie is an undeniably seductive, voluptuous wine that takes little experience to appreciate.

The first view one has of Côte Rôtie (literally translated, "the roasted hillside"), which sits on the western bank of the Rhône with a perfect southerly exposure, is quite unforgettable. Just 20 minutes by car south of Lyons is the tiny, rather drab town of Ampuis, and looming over the town are the precipitously steep terraced slopes of Côte Rôtie. Except for the vineyards along the Mosel River in Germany, there are none in all of Europe that appear so vertical and forbidding to maintain as those of Côte Rôtie. Cultivated entirely by hand, the narrow terraces of vines and difficult footing have made the use of machines impossible, and in many places even oxen and horses are useless. Undoubtedly, the huge expense of human labor has caused many a less hearty grower and winemaker to look elsewhere for a career in winemaking.

Côte Rôtie has a remarkably long history, and of course there are a handful of legends surrounding the established facts. One school of thought attributes the origin of these vineyards to the ancient Greeks, claiming they introduced viticulture to Côte Rôtie in the sixth century B.C. This line of thought has its critics who claim it was the Romans, in the first century A.D., who planted vines on these steep hillsides. It is this latter theory that seems more plausible, given the stature of the city of Vienne as a center for Roman activity. Vienne, only five miles away, is still a hallowed site for Roman ruins, particularly the temples of Livia and Augustus, believed to have been constructed 100 years before Christ's birth. Whichever theory is true, it seems doubtful that the look of these vineyards has changed much over the last 1,900 years. There can be no doubt, however, that the size of the area under vine has increased, and will continue to do so given the great demand for this wine and the higher and higher prices Côte Rôtie commands. At present, 320 acres that at best are capable of producing less than 50,000 cases of wine are planted. This includes all of the hillside vineyards and a burgeoning, even alarming, number of new vineyards above the hills on the level plateau behind the town of Ampuis. Much of the plateau is officially within the Côte Rôtie appellation boundaries, and expansion will no doubt continue in these less desirable spots. While wine pro-

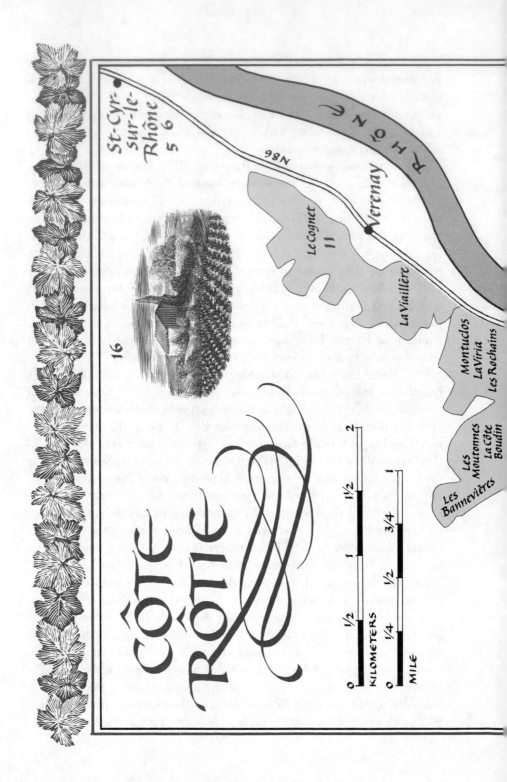

CÔTE RÔTIE

St-Cyr-
sur-le-
Rhône
5 6

16

N86

RHÔNE

Le Cognet
11

Verenay

La Viaillère

Montuclos
La Viria
Les Rochains

Les Moutonnes
La Côte Boudin

Les
Bannevières

KILOMETERS
0   ½   1   1½   2

MILE
0   ¼   ½   ¾   1

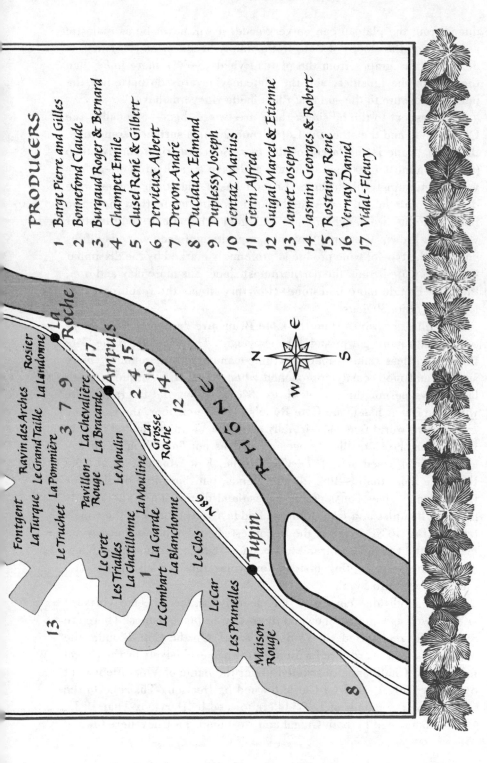

duced from the plateau can be very good, it will never be as majestic as that from the slopes of Côte Rôtie simply because the soil is not as desirable, the grapes from the plateau yield 15–30% more juice than those from the hillsides, and the plateau vineyards do not enjoy the perfect exposure to the sun that the hillside vineyards have.

With respect to the hillsides, there are two of them—one called the Côte Blonde and the other the Côte Brune. From a surface perspective, the Côte Brune is the larger of the two. Both are frighteningly steep (they are almost 1,000 feet in height and have a gradient of 30–35°) as well as stunningly photogenic. Legend has it that their names were derived from a feudal lord named Maugiron who bequeathed these two hillsides to his two daughters, one with golden blond hair and the other with dark brown. Certainly the soil composition of each slope is different, and the type of wine produced profoundly marked by the dissimilar soils. The Côte Brune, the northernmost slope, has more clay and iron, the Côte Blonde more limestone. How this affects the resulting wines is usually quite obvious.

As a rule, the wines from the Côte Brune are darker in color, more tannic, with more power and obvious weight. The wines from the Côte Blonde are less tannic, more perfumed and fragrant, rounder, more supple, and more easily approached when young. Côte Rôtie's appellation laws permit the use of up to 20% Viognier, the fragrant white wine grape that has made Côte Rôtie's closest neighbor, the Condrieu appellation, world famous. Virtually all of the Viognier planted in Côte Rôtie is on the Côte Blonde because it does not flourish in the heavy clay-and-iron-based soil of the Côte Brune. Few winemakers at Côte Rôtie use more than 5–10% in their blends, but those that do all agree that Viognier gives considerable finesse and distinction to the already majestic bouquet of a Côte Rôtie and adds a velvety note to the wine's texture. But 100% Syrah is the uncontested preference of most winemakers, and the modern trend has been to reduce the amount of Viognier in the wine, opting instead for wines that for all intents and purposes are pure Syrah.

The two hillsides consist of increasingly famous specific vineyard sites as well as equally renowned *lieux-dits*, or place names. There are 54 officially recognized vineyards or *"mas."* On the Côte Blonde, the most famous vineyards are La Mouline (owned exclusively by the Guigal family), La Chatillonne (marketed under the name of Vidal-Fleury but owned by Guigal), and La Garde (owned by Dervieux-Thaize). On the Côte Brune the names of La Viaillère (owned by Dervieux-Thaize), La Landonne (owned by both Guigal and Rostaing), La Chevalière (owned by several growers, most notably Jasmin), and La Turque (a Guigal vineyard) can all be found on bottles of Côte Rôtie. Other *mas* or vineyards of Côte Rôtie include La Viria, Le Truchet, Les Triottes, Tharamon de Gron, Les Sévenières, Rosier, Les Rochains, Les Prunelles, La Pommière, Le Pavillon Rouge, Nève, Les Moutonnes, Le Moulin, Montuclos, Montmain, Le Mollar, Les Lézardes, Lancement, Les Journaries, Janville, La Guillambaude, La Balaiyat, Le Grand Taille, Les Grandes Places, La Garelle, La Giroflavie, Les Germines, Les Gagères, La Fuzonne, Le Fourvier, Le Cret, La Côte Baudin, Corps des Loups, Combe de Calon, Le Combart, Le Cognet, Le Clos, Chez Guerard, Chez Gaboulet, La Chevalière, Le Chavaroches, Chambretout, Le Car, La Brocarde, Les Bannevières, La Blanchonne, Bassemon, and Les Arches. Nevertheless, the vast majority of Côte Rôties on the market will usually not be designated by a single vineyard, but are simply called "Côte Rotie, Côte Blonde et Brune," referring to the fact that the wine is made from grapes grown on both hillsides. If the wine does not indicate either the Côte Blonde or Brune or both, you can be sure that the wine has been produced largely from vineyards on the less desirable plateau.

For the last decade, the production of high-quality Côte Rôtie has been dominated by the Guigal family, who has increased its vineyard holdings and taken the quality of its winemaking to the highest possible level. Their winemaking philosophy has also had a profound influence on other growers, some of whom are quite open in their criticism of the Guigals' introduction of new oak barrels to age Côte Rôties, and of their concept of vineyard-designated, luxury-priced Côte Rôties. Despite general philosophical disagreements of how Côte Rôtie is to be made and aged, there is no question that the overall quality of winemaking in this tiny appellation is extremely high. Guigal does indeed produce the appellation's most glamorous wines, but superb Côte Rôtie is also made by a bevy of committed growers such as Dervieux-Thaize, Gentaz-Dervieux, Rostaing, Jasmin, Barge, Champet, Burgaud, Jamet, and Duclaux.

RECENT VINTAGES

1986—Côte Rôtie received a great deal of rain in late August and early September, but the harvest itself occurred under ideal conditions. The grapes were plentiful and healthy, and this should be a good, sometimes very good, abundant vintage of quick-maturing, easy to appreciate wines. Optimum maturity: 1990–1998.

1985—I believe time will establish that Côte Rôtie enjoyed the greatest success of all appellations of France in 1985. The wines are splendidly concentrated, very deep in color, somewhat low in acidity but magnificently perfumed and capable of aging for 10–15 years. They will, however, drink well young. Virtually everyone had great success in 1985, but it was a particularly great year for Dervieux-Thaize, Gentaz-Dervieux, Guigal, Jasmin, Rostaing, and Vidal-Fleury. Nineteen eighty-five will also be remembered as the year the Guigal family purchased the great Rhône winemaking firm of Vidal-Fleury. Optimum maturity: 1988–2000.

1984—Notwithstanding the vitriolic press this vintage received prior to any grapes being harvested, many of the wines have turned out to be quite good, well concentrated, and capable of 5–10 years of life. There are even a handful of real stars in this vintage. For example, Burgaud, Dervieux-Thaize's La Viaillère, Gentaz-Dervieux, Guigal's La Mouline and La Landonne, Jasmin, and in particular Rostaing's Côte Blonde are among the finest wines made in France in 1984. Optimum maturity: 1987–1994.

1983—Considered a great classic year, the 1983s are infused with a tremendous lashing of tannin that precludes enjoyable drinking until at least 1990. Deeply colored, full-bodied, rather tough wines were the result of a season marked by a swelteringly hot, dry summer. This is clearly a vintage for the patient, so don't be surprised to see a handful of revisionist writers decrying it in a few years as being "too tannic." Guigal's La Mouline and La Landonne are pure perfection in 1983, but Rostaing, Jasmin, Dervieux-Thaize, Gentaz Dervieux, B. Levet, and Burgaud also excelled. The 1983s require cellaring until at least 1990, and will indeed make "old bones"—drinking well into the next century. Optimum maturity: 1993–2010.

1982—There was no question that Mother Nature provided outstanding raw materials for the growers to work with in 1982, but the torridly hot harvest conditions created numerous fermentation problems that resulted in some wines becoming volatile and extremely fragile. Few of Côte Rôtie's small growers are equipped to cool their old open oak fermenters and therein was the principal problem plaguing an otherwise fine vintage. In complete contrast to the tannic, now closed and dormant 1983s, the 1982s at their best are remarkably seductive, voluptuous, intense wines that can easily capture a taster's undivided attention. As flattering as some reports are, they must be monitored with a degree of caution since natural acidities are low. Some wines have surprisingly high levels of volatile acidity. Guigal and Gentaz-Dervieux turned in superstar performances in 1982. Honorable mentions would no doubt go to Barge and Champet, but elsewhere in Côte Rôtie be cautious and taste before committing to any sizeable purchase. Optimum maturity: 1987–1997.

1981—This is the least successful vintage for Côte Rôtie of the decade. The wines are adequately concentrated, decently colored, but rarely seem to charm or provide the exhilarating level of pleasure that Côte Rôtie so often can. They are rather compact, one-dimensional wines, although the Guigal top cuvées La Mouline and La Landonne are excellent. This is not a vintage to lay down, and though one is unlikely to be disappointed by the 1981s, they should be consumed over the next 5–6 years as they are not likely to improve further. Optimum maturity: now–1990.

1980—A terribly underrated vintage, the 1980s offer captivating drinking today, yet their balance should ensure at least another 3–5 years of positive evolution. The wines are surprisingly deep in color, round, very fruity, and supple. As Côte Rôties go, they are not massive or particularly concentrated, but they are charming, elegant, and delicious. Guigal's La Mouline and La Landonne are exceptional. Optimum maturity: now–1992.

1979—As is the tendency everywhere after a great vintage, the subsequent year becomes lost in the hype and publicity surrounding "the great one." Such was the problem for the 1979s, conceived in the shadow of the 1978s, the northern Rhône's finest overall vintage since 1961. The Côte Rôties are all fully mature except for Guigal's La Landonne and Dervieux-Thaize's La Viaillère. The 1979s are rich, full-bodied, rather chunky wines with good character. They can be safely drunk over the next 5–9 years. Jasmin's Côte Rôtie is totally charming and *à point* (or fully mature). Optimum maturity: now–1994.

1978—A great and memorable vintage, the 1978 Côte Rôties are splendidly concentrated, impeccably balanced, gorgeously perfumed, and will keep improving for another decade. Everyone did something special in 1978, and until the Guigal family assumed control in 1985, this was the last great vintage for the house of Vidal-Fleury. Guigal's La Mouline and La Landonne are the sort of stuff that creates legends along the lines of such immortal wines as the 1929 and 1945 Mouton-Rothschilds, or 1947 Cheval Blanc or Pétrus. Optimum maturity: 1988–2005.

OLDER VINTAGES

Given the minuscule production of Côte Rôtie, rarely does it appear on the auction market, the older vintages are only likely to come out of some remarkably perceptive collector's cave. Nineteen seventy-seven was a viciously cruel vintage overall for France, though not bad in Côte Rôtie, but those wines should be drunk up. Nineteen seventy-six is a great vintage in Côte Rôtie and the wines can be kept for another 5–10 years, much like the burgundies of that year. The 1975 vintage was a disastrously bad one, and 1974 almost as poor. Nineteen seventy-three was adequate, 1972 better than elsewhere in France, 1971 very good but now showing signs of fatigue, and 1970 very much the same.

In the sixties, 1969 was a fabulously great vintage for Côte Rôtie. The La Mouline of that year is one of the single finest wines I have ever tasted. Nineteen sixty-four is an excellent vintage, as is 1961, but it is very unlikely that any of these wines will be found in the marketplace.

A Personal Rating of the Côte Rôtie Producers

*****(OUTSTANDING PRODUCERS)*

Gentaz-Dervieux	Robert Jasmin
E. Guigal	René Rostaing

****(EXCELLENT PRODUCERS)*

Gilles and Pierre Barge	Albert Dervieux-Thaize
Bernard Burgaud	Joseph Jamet
Emile Champet	Vidal-Fleury (before 1979 and after 1984)

***(GOOD PRODUCERS)*

Chol de Boisseyt	André Drevon
Claude Bonnefond	Edmond Duclaux
M. Chapoutier	Alfred Gérin
René and Gilbert Clusel	Paul Jaboulet Ainé
Delas Frères	L. de Vallouit

GILLES AND PIERRE BARGE ****

Gilles Barge, son of Pierre Barge, is gradually assuming full control and authority over this small domaine he owns with his father. Gilles is one of the younger growers in Côte Rôtie and is also one of the few individuals who seems to sense winemaking from a global point of view. An articulate man, Gilles Barge spoke out strongly against filtration, which he experimented with several years ago only to be saddened by the results. His wines spend two years in large wooden foudres (large oak casks), although in 1985 he purchased six new burgundy barrels, openly admitting that his use of new oak barrels was influenced by Guigal's belief in them. The family owns and rents 11 acres of vines of which 80% are on the Côte Brune. One-half of their vines are 35–40 years old, one-third 12 years old, and the remainder very young. His Côte Rôtie is made with 4–5% Viognier. The young, wiry Barge thinks most vintages of his Côte Rôtie are at their best between 5 and 10 years of age, but he claims great vintages like 1978 will keep 20 years. Gilles and his father also have begun to produce several barrels of Condrieu each year that also looks to be a winner.

VINTAGES

1985—*Côte Rôtie*—Very deeply colored, the 1985 has deeply concentrated fruit, a fragrant bouquet of blackberries, a touch of vanillin from partial aging in new casks, full body, and a very long, ripe, tannic finish. Anticipated maturity: 1991–2000. Last tasted 6/86.
•
90

1984—*Côte Rôtie*—Medium ruby in color, the 1984 has rather high acidity, a spicy bouquet of cherries and saddle leather, medium body, and a lean, rather dry finish. Anticipated maturity: now–1990. Last tasted 8/86.
•
82

1983—*Côte Rôtie*—A super bouquet of cassis and spice is first-rate. On the palate, the wine is fleshy, full-bodied, very tannic, and quite hard. Great patience is required. Anticipated maturity: 1993–2000. Last tasted 6/86.
•
89

1982—*Côte Rôtie*—A nicely concentrated, robust, somewhat coarsely textured wine, the 1982 is a dusty, rather awkward, clumsy wine that should be drunk over the next 5–8 years because of its fragility. Last tasted 6/86.
•
82

BERNARD BURGAUD ****

This 30-year-old winemaker whose winery is located on the top of the ridge overlooking Côte Rôtie in Le Champin should be taken very seriously. His father recently died, but he obviously trained his son well. The four vintages they have produced here are all excellent, with Burgaud's 1984 one of the top wines of this vintage. Burgaud owns 7.4 acres, two-thirds on the hillside and one-third on the plateau. I noticed he had six new barrels (a tiny percentage of the total) in his cellar, an underground, cool cave that is meticulously kept. Production is only 800 cases in a good year. The wine is fermented at a very high temperature for extraction purposes, kept 18 to 26 months in small barrels, and bottled unfiltered. Despite only four vintages behind him, Burgaud appears to be one of the up and coming stars of this appellation. The fact that he also produces one-third of his wine from the plateau is an encouraging sign for that much maligned segment of the Côte Rôtie appellation. His style of wine is one of exceptional elegance and purity of flavors. There are more concentrated and certainly more powerful wines made in Côte Rôtie, but only Jasmin's exquisite Côte Rôtie is more elegant than that of Burgaud.

VINTAGES

1985—*Côte Rôtie*—By comparison with the elegantly wrought wines
· Burgaud produced in previous vintages, the 1985 is a rather
91 corpulent, dense, powerful wine. Yet the wonderfully clean, ripe blackcurrant fruitiness is abundantly displayed with good acidity as well as marvelous depth and length. Anticipated maturity: 1989–1997. Last tasted 6/86.

1984—*Côte Rôtie*—This wine rivals the best wines of Côte Rôtie and
· anything else produced in France in 1984. Very deeply colored,
88 fragrant, rich and supple on the palate, but well defined with solid backbone, this is a real sleeper. Anticipated maturity: 1988–1996. Last tasted 12/86.

1983—*Côte Rôtie*—Surprisingly, the 1983 appears to me to be not as
· deep or as concentrated as either the 1984 or 1985, though Bur-
87 gaud strongly argues that he believes his 1983 is better. It relies on its elegant, peppery, raspberry-scented bouquet and me-dium-bodied, graceful flavors rather than pure muscle and flesh to disarm the taster. Anticipated maturity: 1988–1996. Last tasted 2/87.

1982—*Côte Rôtie*—Fully mature, supple, round, and fruity, the 1982
· marked Burgaud's debut vintage. Though very attractive and
85 well made in the fiery temperatures of this vintage, it does not show the class and elegance of subsequent offerings. Drink over the next 2–4 years. Last tasted 6/86.

EMILE CHAMPET****

The tiny, hyperactive, wiry Emile Champet could easily be mistaken for one of Steven Spielberg's devilish gremlins. He is an extremely busy man, having significant interests in the vegetable and flower business. The animated Champet was not the least bit cooperative in scheduling or showing up for business appointments with me, but once caught in his cellars, was immensely enjoyable to talk to and taste with. Quick-talking, fidgety, and colorful, Champet operates from an old cellar that consists of a conglomeration of small old barrels, medium-sized old barrels, and large, ancient foudres. Needless to say, it hardly inspires confidence in his winemaking, but like so many small growers in France, the decrepit cellar conditions are quite deceiving when it comes to evaluating the finished wine. Champet, who is in remarkable physical condition and whose wrinkled, sun-beaten face suggests he is in his fifties, owns almost four acres of vines that produce close to 800 cases of wine. His vines are primarily situated in the Côte Brune, with a choice parcel within the famous vineyard La Viaillère. He blends 5% Viognier with his wine and tends to bottle his Côte Rôtie after 18 months of maturation in one of the types of wood barrel he has. Champet prefers to drink his Côte Rôtie between five and ten years old, and is proud of the fact that he makes a natural wine that is never filtered. Stylistically, I find Champet's Côte Rôtie the closest thing to a big Côte de Nuits burgundy (a spicy, aggressive Chambertin comes to mind instantly) than any Côte Rôtie made by his peers.

VINTAGES

1985—*Côte Rôtie*—Champet did not have the great success that many of his peers enjoyed in this vintage. Nevertheless, this is still an
86   appealing wine with a rustic, full-bodied, intensely spicy, peppery-scented aroma, very good concentration and hard tannins, as well as annoyingly high acidity. It is quite different in style from other 1985s. Anticipated maturity: 1991–2000. Last tasted 7/86.

1984—*Côte Rôtie*—The burgundian, spicy, animal-scented bouquet conjures up the smell of a fine Premier Cru Gevrey-Chambertin.
85   Nicely colored with good concentration, this is a complex, round, interesting offering from Champet. Anticipated maturity: 1987–1993. Last tasted 7/86.

1983—*Côte Rôtie*—Surprisingly agreeable for a wine from this vintage, the 1983 has a sumptuous, fragrant bouquet, rich, generous fla-
88   vors of ripe cherries, medium to full body, and moderately soft tannins. Quite accessible, it should provide excellent drinking over the next decade. Last tasted 7/86.

1982—*Côte Rôtie*—Fully mature, but capable of holding until at least 1990, this seductive, supple, savory mouthful of wine is broadly
87   flavored, velvety, quite spicy, and again extremely burgundian-like in personality. It should be drunk over the near term. Last tasted 1/87.

CHAPOUTIER ***

This famous Rhône Valley négociant and vineyard owner is discussed in depth in the chapter on Hermitage (see page 84) since the firm is based in Tain L'Hermitage. However, Chapoutier does produce good rather than thrilling Côte Rôtie from the family's 6.7 acres of vineyards. Forty percent of their total production comes from these vineyards, while the other 60% of their Côte Rôtie is made from grapes purchased from other growers, so Chapoutier produces a considerable amount of this appellation's tiny production. As with many of the Chapoutier wines, there are two cuvées made—a regular vintage dated Côte Rôtie and a blend of various years entitled "Grand Cuvée." The latter are lots blended by Chapoutier and targeted for both consumers and restaurants that desire a fully mature wine. I have tasted some delicious examples of his Grand Cuvée, but also some dull, lifeless ones. One is always kept guessing as to the precise quality of a particular lot since the quality of the vintages that make up the blends differ so dramatically. Chapoutier's Côte Rôtie can age well, as the 1959 consumed in June 1986 so poignantly demonstrated. However, while it is certainly good, I tend to think of the Côte Rôtie made here as reliable rather than exciting or particularly inspirational. The wine is traditionally made and remains in large wood foudres until bottled. Recent vintages seem close to maturity upon release and appear to lack the depth and richness to last beyond 7–9 years. In short, I would rate many other wines from Chapoutier ahead of their Côte Rôtie, but should you see old vintages from the fifties, they are well worth purchasing.

VINTAGES

1985—*Côte Rôtie*—Potentially, this may be Chapoutier's best Côte
·   Rôtie in years. It will not be long-lived, but for drinking over the
84   next 5–7 years, few could deny its supple, smooth, black cherry
        fruitiness and easygoing charm. It also has a great deal of alcoholic punch to it. Anticipated maturity: 1987–1992. Last tasted 6/86.

1984—*Côte Rôtie*—Rather light, but certainly pleasant to drink in a
·   one-dimensional sort of way, the 1984 should be drunk over the
78   next 3–4 years. Last tasted 1/87.

1983—*Côte Rôtie*—More muscular and tannic than the 1985, Cha-
·   poutier's 1983 has adequate depth, medium to full body, some
83   tannin to shed, but overall seems to lack depth and definition
        given the vintage. Anticipated maturity: 1988–1992. Last tasted 11/86.

1982—*Côte Rôtie*—Supple, fruity, medium- to full-bodied, low in acid-
·   ity, this wine is somewhat succulent and alluring in a simple
82   fashion. This should be drunk over the next 4 to 5 years. Last
       tasted 6/86.
1981—*Côte Rôtie*—Fully mature, rather light, slightly dry and hard in
·   the finish, this wine appears to be losing its fruit and should be
75   drunk up. Last tasted 12/86.

RENÉ AND GILBERT CLUSEL ***

As is increasingly the trend not only in the Rhône Valley but also in
Burgundy, René Clusel and his son Gilbert are growers who previously
sold their crop to one of the large négociants. In 1980 they decided to
estate bottle their own production rather than sell their grapes. At
present, the Clusels own 6.2 acres of vines, two-thirds located in the
less desirable parts of the appellation outside the famous Côte Blonde
and Côte Brune. René Clusel is just beginning his retirement, so son
Gilbert, a suspicious, uneasy man, is now in full control. The underground cellar of Clusel's is one of the coolest and deepest in Côte Rôtie,
and is kept in impeccable condition. The wine here is given a relatively
long maceration (or time on its skins) and then spends 18–24 months in
small oak barrels, of which a few are new. The wines are certainly
good, rather hard and more austere than other Côte Rôties, and they
possess a certain rustic quality. They are capable of aging for 7–10
years.

VINTAGES

1985—*Côte Rôtie*—For a 1985 Côte Rôtie, Clusel's wine is notably less
·   successful than others. Medium ruby, rather loosely knit, low in
84   acidity, but soft and accessible, this wine will have to be drunk
       over the next 5–6 years. Last tasted 6/86.
1984—*Côte Rôtie*—Rather rustic and slightly coarse, this overtly spicy,
·   medium-bodied wine has narrowly focused fruit flavors and a
76   short, somewhat hard finish. Last tasted 6/86.
1983—*Côte Rôtie*—This is Clusel's best effort since he began to estate
·   bottle his own production in 1980. Dark ruby, with a berry-
87   scented, tarry, spicy bouquet, full body, plenty of concentration
       as well as tannin, and at present in need of 4–5 years of bottle
       age. Anticipated maturity: 1990–1995. Last tasted 10/86.

DELAS FRÈRES ***

This négociant is just outside Tournon and produces a small amount of
good rather than great Côte Rôtie from their ten acres of vineyards

at Côte Rôtie. The stars in the Delas house are its fabulous Hermitage Cuvée Marquise de la Tourette (see page 104) and their exquisite Condrieu. Their Côte Rôtie is made in the modern style, fermented in stainless steel, filtered after malolactic, fined by bentonite, and filtered again before bottling. The Côte Rôtie spends up to two years in two- and three-year-old barrels and foudres prior to bottling. The cellar of Delas is air conditioned, one of the few in France to have this luxury. The Côte Rôtie is made completely from vineyards on the Côte Brune, and 5% Viognier is added to the blend to add complexity and softness. Delas is owned by the well-known champagne house of Deutz, and maintains a curiously low profile in the marketplace, somewhat surprising in view of the quality of their top wines. Prices are rather moderate for Côte Rôtie, so values are to be had. Delas calls it Côte Rôtie Maugiron, in recognition of the legendary landholder.

VINTAGES

1985—*Côte Rôtie*—Less concentrated than the other top Côte Rôties, the 1985 is lighter and more supple, quite surprisingly so for a wine from the Côte Brune. It is deliciously fruity, quite low in acidity, but also uncomplicated. Drink over the next 5–7 years. Last tasted 6/86.

·
84

1983—*Côte Rôtie*—Much deeper in color and richer in concentration than the 1985, the 1983 has a big, gamey, black cherry-scented bouquet, clean, rich, medium- to full-bodied flavors, and a chewy, hearty texture. Drink it over the next 5–7 years. Last tasted 6/86.

·
86

1982—*Côte Rôtie*—Sweet, ripe, toasty, berry fruit aromas suggest a fully mature wine. On the palate, the wine is soft, nicely concentrated, velvety in the finish, and should be drunk up over the next 4–5 years. Arguments will no doubt abound with respect to whether it will keep. Last tasted 9/86.

·
86

ALBERT DERVIEUX-THAIZE ****

At the northern end of Côte Rôtie, in the tiny town of Verenay, the warm, friendly, diminutive, yet authoritative Albert Dervieux resides and makes his exceptional Côte Rôtie. Dervieux is a must visit for Côte Rôtie enthusiasts. He has been the president of the growers' association since 1953 and is filled with information. His bushy eyebrows become increasingly animated as he enthusiastically and proudly unleashes fact after fact about his beloved Côte Rôtie. His wines are very traditionally made, very long-lived, and among the most backward when released.

Dervieux uses 5% Viognier in the blend for his Côte Rôtie called "La Garde," and keeps all of his wines in large old foudres for two to two and a half years. No new wood barrels are employed here since Dervieux believes they mask the true character of Côte Rôtie. For that reason he is quick to criticize Marcel Guigal, the appellation's leading proponent of new oak barrels. Dervieux produces 1,200–1,500 cases from three different Côte Rôtie vineyards that total eight acres of vines. They are called Fongent when from 15-year-old vines on the Côte Brune, La Garde from 15–25-year-old vines on the Côte Blonde, and his top wine, La Viaillère, from 55-year-old vines on the Côte Brune. His wines are egg white-fined but never filtered, simply allowed to settle and fall brilliant naturally. Dervieux, who is the brother-in-law of Marius Gentaz-Dervieux, has argued strongly but unsuccessfully with the other growers to limit the yield of juice produced to 35 hectoliters rather than 40, a rarity given the fact that most of France's viticultural regions produce twice this much wine in a good vintage. There can be no question that Dervieux-Thaize produces some of Côte Rôtie's best wines, yet all of his wines need time in the bottle, especially his best wine, La Viaillère. If his wines have a weakness, it is that they can be less consistently good in the so-called off years (i.e., 1984, 1980, 1977) than those of his peers. There is no doubt that in the top vintages (1985, 1983, 1978, etc.) he produced wines of exceptional quality that will age as well as any produced in this appellation. In comparative tastings of Dervieux-Thaize's Côte Rôties against other notable producers the differences are immense. More tannic and brutal in their youth than those of Jasmin or Guigal, the wines of Dervieux age into rich, full-bodied, rather virile wines with earthy, saddle leather scents intertwined with spring flowers and ripe berry fruit. In fact, their taste confirms what Dervieux says about them: "Je fais un vin solide et tannique." If Jasmin's wines are the Volnays of Côte Rôtie and Guigal's the Clos Vougeots, then Dervieux's are its Chambertins.

VINTAGES

1985—*Côte Rôtie La Viaillère*—A fabulously promising wine, Dervieux's 1985 La Viaillère has a deep, dark ruby color, a huge,
·   exotic, earthy, fruity, undeveloped bouquet, super ripeness and
92   richness, and great length. Anticipated maturity: 1991–2004.
      Last tasted 6/86.

1985—*Côte Rôtie La Garde*—In contrast to the more sturdy, tannic La
·   Viaillère from the Côte Brune, Dervieux's La Garde from the
92   Côte Blonde is more supple and velvety, yet still fully capable of

a decade or more of evolution in the bottle. It has layers and layers of fruit, sensational intensity and color, and ripe, round tannins. Anticipated maturity: 1989–2000. Last tasted 6/86.

1985—*Côte Rôtie Fongent*—The only problem with Dervieux's Fongent
·   is that I tasted it in the company of his other two wines, which
87 are unquestionably superstars in 1985. The Fongent is lush, but finishes harder, and though admirably concentrated, it does not have the great depth of La Garde and La Viaillère. Anticipated maturity: 1991–2000. Last tasted 6/86.

1984—*Côte Rôtie La Viaillère*—Given the vintage's so-so reputation,
·   one is likely to be surprised by the quality of Dervieux's La
86 Viaillère. Rather deep in color, quite concentrated, perfumed and ripe, this full-bodied wine could take some cellaring. Anticipated maturity: 1988–1994. Last tasted 6/86.

1984—*Côte Rôtie La Garde*—A very forward, attractive bouquet is im-
·   mediately enticing. On the palate the wine is less impressive
80 though certainly sound. High acidity gives the wine a certain tartness, but the fruit is there. Drink over the next 4–5 years. Last tasted 6/86.

1984—*Côte Rôtie Fongent*—Quite high in acidity, which will no doubt
·   keep this wine tart and refreshing, the 1984 Fongent also has a
84 good concentration of berry fruit. Medium-bodied and not very tannic, I find it difficult to predict how this wine will age. Last tasted 6/86.

1983—*Côte Rôtie La Viaillère*—Dervieux's 1983 La Viaillère is clearly
·   the best of his offerings from this fine vintage. One can see what
90 old vines can do in a top year. Dark ruby, firm, concentrated and robust, this is a very concentrated yet tannic wine with plenty of length and tannin to match its power. Anticipated maturity: 1993–2000. Last tasted 9/86.

1983—*Côte Rôtie La Garde*—Significantly less powerful and concen-
·   trated than Dervieux's La Viaillère, the 1983 La Garde is supple,
85 smooth, fruity, moderately dark in color, but still closed and unevolved. Anticipated maturity: 1990–1997. Last tasted 6/86.

1983—*Côte Rôtie Fongent*—Deep in color, with a tarry, very spicy
·   (cinnamon and saddle leather) bouquet, ripe and quite tannic,
86 this wine from Dervieux's vineyard on the Côte Brune is closed in, promising, and well made, but needs time. Anticipated ma-turity: 1990–1998. Last tasted 9/86.

1982—*Côte Rôtie La Viaillère*—For a Dervieux wine, the 1982 La
·   Viaillère is quite well developed, open knit, forward, richly

87   fruity with a bouquet of overripe cherries, caramel, and damp wood. Drink this precocious wine over the next 5–6 years. Last tasted 6/86.

1981—*Côte Rôtie La Viaillère*—Deep in color with some amber at the
·   edge, the 1981 is hard-edged, still rather closed and tannic. Does
78   it have the fruit to outlast the tannin? It seems to me to be a gamble. Anticipated maturity: 1990–1995? Last tasted 9/86.

1978—*Côte Rôtie La Viaillère*—Still very muscular, very tannic, and
·   presumably set to enjoy a long life, this dark-colored, full-bod-
89   ied, chewy, rich Côte Rôtie has the depth of fruit to stand up to the tannin. Anticipated maturity: 1990–2000. Last tasted 6/86.

1971—*Côte Rôtie La Viaillère*—Most of the 1971 Côte Rôties I have
·   tasted have been quite mature for some time. This offering from
90   Dervieux has reached its plateau of maturity, but remains vividly fresh and alive and capable of aging for another 5–9 years. An enormous bouquet of grilled nuts and smoky, berry fruit leads one to a sumptuous, velvety, broadly flavored wine that is impeccably made, and is a striking example of how complex a Côte Rôtie can be. Drink over the next 5–9 years. Last tasted 6/86.

EDMOND DUCLAUX ***

The youngish Duclaux, with his ruddy complexion and thinning black hair, is one of Côte Rôtie's most enthusiastic growers. Until 1978 he sold the wine made from his 7.5 acres of vineyards located exclusively on the Côte Blonde to the likes of such firms as Guigal, Delas, and Chapoutier. Then with the encouragement of his mentor, Robert Jasmin, Duclaux began to estate bottle his entire production. Not surprisingly, Duclaux's wines resemble those of Jasmin. They are fragrant, seductive, forward, and have ripe aromas and broad, supple flavors that suggest early drinkability and maturity. Duclaux likes to keep his wines in barrels for two years and normally uses no more than 5% Viognier in the blend. However, in 1986 he intends to increase the percentage of Viognier because his crop of that grape was abnormally large. Duclaux will have none of the idea that new barrels are beneficial for his Côte Rôtie. Highly influenced by Robert Jasmin and Gentaz-Dervieux, the latter of whom has barrels that are almost 100 years old, Duclaux points out that new barrels are for winemakers who like to play tricks with their wines, thereby disguising the true flavors and concentration of fruit. Duclaux's vineyard, called the Maison Rouge, at the very southern end of the Côte Blonde, has vines that were planted in 1924, 1943, and 1963. Like many of the small growers in Côte Rôtie, Duclaux also grows vegetables and flowers to supplement his income. He is a serious young grower who will no doubt merit more and more attention as his wines receive wider distribution.

VINTAGES

1985—*Côte Rôtie*—Duclaux believes his 1985 is the finest wine he has
·   yet produced. A textbook Côte Blonde wine, the 1985 has a
89   captivating crushed berry fragrance, rich, lush, almost sweet, jammy flavors, very long finish, and enough backbone to ensure further evolution. Anticipated maturity: 1989–1996. Last tasted 6/86.

1984—*Côte Rôtie*—Duclaux readily admits that his 1984 is on the light
·   side. Nevertheless, it is ideal for drinking now. Soft, moderately
82   intense scents of raspberry fruit are very Volnay-like. On the palate, the wine is a little short in the finish, but elegant, medium-bodied, and fully mature. Drink over the next 3–4 years. Last tasted 6/86.

1983—*Côte Rôtie*—Because of the power in this wine, Duclaux kept his
·   1983 in oak for 30 months, rather than the normal 24 months. It
85   is still a hard, tannic wine, and though one can see that the ripeness and fruit intensity are there, I believe even Duclaux feels the wine would have benefited from being bottled earlier since it could have been even fruitier. Anticipated maturity: 1990–1996. Last tasted 6/86.

1982—*Côte Rôtie*—Soft, broad flavors show very good ripeness and
·   concentration, but this precocious, delicious Côte Rôtie requires
85   drinking over the next 4–5 years because of low acidity. It is quite charming, and very smooth and seductive on the palate. Last tasted 10/86.

MARIUS GENTAZ-DERVIEUX *****

One of Côte Rôtie's greatest winemakers, Marius Gentaz, who is the brother-in-law of Albert Dervieux, produces a scant 600–800 cases of wine from his three acres of vines on the Côte Brune. Consequently, his winemaking genius will never be widely known. Gentaz, who appears to be in his sixties, abhors new oak barrels (some of his barrels are 100 years old) and believes in no filtration, a process that he claims ruins the character of the wine. He usually keep his wines in wood 20–22 months prior to bottling. Gentaz, a very hard worker with an enthusiastic personality who now has to allocate his wine because of its emerging popularity, says his vines average 20 years in age. In describing his wine, Gentaz claims it is best drunk between 10–12 years of age, but comments that it is often drunk earlier. I find his wines among the very finest of the appellation. They are not as powerful and as deep as those of Guigal, nor as rustic and backward as those of his brother-in-law, Dervieux. They are elegant wines that seem slightly more concentrated and denser colored than those of his neighbor Robert Jasmin. His wines are often among the best two or three in the so-called off years such as 1984 and 1981.

VINTAGES

1985—*Côte Rôtie*—An exceptional wine in all respects, Gentaz feels
· this is his best vintage in the last decade. Very dark ruby, with
94 a huge, intensely perfumed bouquet of ripe fruit, a luscious, deep, velvety texture with enough tannin for 10 years of evolution, this wine is already quite accessible. Anticipated maturity: 1990–2000. Last tasted 6/86.

1984—*Côte Rôtie*—One of the very finest 1984s in Côte Rôtie, Gentaz
· unfortunately made only 325 cases. Quite dark in color, it has a
87 surprisingly rich, intense bouquet of plummy fruit. On the palate, this wine has very good depth and length with some hard tannins in the finish. Anticipated maturity: 1989–1995. Last tasted 6/86.

1983—*Côte Rôtie*—Now rather closed and tannic, the 1983 Côte Rôtie
· of Gentaz has outstanding underlying richness and length, but
91 needs a good 5–6 years of further cellaring. Anticipated maturity: 1992–2000. Last tasted 11/86.

1982—*Côte Rôtie*—In contrast to the tannic, hard, firm, closed 1983,
· the 1982, while quite tannic for a Côte Rôtie from this vintage,
91 is much more open and opulent on the palate. It would be a shame to drink it now, but it will certainly come forth long before the 1983, and provide just as much flavor concentration and complexity. Anticipated maturity: 1988–1996. Last tasted 12/86.

1981—*Côte Rôtie*—A stern, rather tough textured Côte Rôtie with very
· good depth of fruit, but a rather austere character, this wine
84 may just need time, but it may also dry out before the tannins resolve. It is a bit of a gamble. Anticipated maturity: 1988–1994. Last tasted 10/86.

1978—*Côte Rôtie*—Superb now, this wine has a full-blown bouquet of
· rich plummy fruit, lush, supple, deeply concentrated flavors,
91 medium to full body, and soft tannins in the lengthy finish. Drink over the next 5–6 years. Last tasted 12/84.

ETIENNE AND MARCEL GUIGAL *****

In the decade of the eighties, the house of Guigal, located directly on a dangerous curve of the narrow road that passes through the tiny town of Ampuis, has emerged as the dominant producer of outstanding Rhône wines. The Guigals—father Etienne, now in semiretirement, and son Marcel, a workaholic as well as genius—are rather unlikely stars. The house of Guigal is both a négociant and an important vineyard owner in Côte Rôtie. It was founded only in 1946, an infant by the standards of old-line Rhône négociants such as Paul Jaboulet Aîné (founded in 1834), Chapoutier (founded in 1808), or Ampuis's other famous house, Vidal-Fleury (founded in 1780). The elderly, quiet, extremely shy Etienne Guigal learned his trade while working at Vidal-Fleury, departing after 22 years to form his own firm in 1946. Since the early seventies, his son, the bespectacled, béreted, birdlike Marcel, has taken charge. The result has been the transformation of very good wines to not only spectacular wines but some of the finest in the world. In addition, the fame and superstar status that Marcel has been accorded both at home and abroad has led to some ambitious empire building, most notably the acquisition of the firm of Vidal-Fleury in 1985. The Guigals have also gazed south at several significant properties in Condrieu, but as of this writing no further extension of their Rhône wine kingdom has taken place.

The dominance of the Guigal family has not gone unnoticed, and the Guigal winemaking style has its critics, mostly those who produce inferior wine and who seem blinded by jealousy. Paradoxically, they do not seem to appreciate or realize that Guigal's great success has created significantly more interest in the wines of the entire Rhône Valley, including their own.

Guigal's style of winemaking is unique not only in Côte Rôtie but in all of the Rhône Valley. First, he is the Rhône's greatest exponent of the judicious use of new oak barrels for aging his wines. Some of his wines may see only several months in new oak—his Condrieu for example—but his single-vineyard Côte Rôties sojourn 30–36 months in new oak. Second, because of the fact that Guigal's red wines spend such a long time in both small oak and large oval foudres, his wines rarely have to be fined or filtered since they are allowed to settle naturally. The results are wines that have explosive richness and length on the palate but also impeccable balance and aging potential. They are uncompromisingly made and bottled and released only when Marcel Guigal believes they can be appreciated fully. His critics argue that his reds are often too alcoholic and oaky, a criticism that is totally unjustified, particularly to anyone who takes the time to taste his wines.

Guigal produces four separate Côte Rôties. The regular cuvée, made from the house's own holdings and purchased grapes from small growers, is a very fine, sometimes exceptional Côte Brune and Blonde blend. There are three vineyard-designated Côte Rôties. The most famous is from the Côte Blonde vineyard called La Mouline, a legendary wine despite the fact that its first vintage was as recent as 1966. If I were forced to name the single greatest red wine in the world, La Mouline's 1969, 1976, 1978, 1983, and 1985 would all be in the running. It is staggeringly perfumed and concentrated, combining a velvety texture and old vine intensity (the average age of the vines is 75 years) with enough backbone to keep it going for more than a decade. The problem is that only 600 cases of it are produced and demand for it has led not only to theft but to private clients of Guigal threatening him with physical harm if he does not increase their allocation to more than several bottles. Virtually every two- and three-star Michelin restaurant wants it on their wine list, so Guigal's biggest problem is simply how to allocate this monumental wine fairly.

In 1978, Guigal offered a second vineyard-designated Côte Rôtie. This wine, called La Landonne, is from the Côte Brune, and Guigal does not have an exclusive on it. Another superb grower, René Rostaing, also makes a La Landonne. Guigal's La Landonne, produced from vines that are just now approaching ten years of age, is a black purple-colored wine, incredibly concentrated, smoky and exotic to smell, but obviously more tannic than the voluptuous, seductive La Mouline. If La Mouline begs to be accompanied by Mozart, La Landonne demands the sound and fury of Tchaikovsky. Guigal claims that the 1978 and 1983 La Landonnes will age for 40–50 years, twice the longevity of La Mouline.

Guigal's designating specific vineyards Côte Rôties has caused other growers to be critical, claiming that the best wines are often blends from both the Côte Blonde and Côte Brune. However, I know of no other Côte Rôtie that can match either the overwhelming complexity of La Mouline or the balanced power and richness of La Landonne, except perhaps Guigal's newest vineyard-designated Côte Rôtie inaugurated in 1985, La Turque. This wine comes from a tiny sheltered parcel of vines on the Côte Brune previously owned by Vidal-Fleury. It may turn out to be the quintessential Côte Rôtie, and when Guigal releases this wine in 1988, I am sure it will be priced in the stratosphere.

The Guigals are the dominant producers of Côte Rôtie, yet their total production as both growers and négociants is still a meager 15,000 cases. With 30 acres, they are the most important owners and holders in Côte Rôtie. While they have augmented their production significantly in the last decade, the quality of all the wines made here continues to improve. Despite Marcel Guigal's superstar status, hard work, not complacency, is the rule here. Tasting a Guigal Côte Rôtie is indeed a special event, and, of course, they deserve to be in any serious wine collection. As the tasting notes demonstrate, I have never tasted through a greater lineup of wines. I don't believe there is another winemaker or wine-producing estate in the world that has ever put together such an array of monumental wines as these.

VINTAGES

1985—Côte Rôtie Côte Blonde et Brune—Like many northern Rhônes
from this vintage, the 1985 regular cuvée is deliciously ripe,
90   round, precocious-tasting wine, but quite deep, concentrated
and long, with a creamy texture and smoky bouquet. Anticipated
maturity: 1988–1996. Last tasted 6/86.

1985—Côte Rôtie La Mouline—The 1985 La Mouline is similar in style
to the 1982. Decadently ripe, perfumed and rich, with layers of
100   sweet, smoky fruit, this hedonistic wine offers as complex and
as sensuous a taste of wine as money can buy. Anticipated maturity: 1989–2000. Last tasted 6/86.

1985—Côte Rôtie La Landonne—An extraordinary wine, even richer
and longer on the palate than the La Mouline, La Landonne's
100   1985 has a full-intensity bouquet of smoky, plummy fruit and
grilled almonds. This is an enormously concentrated wine of
remarkable dimension and depth. Anticipated maturity: 1995–
2010. Last tasted 6/86.

1985—Côte Rôtie La Turque—This wine, Guigal's first effort from this
vineyard, has already received deity status in western European
100   wine circles. Only 333 cases were produced, and if one were to
kill for a wine, this might be the one to do it for. It meets, then
exceeds, all parameters for judging wine—calling it great seems
somehow woefully inadequate. It has the power and enormous
concentration of La Landonne, as well as the sheer, decadent,
self-indulgent pleasures of the voluptuous La Mouline. It is the
quintessential Côte Rôtie. When it is released in 1988, the price
should be equally celestial. Anticipated maturity: 1990–2005.
Last tasted 6/86.

1984—*Côte Rôtie Côte Blonde et Brune*—The bouquet reveals plenty of
· complex berry and smoky scents, but on the palate the wine
84 shows rather high acidity though decent flavor concentration.
Anticipated maturity: 1988–1992. Last tasted 6/86.

1984—*Côte Rôtie La Mouline*—A fabulous, well-evolved bouquet of
· sweet hickory wood and berry jam is top-flight. However, the
88 palate impression, while quite good and deep, is shorter than
other top vintages of La Mouline. Nevertheless, this is still a
very impressive wine. Anticipated maturity: 1988–1996. Last
tasted 6/86.

1984—*Côte Rôtie La Landonne*—Darker in color than La Mouline, with
· an intense, smoky, grilled nut bouquet, rich, intense flavors, full
88 body and surprising tannin, the 1984 La Landonne will take
some aging. Anticipated maturity: 1990–2005. Last tasted 6/86.

1983—*Côte Rôtie Côte Blonde et Brune*—Guigal's most tannic regular
· Côte Rôtie since the 1961, the 1983 has a huge bouquet of toasty,
90 berry fruit, great extraction and depth of fruit, loads of tannin,
and considerable length. Anticipated maturity: 1990–2005. Last
tasted 12/86.

1983—*Côte Rôtie La Mouline*—This wine, which normally overwhelms
· one's senses with its pleasurable onslaught of complex smells
100 and flavors, is more tannic and less immediately hedonistic in
this vintage. It may evolve along the lines of the spectacular
1969 since it has extraordinary depth, length, and unbelievable
concentration. Anticipated maturity: 1990–2005. Last tasted
6/86.

1983—*Côte Rôtie La Landonne*—A profound, backward wine that
· shows all the characteristics of the greatest wines. It is dense in
100 color with a blossoming bouquet of immense and differing sen-
sations of ripe fruit and smoky, toasty oak. On the palate, there
is staggering depth and extract, layers and layers of fruit, and
a finish that seems to last and last. Guigal thinks the wine will
last for 40 years. Anticipated maturity: 1995–2010. Last tasted
6/86.

1982—*Côte Rôtie Côte Blonde et Brune*—I have experienced some bot-
· tle variation with this wine, ranging from very good examples to
87 several superb ones. Guigal admits to three different bottlings
occurring over a long period. Regardless, all of the 1982s exhibited broad, lush, ripe, delicious fruit, a very velvety texture,
and dark color. Anticipated maturity: 1987–1993. Last tasted
12/86.

1982—*Côte Rôtie La Mouline*—A textbook La Mouline, extremely se-
• ductive, lush, very ripe, gorgeously perfumed and fragrant, this
98 sublime wine is difficult to resist drinking now because of its low
acidity, yet patience will no doubt reward one with even greater
thrills. The intense, smoky, flowery, ripe berry-scented bouquet
is inspirational; the smooth, long, layers of velvety fruit unforgettable. Anticipated maturity: now–1997. Last tasted 12/86.

1982—*Côte Rôtie La Landonne*—Again, La Landonne shows the char-
• acter of a wine from the Côte Brune—very smoky, significantly
96 more tannic and unevolved when compared with the La Mouline.
It is extremely promising as the fabulous depth and amazing
length and purity of Syrah fruit suggest so unequivocally. Anticipated maturity: 1992–2010. Last tasted 12/86.

1981—*Côte Rôtie Côte Blonde et Brune*—While not one of Guigal's
• notable stars, he still managed in this rather mediocre vintage to
84 produce a wine with good depth and a spicy, straightforward
character with only a touch of austerity. Anticipated maturity:
now–1992. Last tasted 12/86.

1981—*Côte Rôtie La Mouline*—Not so impressive from the cask, in the
• bottle the 1981 La Mouline has evolved extremely well and is
89 showing much greater flavor dimension than I thought possible.
Deep in color, more reserved, or should I say not as overwhelming as usual, this medium- to full-bodied wine has loads of fruit
and character in a slightly lighter style. Anticipated maturity:
now–1994. Last tasted 12/86.

1981—*Côte Rôtie La Landonne*—For a La Landonne, this wine is more
• open and forward than usual, but it still has at least a decade of
90 further evolution. Dark ruby with the telltale smoky, rich, multidimensional bouquet, this medium- to full-bodied wine has outstanding concentration for the vintage. Anticipated maturity:
1990–2000. Last tasted 12/86.

1980—*Côte Rôtie Côte Blonde et Brune*—A "plain Jane" sort of Côte
• Rôtie, fruity, nicely colored, but as Michael Broadbent would
84 possibly say, rather "foursquare." Meaty and substantial, it does
not seem to have much complexity. Drink over the next 4–5
years. Last tasted 12/86.

1980—*Côte Rôtie La Mouline*—No greater red wines were made in
• France in 1980 than that of La Mouline and its burlier, more
96 tannic sibling, La Landonne. The La Mouline has the full-intensity, rather magical bouquet of exuberant fruit, hickory wood
smoke, and layers of crushed berry fruit. Voluptuous and deep

on the palate, this is another exceptional wine from what is arguably the world's greatest vineyard. Anticipated maturity: now–2000. Last tasted 12/86.

1980—*Côte Rôtie La Landonne*—Perhaps even more concentrated than
· La Mouline, the La Landonne is also more tannic and not as
96 obviously sensual, but just be patient. The dense, dark color, the tarry, plummy, and of course roasted bouquet, the great depth and tannic bite, all suggest that cellaring of another several years is mandated. Anticipated maturity: 1990–2005. Last tasted 12/86.

1979—*Côte Rôtie Côte Blonde et Brune*—An underrated wine, richly
· fruity with the smell of grilled herbs, fresh tomatoes, and berry
86 fruit, this lush, full-bodied wine is drinking well now and should continue to hold for 5–6 more years. Last tasted 6/86.

1979—*Côte Rôtie La Mouline*—Curiously, this wine never exhibited
· much character or charm from the barrel, and for the first 6
90 months after bottling, it seemed slightly oxidized. However, this was just a passing phase because the 1979 La Mouline has developed stunningly and is now at its plateau of maturity—rich, smoky, deep, and extremely long. Anticipated maturity: now–1997. Last tasted 12/86.

1979—*Côte Rôtie La Landonne*—Still young, dark purple/ruby in color,
· this is a sleeping giant of a wine—chewy, rich and tannic, rather
92 closed, but obviously very, very concentrated. Guigal's 1979 La Landonne is an extremely promising wine. Anticipated maturity: 1990–2005. Last tasted 12/86.

1978—*Côte Rôtie Côte Blonde et Brune*—Fully mature, but capable of
· lasting for at least another decade, the 1978 vintage, a great one
88 for the Rhône and Guigal, combines power and super concentration with grace and balance. Dark ruby, still richly fruity, yet showing some amber at the edge, this full-bodied, plump wine offers ideal drinking over the next 5–7 years. Last tasted 12/86.

1978—*Côte Rôtie La Mouline*—An astonishing wine, as good as the
· great 1969 and 1976 La Moulines and potentially longer lived
100 than the 1985, the huge bouquet of crushed berry fruit, grilled meats, and floral scents dazzles the olfactory senses. On the palate, the layers of flavors are overwhelming and virtually endless. Accessible now, this promises to be even greater in 4–5 years—a tour de force! Anticipated maturity: 1990–2000. Last tasted 12/86.

1978—*Côte Rôtie La Landonne*—The debut vintage for Guigal's La
· Landonne continues to live up to the raves it received from cask
97 tastings done in the late seventies. The intense, almost overdone
bouquet of smoky, exotic fruit carries one's nose to the brink of
paradise. On the palate, the wine is explosively rich and full-
bodied, has loads of tannin, and should age majestically for at
least another 15 years. Anticipated maturity: 1990–2005. Last
tasted 12/86.

OLDER VINTAGES

For Guigal's regular Côte Rôtie, the older top vintages include a still
rather firm 1976 and great 1964 and 1961, the latter two wines fully
mature but so, so seductively rich and velvety. Nineteen seventy-eight
was the first vintage for La Landonne, 1966 for La Mouline. Interestingly, with the exception of the magnificent and perfect 1969 and 1976
La Moulines, the other vintages prior to 1978 exhibited less strength
and vigor, and seemed to age much quicker. The employment of new
oak barrels by Marcel Guigal, and the reduction in the amount of Viognier in the final blend since 1978, has given La Mouline more backbone, depth, and aging potential. The 1966, 1970, 1971, 1973, 1974, and
1977 La Moulines should be drunk up. I have never tasted the 1967,
1968, 1972, or 1975, but they are said by Guigal himself to be "fatigué."

PAUL JABOULET AINÉ ***

This great house, founded in 1834, is located in Tain L'Hermitage. Its
fame rests in large part on the quality of its greatest red wine, the
extraordinary Hermitage La Chapelle. However, like most négociants,
the Jaboulets make an entire line of Rhône wines, with Côte Rôtie being
one of them. (For a more complete discussion of this firm, see page 116
in the chapter on the wines of Hermitage.)

The current generation of Jaboulets that now runs this house consists
of the jovial father, Louis, and his three sons: Jacques, who runs the
wine cellars; Philippe, who looks after the vineyards; and the best-
known of all, the handsome, ruddy-faced Gérard, who travels exten-
sively as an articulate spokesman for not only the wines of his family
but those of the entire Rhône Valley. The Rhône could hardly ask for a
better ambassador for their wines.

Their Côte Rôtie is consistently good, but they own no vineyards in
this appellation and therefore must depend exclusively on purchases
from growers to obtain the grapes for their wine. Certainly, the Jaboulet
Côte Rôtie (Les Jumelles, or the twins) is not in the same exalted class

as the firm's Hermitage. It seems to be a wine made to be drunk young, usually within its first decade of life. (For example, my experience with older vintages has been mixed; a 1970 and 1967 tasted in 1986 were quite tired even though they had been stored perfectly.) The Jaboulets use 3% Viognier in their blend and keep the wine 12 months in oak barrels prior to bottling. As the tasting notes demonstrate, the best recent vintages for the firm's Côte Rôtie have been 1976, 1978, and 1985, followed by 1983 and 1979.

VINTAGES

1985—*Côte Rôtie*—The Jaboulets believe this to be their best Côte
· Rôtie since the fine 1976. It is rather low in acidity and preco-
86 cious, but has heaps of lush blackberry fruit, medium to full body, and a velvety long finish. Anticipated maturity: 1988–1994. Last tasted 6/86.

1984—*Côte Rôtie*—Quite well made given the vintage, the 1984, though
· somewhat one-dimensional, is round and fruity, clean, elegant,
83 and attractive for drinking over the next 5 to 6 years. Anticipated maturity: now–1991. Last tasted 6/86

1983—*Côte Rôtie*—Rather tannic and stern on the palate, the 1983 has
· a medium garnet color, a ripe berry, somewhat gamelike smoky
86 nose, but is still quite firm and closed. It seems to have the depth of fruit to outlast the tannins. Anticipated maturity: 1990–1995. Last tasted 6/86.

1982—*Côte Rôtie*—Similar to the 1985, only lighter in style, quite soft
· and supple, very fruity, and ready to drink, this full-bodied,
85 rather exotic wine will provide delightful drinking over the next 5–6 years. Last tasted 9/86.

1981—*Côte Rôtie*—Rather straightforward, somewhat austere and un-
· dernourished, this medium-bodied wine has the smoky, game-
74 like bouquet so typical of many Côte Rôties, but lacks generosity. Anticipated maturity: now–1990. Last tasted 11/85.

1980—*Côte Rôtie*—Rather light for a Côte Rôtie, but fully mature or *à*
· *point,* as the French say, with a smoky, bacon fat nose intermin-
82 gled with berry fruit, soft, medium-bodied, not concentrated but certainly fine for uncritical tasting, this wine has a touch of sharp acidity in the finish. Anticipated maturity: now–1989. Last tasted 12/84.

1979—*Côte Rôtie*—Ripe, rich, open-knit, toasty, soft, fruity flavors
· show little tannin. The amber edge to the color also suggests full
84 maturity. While the 1979 could use a bit more stuffing, it is quite

pleasant, but should be drunk up. Anticipated maturity: now–1989. Last tasted 11/86.

1978—*Côte Rôtie*—There is a lot of concentration, and I believe prom-
·   ise, to this wine, but the acidity remains a bit high as the tannins
85?   begin to melt away. The color remains sound, the depth and
           ripeness are present, but will the wine come together? Antici-
           pated maturity: now–1993. Last tasted 11/86.

OLDER VINTAGES

The 1976 may well be Jaboulet's finest Côte Rôtie in the last 20 years. Very fragrant, rich, intense with all its components in balance, it is a voluptuous, delicious wine for drinking over the next 4–5 years. The 1971 and 1970 are showing fatigue, and unless the wines are from large bottle formats or from very cold cellars, they should be consumed immediately.

JOSEPH JAMET****

Joseph Jamet is unquestionably one of the finest growers in Côte Rôtie. He owns just under nine acres of well-situated hillside vineyards. The wines are very traditionally made here. There is no destemming and the wine spends a long time on the skins—usually three weeks. Afterwards, Jamet ages his wines at least two years in oak barrels prior to bottling. One year is spent in large old wooden foudres, and the second year in small used oak barrels. His wines are deeply colored, have the characteristic smoky, bacon fat aroma, often the scent of raspberry jam, and according to Jamet, "les aromes des violettes."

VINTAGES

1985—*Côte Rôtie*—Extremely concentrated, this wine, which is nearly
·   black in color, shows immense potential, but unlike other 1985s
90   is quite closed. Very full-bodied and very concentrated, it should
           age very well. Anticipated maturity: 1990–2000. Last tasted
           10/86.
1984—*Côte Rôtie*—Jamet prefers his 1984 to his 1985. Unquestionably,
·   his 1984 is quite successful. Deep in color with raspberry and
87   floral scents as well as vanillin, it is a round, generous, richly
           fruity wine with good balance. Anticipated maturity: 1988–1994.
           Last tasted 10/87.
1983—*Côte Rôtie*—A typical 1983, Jamet's wine is deep in color, but
·   tight and very tannic. However, it already hints at being a very
88   complex, rich, deeply concentrated wine. The impressive depth

and length are quite obvious despite all the tannin. Last tasted
10/86.

1982—*Côte Rôtie*—Much more supple and flattering to taste than the
1983, Jamet's 1982 is richly fruity, has a full-intensity, smoky,
87 hickory-scented bouquet, good, rich, jammy fruit on the palate,
and medium to full body. Drink over the next 5–7 years. Last
tasted 1/87.

ROBERT JASMIN *****

The domaine of the warm, inviting, friendly Robert Jasmin is a must
visit for those wanting to taste great wine as well as meet one of the
most serious winemakers in the Rhône. Jasmin owns just under ten
acres of vineyards split evenly between the Côte Blonde and Côte
Brune. His yield is very conservative, only 1,000 cases of wine from
vines that average 25–30 years of age. Jasmin, a handsome, rather
large-framed man, uses no new oak barrels, but does employ many two-
and three-year-old troncais oak barrels that he purchases from Burgundy growers, who he claims use "a lot of new oak to disguise a lack
of concentration." His wines are considered by many to be the most
elegant and polished wines of Côte Rôtie. They are certainly very easy
to drink young, being made in a lush, supple style, yet seem to magically hold and frequently deepen in the bottle despite their precocious
appeal. Jasmine used to employ a hefty 10–20% Viognier in his Côte
Rôtie, but since 1983 claims he has eliminated it totally.

Jasmin, who has a great appetite for his own wine, keeps two cellars.
First-time visitors, unless they demonstrate great admiration for his
wines, are not likely to get past the primary, rather drab cellar in what
looks like a garage. However, repeat or overly enthusiastic visitors who
seem enthralled with his wines may well merit a visit to the private
cellar below Jasmin's house where his best lots are kept for his personal
consumption and a few lucky importers whom Jasmin admires, most
notably his English representatives from Wiltshire, Robin and Judith
Yapp. Jasmin's great pride and enthusiasm have always kept me from
spitting out his wine when tasting (it is the only place I do not spit) for
fear of showing what I am afraid he would interpret as disrespect.

Jasmin's Côte Rôtie is an intense, majestically perfumed wine that
one could call the most burgundian-like of this appellation. He believes
in drinking it young—he claims it is at its best in five years, but certainly both his 1978 and 1976 are hardly near their prime. The notes
that follow are for Jasmin's regular cuvées, not his splendid reserve lots
kept for his best customers.

VINTAGES

1985—*Côte Rôtie*—Jasmin believes this is his best wine since his father's 1947. It is already delicious to drink, broadly flavored with

90   an intense bouquet of ripe berry fruit and floral scents. It will be hard to resist drinking up, but it should hold and hopefully develop well for 6 to 8 years. Anticipated maturity: now–1994. Last tasted 6/86.

1984—*Côte Rôtie*—Better from the bottle than from the cask, Jasmin's 1984 has turned out quite well. It is a very fruity, well-colored

85   wine with a good, moderately rich, ripe bouquet of raspberry, cedary aromas, a touch more acidity than the 1985, but good balance in a lighter, less concentrated style. Anticipated maturity: now–1992. Last tasted 1/87.

1983—*Côte Rôtie*—A much more evolved and accessible wine than other 1983s, Jasmin's Côte Rôtie can be drunk today or cellared

90   for up to a decade. It has a big, forward, ripe bouquet of fruit and spices, fleshy flavors, and for a wine from Jasmin, quite a tannic bite to it. Anticipated maturity: 1988–1996. Last tasted 12/86.

1982—*Côte Rôtie*—Velvety, fully mature, a bit low in acidity, but as good and as broadly flavored and plump as it is, it lacks the

87   concentration of the 1983 and 1985. Anticipated maturity: now–1992. Last tasted 12/86.

1981—*Côte Rôtie*—Still very youthfully colored, with a light to moderately intense berry fragrance, the 1981 seems to have decent

81   fruit to outlast the tannins. The acidity is a trifle high, and the overall impression is one of restrained elegance. This wine should continue to drink well for 5 to 6 years. Last tasted 1/87.

1980—*Côte Rôtie*—A touch of coarseness in the 1980 detracts from an otherwise decent effort. It is deeper in color than the 1981, but

79   with less bouquet, and gives an austere, rather dry palate impression that begs for more fruit and charm. Rather atypical for a Jasmin Côte Rôtie. Anticipated maturity: now–1992. Last tasted 6/86.

1979—*Côte Rôtie*—The 1979 was delicious to drink from the cask and despite its precocious appeal, this wine has seemed to deepen

85   and broaden on the palate as it has aged. Medium ruby color, very fragrant with crushed raspberry fruit, spicy oak, and a smoky game bird smell, it is completely mature. Anticipated maturity: now–1990. Last tasted 6/86.

1978—*Côte Rôtie*—This is a sensational wine. Can the 1985 be better
· than this? Still deep in color with no amber, the 1978 has the
92 full-intensity bouquet of spring flowers and very ripe fruit. The
texture is rich, creamy, long, and impeccably balanced. Quite
concentrated, quite complex, and very captivating, this is superb Côte Rôtie. Anticipated maturity: now–1992. Last tasted
6/86.

1976—*Côte Rôtie*—Undoubtedly a great wine, yet somewhat firmer and
· more austere than the more succulent 1978, the 1976 is a rather
90 brawny, meaty wine that seems (for Jasmin) to emphasize power
rather than finesse. It is just now coming into its own. Anticipated maturity: now–1994. Last tasted 9/86.

RENÉ ROSTAING *****

The young businessman René Rostaing makes tiny quantities of Côte
Rôtie as a hobby. However, one taste of his wine will no doubt convince
anyone that Rostaing is not only serious but a star of this appellation.
His tiny cellar, which is air conditioned, is by the river in Ampuis, just
a block away from that of Emile Champet. Rostaing, a sort of French
yuppie, is in the real estate business and manages apartment buildings
in nearby Condrieu. He has only five acres of vines and from that
produces 500 cases of Côte Rôtie. His winemaking skills are evident,
having learned them from his father-in-law, Albert Dervieux, although
I suspect Dervieux's hostility to the use of new oak barrels was not
passed on since Rostaing routinely employs 30% new oak while aging
his Côte Rôties for two to three years in the cask. Another fervent
believer in neither fining nor filtering of wines for fear of removing
flavor, Rostaing produces a Côte Blonde, a Côte Brune, and a very
special Côte Brune from his portion of the La Landonne vineyard where
his vines average 70 years in age.

Rostaing is critical of the French for paying little attention to Côte
Rôtie. He likes to cite a survey done in Lyons, France's third largest
city and one with a great gastronomic reputation, only 23 miles from
Côte Rôtie. According to the survey, only one out of 50 of Lyons's
residents has ever heard of Côte Rôtie, and only one out of 500 claimed
to have ever tasted it. Rostaing says that there is just not enough money
paid for a good Côte Rôtie to justify the backbreaking labor on the
slopes, so growers are forced to seek other employment to supplement
their income. Yet he intends to augment his vineyard holdings, a plan
that every wine-lover should applaud given the superb wines he is

capable of making. His wines are very structured, very ageworthy Côte Rôties with a style all their own. The use of a healthy percentage of new oak suggests Guigal, but Rostaing's wines are less opulent and less powerful than Guigal's. Perhaps the best way to describe the style of wine he produces is to say it is a synthesis between that of his father-in-law Dervieux-Gentaz, with the new oak influence reminiscent of Guigal. Rostaing's tiny production precludes many a wine enthusiast from ever seeing a bottle, and virtually all of his wine is sold only to people who he says "have a greater understanding and appreciation of it." Consequently, Rostaing exports all of his wines and they are well worth a special effort to find.

VINTAGES

1985—*Côte Rôtie La Landonne*—Black/purple in color with a very con-
· centrated, powerful, ripe feel on the palate, the 1985 La Lan-
93 donne has sensational extract, a fabulous bouquet, and length that just goes on and on. A great wine. Anticipated maturity: 1993–2005. Last tasted 6/86.

1985—*Côte Rôtie Côte Blonde*—A super wine, Rostaing's Côte Blonde
· is a more velvety, softer wine than the more obviously tannic La
92 Landonne. Voluptuous on the palate, with a staggering bouquet of roasted nuts and ripe, jammy fruit, this wine offers a smorgasbord of exotic aromas and flavors. Anticipated maturity: 1989–2000. Last tasted 6/86.

1984—*Côte Rôtie La Landonne*—A good wine that suffers in compari-
· son with Rostaing's super 1984 Côte Blonde, the La Landonne
85 is broadly flavored, a bit tough and tannic, but concentrated and flavorful. Anticipated maturity: 1991–1998. Last tasted 6/86.

1984—*Côte Rôtie Côte Blonde*—Perhaps the finest wine (for sheer
· class) produced this vintage in Côte Rôtie, the 1984 Côte Blonde
90 may also be one of the best half-dozen wines made in France. Sweet, super ripe flavors hardly suggest a mediocre year. Extremely deep, lush, and velvety, this is a knockout. Anticipated maturity: now–1994. Last tasted 6/86.

1983—*Côte Rôtie La Landonne*—More impressive immediately after
· bottling than at present, the 1983 La Landonne is quite tannic,
87 very closed, and clearly in need of a decade of cellaring. The depth of fruit appears sufficient to outlast the considerable tannic clout. Anticipated maturity: 1993–2000. Last tasted 12/86.

1983—*Côte Rôtie Côte Blonde*—As closed and tannic as the La Lan-
· donne, but the bouquet and flavors suggest a slightly more fruity
87 wine with less body and toughness. Nevertheless, this wine begs
for cellaring. Anticipated maturity: 1991–2000. Last tasted 1/87.

1981—*Côte Rôtie Côte Blonde et Brune*—Quite austere and reserved,
· with plenty of tannin and good underlying fruit, this wine is
82 somewhat of a gamble given the dominant tannins. Am I being
too generous with the rating? Anticipated maturity: 1990–1996.
Last tasted 6/86.

1981—*Côte Rôtie Côte Blonde*—Fully mature, the 1981 has a full-inten-
· sity bouquet of peppery, raspberry fruit, soft, melted tannins, a
87 lush, ripe texture, and very fine length. Drink over the next 5–6
years. Last tasted 5/86.

DE VALLOUIT***

This firm is not located in Ampuis but further south in St.-Vallier. It is
an established company, having been founded in 1922, and has kept, at
least in the major export markets, a surprisingly low profile, particularly
in view of the fact that Madame de Vallouit owns 24 acres in Côte
Rôtie, making her one of the two largest growers. The firm also operates
as a négociant, producing a full range of Rhône wines from Côtes du
Rhône, Gigondas, Châteauneuf-du-Pape, St.-Joseph, and Hermitage.
Production of Côte Rôtie averages 4,400 cases out of the appellation's
approximate total production of 50,000. I find it interesting that little is
said about this firm, yet the limited tastings I have done of their Côte
Rôties have demonstrated quite good wines that are filled with flavor
and seem uncompromisingly made and rather undervalued in the
scheme of things in the northern Rhône.

VINTAGES

1985—*Côte Rôtie*—This is the finest Côte Rôtie I have tasted from
· de Vallouit. Powerful, intense aromas of pepper and crushed
89 raspberry fruit jump from the glass. On the palate, the wine is
expansively flavored, quite forward, but should age well. Anticipated maturity: 1989–1995. Last tasted 3/87.

1984—*Côte Rôtie*—Slightly high in acidity with perhaps not enough
· flesh to cover the bones, Vallouit's 1984 is quite spicy in aroma,
78 medium ruby in color, has an attractive gamey character, but is
too angular. Anticipated maturity: now–1991. Last tasted 11/86.

1983—*Côte Rôtie*—Deep ruby in color with a huge bouquet of smoky,
· gamey, peppery fruit, this full-bodied wine is much more acces-
88 sible than many of the now rather closed 1983s. It has admirable
concentration, a broad, lush texture, and moderate tannins. Anticipated maturity: now–1994. Last tasted 8/86.

1982—*Côte Rôtie*—Very ripe, richly fruity aromas of plums and spicy
· oak are quite captivating. On the palate, the wine is lush, ripe,
87 very velvety, and seems fully mature. I would drink it over
the next 5 years for its exuberant, exotic richness. Last tasted
12/86.

1978—*Côte Rôtie*—The 1978 Vallouit is medium ruby with a rather
· vegetal, peppery, smoky aroma that is interesting, but not typi-
? cal. The "green" flavor persists on the palate backed by plenty
of body as well as tart acidity and sharp tannins. Judgment
reserved. Last tasted 12/83.

*VIDAL-FLEURY*****

Founded in 1781, this is the oldest and, until the late seventies, one of
the most respected houses in the Rhône Valley, operating as both a
négociant and grower with 20 acres of vines in Côte Rôtie gorgeously
situated on both the Côte Blonde and Côte Brune. For decades, Joseph
Vidal-Fleury ran this house with meticulous care and great passion.
One of his star pupils was Etienne Guigal, who left in 1946 to begin his
own house. In 1976, Vidal died, and while the firm still continued to
produce some superlative wines, the great consistency of the past was
replaced by irregularity, uncertainty, and a general lack of leadership.
The crusty old cellarmaster, M. Battier, appeared to become more
difficult each time I paid the house a visit, and seemed to be leaving
very good lots of wine entirely too long in the old chestnut barrels,
causing many of them to become oxidized and dried out. It was a
particularly depressing thing for this writer to see since the first great
Côte Rôties I tasted, the 1959, 1964, 1966, and 1969, were all from
Vidal-Fleury.

Rumors in the early eighties continually suggested that Vidal-Fleury
was up for sale, and in fact in 1985 the house was purchased by the
Guigal family whose first vintage was, fortuitously, the sensational
1985. Marcel Guigal was quick to make it clear that both houses would
retain their separate identities, and the name Vidal-Fleury would neither be changed nor become a second label for Guigal. Yet changes are
well under way. Guigal did adopt Vidal-Fleury's best vineyard site (the
La Turque) for Guigal's third vineyard-designated wine, but left the

other outstanding Vidal-Fleury vineyards, La Chatillonne, Le Clos, La Pommière, and Pavillon Rouge, for exclusive use by Vidal-Fleury. Of course, Guigal's philosophy of vinification and cellar techniques will be followed at Vidal-Fleury, but in actuality the styles of both houses were not that far apart to begin with, except for Guigal's infatuation with new oak barrels. Guigal himself does not manage his new acquisition but has hired Jean Pierre Rochias, a former employee of the famous Bordeaux house of Cordier, to oversee the day to day affairs. The run down wine cellar and facilities at Vidal-Fleury will undoubtedly get a facelift, and, as one can already see from tasting the excellent 1985s, Vidal-Fleury's reputation, which suffered between 1979 and 1984, is ready to rebound strongly. I suggest that readers be careful with the wines from Vidal-Fleury made between 1980 and 1984 since they are extremely variable due to the fact that the house had no consistent policy with respect to bottling dates. Early-bottled Côte Rôties can be fresh and alive, whereas those left three or more years in wood have become tired and oxidized. This would apply equally to the firm's line of négociant wines, such as their Côtes du Rhône, Châteauneuf-du-Pape, Crozes-Hermitage, St.-Joseph, Cornas, and Hermitage. However, from 1985 forward, there appears to be no problem of this nature. Vidal-Fleury under Guigal will continue to offer approximately 7,000–10,000 bottles each year of its special vineyard-designated Côte Rôtie, La Chatillonne.

VINTAGES

1985—*Côte Rôtie La Chatillonne*—Very ripe and fat with heaps of
· blackberry fruit, the 1985 La Chatillonne has excellent depth
89 and richness, rather low acidity, but undeniable charm. It will
develop quickly. Anticipated maturity: now–1994. Last tasted
6/86.

1985—*Côte Rôtie Côte Blonde et Brune*—Every bit as good as the sin-
· gle-vineyard bottling of La Chatillonne, this wine is dense in
89 color, quite concentrated, richly fruity, has a creamy texture,
and a bit more backbone than the Chatillonne. Impressive. Anticipated maturity: 1990–1998. Last tasted 6/86.

1984—*Côte Rôtie Côte Blonde et Brune*—Rather austere, quite tannic
· and lean, with annoyingly high acidity, this is a meagerly en-
78 dowed wine with little future. Anticipated maturity: now–1990.
Last tasted 6/86.

1983—*Côte Rôtie La Chatillonne*—The 1983 is disappointing, particu-
· larly given the vintage; it is rather austere, quite dry and hard
78 with barely adequate fruit, a dusty texture, and excessive tan-

nins in the finish. It is likely to only dry out further. Last tasted 6/86.

1983—*Côte Rôtie Côte Blonde et Brune*—No doubt sloppy cellaring · accounts for the oxidized, excessively stale taste to this hollow 65 wine. Pass it by. Last tasted 6/86.

1980—*Côte Rôtie Côte Blonde et Brune*—The 1980 is plump, decently · colored, fruity, rather one-dimensional, but shows no oxidation 82 or staleness. Drink over the next 2–3 years. Last tasted 11/85.

1980—*Côte Rôtie La Chatillonne*—Rather like the regular bottling, the · 1980 La Chatillonne is lighter and marginally less interesting in 81 its bouquet. It needs drinking up. Last tasted 12/84.

1979—*Côte Rôtie La Chatillonne*—Vidal-Fleury's 1979 Chatillonne is · medium ruby with a moderately intense bouquet of berry fruit 83 and spices. It could use some more flesh and concentration, but is attractive in a lighter, more elegant style. Anticipated maturity: now–1990. Last tasted 1/86.

1978—*Côte Rôtie Côte Blonde et Brune*—A great wine, the 1978 has · the huge bouquet of intense, jammy, cassis fruit as well as 90 roasted nuts that makes Côte Rôtie so special. Very concentrated, lush, and full-bodied, this impressive wine is just now reaching its apogee. Anticipated maturity: now–1995. Last tasted 1/87.

OLDER VINTAGES

The very first great Côte Rôties I tasted were those of Vidal-Fleury. I had the 1959 only once, in the mid-seventies, at which time it was superb, but by then had no place to go except down. The 1966, of which I had several cases at one time, peaked in the early seventies and has now faded. The 1969 is fully mature and quite exceptional, still loaded with fruit, very fragrant, and should keep well for at least another 5–6 years.

Other Côte Rôtie Growers

Guy Bernard (Ampuis)

Chol-Domaine de Boisseyt (Chavanay)—Chol owns two acres on the Côte Blonde, and both his 1983 and 1982 showed a classy, very fine style made for long cellaring. I wish I knew his wines better.

Claude Bonnefond (Ampuis)

Marius Chambeyron (Ampuis)

André Drevon (Ampuis)—Drevon produces easy to drink, fruity, supple Côte Rôties that mature early and therefore should be drunk within 7–8 years of the vintage.

François Gérard (Ampuis)—Gérard, who produces both Côte Rôtie and Condrieu, owns 6.2 acres of vines at Côte Rôtie from which he makes about 1,000 cases of wine. His acreage is totally on the Côte Blonde. His 1982 is soft, velvety, and quite good; his 1984 very acidic and unpleasant.

Domaine Gérin (Ampuis)— With the help of American capital this estate was created in the late sixties. Alfred Gérin, the mayor of Ampuis, heads the firm, which owns 24 acres of vines situated on the plateau. The wines were mediocre in the seventies, but in 1980, 1982, and 1983 the quality seemed higher and the wines deeper and more interesting. Prices are fair and the production is large. This is an estate that seems to be moving up the ladder of quality.

Bernard Levet (Ampuis)—This young grower, who keeps his cellar right on the traffic-laden main road that runs through Ampuis, burst on the scene with a dense, powerful, potentially long-lived 1983. It is too soon to judge Levet, but he could well prove to be a producer to follow. His production is tiny (under 1,000 cases).

Henri Minot (Ampuis)

Louis Remiller (Ampuis)

Georges Vernay (Condrieu)—The great master of Condrieu produces a rather lean, high-acid, angular Côte Rôtie from 3.7 acres of vines. It has never impressed me.

CONDRIEU AND CHÂTEAU GRILLET

France's Most Decadently Fruity and Opulent Wines

CONDRIEU AT A GLANCE

Type of wine produced:	White wine only
Grape varieties planted:	Viognier
Acres currently under vine:	Condrieu (57), Château Grillet (7.4)
Quality level:	Exceptional, one of the rarest and most unique wines in the world
Aging potential:	1–4 years; Grillet will keep 4–8 years
General characteristics:	An exotic, often overwhelming tropical fruit fragrance intertwined with floral aspects; a low-acid, very rich wine that is usually quite short-lived
Greatest recent vintages:	1985, 1983, 1982
Price range:	$12–$30

Condrieu has always been one of the rarest of white wines. Virtually everything about it is unique. First of all, the grape that produces Condrieu is the little-known Viognier. Where it came from and how it got to the hillsides of this quaint Rhône village have never been established. Despite the paucity of historical documentation, most of the local storytellers seem to recite the same tale. Their account is that the Viognier was transplanted in the third century A.D. by Romans who had pirated it out of Dalmatia (now Yugoslavia). Regardless of the truth of this story, whoever brought the Viognier grape to Condrieu deserves a great deal of thanks from wine-lovers everywhere.

The Viognier is a curious grape, hard to grow and never as prolific a producer as many growers desire. It ripens unevenly and at its point of fruit maturity can become overripe in a matter of hours. In short, it is one of the most troublesome grapes to cultivate. In France there is very little of it planted. Condrieu has only 57 acres planted with Viognier, although there are moves underfoot to increase the appellation's acreage to 50 hectares (about 104 acres). Château Grillet, Condrieu's neighbor several kilometers to the south, has almost eight acres of Viognier. Elsewhere the only Viognier to be found in France is in the southern Rhône where several experimental vineyards, particularly the Domaine Ste.-Anne in Gervais and Château Estève near Uchaux, are working with the Viognier. In addition, Viognier is found in Côte Rôtie, where tiny amounts are grown on the Côte Blonde and vinified together with the Syrah. Lastly, there are some illegal plantings in Châteauneuf-du-Pape.

Nevertheless, the Viognier produces wines that are remarkably alluring and exotic. The personality traits of this grape in the top vintages are its stunning, overwhelming fragrance that resembles scents of honeysuckle, pears, peaches, and apricots; a lush, opulent, almost unctuous and viscous texture; full body; and plenty of length and alcoholic headiness. The wine writer Jancis Robinson says it produces "full-bodied, golden wines with a haunting and tantalizingly elusive bouquet." On the negative side, the wine is low in acidity and generally not capable of aging. I have always found Condrieu to be one of the most luscious, intense, complex wines one could ever hope to taste, but it must be drunk within its first two or three years of life. There is only one exception to this rule, Château Grillet, which can handle cellaring up to eight to ten years in specific vintages.

Condrieu, like Côte Rôtie, is located on the western bank of the

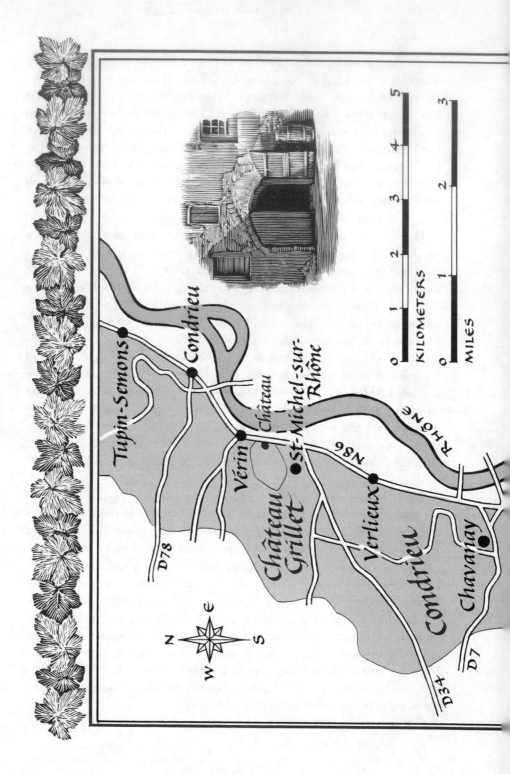

Tupin-Semons

Condrieu

Château

Vérin

St-Michel-sur-Rhône

Château Grillet

N86

RHÔNE

Verlieux

Condrieu

Chavanay

D78

D34

D7

N
W E
S

KILOMETERS
0 1 2 3 4 5

MILES
0 1 2 3

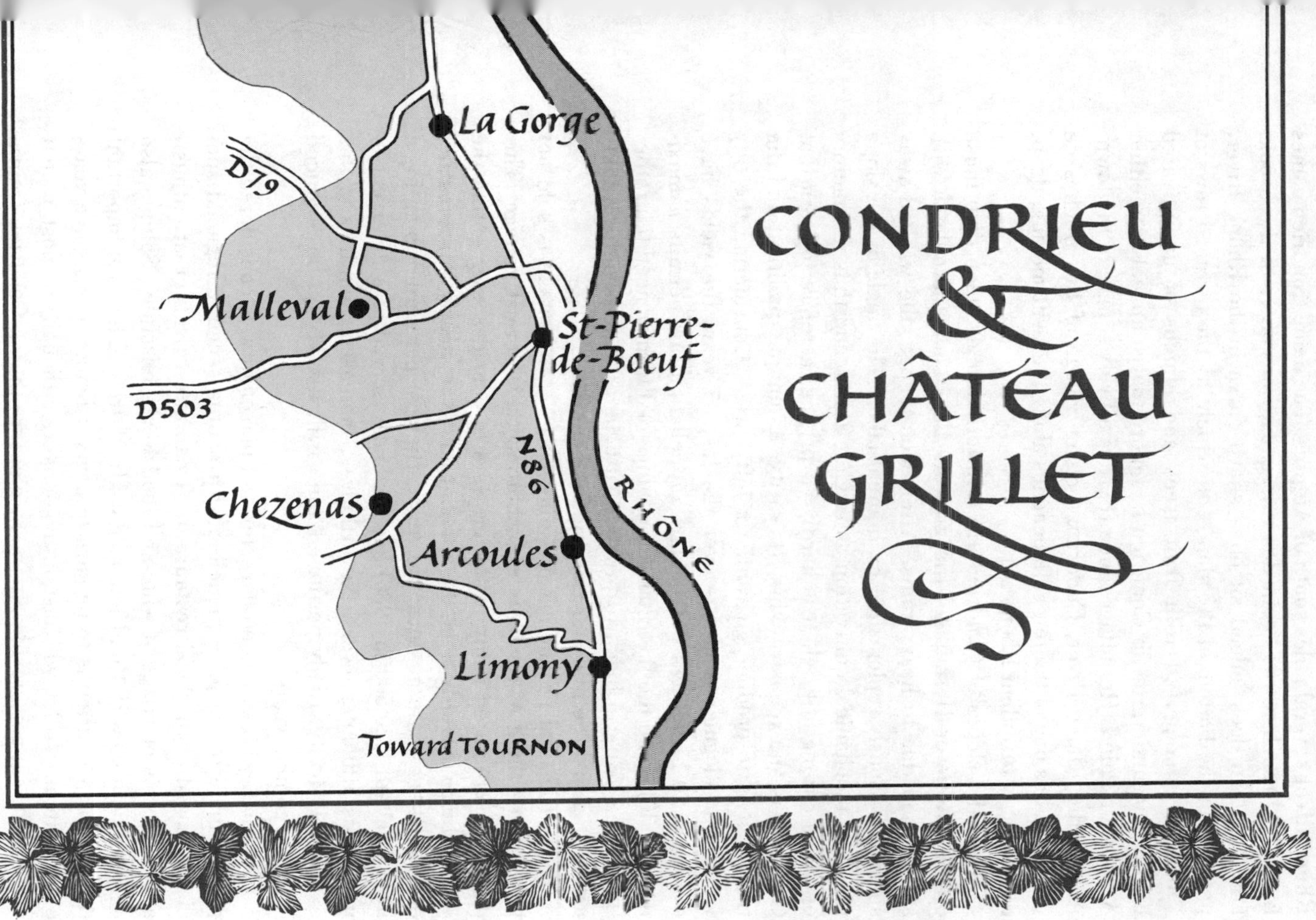

CONDRIEU & CHÂTEAU GRILLET

RHÔNE

La Gorge

St-Pierre-de-Bœuf

N 86

Arcoules

Limony

Toward Tournon

D79

Malleval

D503

Chezenas

Rhône River several miles south of Ampuis. The name Condrieu comes from the French words "coin des ruisseaux," or corner of the brook, and the town does indeed sit on a sharp curve in the Rhône River, perched at the bottom of the slopes on which lay the terraced rows of Viognier, interspersed with fruit trees and clumps of uncultivated bushes and undergrowth. Condrieu has more tourist appeal than either Ampuis or Tain L'Hermitage since there is a lively square in the town. Across the Rhône River, Condrieu's sister village of Les Roches de Condrieu has one of the few safe beaches along the swift-moving, deep, dangerously turbulent Rhône.

While the slopes of Condrieu are less forbiddingly steep than those of Côte Rôtie or Hermitage, the growers have similar problems with soil erosion due to heavy rains. After each deluge, the washed-away soil is laboriously replenished by manual labor. The angle of the slope prevents mechanical cultivation as in Côte Rôtie, and thus no tractors or plows can be utilized. It is hardly surprising therefore to learn that Condrieu is an expensive wine. Its rarity, its unique qualities, and the trouble it is to produce guarantee a lofty price. Considering the tiny yields the Viognier renders—over the last 35 years the yields have averaged 20 hectoliters per hectare (appellation law permits a maximum of 30)—and the fact that young vines of Viognier need ten rather than three years to begin to produce sufficiently, one is quite frankly astonished that the price for Condrieu is not higher.

Today the total production of Condrieu in each vintage is sold out long before the growers have even bottled their newest vintage. This demand has caused many of the growers to consider augmenting the size of their vineyards since the appellation covers nearly 500 acres and only 57 of these are in vines. However, the cost per acre of planting a new vineyard ($20,500 in 1986) has obviously served as a deterrent to many less affluent growers. Nevertheless, increased quantities of this explosively fruity, richly perfumed wine will, thankfully, be produced over the coming years.

Condrieu, with so much character and personality, is considered the perfect mate to the pike quenelles with nantua sauce, a regional specialty served at the local restaurants. I can attest (with great enthusiasm) that this marriage of wine and food works blissfully. Salmon also seems to go well with Condrieu, as does fresh trout. The most important thing about Condrieu is to be sure to drink it before it turns five years old. Château Grillet will last much longer, although in most recent vintages it will not provide any more pleasure than a Condrieu from a top grower.

RECENT VINTAGES

1986—The quality of the 1986s should be good, although much higher in acidity and less opulent than the 1985s. However, the quantity was down 40% compared to 1985 because of hailstorms during the summer. Optimum maturity: 1988–1991.

1985—While the overall acidities are quite low, there can be no doubt that for those who prefer Condrieu at its flamboyant best—explosively rich, full-bodied, unctuous, and loaded with ripe fruit—this is the vintage to seek out. The wines are dramatic, sensationally perfumed, and gorgeous to drink. Optimum maturity: now–1989.

1984—Some growers prefer the higher acid, leaner, more restrained style of the 1984s to the blockbuster 1985s. The 1984s have nowhere near the size and power of the 1985s, but are certainly good. Optimum maturity: now–1990.

1983—A top-notch vintage, the 1983s should be consumed immediately before they begin to fade and lose their fruit. They were full-bodied, unctuous wines with heaps of fruit, but I have long ago drunk up my tiny supply.

1982—Again, the 1982s were superb in Condrieu, somewhat similar in style to the 1985s. They should all have been consumed by now.

OLDER VINTAGES

Only Château Grillet has consistently shown the ability to age gracefully. The top older vintages for Château Grillet were 1970, 1971, and 1978, all of which should now be consumed.

A Personal Rating of the Condrieu Producers (Including Château Grillet)

*****(OUTSTANDING PRODUCERS)

Delas Frères
Pierre Dumazet
Etienne Guigal

Paul Multier (Château du Rozay)
Georges Vernay (Coteaux de Vernon)

****(EXCELLENT PRODUCERS)

Jean Pinchon

Georges Vernay (regular bottling)

***(GOOD PRODUCERS)

Antoine Cuilleron
Château Grillet

Robert Jurie-des-Camiers
Pierre Perret

ANTOINE CUILLERON***

The elderly Cuilleron, who must be approaching his mid-sixties, owns only 2.5 acres of Viognier vines from which he produces a good, relatively straightforward, cleanly made Condrieu with the telltale aroma of pears and honeysuckle. His wine is fermented in spotless stainless steel and then aged in small oak barrels for 12–16 months.

VINTAGES

1985—*Condrieu*—Light to medium straw in color, the ripe pear-
·   scented fragrance of the Viognier seems readily apparent in this
86   medium-bodied, rather stylish wine that has better acidity than
         many 1985s. Anticipated maturity: now–1989. Last tasted 6/86.

1984—*Condrieu*—Quite light for a Condrieu, but nevertheless delight-
·   fully refreshing, crisp, medium-bodied, and very flowery. Tasted
82   blind, I would have thought this was a Mosel. Drink up. Last
         tasted 6/86.

DELAS FRÈRES*****

This négociant owns one of the choicest vineyard sites in Condrieu. Called Le Clos Bouché, this five-acre steep hillside vineyard produces one of the finest Condrieus of the appellation. The Delas staff vinifies its Condrieu in stainless steel at a very low temperature, blocks the malolactic fermentation, gives it a brief respite in small oak barrels, and bottles it in the spring following the vintage. It is among the most perfumed and unctuous styles of Condrieu produced. Not surprisingly, it is not inexpensive. For some unknown reason, the great quality of this firm's Condrieu has remained in large part a secret.

VINTAGES

1985—*Condrieu*—A classic Condrieu, the 1985 has an intense, over-
·   whelming fragrance of spring flowers and pears. Quite rich, unc-
90   tuous, and full-bodied on the palate, this wine should be drunk
         by mid-1988. Last tasted 12/86.

PIERRE DUMAZET*****

This micro-estate of one acre would otherwise not merit a mention but for the fact that their wines are among the very best of the appellation. The vineyard, located near the hamlet of Limony, is the steepest of the appellation. The wine is explosively rich, as well as wonderfully perfumed, and it is a shame there is so little of it to go around (about 150 cases a year). The Dumazet family, which has been making wine from this site for over a century, ages their wine for 12–18 months in oak barrels prior to bottling.

VINTAGES

1985—*Condrieu*—a large-framed, dramatic Condrieu, the 1985 oozes
· with scents of lychee nuts, apricots, and the perfume of overripe
92 melon. Low in acidity, it should be drunk before the end of 1989. Last tasted 3/87.

CHÂTEAU GRILLET***

The legendary Château Grillet produces not only the Rhône Valley's most famous white wine, but one of the most celebrated wines of France. It is unique in many respects. For one thing, it is an appellation unto itself; for another, it is France's smallest appellation. And there is not much of it made. The 7.4 acres of vineyards, which sit 500 feet above the Rhône in a perfect amphitheater with a superb south-southeasterly exposure, are drenched in sunlight during the growing season. The grape, like that of Condrieu only a mile away, is the fickle Viognier, but at Château Grillet the soil is lighter and more fragmented with a great deal of mica in it. From this privileged, hallowed site comes about 1,000 cases of a wine that sells at prices two to three times higher than that of the finest Condrieu. Château Grillet is also distinguished by its brownish/yellow bottle, the only one of its type in use in France. And close inspection will reveal that it holds only 70 centiliters, not 75 as do all other standard French wine bottles. Since 1830, Château Grillet has been owned by the Neyrat-Gachet family. The current proprietor is the elderly, aristocratic-looking André Canet who resides in Lyons but obviously spends a great deal of time at Grillet.

Is Château Grillet a better wine than the top Condrieu? Certainly, well-heeled collectors are drawn to this wine because of its rarity, expense, and mystique, but my experience, which includes virtually all the Grillet vintages since 1967, has shown that this wine usually fails to live up to expectations. It is ironic that Rhône wines as a general rule are notoriously undervalued and underappreciated, yet the region's most famous white wine is no doubt overpriced and overrated. Such is sometimes the state of things in the wine world.

This is not to suggest that Grillet has not made some fine wines. The 1967, 1970, 1972, and 1976 were all delicious, very good rather than stupendous expressions of winemaking art. However, recent vintages have been quite light, sometimes even watery and underripe. Most observers (which includes the local cognoscenti in Condrieu) make much of the fact that Grillet consistently harvests two to three weeks before the better growers, apparently unwilling to risk the chance of fall rains. Guigal in particular argues that this robs the wine of much of its richness since the grapes are not fully mature. And the growth of the vineyards from 4.2 acres in 1971 to the present 7.4 acres has been accompanied by a doubling of production, a large percentage of which comes from very young vines that do not give the richness in juice that old vines do. Finally, many feel that the continued practice of aging the wine in cask for 18 months is foolish and overwhelms the delicate fruit. All of these factors help explain why recent vintages are less than inspired. Reports continue to circulate that this domaine will eventually be sold. However, much of this speculation seems nothing more than wishful thinking on the part of several powerful Rhône families who would like nothing better than to add Château Grillet to their portfolios.

VINTAGES

1984—*Château Grillet*—Quite light in both body and flavor, the 1984 has very high acidity, an undernourished feel on the palate, but enough fleeting aromas of the Viognier to give it some appeal. Anticipated maturity: now–1989. Last tasted 12/86.
•
78

1983—*Château Grillet*—Given the vintage and the great success vignerons in nearby Condrieu had, one would have expected a great deal more flavor and body. Elegant aromas of spring flowers and spicy oak are attractive. On the palate, the wine is medium-bodied, excessively understated, and polite. It offers good, uninspired drinking at a ridiculously high price. Anticipated maturity: now–1990. Last tasted 7/86.
•
82

1982—*Château Grillet*—Of recent vintages of Grillet, the 1982 shows the most flavor concentration and character. In addition, it seems to be holding up in the bottle better than the Condrieu wines of this vintage. There is a very enticing bouquet of flowers and fruit. On the palate, the wine shows a good measure of glycerine, good acidity, and a fine finish. Drink over the next 2–3 years. Last tasted 7/86.
•
86

1981—*Château Grillet*—All the right aromas and flavors are present, but one wishes this wine were deeper and bolder. It is a very delicate wine, medium-bodied, understated, graceful, but a little straightforward and short in the finish. Drink up. Last tasted 7/86.
•
84

ETIENNE GUIGAL *****

Guigal's Condrieu is not only that excellent firm's finest white wine, but it is a wine that Marcel Guigal takes great care and pride in making. The Guigals own no vineyards (although they are aggressively looking to buy), but purchase the grapes and vinify the wine at their cellars in Ampuis. There have been continual experiments with aging their Condrieu in new oak barrels, a tactic that other producers vehemently denounce as lunacy. However, after using too much new oak in 1982, Guigal has now reached a formula that seems to work well. Currently, 40% of his Condrieu spends three months in new oak and is then blended with the 60% that has remained in stainless steel tanks. The wine is bottled in April following the vintage. Guigal believes this gives his Condrieu the structure that it often lacks while not sacrificing any of its decadently rich, unctuous fruitiness. Guigal produces, on average, 450 cases of Condrieu, not nearly enough to satisfy customer demand. But he expects to gradually increase the amount of Condrieu produced.

VINTAGES

1985—*Condrieu*—For me, this is Guigal's best Condrieu yet. A multi-
·   dimensional bouquet of flowers, apricots, and subtle oak is to-
91 tally delightful. On the palate, the wine is very concentrated, lush, and full-bodied, but also has some structure to it. It will keep better than others, but should be drunk before the end of 1988. Last tasted 12/86.

1984—*Condrieu*—A much lighter and less concentrated wine than the
·   1985, Guigal's 1984 is fragrant, spicy with good fruit as well as
85 good acidity. Drink up. Last tasted 6/86.

PAUL MULTIER (CHÂTEAU DU ROZAY) *****

This estate was founded only in 1978 by the late Paul Multier, who had worked for Condrieu's largest and most successful grower, Georges Vernay. It was in 1978 that he began to estate bottle his own wine. His once boldly painted, now faded pink, turreted château high on a hill behind the town of Condrieu is called Château du Rozay, and the Multier family have lived there since 1898. His son, Jean Yves, in his mid-twenties, presides over the estate and tends to the making of the wine. The vines are planted on 2.5 acres of a particularly desirable part of the Condrieu hillside called Coteau de Chéry. Jean Yves Multier is a remarkably frank, open man who proudly boasts that their vineyard is always picked at least two to three weeks after Château Grillet's, ensuring that they have obtained the super ripeness (or *sur-maturité*) in the Viognier that they desire. The wine is fermented in stainless steel tanks and aged several months in large wooden barrels prior to bottling in May following the vintage. Multier opposes new oak barrels for aging Condrieu, and is in total agreement with the view that Condrieu must be drunk within three to four years of the vintage. To prove his point, he opened a 1979 in June 1986 to demonstrate how this wine, which was excellent in 1981, had lost its fruit and taken on a completely oxidized character.

VINTAGES

1985—*Condrieu*—Multier seems less enthusiastic about this wine than
·   I am. Though it does not quite compare to the monumental
86   Condrieu made here in 1983 and 1981, it is still a powerful, alcoholic, rich, big-styled wine with gobs of fruit, but is a little deficient in acidity. Drink it before the end of 1989. Last tasted 6/86.

1984—*Condrieu*—The 1984 is somewhat angular and acidic for a Condrieu. Those who prefer their wines light and very crisp may
·
82   appreciate this style more than I did. It is cleanly made and vibrantly fresh, but lacks flesh and length. Drink up. Last tasted 6/86.

PIERRE PERRET***

Perret, whose cellars are in nearby Chavannay, produces one of the lightest, least unctuous styles of Condrieu. He ferments his wine in stainless steel and tends to harvest his five acres of 40-year-old vines earlier than other growers. His production averages about 600 cases of wine per year, and his wines, even more so than the other wines of Condrieu, should be drunk within 2–3 years of the vintage.

VINTAGES

1985—*Condrieu*—One of Perret's best Condrieus, the exuberant, flow-
·   ery, tropical fruit bouquet, creamy, full-bodied flavors, and
86   rather low acidity beg for this wine to be drunk before the end of 1988. Last tasted 6/86.

1984—*Condrieu*—Tart, light, somewhat thin and watery, I would be
·   hard pressed to identify this wine as a Condrieu in a blind tast-
72   ing. Last tasted 6/86.

JEAN PINCHON****

Pinchon is a pleasant though reserved man in his late fifties. He is contemplating retirement now that his son-in-law has expressed an interest in taking over the domaine, which consists of 3.8 acres of vines. In a big vintage, Pinchon produces about 600 cases of wine. His cellars are below his home in Condrieu. Unlike his peers, Pinchon is the last to bottle his Condrieu, preferring to see it get at least 20–24 months in his ancient oak barrels. In addition, he is not a believer in drinking Condrieu too young, claiming it is at its best when five to six years old, and can be kept a decade before its perfume of tropical fruit and flowers fades away. I do not agree with this, but I will acknowledge that Pinchon's Condrieu does seem to keep in the bottle longer than those of other growers. Even though great chefs such as Bocuse and Troisgros are constantly requesting increases in their allocations, Pinchon seems totally unaffected by the incessant demand for his wines. I find them among the best balanced and harmonious of Condrieus. They have the flamboyant, dramatic fruitiness of Condrieu, but never seem to be overblown or overwhelming.

VINTAGES

1985—*Condrieu*—The 1985 has the full-intensity, exotic, extroverted
·   bouquet of the Viognier, as well as rich, full-bodied flavors and
89   excellent, crisp acidity for balance. Anticipated maturity: now–
             1991. Last tasted 6/86.
1984—*Condrieu*—An elegant, stylish wine that is considerably less
·   powerful and unctuous than either the 1983 or 1985. Neverthe-
84   less it is attractive in a lighter style. Drink before the end of
             1987. Last tasted 6/86.
1983—*Condrieu*—Now at its peak, Pinchon's 1983 has an exotic,
·   peach-scented bouquet, and viscous full-bodied flavors comple-
87   mented nicely by crisp acidity. Drink up. Last tasted 12/86.

GEORGES VERNAY****

The stocky, heavily jowled Georges Vernay is, for all intents and purposes, Mr. Condrieu. Not only is he the long-standing president of the growers' association, but he produces and bottles over 50% of the appellation's total output. He owns 15 acres of vineyards, but supplements his own yields with purchases from growers. Despite just turning 60, Vernay is always on the move, flitting around Condrieu dispensing words of encouragement, giving advice, and working extremely hard to extract from one of the wine world's most temperamental grapes as fine a wine as it is possible to make. Vernay produces three types of Condrieu. For the locals, he makes a sweet Condrieu called Vin de Noël that is sold only to private customers and never exported. The bulk of his production is his dry, full-bodied, delicious Condrieu. A tiny percentage of this production is from a specific vineyard called the Coteaux de Vernon. It is his finest Condrieu, and usually the best wine made in the appellation. Unfortunately, only about 330 cases are produced from this vineyard planted with vines that average 35 years of age, located on a steep slope opposite Condrieu's most famous restaurant, Beau Rivage. While his regular Condrieu is bottled in March following the vintage, the Coteaux de Vernon spends an additional six months in both new and old oak barrels prior to bottling. Vernay ferments all of his Condrieu in spotless stainless steel tanks and always puts them through a malolactic fermentation. While he employs some new oak barrels each year, he says one must be judicious in the use of these so as not to overwhelm the ripe, seductive fruit of the Viognier with toasty, vanillin aromas of new oak.

VINTAGES

1985—*Condrieu*—This is classic Condrieu, quite concentrated, rich,
·   somewhat high in alcohol, but very perfumed and unctuous on
87   the palate. Drink over the next 2–3 years. Last tasted 12/86.

1985—*Condrieu Coteaux de Vernon*—One of the two finest Viognier-
·   based wines I have ever tasted. Unbelievably concentrated, it
92   has layers of an exotic melange of tropical fruit. Stunningly long,
       it overwhelms the palate with a dazzling display of flavors and
       aromas. Drink over the next 3 years. Last tasted 1/87.

1984—*Condrieu*—Vernay's regular cuvée of 1984 is light, a little tart
·   and even watery for one of his wines, but pleasant in a straight-
83   forward way. Drink up. Last tasted 6/86.

1984—*Condrieu Coteaux de Vernon*—A much more amply proportioned
·   wine, this exotic-scented wine has aromas of ripe pears and a
87   mineral fragrance. Medium- to full-bodied with good, crisp acid-
       ity, this wine may be cellared 4–5 years, an anomaly for a Con-
       drieu. Last tasted 6/86.

Other Condrieu Producers

Pierre Corompt

Emile David

André Dézormeaux—This highly esteemed grower has three acres of vines and is reputed to make fat, tasty, deeply flavored wines. I have never had the opportunity to taste Dézormeaux's Condrieu.

Robert Jurie-des-Camiers—This small grower, who lives outside Lyons in St.-Genis Laval, owns three acres of vines. The wine rests one year in tanks prior to bottling. I was impressed with both a 1983 and 1985 from this grower, but have never seen his wines outside France.

Vidal-Fleury—The Guigal family now owns this famous firm in Ampuis. Traditionally, a decent rather than exciting Condrieu was produced. It is expected that Vidal-Fleury will continue to produce a Condrieu, made to the specifications of Marcel Guigal.

HERMITAGE

The Manliest of All Wines?

HERMITAGE AT A GLANCE

Types of wine produced:	Red and white wine
Grape varieties planted:	Syrah for the red wine; primarily Marsanne and some Roussanne for the white wine
Acres currently under vine:	380
Quality level:	Exceptional for the red wines, good to exceptional for the white wines
Aging potential:	Red wine: 5–30 years White wine: 3–15 years
General characteristics:	Rich, port-like, viscous, very full-bodied, tannic red wines. Full-bodied white wines with a unique scent of herbs, minerals, nuts, and peaches
Greatest recent vintages:	1985, 1983, 1979, 1978, 1972, 1970, 1966, 1961
Price range:	$12–$35

The huge Hermitage hill that looms over a sharp bend in the Rhône River is a formidable sight, particularly from across the Rhône in Tournon. The appellation of Hermitage is not large. There are only 380 acres of vines, seemingly chiseled into the granite rock, from which both red wine from the Syrah grape and white wine from the Roussanne and Marsanne grapes are made. Despite increased interest and prices in what can be exceptional wines, the wines of Hermitage are still remarkably undervalued. I am convinced that if I ever sat down with all my tasting notes and tried to come up with the finest 50 wines I have ever had, at least 20% of them would be from Hermitage, an impressive percentage.

Hermitage has a long and colorful history. John Livingstone-Learmonth, in his excellent book on the wines of the Rhône, states that vines were first brought to Hermitage in 500 B.C. by the Greeks. The most often quoted legend of this famous hill is that in the thirteenth century a crusader, Gaspard de Stérimberg, wounded in the wars of that period, sought refuge on top of this hill and subsequently built a chapel there. The modern, reconstructed version still sits alone near the crest of the hill and is owned by the Jaboulet family, who call their best red Hermitage "La Chapelle" and their white Hermitage "Gaspard de Stérimberg." There are other stories that have no doubt been equally embellished, but it is this legend which has endeared itself to most of the story tellers.

Few realize it, but in the early nineteenth century Hermitage was France's most expensive red wine, selling at prices above Lafite-Rothschild and Haut-Brion. Additionally, it is also a well-documented fact that Hermitage was used to add color, strength, and structure to Bordeaux in the nineteenth century. In fact, Hermitage was so prized an addition to the wines of Bordeaux that Châteaux actually promoted them as being "Hermitaged."

Among wine connoisseurs who seek quality, not merely prestige, Hermitage remains a revered name. I doubt that it is as massively portlike and viscous as it may have been 50 or 100 years ago, and as for its reputation as France's manliest wine, I would give this chauvinistic award to Cornas, the southern neighbor of Hermitage. Nevertheless, Hermitage can be stupendous wine in the hands of the best growers and producers. The 1929 white and red Hermitages of Chave (drunk most recently in 1986), the 1959 and 1961 La Chapelles of Paul Jaboulet, the 1929 Chapoutier white Hermitage (drunk in 1985), as well as an unlabeled bottle of 1922, are six wines that give irrefutable evidence to

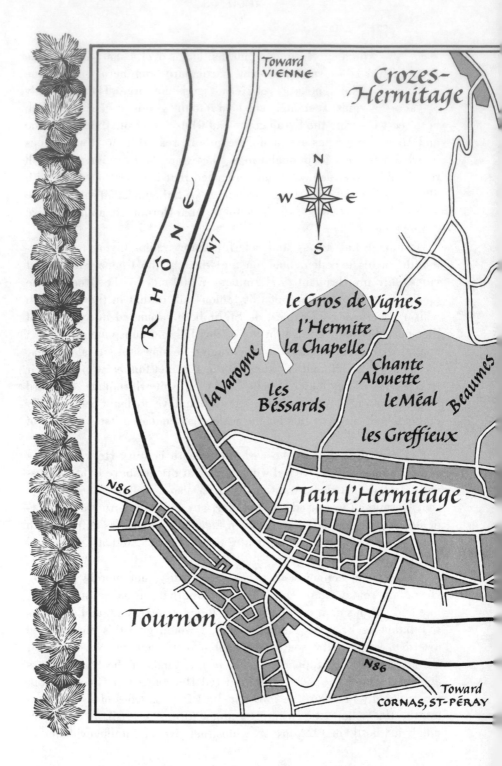

HERMITAGE

la Maison Blanche

la Pierelle

l'Homme

les Rocoules

les Murets

la Croix

les Diognières

D109

A7

D532

D101

N7

RHÔNE

Toward VALENCE

the enormous aging potential of Hermitage. Why is it then that Hermitage does not fetch the price of a Bordeaux first-growth or a Burgundy Grand Cru?

Another explanation why Hermitage is no longer France's most expensive red wine is that it is generally not easy to taste young. Often quite tannic, with intense aromas of licorice, tar, smoky, peppery, berry fruit, and frequently a gamelike scent, it is a remarkably complex, intense wine that offers a much more challenging range of impressions compared to a fine young claret. A young claret's classic aromas of blackcurrant fruit intermingled with toasty, vanillin, oaky scents are something many consumers find much easier to understand and have had much more experience with. It is with age—a minimum of five to seven years for a decent vintage, a decade for a top vintage—that Hermitage develops the profound, enticing bouquet and rich, velvety flavor for which it is known. Only then can one begin to comprehend why it has been such cherished and greatly revered wine.

Perhaps part of the problem is the image the Syrah grape has in the world's viticultural regions outside of France. Americans have largely turned their backs on California's wines called "Petite Sirah" which, as England's Jancis Robinson points out in her book *Vines, Grapes, and Wines,* is not even Syrah, but rather a bland grape named "Durif" that produces less than inspired wine. In Australia, fine Syrah can be found everywhere but is inexplicably thought of as less sexy and desirable than the glamorous Cabernet Sauvignon or Pinot Noir, despite the fact that Australia's greatest wine, the Penfolds Grange Hermitage, is a totally Syrah wine.

Prices for Hermitage, however, are moving up as the glories of these wines, produced in quite limited quantities by only a handful of growers and négociants, have become more widely publicized. Amazingly, there are only 16 producers of Hermitage wine, each producing a distinctive, unique style apart from that of the others.

Hermitage's huge, steep hill in actuality consists of three different slopes sprinkled with specific vineyard sites, or as the French say *mas,* and varying types of soil. Virtually every producer of Hermitage will state unequivocally that it is these vineyards, and the proportion of wine produced from each, that dictates the character of his Hermitage.

The steepest part of the Hermitage hill is directly behind the dull little commercial town of Tain L'Hermitage, where the elevation reaches nearly 1,000 feet. At the top is the Jaboulet-owned, tiny chapel from which Jaboulet takes the name La Chapelle for its red Hermitage. The principal vineyard here is Les Bessards, and the wines produced from its granite soil are the deepest in color, most intense in flavor, and often the richest and fullest in body, with a great deal of tannin. Further down the slope is Le Méal, also a top site for great Hermitage. Méal is reputed to produce very fragrant, supple, intensely fruity wines. At the very bottom of the hill is Les Greffieux, which has the richest soil and produces lighter, more perfumed, velvety-textured wines with great finesse. Les Greffieux is also one of the best locations for the white wine varietals, Marsanne and Roussanne. These are the three most highly prized vineyards, and traditional thinking has it that the greatest wines of Hermitage must be made from a blend of all three locations. However, there are other notable vineyards (see map on pages 86–87).

For the finest white Hermitage, the three vineyards of Les Rocoules, Chante-Alouette, and Les Murets are deemed the best. Chante-Alouette is owned exclusively by the Chapoutier firm and their white wine from the rocky, granite soil is one of the finest and longest lived of the appellation. Chante-Alouette sits higher up the slope than either Les Murets or Les Rocoules. I have tasted equally superb white Hermitage from both vineyards, but Les Murets seems to have a better reputation among the local cognoscenti. Other recognized vineyard sites are L'Hermite, the highest vineyard; Beaumes, in the middle of the hill and known for its fruity, aromatic, soft red and white wines; Les Diognères, located at the eastern end of the hill, which is noticeably less steep and a consistent producer of dense-colored, powerful, tannic wine; and La Maison Blanche, known for its white wine. Other vineyards that make red wine but are less renowned include L'Homme, Gros des Vignes, La Croix, La Pierrelle, Signaux, Varoque, and Croix de Jamanot.

Only a few growers and producers designate their Hermitage by vineyard, since an assemblage of wine from different parcels has been considered the best way of producing a great Hermitage. Those producers who do indicate a vineyard name on their Hermitage include Marc Sorrel, whose Le Gréal (a blend of wine from Greffieux and Le Méal) is used for their red wines, and Jules Fayolle, who cites Les Diognères as the source for his red Hermitage. As it happens, the best-known and frequently the greatest red Hermitage, La Chapelle of the Jaboulet firm, is named after the tiny chapel that sits on the top of a majestic hill rather than for any specific vineyard. The other great Hermitage is that of Gérard Chave, whose family has been making Hermitage merely since 1481. He normally produces his superb red Hermitage from at least seven different vineyards, with remarkable, often spectacular results.

Hermitage is quite a long-lived wine, although I doubt that it has the potential today to improve in the bottle and last beyond 30–35 years. I suspect this is more than adequate for today's generation of wine drinkers, who show little inclination to defer gratification. Hermitage draws its aging capacity from itself, since only a handful of growers employ small new oak barrels to give the wine extra tannin and the toasty, oaky character found in many wines from Bordeaux and Burgundy. Even those producers who do use some new oak barrels employ them conservatively, feeling, quite justifiably, that Hermitage has all the natural concentration, tannins, and fruit necessary to last and evolve for decades.

If red Hermitage has become increasingly popular, few wine enthusiasts yet seem to comprehend the white wines of Hermitage. Two white grape varietals are permitted at Hermitage, the Marsanne and Roussanne. The latter has virtually disappeared in the northern Rhône because the vine was susceptible to the disease called oidium, but new plantings are taking place with a disease-resistant clone. Marsanne is widely planted in Hermitage and tends to produce a strongly scented wine that Jancis Robinson claims "smells not unpleasantly reminiscent of glue." More flattering is John Livingstone-Learmonth's statement that some note the taste of "nuts, peaches and apricots." Personally, I have preferred the scent of pure Roussanne, which I would describe as the aroma of honeysuckle and sometimes almonds, to that of Marsanne, which can be dull and heavy. But in ideal years there is no doubt that the scent of peaches and apricots is more than just an olfactory flight of fancy—it can be detected. As white Hermitage ages, it takes on a golden color; I find the scent of smoky hazelnuts extremely strong in the top old white Hermitages such as Chave's and Chapoutier's Chante-Alouette. White Hermitage can be unbelievably long-lived. In 1986 I drank (with enormous pleasure) both the 1929 Chave and Chapoutier. Besides the famous taste of nuts that is attributed to them, both had exceptional richness and depth as well as amazing freshness. Despite the fact that white Hermitage is hardly a household name, the strong personality of this wine makes it an ideal accompaniment to many of the innovative and exotic dishes now featured in chic restaurants.

While the appellation controls of Hermitage permit up to 15% white Hermitage in the blend of red wine, no producer admits to adding more than 2–5% to his wines. One perceivable trend in Hermitage that has emerged in the eighties is the production of tiny quantities of the legendary, nectarlike *vin de paille*, or straw wine. This wine was produced as a matter of course in the nineteenth century with late-harvested grapes left out on straw mats for a month or more to dry out and become raisins. Chave produced an Yquem-like Vin de Paille in 1974, which, when I last drank it in 1986, was decadently rich, perfumed, and indeed special. In 1982 Chapoutier also produced an exceptional though tiny quantity of Vin de Paille. Finally, Ferraton made a great Vin de Paille in 1985, so one hopes to see more and more of this unique, very rich, powerful, sweet wine made by the producers of Hermitage.

RECENT VINTAGES

1986—It was a very abundant crop in Hermitage with the white wines significantly less powerful and concentrated than the big, occasionally overblown 1985s. As for the reds, they show good concentration, are medium-bodied, elegant, and fruity but early maturing. Optimum maturity: 1990–1998.

1985—The red wines from this vintage were not as successful in Hermitage as in Côte Rôtie. Nevertheless, the red wines are intensely fruity, somewhat fat, low in acidity, but very perfumed, round and generous, with very good tannin contents. They are precocious wines and will no doubt mature rapidly, giving great pleasure soon. The one exception is Chave's red wine, undoubtedly the best of the appellation in 1985, and one that will last for 25 years. The white wines are very, very concentrated, sometimes a trifle exaggerated, but immensely interesting, rich, full-throttle wines with somewhat elevated levels of alcohol. Chapoutier's Chante-Alouette and Chave's white wines are sensational. It appears they will have to be drunk early, but they are sumptuous wines. Optimum maturity: now–1997.

1984—Again, less successful for the red wines than in Côte Rôtie; however, 1984 was certainly good for the white wines. At first, they seemed lean and highly acidic, but in the bottle they have exhibited a generally lighter style, plenty of finesse, and while they are not blockbusters, they certainly are quite pleasurable. The 1984 reds are quite light and will mature rapidly. Chave's white and red Hermitages are notable successes in 1984. Optimum maturity: now–1992.

1983—This is a great year in Hermitage, superior even to Côte Rôtie. However, this is a true *vin de garde* vintage since the dry, hot summer produced modest quantities of very rich, very tannic, hard wines that will, I am afraid to say, require at least another decade of cellaring. The wines were fabulous from the cask but have since closed up completely and it is a waste to drink them now. Arguments will no doubt rage well into the next century as to whether Chave or Jaboulet produced the greater red Hermitage, but both wines are monumental efforts that should not be touched before the year 2000. Great efforts were also turned in by Delas Frères, Guigal, Sorrel, and Ferraton. As for the white wines, they are excellent, but clearly not as consistently exceptional as the red wines. Is 1983 better than 1978? While some producers say yes, I still have to give the nod to the 1978s, but certainly the 1983s are indeed very special. Optimum maturity: (reds) 1993–2020; (whites) now–1995.

1982—Potentially an exceptional vintage, 1982 was also an extremely troublesome year for producers because of the torrid heat during the harvest that resulted in overheated fermentations and spoilage. The top red wines, such as those of Chave, Fayolle, and Jaboulet's La Chapelle, are velvety, rich, broadly flavored wines with considerably more appeal now and over the next 5–10 years than the more highly rated 1983s. Rich and perfumed, but low in acidity, the wines will develop quickly. As for the whites, they are all fully mature and because of their low, fixed acidities should be drunk up. This is a tricky vintage to purchase blindly. For example, two fine growers, Ferraton and Sorrel, both made poor wines (no doubt because they were unable to control the temperature of their fermentations). Optimum maturity: (reds) now–1997; (whites) now.

1981—To date, I find this the least attractive vintage for Hermitage in the eighties. The wines are tart, somewhat undernourished, angular, and lacking both charm and flesh. Jaboulet, who first deemed the quality insufficient to declare a La Chapelle, changed his mind, mistakenly in my view. Even Chave's 1981 is, by his standards, a delicate, austere wine. Surprisingly, one of the best 1981s came from the small grower Michel Ferraton. Guigal also made a good wine in 1981. The white wines are more interesting, but overall still unexciting. I doubt that any of these wines will improve, so it is advisable to drink them now.

1980—An underrated vintage, the 1980s will offer supple, fruity, attractive drinking for the next 5–6 years. They are not big, deep, dramatic wines, but rather round, elegant, and soft with plenty of clean fruit and charm. The white wines have stood up to bottle age well and should be drunk up. This is certainly a good rather than poor vintage, as suggested by a number of writers in August

1980, a good 6 weeks before the harvest commenced! Optimum maturity for both red and white wines: now–1993.

1979—This is an excellent vintage for red wine and a good one for white. For the reds, 1979 was simply caught in the classic vinous scenario—a very fine year receives little or no publicity because the preceding year was a great one, and the wine press had exhausted its supply of raves. Thus 1979, coming after the superb 1978 vintage, seemed something quite inferior. In actuality the wines are not far from the heights reached by the 1978s. They are developing more quickly than the 1978s and have exceptional color, excellent depth, and in the case of Jaboulet's La Chapelle, Delas's Cuvée Marquise de la Tourette, and Sorrel's Le Méal, will easily arrive in the next century in fine shape, good cellar conditions permitting. Curiously, Chave's 1979, though quite good, is not at the level one might expect. Optimum maturity: (reds) 1988–2000.

1978—This is the greatest vintage for Hermitage producers in the last 25 years. The top wines are still infants in terms of their evolution. Rich, profoundly concentrated, tannic yet complex, fragrant wines were produced that will in some cases last 40–50 years. I believe the 1978s have more depth and fruit than the 1983s, and for that reason believe 1978 is superior. Chave made a simply stunning wine that will provide monumental drinking in 20 years. As sublime as Chave's 1978 is, the 1978s from Sorrel, Delas, and the La Chapelle of Paul Jaboulet are equally grand and potentially as long-lived. Unfortunately, the only place these wines are likely to show up is at wine auctions. Optimum maturity: (reds) 1992–2015.

OLDER VINTAGES

Nineteen seventy-seven was a poor vintage, 1976 rather highly regarded but I believe vastly overrated, and 1975, 1974, and 1973 all quite mediocre. The sleeper vintage of the seventies is the terribly underrated 1972. Jaboulet's La Chapelle is outstanding in 1972 and equal, perhaps superior to, the very good years of 1970 and 1971. In the sixties, 1961 produced a La Chapelle that remains one of the three or four greatest red wines I have ever tasted. Nineteen sixty-four was very fine, as was 1966. Certainly 1969 and 1962 were good, but somewhat less concentrated. Old vintages of Jaboulet's La Chapelle that turn up on the market from these years should all be in fine drinking form if they have been well cellared.

A Personal Rating of the Hermitage Producers
Red Hermitage

*****(OUTSTANDING PRODUCERS)*

J. L. Chave   Paul Jaboulet (La Chapelle)
Delas Frères (Cuvée Marquise
de la Tourette)

****(EXCELLENT PRODUCERS)*

M. Chapoutier (Cuvée   E. Guigal
Numéro)   M. Sorrel (before 1980, after
B. Faurie   1982)

***(GOOD PRODUCERS)*

M. Chapoutier (other cuvées)   J. L. Grippat
Jules Fayolle   Paul Jaboulet (regular cuvée)
M. Ferraton   de Vallouit

**(AVERAGE PRODUCERS)*

Desmeure   L. Revol
Jaboulet-Vercherre   Union des Propriétaires

White Hermitage

*****(OUTSTANDING PRODUCERS)*

M. Chapoutier (Cuvée   J. L. Grippat
Numéro)
J. L. Chave

****(EXCELLENT PRODUCERS)*

M. Chapoutier (Chante-   M. Sorrel (after 1982)
Alouette)

***(GOOD PRODUCERS)*

Delas Frères   E. Guigal
B. Faurie   Paul Jaboulet (after 1982)
M. Ferraton (after 1982)

**(AVERAGE PRODUCERS)*

Desmeure   L. Revol
Jaboulet-Vercherre   Union des Propriétaires

CHAPOUTIER ***–****

There is no one more enthusiastic, animated, and amicable than the diminutive Max Chapoutier, who I am sure has told every visitor that he is "the smallest" producer in the Rhône Valley. Despite his lack of height, his presence in the Rhône and the international wine scene is enormous. His marketing genius has engineered the placement of his wines in every important market in the world. This firm, located right in Tain L'Hermitage, was founded in 1808. Chapoutier is a very important vineyard owner with over 175 acres of vines in five appellations, Hermitage, Crozes-Hermitage, Saint-Joseph, Côte Rôtie, and Châteauneuf-du-Pape. His estate in Châteauneuf-du-Pape, called La Bernadine, is the largest, comprising 67 acres, but Chapoutier is also a very important grower in Hermitage, owning all of the famous Chante-Alouette vineyard and other parcels that total 59 acres, plus 17 acres under *fermage* or lease. The firm also operates as négociants, augmenting their own production with purchased grapes.

The Chapoutiers are quick to point out that their wines are among the most traditionally made in the Rhône Valley. The red wines are vinified at warm temperatures and aged up to three years in a combination of large oak and chestnut foudres and small barrels. They still ferment their Côte Rôtie and Hermitage in open wood vats and crush the grapes by actual foot stomping. This is a passionately run family business with father Max and his two sons always exhibiting great enthusiasm for their wines. However, the innovative spirit of Max Chapoutier caused him to break away from tradition in 1965 and begin to offer not only his Hermitage but also his Châteauneuf-du-Pape and Côte Rôtie as blends of several vintages that he called Grandes Cuvées. His intention was to produce a wine from this blend that was consistent and ready to drink upon release. It would not replace his vintage-dated Hermitage, but supplement it. It was a brilliant idea, for restaurants throughout France rushed to put it on their wine lists. The success of the non-vintage Grande Cuvée led to the introduction of his Prestige Cuvées, which are also blends of different vintages but are in effect the finest lots of wine that Chapoutier believes he has made. Called "Cuvées Numérotées," these are rare editions of Chapoutier's finest wines, and compared to the modest prices his other wines sell for, they fetch very high prices. Production of his luxury red Hermitage called Le Pavillon has ranged between 220 and 900 cases, and his white Hermitage, called Cuvée de L'Orvée, about 400 cases. Max Chapoutier is not known for being modest about his wines, but the Cuvées Numérotées live up to their billing. I only wish that more was revealed about the vintages used for the blends and the bottling dates so that one could know a little about its history rather than simply relying on the fact that Chapoutier says it is the best wine he can produce. Chapoutier released his first Cuvées Numérotées in 1956 and only his third series of luxury cuvées as recently as 1986.

In summary, Chapoutier produces three different levels of red and white Hermitage: the outstanding red and white luxury blend, the Cuvées Numérotées; his vintage-dated red Hermitage called La Sizeranne and his famous white Hermitage, Chante-Alouette; and a Grande Cuvée of both white and red Hermitage that I find variable, ranging from very good to somewhat dull. At times, this all seems rather confusing.

Chapoutier's traditional style of Hermitage tends to produce robust red wines that seem less concentrated and complex than those of Jaboulet or Chave. However, his white Hermitage is superb, aging as well as that of Chave's, and is vastly superior to that made by Jaboulet. The Chapoutier firm is a great success story. Certainly, the consistent quality of the company's wines, their realistic, very fair prices, and the dynamic, extremely agreeable personalities of Max Chapoutier, his charming wife, and their gregarious sons have all contributed enormously to this family's reputation and good fortune.

VINTAGES

1985—*Hermitage La Sizeranne (red)*—Like many of the red Hermitage
·   wines from this vintage, Chapoutier's 1985 is rather low in acid-
88   ity, but quite richly flavored, full-bodied, deep, velvety, and
        loaded with peppery, cassis fruit. It will mature quickly. Antici-
        pated maturity: 1989–1996. Last tasted 6/86.

1985—*Hermitage Chante-Alouette (white)*—Power, intensity, and au-
·   thoritative flavors are the rule here rather than restraint and
90   finesse. This is quite a large-scaled wine with explosive richness
        and a significant alcoholic punch. Drink over the next 5–7 years.
        Last tasted 6/86.

1984—*Hermitage La Sizeranne (red)*—Much of Chapoutier's 1984 is
·   being allocated for his Grande Cuvée. This wine is lean, high in
78   acidity with moderately intense, dusty, spicy, cherry fruit.
        Somewhat light. Anticipated maturity: now–1992. Last tasted
        6/86.

1984—*Hermitage Chante-Alouette (white)*—Quite excellent, the 1984
·   Chante-Alouette has a stony, mineral fragrance, very fine rich-
88   ness, surprising ripeness, good acidity, full body, and good

length. It is better balanced than the 1985. Anticipated maturity: 1988–1998. Last tasted 6/86.

1983—*Hermitage La Sizeranne (red)*—This is a very good vintage for
·
87   Chapoutier. Their Hermitage is more open knit and accessible than others, but still quite tannic, very peppery and spicy, full-bodied, with a long, rich, ripe finish. Anticipated maturity: 1990–1998. Last tasted 12/86.

1983—*Hermitage Chante-Alouette (white)*—Not as rich as the outstand-
·
85   ing reputation of this vintage might suggest, the 1983 white Hermitage from Chapoutier has plenty of flesh and body as well as flavor, plus very good length and decent acidity. Drink over the next 5 years. Last tasted 10/86.

1982—*Hermitage La Sizeranne (red)*—Much more advanced than the
·
87   1983, the 1982 has a spicy, full-intensity bouquet of ripe cherry fruit, a spicy, leathery aroma, velvety, fat flavors, lush texture, and an alcoholic finish. Ready to drink now, this vintage should provide pleasure for at least another decade. Last tasted 6/86.

1982—*Hermitage Chante-Alouette (white)*—The low acidity of the 1982
·
82   suggests that it should be drunk up. It has a lot of body and good depth, but finishes without much zip or zest. Drink up. Last tasted 6/86.

1981—*Hermitage La Sizeranne (red)*—This is a one-dimensional Her-
·
79   mitage from Chapoutier. It is not austere and angular like many wines of this vintage, but round, fruity, chunky, and straightforward. Anticipated maturity: now–1990. Last tasted 6/86.

1981—*Hermitage Chante-Alouette (white)*—Slightly more successful
·
82   than the red wine of 1981, the white Hermitage is medium-bodied, somewhat short in the finish, but crisp and fresh, with a fragrance of wet stones. Drink over the next 5–6 years. Last tasted 4/86.

N.V.—*Hermitage Grande Cuvée (red)*—These cuvées change yearly, so
·
83   evaluation is of little value. However, the style of this particular one offers soft, round, mature aromas and flavors. This cuvée, tasted in 9/86, is lighter than normal, medium ruby in color, smoky, spicy, and totally ready. Drink up.

N.V.—*Hermitage Grande Cuvée (white)*—Again, I am not sure the
·
84   blend of Grande Cuvée you taste will be the one I tasted (the chances are that it will not), but given the fact that Chapoutier likes these wines to be consistent, the white Grande Cuvée has broad, round, substantial flavors and a good measure of power. Last tasted 9/86.

N.V —*Hermitage Le Pavillon "Numérotées" (red)*—This luxury cuvée,
·   only the third one offered by Chapoutier since the debut Le
88   Pavillon was released in 1956, is very dark in color with a big,
         smoky, peppery bouquet dominated by scents of raspberry and
         chocolate. On the palate, it is quite rich and chewy, almost
         viscous, with a long, lush finish. A total of 10,800 bottles of this
         wine was released in 1986. Anticipated maturity: now–1996.
         Last tasted 10/86.

N.V —*Hermitage Cuvée de L'Orvée "Numérotées" (white)*—This is a
·   sensational wine. Released in 1986, only 4,800 bottles (400
92   cases) were produced. This straw-colored wine has a rich, com-
         plex bouquet of grilled nuts, minerals, and spicy fruit. Quite full-
         bodied, but impeccably balanced by its crisp acidity, this big,
         rich wine is as good as white Hermitage can get and seems to
         have the balance to get even better. Anticipated maturity: now–
         1996. Last tasted 10/86.

1982—*Hermitage Vin de Paille (white)*—Chapoutier produced this nec-
·   tarlike, sweet wine in 1982 for the first time. Only 100 cases
92   were made. It is an amazing wine, quite unique and different
         from any sweet wine I have tasted. It has very crisp acidity, 255
         grams of residual sugar, amazing power, length, and complexity.
         It should last for 50 or more years. Last tasted 6/86.

1978—*Hermitage La Sizeranne (red)*—A huge bouquet of hickory wood,
·   ripe plums, saddle leather, and exotic spices is indeed quite
90   special. On the palate, the wine is fully mature, has great con-
         centration, superb length, and is certainly the best recent red
         Hermitage Chapoutier has produced. Anticipated maturity:
         now–1997. Last tasted 6/86.

1967—*Hermitage La Sizeranne (red)*—A very mature bouquet of
·   prunes, cedar, and sweaty leather suggests that this wine has
84   passed its apogee. Quite velvety and broad on the palate, but
         drying out in the finish. Drink up. Last tasted 6/86.

1929—*Hermitage Chante-Alouette (white)*—One of the greatest white
·   wines I have ever tasted, the 1929 Hermitage, which had been
96   recorked and topped off, had a deep golden color and an exhila-
         rating bouquet of toasted hazelnuts, rich, round, velvety flavors
         of butter, figs, and smoky fruit. The finish seemed to go on and
         on. Of course, such a wine is no longer available commercially,
         but this wine and the old white Hermitages I tasted with Gérard
         Chave (the 1929, 1952, 1967) poignantly demonstrate the aging

potential of these underrated, often underpriced white wines. Last tasted 6/85.

J. L. CHAVE *****

There can be no doubt that Gérard Chave, the most recent Chave in a family of growers that has been making Hermitage since 1481, is one of this planet's greatest winemakers. If I have trouble writing objectively about Chave, it is because of the fact that there is so much about the man himself that I admire. Chave, born in 1935, lives in the tiny, one-horse village of Mauves, across the river from Tain L'Hermitage and just south of Tournon. One blink of the eye when passing through Mauves and the passerby would no doubt miss the tiny, faded and rusting, brown and white metal sign hanging from the wall of a building inconspicuously announcing the cellars of J. L. Chave. The big, sad, basset hound eyes and long, pointed nose of Gérard Chave suggest sympathy and warmth immediately. For all his achievements, Chave is a remarkably modest man who remains unwaveringly committed to his passion—making wine in the same manner as his father before him, with no technological razzle dazzle, and no compromises for consumers who want their wines to be already mature when released.

Chave is no provincial-thinking man blindly carrying on a tradition, however. Several trips to California and a keen sense of curiosity have informed him of the wonders, as well as dangers, of centrifuges and German micropore filtering machines that can clarify and stabilize a wine in a matter of minutes (as well as remove most of its flavor) so that no winemaker will ever have to worry about an unstable bottle. Yet he will have none of these methods, which he calls "the tragedy of modern winemaking." In his deep, damp, cobwebbed cellars, over 500 vintages of the Chave family's Hermitage have been allowed to clarify and sta-bilize naturally without the aid of chemicals or machines. No flavors have been sacrificed, and Chave sees no reason to change since the old way, though much more troublesome and fraught with increased risk, produces wines of greater flavor, dimension, and depth.

Chave is not averse to experimentation if it can be proved that his wine will be better because of it. For instance, new oak barrels, pi-oneered by Marcel Guigal for his Côte Rôtie and now *à la mode* in other houses in the Rhône Valley, have given Chave reason to reflect. Despite the fact that Chave firmly believes that the intense richness of fruit produced at Hermitage does not need to age in new oak barrels to give structure, he did purchase *one* new barrel in 1985 to age one batch of his red Hermitage. Though a great admirer of Marcel Guigal, he believes that the toasty, vanillin character imparted by this new oak barrel to his Hermitage not only changes the character of the wine, but disguises its identity—all to the detriment of *his* Hermitage. Nevertheless, Chave was willing to make the experiment.

He now owns 27 acres on Hermitage hill. His production ranges between 2,000–3,000 cases of Hermitage and 250 cases of excellent red St.-Joseph. (The latter seems to be a well-kept secret.) In 1985 he acquired 7.4 acres of vines that were originally part of another estate, the Domaine L'Hermite of Terence Gray, so we can all be thankful that additional quantities of his splendid wines will be available.

Chave's style of winemaking is totally traditional. His white Hermitage is made from a blend of 90% Marsanne and 10% Roussanne, and aged after malolactic fermentation in both vats and old wooden barrels for 14–18 months. His white Hermitage, which along with Chapoutier's Chante-Alouette is the longest-lived, is even more complex. It is not filtered and does indeed throw a sediment like a red wine. It is a wine that will evolve for at least a decade in those vintages where the balance is correct. In 1974, Chave made a Vin de Paille that I have been fortunate enough to taste several times. It is the best wine of this type I have seen, yet he has not made it again nor has he any plans to commercialize it.

As for his red wine, perhaps the most important distinction is that Chave, along with Chapoutier, is always the last grower to harvest, pushing his grapes to their maximum maturity, which in turn provides the super-ripeness and richness of a great wine. Of course, putting off the harvest is risky because of the torrential rains that tend to plague France in October. Chave keeps the wine made from the different vineyards on Hermitage hill separate for one year as they age in various types and sizes of oak barrels and the larger foudres. In most years, he usually makes wine from seven or eight different vineyards. After a year apart, Chave begins the tedious process of making his blend, which is where his formidable tasting abilities come forth. After he has decided on the blend—and he is quick to say that each year the character of the wine from these vineyards is the same although their quality will be different—the red wine spends 8–10 more months in wood and is then bottled unfiltered. His red Hermitage is, it seems to me, an immortal wine in the top vintages. Will it peak in 20 or 30 years? Chave's red Hermitage is not as opulent nor as flashy as Jaboulet's La Chapelle and can also be less consistent. However, though it starts life slowly, it never fails to impress after seven or eight years in the bottle, and in his great vintages, 1978, 1983, and 1985 for example, only a half-dozen producers in France made better wine.

VINTAGES

1985—*Hermitage (red)*—Tasted prior to bottling, it seems without
·   question that Chave produced the best red Hermitage of this
91   vintage. Yet for Chave 1985 was not a year he cares to remember. Holding back the tears, he sadly states that his beloved mother, as well as his faithful sidekick, his dog, passed away that year. A sentimentalist, Chave is likely to put little of this vintage into the huge reservoir of old vintages that his family has faithfully cellared throughout this century. His 1985 avoids the oversupple style of some of the other reds of this vintage. Perhaps similar to the 1982, the 1985 is a voluptuous wine with deep cassis fruit, plenty of body, excellent concentration, and good tannins. Anticipated maturity: 1990–2005. Last tasted 6/86.

1985—*Hermitage (white)*—Particularly powerful in 1985, Chave's
·   white Hermitage is a blockbuster. A huge aroma of pineapple,
92   wet stones, spring flowers, and honey is sensational. On the palate, the wine is very intense, long, broadly flavored, lush, and extremely rich. It is a trifle low in acidity, but what a mouthful of wine! Anticipated maturity: 1988–1996. Last tasted 6/86.

1984—*Hermitage (red)*—Gushing with aromas of ripe, sweet, berry
·   fruit, this medium-bodied, very elegantly wrought wine has soft
86   tannins and surprisingly good concentration. It's very appealing for near-term drinking. Anticipated maturity: now–1994. Last tasted 12/86.

1984—*Hermitage (white)*—Much lighter and less powerful than the
·   1985, the 1984 is fruity, and has the nutty, honeysuckle fra-
85   grance often attributed to Chave's wines plus good acidity, medium body, and a lovely freshness. Anticipated maturity: now–1996. Last tasted 2/87.

1983—*Hermitage (red)*—While Chave will not admit which vintage he
·   prefers, 1983 or 1985, it seems to me that his 1983 is a true
93   superstar and will outlast the 1985 by at least a decade. For now, it is less charming and exotic than either the fat, ripe, succulent 1985 or 1982. Deep dark ruby in color, it has a profound concentration of ripe, smoky, berry fruit and oriental spices, full body, great depth and length as well as amazing tannin that will take it well into the next century. Anticipated maturity: 1995–2025. Last tasted 12/86.

1983—*Hermitage (white)*—Very aromatic with a wonderful variety of
· scents (honeysuckle, pineapple, stony minerals), this is a grace-
90 ful wine that balances power with finesse. Chave says he will
not drink it until 1995. Anticipated maturity: 1988–2000. Last
tasted 12/86.

1982—*Hermitage (red)*—Like many of Chave's wines, the 1982 has
· gotten deeper and richer in the bottle after starting life a little
92 diffuse and awkward. It is much more evolved than the 1983
(a normal characteristic of this vintage), very rich, silky
on the palate with gobs of fruit. Quite delicious now, it will obviously get better. Anticipated maturity: 1989–2000. Last tasted
6/86.

1982—*Hermitage (white)*—I have had some bottle variation with this
· wine, but the last two times tasted it has been superb. Very rich,
86– ripe, intense, and maturing much more quickly than the 1983, it
92 has a good lashing of alcohol, a heady fragrance, and glorious
ripe richness—can it really get any better? Anticipated maturity: now–1992. Last tasted 6/86.

1981—*Hermitage (red)*—Rather austere and lacking fruit, this wine
· offers a light-intensity, cherry fruitiness, some earthy, herbal
80 notes, medium body, and an ungenerous finish. This is not a
strong effort from Chave. Anticipated maturity: now–1992. Last
tasted 6/86.

1981—*Hermitage (white)*—Like the red 1981, this wine's personality is
· one of leanness and restraint, with a herbaceous, peppery nose,
78 high acidity, and only adequate length. It is quite light for a
Chave Hermitage. Drink up. Last tasted 6/86.

1980—*Hermitage (red)*—Soft, fruity, straightforward, and totally ma-
· ture, this wine is Chave's least favorite vintage of the eighties,
78 and I must agree with him. Drink it over the next 4–5 years.
Last tasted 6/86.

1980—*Hermitage (white)*—Certainly better than the 1980 red Hermi-
· tage, this medium-bodied wine shows a ripe, complex bouquet
84 of tropical fruit and smoky nuts and herbs. On the palate, it is
fresh, soft, and fully ready to drink. It will not keep. Last tasted
6/86.

1979—*Hermitage (red)*—This is a perfect example of my statement
· about Chave's wine starting off slowly. After bottling in 1981,
86 this wine seemed light in color and rather insubstantial. Two
years later the color seemed deeper and more body was apparent. Now it is a totally delicious wine, not a superstar like the

1978 or 1983, but wonderfully elegant, ripe, round, full-bodied, and generously flavored. Drink it over the next 5–6 years. Last tasted 6/86.

1979—*Hermitage (white)*—Medium gold in color, quite spicy on the
·
86   nose with scents of nuts, apricots, and dried fruit, medium-bodied, round, fresh, and very attractive, this stylish, graceful wine should continue to evolve well. Anticipated maturity: 1985–1993. Last tasted 4/84.

1978—*Hermitage (red)*—Have I been too stingy? For me, this is
·
96   Chave's single finest wine in recent vintages. It remains an infant, so drinking it now is, I suspect, infanticide. Memorizing its aromas, its flavors, its texture, and its length is a quick education in what great wine is all about. Powerful yet harmonious, staggeringly rich and deep, this wine is loaded. Save it for the turn of the century. Anticipated maturity: 1995–2025+. Last tasted 6/86.

1976—*Hermitage (red)*—For whatever reason, I have found this wine
·
77   excessively lean, unforthcoming, and terribly tannic and dry on the palate. Perhaps I have been unlucky, but I fear this wine is losing what little fruit it had. Last tasted 7/84.

1969—*Hermitage (red)*—Not terribly impressive, the 1969 is fully ma-
·
80   ture, seems rather lightweight, and finishes short. Yet it provides a decent drink. Last tasted 5/83.

1967—*Hermitage (red)*—Medium dark ruby with an amber/orange rim,
·
91   the 1967 has an intense smoky, creamy, seductive bouquet, long, very generous flavors of berry fruit backed up by ripe, soft tannins, and a good deal of body. The 1967 should keep for at least another decade. Last tasted 6/86.

1967—*Hermitage (white)*—Heavenly aromas of grilled nuts, dried
·
92   dates, tropical fruit, and exotic spices are tantalizingly marvelous. On the palate, this wine gushes with generous portions of ripe fruit. Quite fresh. Last tasted 6/86.

1952—*Hermitage (white)*—Tasted with Chave as a prelude to his 1929,
·
93   I was stunned by this wine's richness and fullness as well as complexity. Is anyone other than Chave prepared to cellar white Hermitage this long? Last tasted 6/86.

1935—*Hermitage (red)*—Chave's birth year, 1935, hardly an inspira-
·
92   tional vintage in French wine lore, produced a magnificently scented, smoky, gamey-scented wine, still dark in color, and still oozing with rich, ripe fruit. An amazingly fresh wine. Last tasted 6/86.

1929—*Hermitage (red)*—Pulled directly from Chave's cellar and never
. recorked, this medium ruby wine with a pinkish, amber edge
86 had an ashtray, cigar-type aroma, some plummy fruit on the
palate, good acidity, and was still very much alive, if fading.
Chave said he had tasted from better bottles. Next to the lowly
regarded 1935, the 1929 suffered in terms of richness, complexity, and length, but at 57 years of age was still quite a mouthful
of wine. Last tasted 6/86.

1929—*Hermitage (white)*—The 1929 had a very deep golden color and
. an aroma not unlike a very old vintage of Yquem. Toasty hazel-
88 nut aromas, some oxidation, yet dry, rich, heavy, and intense.
This wine has plenty of fruit left. Again, this bottle came from
Chave's cave and had never been recorked. He served it with
foie gras, which was ideal. Quite excellent as a wine; stupendous
considering its age. Last tasted 6/86.

DELAS FRÈRES ***–*****

This company keeps a surprisingly low profile in spite of the fact that
several of the wines are of exceptional quality. It is an old house,
founded in 1836, and it remained family owned until 1978. That year,
Delas was purchased by the champagne firm of Deutz. In 1981, Delas
left the quaint, touristic town of Tournon, which sits across the Rhône
River opposite Tain L'Hermitage, and moved into a spacious, modern
facility several miles north in Saint-Jean-de-Muzols. The pride of Delas
is the estate-bottled northern Rhône wines from their 23 acres of vines
in Hermitage, 10 acres in Côte Rôtie, 5 acres in Condrieu, and 2.5 acres
in Cornas. Delas produces an entire range of Rhône wines from the
other appellations using purchased grapes and/or wine to complete the
portfolio. The southern Rhône wines offered by Delas are not of the
quality level of their northern Rhône estate-bottled wines, a fact that
they acknowledge.

The production of 100,000 cases a year belies the modest image this
house seems to promote. The cellars are extremely modern and immac-
ulate at Delas, and this is the only house in the northern Rhône to have
all its aging cellars (which are aboveground) air-conditioned. The oenol-
ogist for Delas, Jacques Bourut, is obsessed with technically stable and
clean wines, and sounds quite Californian in pursuing this goal with all
the modern means possible—no malolactic fermentation for the white
wines, two filtrations and bentonite clarifications. Yet the top wines still
seem to be full of flavor, and it is only the lower-level, moderately
priced wines such as their Crozes-Hermitage and Côtes du Rhône that

lack character. The white Hermitage, called Marquise de la Tourette, is fermented very slowly at low temperatures and does see some time in small oak barrels. Although the product of a modern vinification, it is quite good and flavorful. Delas draws its grapes for the white Hermitage from the vineyard called Domaine L'Hermite. The red Hermitage, also called Marquise de la Tourette, is unquestionably the firm's greatest wine (along with its Condrieu). The red Hermitage spends 18 to 24 months in two-year-old barrels purchased from a producer in Pommard, as well as several months in large wooden foudres. It is an impeccably clean wine but quite rich and full-bodied. In comparing the Delas red Hermitage to the opulent, fleshy, exotic style of Jaboulet's La Chapelle, or the stylish, graceful wines of Chave, it seems as rich in flavor and as fleshy, but tends to have an olive scent and Provençal herbal character in its bouquet to go along with the smoky, hickory wood and rich, berry fruit aromas. It is undeniably a great wine, somewhat overlooked and consequently underpriced, and capable of 10–20 years of evolution in the bottle. Much of its richness and power is no doubt attributable to the fact that 80% of the red Hermitage Delas produces comes from the superb Les Bessards vineyard on Hermitage hill, considered by many to turn out the deepest and richest red wines of any of the vineyards or *mas*.

VINTAGES

1985—*Hermitage Cuvée Marquise de la Tourette (red)*—Very deeply
· colored, the 1985 is quite forward, fat, ripe, richly fruity, full-
88 bodied, low in acidity, but quite concentrated. It will mature
quickly. Anticipated maturity: 1989–1997. Last tasted 6/86.

1985—*Hermitage Cuvée Marquise de la Tourette (white)*—My favorite
· recent vintage of the Delas white Hermitage, this big, rich wine
87 is loaded with fleshy fruit, and has a true hazelnut bouquet intertwined with the scent of apricots. Quite alcoholic and somewhat low in acidity, it will provide delicious drinking early on.
Anticipated maturity: now–1990. Last tasted 6/86.

1984—*Hermitage Cuvée Marquise de la Tourette (red)*—Much lighter
· than the 1985 or 1983, this medium-bodied, moderately intense
83 wine has a strong olive-scented, hickory smoke bouquet, above
average flavor concentration, slightly elevated acidity, but a
good finish. Anticipated maturity: now–1993. Last tasted 6/86.

1984—*Hermitage Cuvée Marquise de la Tourette (white)*—Quite pleas-
· ing for the vintage, the 1984 has round, generous, floral and
84 tropical fruit aromas, good acidity, medium to full body, and the

ultra-clean style of Delas imprinted on it. Anticipated maturity: now–1990. Last tasted 6/86.

1983—*Hermitage Cuvée Marquise de la Tourette (red)*—More open knit
· and developed than many 1983s, this big, fleshy, chewy Hermi-
90 tage has a full-blown bouquet of cured olives, smoke, fennel, and ripe berry fruit. Quite full-bodied, very deep and concentrated, this wine has a considerable future ahead of it. Anticipated maturity: 1993–2005. Last tasted 12/86.

1983—*Hermitage Cuvée Marquise de la Tourette (white)*—Surprisingly,
· the 1983 white Hermitage lacks the character and richness of
82 not only the powerful 1985 but also the 1984. It is, for whatever reason, dull yet fruity, and just too one-dimensional. Drink over the next year. Last tasted 6/86.

1982—*Hermitage Cuvée Marquise de la Tourette (red)*—Forward, rich,
· ripe, intense aromas of Provençal herbs, berry fruit, and smoked
87 beef are quite captivating. Nicely concentrated, medium- to full-bodied, rather soft and velvety, this big, delicious wine is quite evolved and will provide very fine drinking over the next 6–7 years. Last tasted 12/86.

1982—*Hermitage Cuvée Marquise de la Tourette (white)*—Very fatigued
· and seemingly quite tired and losing fruit, the 1982 should be
66 drunk up since the wine is fading and the acidity becoming tart. Last tasted 12/86.

1981—*Hermitage Cuvée Marquise de la Tourette (red)*—Pale in color,
· stale in flavor, and very diluted, this wine was an inexplicable
60 failure at Delas in 1981. Last tasted 10/86.

1980—*Hermitage Cuvée Marquise de la Tourette (red)*—Supple, spicy,
· somewhat herbaceous yet rich fruit aromas mix deftly with
88 scents of tar and very rich, red fruit. On the palate, the 1980 is medium-bodied, soft, quite concentrated, and very long in the mouth. A real sleeper. Anticipated maturity: now–1997. Last tasted 6/86.

1980—*Hermitage Cuvée Marquise de la Tourette (white)*—Aromas of
· vegetation and fennel as well as mineral scents predominate in
78 this straw-colored wine. Round, soft, and quite one-dimensional, this wine should be drunk up. Last tasted 6/86.

1978—*Hermitage Cuvée Marquise de la Tourette (red)*—A magnificent
· bouquet of sweet, oaky, jammy, peppery, berry fruit and licorice
92 is quite enticing. In the mouth, the wine is very full-bodied, even more concentrated than the outstanding 1983, has layers and

layers of fruit, good ripe tannins, and exemplary length. Anticipated maturity: now–2000. Last tasted 12/86.

OLDER VINTAGES
The only notes I have are for the red Hermitage, and I show that a 1973
(tasted in 1981) and 1970 and 1971 (drunk in 1980) were all showing
signs of fatigue and decline. Clearly, the style of Hermitage made here
has changed significantly since the 1980 vintage. As modern-styled as
it is, the Delas red Hermitage should still keep and evolve for 15 or
more years in the top vintages. The white Hermitage should be drunk
within its first 4–5 years of life.

ALPHONSE DESMEURE (DOMAINE DES REMEZIÈRES)**
This small domaine is better known for its red and white Crozes-Hermitage, produced in much greater quantity than its Hermitage. Alphonse Desmeure, a shy and wary man in his early sixties, makes
adequate, occasionally good red Hermitage and interesting, sometimes
very good white Hermitage from 6.2 acres of vines located near the
chapel on Hermitage hill. The white wines seem marginally better than
the lightish, rather uninspired red Hermitage. Perhaps his young son
Philippe, now taking some interest in the cellars, will point things in a
more positive and consistent direction.

VINTAGES
1985—*Hermitage (red)*—This appears to be the best wine I have seen
·   from Desmeure. Deep in color, clean with oodles of jammy,
85   berry fruit, this medium- to full-bodied wine will mature quickly.
    Anticipated maturity: now–1992. Last tasted 10/86.

1985—*Hermitage (white)*—A success for Desmeure, the 1985 white
·   Hermitage is ripe, richly fruity, full-bodied, a little low in acid-
85   ity, but well made, fleshy, and ideal for drinking over the next
    4–5 years. Last tasted 10/86.

1984—*Hermitage (red)*—Medium ruby, spicy, smoky, leather, and
·   cherry scented, the 1984 is a touch high in acidity, but pleasant
78   if slightly one-dimensional. Anticipated maturity: now–1990.
    Last tasted 10/86.

1984—*Hermitage (white)*—A mineral, stony fragrance and the smell of
·   herbs dominate the bouquet of the 1984 white Desmeure. On the
82   palate, the wine is steely, crisp, and well made, though a little
    light. Anticipated maturity: now–1990. Last tasted 10/86.

1983—*Hermitage (red)*—Forward for a 1983 Hermitage, this smoky,
· chunky, full-bodied, solid wine has good depth and richness. It
85 has plenty of tannin, but needs time to develop. Anticipated
maturity: 1992–2000. Last tasted 10/86.

1983—*Hermitage (white)*—An old-style white Hermitage—full-bodied,
· rather heavy, but quite interesting, the 1983 is powerful, oily,
85 and should be drunk over the next 4–5 years. Last tasted 10/86.

1982—*Hermitage (white)*—A bizarre, rather foul aroma suggests a mis-
· hap somewhere in the production of this wine. Undrinkable.
55 Last tasted 6/85.

1981—*Hermitage (red)*—A dirty, musty aroma is pervasive and pre-
· cludes enjoyment of this medium-bodied, soft, lightish wine.
60 Last tasted 11/85.

BERNARD FAURIE ****

Faurie, located in Tournon, is one of the up and coming stars of Hermitage. Of the vintages of Faurie's I have tasted, only his 1981s were
disappointing, and that, of course, was a mediocre to poor year for this
appellation. His style of winemaking seems closest to that of Gérard
Chave in the sense that while his wines are full-flavored, they retain an
elegance and finesse that is obvious, and like those of Chave, start life
very slowly. Faurie produces only 500 cases of red Hermitage and a
scant 50 cases of white. He also produces 200–250 cases of St.-Joseph.
His red wines are fermented in open wooden tanks and given a lengthy
period of skin contact of up to 20 days. Afterwards, the wine rests in
wood for 18 months, is fined once, but never filtered.

VINTAGES

1985—*Hermitage (red)*—Very deep in color, this full-bodied, powerful
· wine admirably balances muscle and finesse. Like many 1985s
88 there is a precocious succulent appeal, but the tannins are there
for longevity. Anticipated maturity: 1991–2001. Last tasted
10/86.

1984—*Hermitage (red)*—Faurie's 1984 is light, elegant, supple, and
· quite attractive to drink now. It lacks a little weight and length,
84 but has good black cherry fruit, a scent of saddle leather, and
round finish. Drink over the next 4–5 years. Last tasted 10/86.

1983—*Hermitage (red)*—Deeply colored, closed and firm as most 1983
· northern Rhônes are, this rich yet full-bodied, tannic wine needs
88 plenty of time in the cellar, but there can be no doubt that it has

the fruit to outlast the tannin. Anticipated maturity: 1993–2005. Last tasted 10/86.

1983—*Hermitage (white)*—Rather one-dimensional, Faurie's 1983
· white Hermitage seems to have plenty of fruit and depth, but as
84 Clive Coates would no doubt say, it just does not "sing." Is it going through an awkward stage? Last tasted 10/86.

1982—*Hermitage (red)*—Quite full-bodied, deep ruby in color, this at-
· tractively proportioned wine has a rich black cherry fruitiness,
85 plenty of power, a solid dosage of alcohol, and avoids the oily, soft character of many 1982 Rhônes. Anticipated maturity: 1989–1997. Last tasted 9/84.

1982—*Hermitage (white)*—A moderately intense bouquet of hazelnuts
· and ripe fruit is attractive. On the palate, the wine is full-bodied,
84 ripe, viscous, a bit heavy, slightly deficient in acidity, but has a long finish. Ready now, it should drink well for 5–6 years. Last tasted 10/85.

1981—*Hermitage (red)*—Few growers and producers in Hermitage had
· successful years in 1981. Faurie's 1981 is a rather medicinal-
62 tasting wine with a hard, sharp nose and bizarre flavors. Pass it by. Last tasted 6/85.

1981—*Hermitage (white)*—Straightforward, heady aromas of wood and
· flowers (honeysuckle?) are attractive if fleeting. On the palate,
82 the wine is chunky, rather weighty, but missing some zip and crispness. Good, but seems to just miss the mark. Drink it up. Last tasted 6/84.

1980—*Hermitage (red)*—One of the sleeper wines of this vintage, Fau-
· rie's 1980 seems quite clearly better than either Jaboulet's La
87 Chapelle or Chave's lightweight, diluted effort in this vintage. Deep in color with a gamelike, smoky, peppery nose, deep, rich flavors, and a good lashing of tannin, this wine is quite impressive. Anticipated maturity: 1988–1996. Last tasted 9/84.

1980—*Hermitage (white)*—Quite good and still rather youthful, the
· 1980 from Faurie has an elegant bouquet of spring flowers and
85 grilled nuts. Medium- to full-bodied, lively and succulent with fresh acidity and good length, this wine shows impeccable wine-making. Drink over the next 5–6 years. Last tasted 10/86.

1978—*Hermitage (red)*—To date, this is the finest effort I have tasted
· from Faurie. Still not at its apogee, this big, very full-bodied,
90 intense, extremely concentrated wine has oodles of blackberry fruit and layers of extract and tannin in the finish. Anticipated maturity: 1988–2000. Last tasted 10/86.

JULES FAYOLLE ET FILS***

The young Fayolle twin brothers, Jean Claude and Jean Paul, are based in the tiny hamlet of Gervans, just to the north of Tain L'Hermitage. An engaging duo, they are far better known for the good white and red Crozes-Hermitage produced from 17.3 acres of well-situated vineyards. However, they can make very good, even excellent red Hermitage from a tiny 3.2-acre parcel within the Les Dionnières (also spelled Diognères) vineyard. The wine (of which there are about 500 cases) is always characterized by a very deep, dark color and lush, deep, blackberry flavors. The problem with Fayolle's Hermitage is that far too frequently there is excessive sulfur in the nose of certain bottles, a shame in view of the otherwise good level of quality attained. No white Hermitage is produced here and prices for the red Hermitage are quite fair. However, bottle variation is a major concern to prospective buyers.

VINTAGES

1983—*Hermitage (red)*—Three bottles have had stinky sulfur aromas which detracted immensely from an otherwise rich, full-bodied, unctuous, deeply flavored, dark ruby/purple-colored wine. Two other bottles I tasted were clean and did not have any trace of sulfur. This is a chancy wine given the irregularity. Judgment reserved. Last tasted 10/86.
· ?

1982—*Hermitage (red)*—A surprisingly rich, broadly flavored, plump, deep wine, Fayolle's 1982 has deep ruby color, a gamey, smoky, plummy bouquet, viscous, cherry flavors, full body, and low acidity. It drinks well now, but will improve for 5–8 years. Last tasted 10/86.
· 89

1981—*Hermitage (red)*—The 1981 has quite ripe aromas for this vintage. On the palate, this wine is chunky, a little dull and short, but certainly a success in this difficult year. Drink over the next 3–4 years. Last tasted 6/86.
· 80

1980—*Hermitage (red)*—Again, the plump, plummy style of Fayolle shows. Deep in color, richly fruity, even fat, this corpulent wine should be drunk now for its uncomplicated character. Last tasted 6/85.
· 78

FERRATON PÈRE ET FILS***

The middle-aged, reflective, gray-haired Michel Ferraton has 10 acres in Hermitage from which he produces both white and red Hermitage, and 15 acres of vines in Crozes-Hermitage. In 1985 he also made a sweet Vin de Paille. Ferraton, whose attractive cellar in Tain L'Hermitage is just around the corner from the city hall and immediately behind that of Sorrel's, is clearly passionate about his winemaking. His white Hermitage, which is 100% Marsanne, has changed to a more modern style in 1984, emphasizing crisp, fresh fruit. Older vintages were rather ponderous, viscous, rich wines with a great deal of character, as well as variability from bottle to bottle. His white wine comes from two *mas* on Hermitage hill, Les Dionnières and Les Murets. His red Hermitage, which can be very good, is from the two vineyards of Le Méal and Les Beaumes. He calls his cuvée of white Hermitage "Le Reverdy," and his red Hermitage "Les Miaux." Due to problems with his 1982, Ferraton began to filter his wines prior to bottling to encourage stability, but he remains very much an artisan winemaker and an extremely meticulous grower who can turn out very fine wine.

VINTAGES

1985—*Hermitage Cuvée les Miaux (red)*—Every bit as concentrated as
   •   his 1983, the 1985 is, however, much softer, very rich and unc-
  90   tuous, with a huge bouquet of wild berry fruit and smoky tar.
       Very intense and full-bodied, this wine should keep well despite
       its precocious appeal. Anticipated maturity: 1990–2000. Last
       tasted 6/86.

1985—*Hermitage Cuvée le Reverdy (white)*—A new style for Ferraton,
   •   the 1985 white Hermitage had its malolactic fermentation
  84   blocked and is a less complex, higher-acid style of wine that has
       more commercial appeal but less interest. Anticipated maturity:
       now–1990. Last tasted 6/86.

1984—*Hermitage Cuvée les Miaux (red)*—Ferraton seems to do as well
   •   as anyone in the so-called off years. His 1984 has very good color
  84   and a moderately intense black cherry bouquet intertwined with
       saddle leather. On the palate, there is good fruit, medium body,
       and a decent finish. Anticipated maturity: 1988–1993. Last
       tasted 6/86.

1984—*Hermitage Cuvée le Reverdy (white)*—Crisp, lean, and austere,
   •   the 1984 is a medium-bodied, straw-colored wine with decent
  78   fruit, a mineral-scented nose, and angular texture. Perhaps it
       will show more character with age. Anticipated maturity: now–
       1992. Last tasted 6/86.

1983—*Hermitage Cuvée les Miaux (red)*—A more tannic, less ap-
   •   proachable version of Ferraton's excellent 1985, the 1983 is quite
  90   full-bodied with a chewy texture, super concentration, a smoky,

tar-scented bouquet, an exceptional finish, and enough tannin to warrant a decade of cellaring. Anticipated maturity: 1995–2005. Last tasted 6/86.

1983—*Hermitage Cuvée le Reverdy (white)*—Stinky, sulfur smells sug-
· gest problems in the wine cellar. On the palate, the wine has
? plenty of depth and richness, but it is impossible to appreciate
without holding your nose. Tasted twice. Last tasted 11/85.

1982—*Hermitage Cuvée les Miaux (red)*—Quite volatile and foaming in
· the glass, this sick, out-of-balance wine is defective and un-
56 drinkable. Tasted three times. Last tasted 12/85.

1981—*Hermitage Cuvée les Miaux (red)*—Ferraton's 1981 is an unqual-
· ified success in what is barely a mediocre vintage. Deep ruby,
87 with an intense, spicy, oaky, plummy, gamey aroma, this peppery, rich, full-bodied, tannic wine will handsomely repay those
willing to cellar it for another 5 years. Anticipated maturity:
1990–1996. Last tasted 12/85.

1985—*Vin de Paille (white)*—Ferraton made a minuscule quantity of
· this wine which statistically has 22% potential alcohol. He har-
93 vested the Marsanne grapes on October 10, 1985, put them on
straw mats, and pressed them on January 15, 1986. It is a wonderfully exotic, opulent, decadently rich wine with oodles of fruit
and a staggering perfume of apricots and peaches. It should
keep for 50–60 years. Unfortunately, less than 100 bottles were
made. Last tasted 6/86.

J. L. GRIPPAT ***–*****

Jean Louis Grippat's cellars are just on the outskirts of the quaint town of Tournon that sits across the Rhône River facing the duller and noisier town of Tain L'Hermitage. Grippat, who is in his early forties, comes from a winemaking family that has been producing both Hermitage and St.-Joseph for over a century. He is an articulate, serious, discreet man who goes to great lengths to explain his winemaking technique, always expressing respect for his peers, and at times even denigrating his own wines. He is quick to admit that his red Hermitage is light and he would like to see it more concentrated. However, as he knows full well, it is his white Hermitage that excites tasters and must be put on allocation because of its superb quality. In a normal year he produces only 400 cases of white Hermitage from the vineyard called Les Murets. His vines there average 40 years of age. His production of red Hermitage is only 200 cases. This is approximately one-third of his total production, the rest consisting of an excellent St.-Joseph white and two St.-Joseph red wines.

Grippat's white wines, which are not as long-lived as Chapoutier's Chante-Alouette or Chave's, are gloriously rich and fruity wines that beg to be drunk during their first four or five years of life. They are aged in tanks for a year, after which they spend two to three months in small oak barrels. In 1985, Grippat purchased three new oak barrels with which to experiment. His red Hermitage is rather light and one-dimensional compared with those from the better producers, but Grippat intends to take steps to increase the color and concentration if he can do so without losing the finesse that he cherishes in his wines. Grippat's red Hermitage will not prove disappointing, but it is the white Hermitage that one should make a special effort to find.

VINTAGES

1985—*Hermitage (red)*—Very soft, medium ruby in color with a light-
·   intensity bouquet of cherry and strawberry fruit, this wine lacks
83   the depth and richness one normally associates with red Hermi-
      tage, but it does have finesse. Anticipated maturity: now 1991.
      Last tasted 6/86.

1985—*Hermitage (white)*—This wine is gloriously fragrant, fat, fleshy,
·   and has layers of apricot-scented fruit, full body, adequate acid-
90   ity, and an impeccably clean finish. It should be drunk over the
      next 3–4 years. Last tasted 6/86.

1984—*Hermitage (red)*—Very supple, quite light in both color and
·   body, but it is attractively fruity in a straightforward manner.
81   Drink over the next 2–4 years. Last tasted 6/86.

1984—*Hermitage (white)*—The scents of honeysuckle and almonds are
·   immediately enticing. On the palate, the wine is fresh, lighter
85   than normal, but very fruity, very charming, and quite nicely
      concentrated for the vintage. Drink over the next 3–4 years. Last
      tasted 6/86.

1983—*Hermitage (red)*—The best of Grippat's recent vintages of red
·   Hermitage, the 1983 has a moderately intense cherry-scented
84   bouquet, medium body, good ripeness and length. Anticipated
      maturity: now–1991. Last tasted 6/86.

1983—*Hermitage (white)*—A gorgeous white Hermitage, the 1983 is
·   less extroverted than the 1985, less alcoholic as well, but deeply
90   fruity and mouth-filling. Its scents of tropical fruit and honey-
      suckle are top-rank. Drink this exuberant, fresh, full-bodied
      wine over the next 2–3 years. Last tasted 10/86.

E. GUIGAL ***–****

This fabulous firm produces exquisite Côte Rôtie (see page 52), but also makes a good quantity of white and red Hermitage. The Guigal family owns no vineyards in Hermitage, but meticulously purchases wine that has been vinified by the grower according to the Guigal formula. Precisely which growers Guigal draws from has never been revealed. However, Guigal produces his red Hermitage from 100% Syrah, refusing to blend in the 15% white wine permitted by law. Just under 2,000 cases of red Hermitage are produced by Guigal. It is a ruby/purple-colored wine, often among the deepest in color of the appellation. Guigal does not fine the wine and will not filter it if it falls brilliant naturally by virtue of its very long aging (3–3½ years) in wooden barrels and large foudres. He is a great believer in long wood aging and is always the last to bottle his red Hermitage. The white Hermitage, of which there are usually about 600 cases per year, is normally made from a blend of 90–95% Marsanne and the rest Roussanne. Unlike Guigal's other wines, which are normally very rich, dramatic expressions of winemaking art, the white Hermitage is somewhat austere, restrained, and overall not as impressive as his red Hermitage. In some vintages it actually tastes green and severe. Among all of the splendidly successful wines in the Guigal stable, I find his white Hermitage to be the least reliable.

With respect to the red Hermitage, Guigal is often much more successful than his peers in so-called off years. For example, his 1974, 1977, and, more recently, 1981 red Hermitages have been among the top two or three best red wines made in this appellation in those years.

VINTAGES

1985—*Hermitage (red)*—This is a very good 1985. Guigal believes the
· wine will turn out like his 1982. Quite rich, very dark in color,
87 with a full-intensity bouquet of peppery, cassis fruit, this full-bodied wine has a good deal of tannin, but the low acidity gives it a precocious appeal. Anticipated maturity: 1990–1998. Last tasted 6/86.

1985—*Hermitage (white)*—Rather high in acidity (an anomaly for this
· vintage), the 1985 has a pearlike, slightly vegetal bouquet and
82 decent ripeness, but overall is restrained and angular. Anticipated maturity: now–1992. Last tasted 6/86.

1984—*Hermitage (red)*—By Guigal's lofty standards, this wine is a bit
· light and insubstantial. The wine has surprisingly good color,
? high acidity, angular, tart flavors, and moderate tannin. Judgment reserved. Last tasted 6/86.

1984—*Hermitage (white)*—Rather short on the palate, quite light, and
·   fresh with simple fruity flavors, this is an understated, exces-
79   sively polite wine that lacks a bit of character. Last tasted 6/86.

1983—*Hermitage (red)*—This must certainly be Guigal's best red Her-
·   mitage to date. Very deep in color, with a huge bouquet of ripe
90   cassis fruit and exotic spices, this full-bodied, splendidly con-
      centrated wine has an unctuous texture, a boatload of tannins,
      and a considerable future. Anticipated maturity: 1990–2005.
      Last tasted 12/86.

1983—*Hermitage (white)*—The telltale bouquet of grilled almonds and
·   wet stones suggests a high-quality white Hermitage. This is one
86   of Guigal's best efforts with a white wine from this appellation.
      Quite youthful, but showing good ripeness and length, this me-
      dium- to full-bodied wine should age well. Anticipated maturity:
      now–1993. Last tasted 12/86.

1982—*Hermitage (red)*—Another unqualified success for Guigal, the
·   1982 is much more fruity and accessible than the tougher 1983,
88   but has deep ruby/black color, a seductive, developed bouquet
      of ripe cassis and black cherries, full body, an unctuous texture,
      and ripe, velvety fruit despite a good lashing of tannin. Antici-
      pated maturity: now–1995. Last tasted 12/86.

1982—*Hermitage (white)*—A chunky white Hermitage on the palate,
·   the 1982 is typically reserved and tight to smell, but has some
84   fleshy fruit and good length. It could have more bouquet. Antic-
      ipated maturity: now–1989. Last tasted 6/85.

1981—*Hermitage (red)*—Surprisingly dark in color, the 1981 from Gui-
·   gal has a big, ripe bouquet of raw beef and cassis fruit. Medium-
87   to full-bodied, deep and concentrated, this wine is quite a
      success given the difficult vintage conditions. Anticipated ma-
      turity: now–1992. Last tasted 10/85.

1981—*Hermitage (white)*—Light straw in color with rather high acidity,
·   this medium-bodied white Hermitage is quite restrained, to the
72   point of being innocuous. Last tasted 6/85.

1980—*Hermitage (red)*—Guigal bottled two separate lots of red Hermi-
·   tage in 1980. One is good—deep in color, spicy and rich in fruit
?   though somewhat short in the finish. The other lot is austere,
      tart, and surprisingly lean. There is no way of telling the differ-
      ence between them before pulling the cork. Last tasted 6/85.

1980—*Hermitage (white)*—Quite dull in bouquet, with simple, straight-
·   forward, rather nondescript flavors. Drink up. Last tasted 6/84.
75

1979—*Hermitage (red)*—Perhaps the best Hermitage of the vintage
·   after Jaboulet's La Chapelle and Sorrell's Le Méal, Guigal's
87   1979 is a big, beefy, intense wine that seems to be evolving
       better than the more highly acclaimed 1978. A huge bouquet of
       cassis and smoked meat is top-notch. Full-bodied, deep and
       tannic, this wine has plenty of life. Anticipated maturity: now–
       1996. Last tasted 12/85.

1979—*Hermitage (white)*—One of Guigal's better efforts with white
·   Hermitage, the 1979 has a stony, mineral-scented bouquet,
85   crisp, medium-bodied flavors, a touch of fennel in the taste, and
       a good, generous finish. It drinks well now, but should hold for
       4–5 years. Last tasted 1/85.

1978—*Hermitage (red)*—Extremely impressive early on, this wine now
·   tastes dull and closed. Is it going through an ungraceful period
85?   or actually just declining without ever fully blossoming? Cer-
       tainly the color is deep, but it finishes with a great deal of as-
       tringence and toughness. Judgment reserved. Last tasted 1/87.

1978—*Hermitage (white)*—Medium golden with a nut-scented smell,
·   this is a rather weighty, full-bodied, slightly oxidized wine made
83   in the old style. It should be drunk over the next 3–4 years. Last
       tasted 6/86.

OLDER VINTAGES

The 1976 red Hermitage from Guigal is a rich, very full-bodied, still
tannic wine that will continue to repay keeping for another 5–7 years.
The good 1974, average 1971, and excellent 1969 all require drinking
up. As for Guigal's white Hermitage, I only know the sherry-like, somewhat maderized 1974, which needs drinking up immediately.

PAUL JABOULET AINÉ ***–*****

I would surmise that the excellent family-owned company of Paul Jaboulet Ainé is the world's best-known producer of high-quality Rhône
wine. Their most celebrated wine is the Hermitage La Chapelle (unquestionably one of the world's ten greatest dry red wines), named not
after a specific vineyard, but after the tiny, white, solitary chapel that
sits atop the steepest part of the Hermitage hill. This famous wine
comes primarily from the two vineyards known as Le Méal and Les
Bessards, where the Jaboulets own 47 acres. In addition, they possess
another seven acres of vines that are used only to produce a regular
cuvée of red Hermitage and 16.8 acres of the La Croix vineyard utilized

to make the firm's white Hermitage, which is named after the thirteenth-century crusader, Gaspard Chevalier de Stérimberg.

The Jaboulet family may be the oldest in the Rhône, but all of the documented family history was destroyed during the French Revolution. The first Jaboulet, Antoine, was born in Tain L'Hermitage in 1807, and founded this firm in 1834. Today the firm, which has opened a new, modern facility south of Tain L'Hermitage, is run with obvious gusto and brilliance by the handsome yet boyish looking Gérard and his brother Jacques. The father, Louis, now approaching 75, is still there (although he officially retired in 1976), full of the *joie de vivre* that seems a particular family characteristic. The Jaboulets, in addition to their 70-plus acres of vineyards in Hermitage, own the 86-acre vineyard of Domaine Thalabert in Crozes-Hermitage that produces the finest wine of Crozes (and which could easily be called the poor man's Hermitage). They also own another 11 acres of young vines or land that is in the process of being planted. From all of these vineyards, the Jaboulets produce only 27,000 cases of wine. As négociants they produce another 175,000 cases, which no doubt contributes to their worldwide reputation and fame.

The increasing fame of the firm's stupendous Hermitage La Chapelle is not difficult to understand. It is an enormously concentrated wine that normally takes a decade to throw off its tannic cloak. Even then it only hints at the majestic perfume and richness that will arise. It is an almost immortal wine in terms of longevity and from the perspectives of quality and complexity is equaled only by a dozen or so Bordeaux Crus Classés and a half-dozen or so burgundies as well as an equal number of other red Rhônes. The wine is conservatively made to last. First, never are more than 40% of the grape bunches destalked, and only the wild yeasts from the vineyard are used to start the fermentation. Second, the maceration period is very long, a total of three weeks unless the skins of the grapes are unhealthy. All of this results in a densely colored, very tannic wine. Afterwards, the wine is put in small one- and two-year-old burgundy barrels purchased from such prominent white burgundy producers as Vincent Leflaive and Etienne Sauzet. The Jaboulets abhor new oak, feeling that their Hermitage needs no additional wood tannins and already has so much size and fruit that new oak would only detract from its inherent qualities. The Hermitage La Chapelle is not clarified at all, but is given a light filtration prior to bottling, a procedure which commenced in 1980. Curiously, Jaboulet is among the first to bottle his Hermitage as it rarely spends more than 12–14 months in wood compared with 36 months-plus for Guigal, 20–

24 months for Chave, and 30 months or more for Chapoutier. Gérard Jaboulet explains that this has always been their method, and one hardly need argue, for the results do indeed speak for themselves.

Most wine enthusiasts think of Hermitage as a thick, chewy wine with a dizzying degree of alcohol. However, the Hermitage La Chapelle, when mature at 15 or 20 years, is virtually interchangeable with a great Pauillac. In addition, the alcohol content rarely exceeds 13%. Much of the enormous impact this wine makes on the palate has simply to do with its fabulous layers of fruit, which comes from vines that average 40 years of age and grow in the granite soil of Le Méal and Les Bessards. Approximately 5,000–6,000 cases of Hermitage La Chapelle are made in an abundant vintage—not nearly enough to satisfy the thirst of increasing numbers of Americans and Englishmen who are this wine's biggest fans.

As staggeringly great as the La Chapelle is, the white Hermitage, the Chevalier de Stérimberg, produced from 60% Marsanne and 40% Roussanne, has, until 1982, been largely a disappointment. The philosophy of making white wine at Jaboulet has been to ferment at very low temperatures, block the malolactic, and bottle the wine in March and April following the vintage, without the wine ever seeing a day in wood cooperage. Far too often this wine has lacked character and flesh, tasting like some technically perfect but flavorless California wine. However, there seems to be an effort by the Jaboulets since 1982 to give their white Hermitage more muscle and character. This certainly holds true for the 1983, 1984, and 1985. Perhaps we can expect better things from this house's white Hermitage. For now, Jaboulet's white Hermitage is a wine to consume within the first 3–4 years of its life.

Lastly, Jaboulet's huge production allows the firm to market many of its wines under other names. The two brands that regularly appear in the marketplace are André Passat and Jaboulet-Isnard. These wines are often considerably less expensive than those labeled Paul Jaboulet Ainé, yet are the same wine, except for the La Chapelle.

VINTAGES

1985—*Hermitage La Chapelle (red)*—Quite deep ruby/purple in color
·   with a full-intensity bouquet of cassis fruit and pepper, this is a
90   concentrated, very full-bodied, soft La Chapelle that has some
     charm and appeal already. Low acidity makes aging beyond 15
     years a gamble, but this wine could well turn out to resemble
     the 1971. Anticipated maturity: 1988–1999. Last tasted 6/86.

1985—*Hermitage Chevalier de Stérimberg (white)*—Perhaps the ripe-
· ness of this vintage has caused this wine to taste richer and more
86 intense than normal. Larger scaled in comparison with previous
efforts, this big, alcoholic wine has scents of peaches and apricots in its bouquet. Drink the next 1–3 years. Last tasted 6/86.

1984—*Hermitage La Chapelle (red)*—I know Jaboulet does not use new
· oak, but I certainly thought I smelled toasty vanillin aromas
85 (from new barrels) in this wine. Medium-bodied, quite soft and
fruity already, this is a very light La Chapelle that will provide
pleasant drinking over the next 6–7 years. Last tasted 12/86.

1984—*Hermitage Chevalier de Stérimberg (white)*—Fragrant floral, wet
· stone scents are of light intensity. On the palate, the wine is one-
78 dimensional, fresh, a little tart, but pleasant. Drink up. Last
tasted 12/86.

1983—*Hermitage La Chapelle (red)*—Gérard Jaboulet believes this is
· the finest La Chapelle since the monumental 1961. I still give a
98 tiny edge to the 1978. However, the 1983 is a profound wine,
closed, very dense in color with a tight yet blossoming bouquet
of ripe blackcurrant fruit, tar, and pepper. On the palate, it is
very, very tannic, amazingly concentrated, quite full-bodied,
and massive in the finish. It is still an infant. Anticipated maturity: 1998–2025. Last tasted 12/86.

1983—*Hermitage Chevalier de Stérimberg (white)*—One of Jaboulet's
· better efforts with a white Hermitage, the 1983 is spicy, fully
85 mature, plump, and fleshy with good fruit and a pleasing, somewhat alcoholic finish. Drink up. Last tasted 4/86.

1982—*Hermitage La Chapelle (red)*—This wine seems to get better
· with each tasting. I first thought it too fat to be classic, but it has
93 firmed up in the bottle. A peppery, rich berry aroma is followed
by a wine with very deep, long, tannic flavors, an opulent, explosive fruitiness on the palate, and super length. It is more approachable and flattering than the tannic 1983, but still a decade
away from maturity. Anticipated maturity: 1996–2010. Last
tasted 12/86.

1981—*Hermitage La Chapelle (red)*—Gérard Jaboulet told me he first
· intended to declassify La Chapelle 1981 into a mere regular
74 cuvée, but he obviously changed his mind. It was a questionable
decision. The wine is austere, with a dusty, leathery aroma and
rather coarse yet sparse flavors. It tastes awkward and charmless. Anticipated maturity: now–1990. Last tasted 9/86.

1980—*Hermitage La Chapelle (red)*—Supple and soft and approaching
full maturity, the 1980 is a good rather than outstanding La
85   Chapelle. The smoky, gamelike aromas, the medium- to full-
bodied texture, and good yet unexciting finish suggest that it be
drunk up. Gérard Jaboulet calls it "honest." Anticipated maturity: now–1990. Last tasted 7/86.

1979—*Hermitage La Chapelle (red)*—An underrated vintage, the 1979
La Chapelle, overlooked because everyone wanted the 1978, can
90   clearly stand on its own merits. Very dark ruby with no sign of
age, this full-bodied wine has excellent concentration, a tarlike,
rich cassis bouquet, quite a bit of tannin, and an impeccably
clean, well-defined finish. Still quite young. Anticipated maturity: 1993–2010. Last tasted 10/86.

1978—*Hermitage La Chapelle (red)*—Perfection. The ruby/purple
color, the staggering concert of aromas ranging from concen-
100   trated, even jammy cassis to smoked meats and exotic spices,
the awesome level of flavor extract, the power, the grace, the
balance, and the length of this sublime wine make it as much a
benchmark for red Hermitage as the quintessential expression
of the noble Syrah grape. It is just now beginning to open. Anticipated maturity: 1995–2025. Last tasted 6/86.

1977—*Hermitage La Chapelle (red)*—I thought I detected the smells of
my mother's fruitcake in the glass. Rather light on the palate,
76   deceptively so in view of the pleasant bouquet, this wine is fully
mature and offers decent, uncritical quaffing. Anticipated maturity: now–1990. Last tasted 2/84.

1976—*Hermitage La Chapelle (red)*—I find quite a few 1976s to be less
exciting than the vintage's reputation suggests. Jaboulet's La
85   Chapelle is a very good wine, but it lacks the extra concentration
and aromatic smorgasbord that makes this wine so special. Full-
bodied, a little dry in the finish with some amber at the edge,
this chunky wine will still keep. Anticipated maturity: now–
1990. Last tasted 12/86.

1975—*Hermitage La Chapelle (red)*—Quite meagerly endowed, this
medium garnet-colored wine hardly suggests the character of La
69   Chapelle. It should be drunk up. Last tasted 6/81.

1973—*Hermitage La Chapelle (red)*—Reminiscent of certain 1976 Bordeaux, the 1973 is quite tasty, but loosely knit, rather ripe and
84   flavorful with only a hint of dilution. This velvety wine is fully
mature, and should be consumed immediately. Last tasted 9/80.

1972—*Hermitage La Chapelle (red)*—This has always been one of my
· favorite La Chapelles, which is surprising given this vintage's
93 reputation in France (no doubt because of the washout in Bordeaux). Still very dark wth some amber at the edge, the 1972
has a majestic bouquet of exotic spices, hickory, smoked meats,
and oodles of ripe fruit. On the palate, the full-bodied, velvety
richness is breathtaking. Approaching its apogee, yet with years
of life left to it, the 1972 La Chapelle is a superb wine that one
could mistake for a top Pomerol. Anticipated maturity: now–
2000. Last tasted 10/86.

1971—*Hermitage La Chapelle (red)*—My notes fail to reveal the first
· time I tasted this wine, but I believe it was between 1973–75,
87 when I bought a case for immediate consumption; every bottle
seemed to get better, so I put away a handful for the eighties.
What all this proves, I suppose, is that the 1971 was gorgeous to
drink early on because of its voluptuousness, and has become
even richer with age. It is among the most elegant of all the La
Chapelles I have drunk. Despite the fact that it has lasted longer
than I guessed, it should be drunk up. Last tasted 10/86.

1970—*Hermitage La Chapelle (red)*—Another great vintage for La Cha-
· pelle, the 1970 has much more life in it than the fully mature
92 1971. The intense perfume of cedarwood, melted caramel, berry
fruit, and toasty scents is fabulous. On the palate, it has the
perfect balance of massive fruit and body with elegance. Anticipated maturity: now–1998. Last tasted 6/84.

1969—*Hermitage La Chapelle (red)*—Less voluptuous and opulent in
· style, the 1969 La Chapelle has a claret-like, restrained richness
87 that seems to require some study and introspection. Dark ruby
with a moderately intense, elegant bouquet, medium to full
body, excellent concentration but a firm backbone, this wine,
while not as dramatic as some, is still very fine. Anticipated
maturity: now–1996. Last tasted 7/86.

1966—*Hermitage La Chapelle (red)*—Layers of velvety fruit carry this
· full-bodied wine. An unctuous, multidimensional wine with a
92 huge, full-intensity bouquet of berry fruit, smoky nuts and saddle leather, the long, lush flavors are something to savor. Drink
up. Last tasted 1/86.

1962—*Hermitage La Chapelle (red)*—Quite mature, the 1962 was, I
· suspect, better 5 or 6 years ago. The aromas of coffee and old
85 leather are attractive. On the palate, this wine is very soft, be-

ginning to drop its fruit, and should be drunk up. Last tasted 12/80.

1961—*Hermitage La Chapelle (red)*—I have only tasted this wine on
· four occasions, the last in February 1986. It is undoubtedly in a
100 class with a 1961 Latour or 1961 Pétrus, and its resemblance to a '61 claret is more than imaginary. It is great for the same reasons that certain 1961, 1947, or 1945 clarets are great. The wondrous level of rich fruit extract is still perfectly intact, only age has added nuance after nuance. Unbelievably concentrated, with a dazzling perfume of ripe fruit, grilled meats, and nuts, this wine is unctuous on the palate with a staggeringly long finish. I have high hopes that the 1978, perhaps the 1983, will be this memorable, for this is a privilege and a thrill to drink. Anticipated maturity: now–2005. Last tasted 2/86.

MARC SORREL ****

One of my fondest memories is of my first visit to the Domaine Sorrel in 1980. The ancient Henri Sorrel was in very poor health at the time, despite which both he and his wife showed remarkable enthusiasm. Until the mid-seventies Henri Sorrel had sold the wine he made from his 8.5 acres of 50-year-old vines superbly located in Le Méal, Les Greffieux, and Les Rocoules to négociants. Based on two ecstatic reports about his wines, one from Mark Williamson of Willi's Wine Bar in Paris and the other from the late Martin Bamford, I visited Sorrel and was overwhelmed by the first two vintages I tasted, a spectacular 1978 and an equally impressive 1979. Henri Sorrel died in 1982 and his son Marc, in his mid-thirites, with little training or experience, assumed control over the domaine. The result was a disastrous group of wines in 1982 that were flawed by excessive volatile acidity. The failures of that year and my documentation of them in my wine journal, *The Wine Advocate*, resulted in my banishment from visiting the domaine for several years. Despite his shortcomings in 1982, Marc Sorrel bounced back in 1983 with very fine wines and has continued to build on those successes.

There are three wines produced by Sorrel. The white Hermitage called Les Rocoules, after the vineyard of the same name, is a solid, fleshy wine with a mineral-and-pineapple-scented bouquet, some oakiness, and full body. Two red Hermitage wines are made. There is a regular cuvée that is good but rarely stunning, and the top-of-the-line red Hermitage called Le Gréal, made from a blend of wine from the Le

Méal and Les Greffieux vineyards. Sorrel's father had called the same wine Le Méal. It can be a stunningly rich, potentially long-lived wine, and in vintages such as 1978, 1979, 1983, and 1985 it is certainly comparable to Jaboulet's La Chapelle and the wines of Chave.

After this turbulent period in the early eighties, the Domaine Sorrel seems to once again be taking its place among the leaders of this appellation.

VINTAGES

1985—*Hermitage (red)*—Surprisingly elegant, soft, with plenty of black
• cherry fruit, this medium-bodied, stylish wine has good color,
85 adequate acidity, and low tannins. Already pleasant. Anticipated maturity: now–1992. Last tasted 1/87.

1985—*Hermitage Le Gréal (red)*—Significantly deeper and more aro-
• matic than the regular cuvée, the Le Gréal has a smoky, toasty,
90 plummy bouquet of excellent ripeness and complexity, and long, rich, very intense flavors of black cherries. This full-bodied wine is loaded with fruit. Anticipated maturity: 1990–2000. Last tasted 1/87.

1985—*Hermitage Les Rocoules (white)*—Scents of tropical fruit such as
• pineapple combine nicely with toasty new oak barrel smells. On
86 the palate, the wine is medium-bodied, rather soft and fleshy, and cleanly made. Drink over the next 3–4 years. Last tasted 1/87.

1984—*Hermitage (red)*—Rather one-dimensional, fruity, and medium-
• bodied, this wine is fully mature and offers straightforward, un-
80 critical drinking. Last tasted 11/86.

1984—*Hermitage Le Gréal (red)*—Surprisingly dark in color, the 1984
• is full-bodied, quite tannic, concentratred and deep, with fine
86 length. It requires cellaring. Anticipated maturity: 1990–1998. Last tasted 11/86.

1984—*Hermitage Les Rocoules (white)*—Some prominent oak domi-
• nates the bouquet. In the mouth, the wine is angular, lean, and
84 lemony with high acidity, but shows a great deal of fruit in the finish. Last tasted 10/86.

1983—*Hermitage (red)*—Very spicy and peppery, this medium- to full-
• bodied wine has good color, good depth of fruit, and a hefty
86 dosage of tannin to shed. Quite well made. Anticipated maturity: 1990–2000. Last tasted 6/86.

1983—*Hermitage Le Gréal (red)*—This wine brings to mind both Chur-
·   chill's and Broadbent's use of the expression "an iron fist in a
90   velvet glove." Deep in color, very spicy, even peppery, with
       loads of ripe black cherry fruit, this full-bodied wine has a lush
       fruitiness but still plenty of tannin to lose. Anticipated maturity:
       1991–2001. Last tasted 6/86.

1983—*Hermitage Les Rocoules (white)*—Pineapples, wet stones, apri-
·   cots, and toasty oak all create a degree of excitement. On the
86   palate, the wine is ripe, full-bodied, a trifle foursquare and
       chunky, but quite concentrated and interesting. It should age
       well. Last tasted 6/86.

1982—*Hermitage Le Gréal (red)*—A failure. The excessive vinegary
·   smells and stewed fruit suggest insurmountable problems in the
55   making of this wine. Avoid. Last tasted 6/84.

1982—*Hermitage Les Rocoules (white)*—Totally lacking acidity, this
·   listless, dull wine is heavy, awkward, and beginning to lose its
61   fruit. Avoid. Last tasted 6/84.

1981—*Hermitage (red)*—A musty nose and lack of fruit and body are
·   this wine's undoing. Barely acceptable, it should be drunk up.
70   Last tasted 6/85.

1980—*Hermitage Le Méal (red)*—Very mushroomy aromas intertwined
·   with pepper and scents of bacon fat are quite complex. Supple,
85   broad flavors continue to express the smoky character exhibited
       in the nose. Medium-bodied, the 1980 Le Méal should be drunk
       over the next 4–5 years. Last tasted 12/84.

1979—*Hermitage Le Méal (red)*—This is a sensational Hermitage.
·   Deep ruby/black in color with an explosive bouquet of toasty
93   oak, tar, licorice, and jammy black cherry fruit, this full-bodied
       wine has stunning layers of fruit, plenty of tannin, and excep-
       tional length. Anticipated maturity: 1995–2008. Last tasted
       7/85.

1978—*Hermitage Le Méal (red)*—This is a momumental effort. It is the
·   only time I tasted a wine and literally begged to buy a few bot-
98   tles. Unfortunately, the feeble Henri Sorrel refused, claiming he
       only had enough stock for his family. I have never seen a bottle
       since I last tasted it with Sorrel in 1980. Black/ruby in color,
       with a majestic bouquet that seemed to inundate the olfactory
       senses with ripe fruit and exotic spices, immense and massive
       on the palate (a clone of the 1977 Taylor Fladgate port), this
       hugely proportioned wine made even the great 1979 Le Méal
       look a little sickly beside it. It had unbelievable length, and for

those lucky enough to have this wine cellared, it should offer considerable challenge to the monumental wines made by Chave and Jaboulet in 1978. Anticipated maturity: 1995–2010. Last tasted 6/80.

UNION DES PROPRIÉTAIRES À TAIN L'HERMITAGE**

In the southern Rhône Valley there are numerous growers' cooperatives, but in the north there are only three. The largest northern Rhône cooperative is in Tain L'Hermitage, with 540 members producing just over 25% of this appellation's wine. It prides itself in being one of the few cooperatives in France to age its wines in small oak barrels, and it employs a cooper full-time just to make barrels.

There is an entire range of northern Rhône wines made here, and if they are to be criticized, it is not for a lack of careful winemaking, but rather for their lack of individuality and blurring (no doubt due to blending) of vintage differences. The wines are soundly made, but far too frequently taste very much alike. The top wines year after year are their white Hermitage and Cornas, of which the latter seems to show the most character, but their red Hermitage wines are also competently made in a thoroughly modern style. Prices for the cooperative's wines are quite fair.

VINTAGES

1984—*Hermitage (red)*—Nicely colored, the 1984 has a dull bouquet
·   with a trace of peppery Syrah fruit, medium body, rather ele-
78   vated acidity, and a tart finish. Anticipated maturity: now–1991.
        Last tasted 1/87.

1984—*Hermitage (white)*—Quite well made, this light straw-colored
·   wine has a light-intensity, floral, fruity bouquet, medium body,
83   crisp acidity, and a solid finish. Though not sublime, it is certainly pleasant, but suffers in comparison to the 1983 and 1982.
        Anticipated maturity: now–1998. Last tasted 1/87.

1983—*Hermitage (red)*—Deep ruby with a tight but forthcoming bouquet of bacon fat and berry fruit, the 1983 is tannic, medium-
·
81   bodied, and just a trifle short and dull. With time, it may show
        better. Anticipated maturity: 1988–1995. Last tasted 1/87.

1983—*Hermitage (white)*—The 1983 is a very good white Hermitage,
·   fleshy and deep on the palate with the aromas of wet stones and
85   nuts. Full-bodied, plump, and flavorful, this wine should drink
        well for 4–5 years. Last tasted 1/87.

1982—*Hermitage (red)*—Slightly softer than the 1983 and seemingly
· just as deep, but lusher and broader on the palate, this is a spicy,
83 chewy wine with a good deal of acidity and tannin in the finish.
Not bad. Anticipated maturity: 1988–1994. Last tasted 1/87.

1982—*Hermitage (white)*—Quite good, round, supple, chewy with the
· scents of almonds and ripe fruit, the 1982 has a lush, full-bodied
85 appeal and is now fully mature, but will hold. Last tasted 1/87.

1980—*Hermitage (white)*—Still quite youthful and fruity with crisp
· acidity, the 1980 is medium straw-colored, spicy, with plenty of
84 fruit and body. No sign of fatigue is apparent. Last tasted 1/87.

Other Producers of Hermitage

Domaine L'Hermite—Terrence Gray, the eccentric Egyptologist, sold
his vineyards to Gérard Chave in 1985 and slipped into retirement.
His wines were often variable but very faithful examples of traditional
Hermitage. Some of his white Hermitage could be stunning, the 1978
and 1980 for example, and in 1983 and 1978 Gray turned out superb
red Hermitage that will last 20 years. Old vintages of Gray's wines
are well worth seeking out.

Jaboulet-Vercherre—This large négociant in Beaune purchases wine
each year from growers and blends it in their cellars. Their red wine
is sold under the name Hermitage-Rochefine and their white is called
Hermitage La Tour Blanche. The quality of the wines is no better
than average. Contrary to what some have surmised, this firm has no
relationship today to Paul Jaboulet Aîné, although Jaboulet-
Vercherre was founded by a member of the original Paul Jaboulet
family in the nineteenth century.

Léon Revol—A modest-sized operation, Revol's offices are located
right in the heart of Tain L'Hermitage. I would like to think I have
been unlucky with his wines, many of which I have found disagree-
able, but I believe the quality here is mediocre at best.

L. de Vallouit—Madame de Vallouit produces 750 cases of good red
and white Hermitage that seem only slightly less exciting than her
Côte Rôtie. Her 1980 and 1981 red Hermitages were disappointing,
the 1982 quite good, the 1983 even better, and the 1985 excellent,
confirming reports that quality here is on the increase. With respect
to the white Hermitage, I have not tasted a vintage since the terrible
1980. However, the 1979 was very good, still quite vivacious and tasty
in 1985. Prices for Vallouit's wines are reasonable, so bargains still
exist.

CROZES-HERMITAGE

The Poor Man's Hermitage?

CROZES-HERMITAGE AT A GLANCE

Type of wine produced:	Red and white wine
Grape varieties planted:	Marsanne and Roussanne for the white wine; Syrah for the red wine
Acres currently under vine:	2,030
Quality level:	Mediocre to good
Aging potential:	White wine: 1–4 years Red wine: 3–10 years
General characteristics:	Tremendous variability in the red wines; white wines are fleshy, chunky, solid, and rather undistinguished
Greatest recent vintages:	1985, 1983, 1978
Price range:	$6–$9

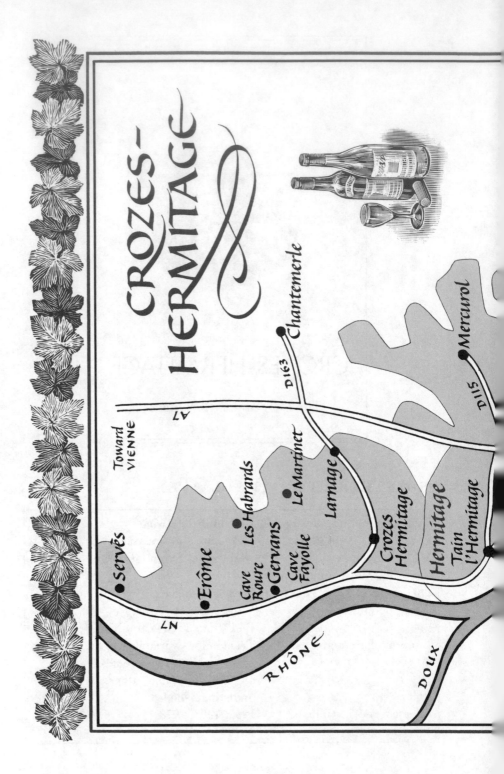

CROZES-HERMITAGE

Toward VIENNE

A7

Servès

Erôme

N7

Les Habrards

Cave Roure

Gervans

Cave Fayolle

Le Martinet

Larnage

Chantemerle

D163

Crozes Hermitage

Hermitage

Tain l'Hermitage

Mercurol

D115

RHÔNE

DOUX

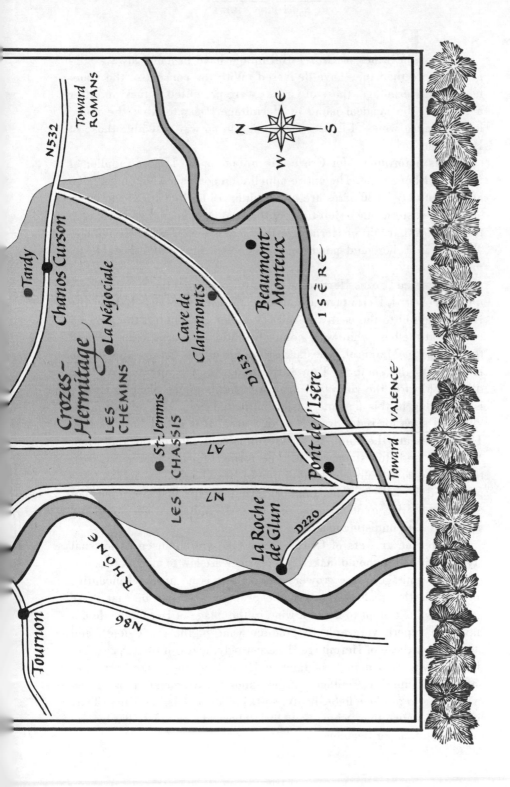

The wines of Crozes-Hermitage have in name always suggested more than they have delivered. With the consent of the winemakers of Hermitage, those of Crozes were permitted to tack on, after a hyphen, the magical name of Hermitage. Despite what the name implies, most wines of Crozes-Hermitage in no way resemble those of Hermitage.

This is unfortunate, for Crozes-Hermitage is the largest supplier of northern Rhône wine. The entire appellation covers a whopping 12,000 acres, but only 2,030 acres are under vine. All of the Crozes vineyards sit on the eastern side or left bank of the Rhône and completely envelop the huge granite hill of Hermitage that looms over Tain L'Hermitage. The soil is richer, and much of the vineyard area is cultivatable by machine.

The best red Crozes-Hermitage tends to come from the granite slopes north of Tain L'Hermitage around the town of Gervans. Behind the Hermitage hill to the east, the soil is sandier and lighter; the growers claim that the best white wine comes from the vineyards in and around the village of Mercurol. The largest sector of the Crozes appellation fans out to the south of Tain L'Hermitage in the direction of Pont d'Isère. Most of the vineyard expansion that is taking place in Crozes is occurring in this flat and easily cultivated area. One of the finest vineyard sites for red Crozes is in this area. It is called Les Chassis. The grapes are the same as for Hermitage, Syrah for the red wine, Marsanne and Roussanne (mostly the former) for the white. And yes, the climate is virtually identical to that of Hermitage. The yield of juice permitted per acre is higher than in Hermitage, but that alone does not explain why the great majority of Crozes-Hermitage wines, both red and white, are undistinguished.

Perhaps the growers of Crozes-Hermitage are confused as to what style of wine they should make. Since prices are low to modest for most Crozes-Hermitage, some growers claim there is no financial incentive to increase the quality. Much of the problem seems to be that those growers who attempt to make a wine in the image of Hermitage do not have the superb vineyards to produce wine of the great depth and structure of those of Hermitage. Interestingly, many of the Crozes producers own small parcels of land in Hermitage and make very fine, sometimes superb Hermitage. At the opposite extreme are those growers aiming to produce light, fruity, soft, innocuous-tasting wines. They lose out because their wines have little character and taste like poorly made imitations of Beaujolais.

The most notable successes here have come from producers such as Jaboulet, Fayolle, Pradelle, Ferraton, and Tardy, who recognize their limitations. They will never be able to equal the majestic richness of a Hermitage, nor can they out-Beaujolais the Beaujolais producers, but they can turn out richly fruity wines with good body and freshness that have appeal and some character.

The top Crozes-Hermitage red wines usually peak two to three years after the vintage and will keep four to five years thereafter. To expect a red Crozes-Hermitage to hold in the bottle for a decade is expecting too much. When they are good, they will offer an interesting yet straightforward, medium-weight, richly fruity wine that may occasionally, and then only vaguely, suggest a Hermitage. As for the white Crozes-Hermitage wines, the best of them should be in the bottle no later than six months after the vintage, and drunk within three years of the vintage for their freshness and vivacity. Both red and white Crozes-Hermitage, when made by the best growers from the top vintages, will satisfy both the palate and the purse.

RECENT VINTAGES

1986—A huge crop of good, soft wine was produced in Crozes-Hermitage in 1986. Some wines will be diluted because of pre-harvest rains and overproduction, but the best cuvées from the hillside vineyards should be quite good and will mature quickly. Optimum maturity: now–1994.

1985—Very supple, round, perfumed wines with good color, loads of fruit, and low acidity were produced in 1985. The whites are fat, deficient in acidity, but tasty; the reds are chunky and capable of providing delicious drinking for 4–5 years. Optimum maturity: now–1991.

1984—Good acidity and a certain toughness will ensure 5–7 years of longevity, but often the level of fruit is not sufficient for the levels of acidity and tannin. Jaboulet's red Crozes-Hermitage Thalabert is a notable exception to this generalization. Optimum maturity: now–1992.

1983—I am a great believer in drinking Crozes-Hermitage quite young, but the 1983s are a true *vin de garde* vintage. Big, beefy, tannic, firm wines were produced that require keeping. Optimum maturity: 1988–1995.

1982—The white 1982s should have been consumed by now. As for the red Crozes-Hermitage, if the grower was able to keep his fermentation temperature from boiling over, the wines have turned out fruity and supple, and are now fully mature. The good examples should be drunk over the next 2–3 years.

OLDER VINTAGES

Nineteen seventy-eight was a superb vintage in Crozes-Hermitage. The Thalabert of Jaboulet is not fully ready, and Raymond Roure's Crozes, Les Picaudières, is still drinking very nicely. These are exceptions, however.

A Personal Rating of the Crozes-Hermitage Producers

****(EXCELLENT PRODUCERS)
Paul Jaboulet (Thalabert)

***(GOOD PRODUCERS)

Cave des Clairmonts	Paul Jaboulet (regular
Collonge	curvée)
Delas Frères (white wine)	Pradelle
J. Fayolle	Raymond Roure
M. Ferraton	R. Rousset
A. Graillot	C. Tardy and Ange

**(AVERAGE PRODUCERS)

A. Bégot	A. Desmeure
Chapoutier	Union des Propriétaries
Delas Frères (red wine)	de Vallouit

ALBERT BÉGOT**

Bégot's cellars are in the very northern part of the Crozes appellation, in the tiny, seemingly lifeless, windswept town of Serves. Bégot's wife actually runs this operation since he works in a factory. Bégot has just under ten acres of vines, and he believes strictly in making a wine only by organic methods—no chemical sprays, no sulfates, no filtration, etc. He seems to have plenty of fruit and depth in his wines, but I believe it is ill-advised for him to age them three years in old wooden casks, which seems to give them a dry, sometimes musty character and a lack of freshness. However, Bégot seems to be content to age his wine in this manner and says he has no problem selling it.

VINTAGES

1981—*Crozes-Hermitage*—Medium ruby with a dusty, rather oxidized
· bouquet, this dry, astringent wine lacked both fruit and charm.
65 Past its prime. Last tasted 6/86.

1980—*Crozes-Hermitage*—Aromas of fading cherry fruit and wet wood
· are fleeting in the glass. On the palate, the wine has barely
69 sufficient fruit to make it palatable. Drink up. Last tasted 6/86.

CAVE DES CLAIRMONTS ***
This domaine was founded only in 1973. It is managed by three families
who have 339 acres divided equally between the production of red and
white Crozes-Hermitage. Their production of 72,000 cases a year is
considerable. All of the vineyards are relatively young and located on
the flat plateau south of Tain L'Hermitage. Their cellars are in Beau-
mont-Monteux. The style of these wines, both red and white, is a very
modern fruity, soft, fresh one designed for maximum commercial appeal. To this firm's credit, prices are also very reasonable. Their white
wine should be drunk within three years of the vintage, the red wine
within four to five years.

VINTAGES
1985—*Crozes-Hermitage (red)*—Quite grapy with good levels of pep-
· pery, cherry fruit, this medium-bodied wine is soft and pleasant.
80 Anticipated maturity: now–1990. Last tasted 12/86.
1985—*Crozes-Hermitage (white)*—Faint flora aromas create some in-
· terest in an otherwise dull, neutral bouquet. On the palate, the
78 wine is chunky, fruity, and has good acidity for the vintage.
Anticipated maturity: now–1989. Last tasted 12/86.
1983—*Crozes-Hermitage (red)*—Deep ruby color with an innocuous,
· light-intensity bouquet of red berries, soft for a 1983, it is me-
75 dium-bodied with a touch of astringence in the finish. Anticipated maturity: now–1992. Last tasted 6/86.
1983—*Crozes-Hermitage (white)*—Not showing much age, this firm,
· rather closed, bland wine has little character or charm, just a
72 simple fruitiness and high acidity. Anticipated maturity: now–
1988. Last tasted 6/86.

CHAPOUTIER **
The large Chapoutier firm produces Crozes-Hermitage not only from
their own 13 acres of vineyards, but also from purchases from growers.
The trade name for both their white and red Crozes-Hermitage is Les
Meysonniers. Chapoutier's wines from Crozes have never been among
my favorites. Frequently high in acidity, underendowed with fruit, and
dimensionless, they offer little value despite their sensible prices.

Given a choice between the two wines, the white seems a safer bet than the red.

VINTAGES

1985—*Crozes-Hermitage Les Meysonniers (red)*—Soft, simple, jammy
· fruit flavors are about the only interesting aspect of this other-
75 wise one-dimensional wine. Drink up. Last tasted 6/86.

1985—*Crozes-Hermitage Les Meysonniers (white)*—Fat, ripe, fleshy,
· and loaded with fruit, the 1985 white Crozes has surprising char-
84 acter and palate presence. Last tasted 6/86.

1984—*Crozes-Hermitage Les Meysonniers (red)*—Light ruby with a veg-
· etal, dusty, spicy aroma, medium body, and delicate flavors, this
69 charmless wine offers little comfort.

1984—*Crozes-Hermitage Les Meysonniers (white)*—Excessively high
· acidity gives this wine a very tart, green, underripe character.
62

COLLONGE (DOMAINE LA NÉGOCIALE)***

This modest-sized estate is located in the best part of the Crozes appellation for producing white wine—Mercurol, in the eastern portion
where the soil is sandy and light. The Collonge family owns 67 acres of
vines from which they produce 10,000 cases of red wine and only 600
cases of white. Recognizing their limitations regarding quality and
price, they make light, fresh, fruity, simple wines that are meant to be
drunk within two to three years of the vintage. The wines, which are
kept in tanks until bottled, are never exciting, but they are sound and
appropriate for uncritical quaffing.

VINTAGES

1985—*Crozes-Hermitage (red)*—This is a round, generously fruity,
· plump, medium-bodied wine with a good deal of gutsy fruit.
82 Anticipated maturity: now–1990. Last tasted 1/87.

1985—*Crozes-Hermitage (white)*—Not complex, the 1985 white Crozes
· is quite cleanly made, fruity, with decent acidity and an ade-
80 quate finish. Drink over the next 1–2 years. Last tasted 1/87.

1984—*Crozes-Hermitage (red)*—Soft, cherry fruit flavors show surpris-
· ing ripeness for this vintage. It is a little short in the finish but
80 sound and satisfactory. Drink over the next 2 years. Last tasted
1/87.

1983—*Crozes-Hermitage (red)*—Quite deep in color, with a straightfor-
·   ward, ripe fruitiness and medium body, the 1983 has good length
83   and a pleasing velvety finish. Last tasted 1/87.
1983—*Crozes-Hermitage (white)*—Showing its age, this wine seems to
·   be losing its fruit and drying out. It should be consumed. Last
74   tasted 1/87.

JULES FAYOLLE ET FILS ***

This small estate, run by twins Jean Paul and Jean Claude Fayolle, has
20 acres of well situated Crozes vineyards on hillside slopes north of
Tain L'Hermitage near the quiet town of Gervans. The Fayolles make
one of the better wines of the appellation. In fact, their red wine is one
example of a Crozes-Hermitage that stands comparison with some Hermitage. They produce 3,600 cases of solid, fleshy, personality-filled red
Crozes-Hermitage, but only 100 cases of good white Crozes. The red is
kept 14–16 months in wood foudres and seems to have the strength and
structure to handle this treatment. Unlike the great majority of Crozes
wines, the red from Fayolle will keep and evolve five to eight years after
the vintage. The trade name for their red and white Crozes-Hermitage
is Les Pontaix.

VINTAGES

1985—*Crozes-Hermitage Les Pontaix (red)*—This is a big, beefy, very
·   concentrated, rather inky-colored Crozes with the smoky, tar-
84   scented bouquet one gets from Hermitage. Its low acidity makes
       it delicious now. Anticipated maturity: now–1992. Last tasted
       6/86.
1984—*Crozes-Hermitage Les Pontaix (red)*—Not a bad effort, the 1984
·   has a light-intensity cherry fruitiness, medium body, and soft,
80   pleasant texture without an excess of acidity. Drink over the
       next 2 years. Last tasted 6/86.
1983—*Crozes-Hermitage Les Pontaix (red)*—A big, thick, unctuous
·   wine that tastes a trifle clumsy, but offers mouth-filling and
84   mouth-coating flavors in a full-bodied format. It will keep until
       1990. Last tasted 6/86.
1983—*Crozes-Hermitage Les Pontaix (white)*—Still fresh and lively,
·   this medium-bodied white Crozes has a slightly herbaceous,
84   pear-scented aroma and good fruity flavors. It should be drunk
       up. Last tasted 6/86.

MICHEL FERRATON***

Ferraton, who can also produce very good red and decent white Hermitage (see page 110), has 15 acres of vines in Crozes-Hermitage not far from Paul Jaboulet's famous Domaine Thalabert. This is a traditionally made red Crozes that spends at least a year in wood prior to being bottled. I have found Ferraton's Crozes, which he calls La Matière, to be rather inconsistent, but there is no doubt that his 1985 is the star of this appellation.

VINTAGES

1985—*Crozes-Hermitage La Matière (red)*—Aside from the Crozes pro-
·   duced by Jaboulet's Thalabert vineyard, this is the best red
87   Crozes I have tasted. Dark ruby in color with a big, full-intensity
      bouquet of cassis fruit and smoky scents, this lush, supple, unc-
      tuous, full-bodied wine is quite impressive. Anticipated matu-
      rity: 1987–1995. Last tasted 6/86.
1984—*Crozes-Hermitage La Matière (red)*—Much lighter than the 1985,
·   Ferraton's 1984 is medium-bodied, fully mature, and cleanly
80   made. Drink over the next 2 years.

ALAIN GRAILLOT***

Alain Graillot's first vintage was 1985. He is renting 40 acres from two elderly women. A serious man, he purchases small two-year-old oak barrels from several growers in Burgundy to age his red wines for 11–12 months. He produces small quantities of good red St.-Joseph, but his main wines are a rich, robust, flavorful Crozes-Hermitage and an even richer, more powerful, tannic single-vineyard Crozes-Hermitage called La Guiraude. Given the commitment to quality at this estate, Graillot should be a producer to follow.

PAUL JABOULET AINÉ***–****

Jaboulet's red Crozes-Hermitage, called Thalabert, is indisputably the finest wine of the appellation. It can in fact taste and smell like a lighter-weight Hermitage. Jaboulet's Domaine Thalabert consists of 86.5 acres in Crozes, and produces approximately 9,000 cases of wine. All of it is red; there is no white wine made at this estate. The vines at Domaine Thalabert average 25–30 years of age. The wine spends 10–12 months in oak barrels prior to being bottled. It is one of the few Crozes reds that actually will improve in the bottle for four to eight years, and can last a decade in vintages such as 1978 and 1983. The Jaboulets also make another red Crozes-Hermitage from purchased wine. In 1985, 42,000 cases of red Crozes-Hermitage were produced. It is usually a sound wine, but much less exciting and less concentrated than the Thalabert.

There is a white Crozes-Hermitage also. Quaintly called La Mule Blanche, it was, like other Jaboulet white wines, neutral and boring until 1983, when the firm clearly started to put a bit more flavor and muscle into their whites. The wine is made from the Jaboulet's own 14.8-acre vineyard, and is unique for the high percentage of Roussanne in it. The blend sought each year is 50% Marsanne and 50% Roussanne. It is a wine to drink within two to three years of the vintage.

VINTAGES

1985—*Crozes-Hermitage (red)*—For Jaboulet's straight Crozes, the
·   1985 is surprisingly good. Quite dark in color, exuberantly fruity,
84   lush, medium-bodied and extremely satisfying to both palate and purse, this wine shows what intelligent winemaking can produce. Anticipated maturity: now–1991. Last tasted 6/86.

1985—*Crozes-Hermitage Thalabert (red)*—Much more voluptuous and
·   opulent than Jaboulet's regular bottling of Crozes, the 1985 Thal-
87   abert has very dark color, full body, outstanding concentration, oodles of cassis, peppery fruit, and a velvety finish. Anticipated maturity: now–1994. Last tasted 6/86.

1985—*Crozes-Hermitage La Mule Blanche (white)*—I agree with Gérard
·   Jaboulet that this is the best white Crozes he has produced. Very
86   ripe and bursting with luscious fruit, this medium- to full-bodied wine should be drunk over the next 1–3 years. Last tasted 6/86.

1984—*Crozes-Hermitage Thalabert (red)*—Quite a success in this vin-
·   tage, the 1984 Thalabert seemed almost as concentrated as Ja-
84   boulet's famous Hermitage La Chapelle. Sweet, round, plummy flavors are generous and supple. Drink over the next 5 years. Last tasted 12/86.

1983—*Crozes-Hermitage Thalabert (red)*—Deep in color with a jammy,
·   berry fruit aroma, the 1983 Thalabert is a more tannic wine than
86   usual. It is still a little hard-edged, but patient cellaring will prove beneficial. Anticipated maturity: 1988–1994. Last tasted 12/86.

1982—*Crozes-Hermitage Thalabert (red)*—Supple, fruity, round, totally
·   ready to drink, this attractive deep ruby-colored wine has heaps
85   of fruit, a freshness to its flavor, and good finish. Drink over the next 3–4 years. Last tasted 4/85.

OLDER VINTAGES

The 1981 is meagerly endowed and will only fade. The 1980 is a very charming, mature, supple wine that seems only slightly less deep than the 1979. One of the finest Thalaberts I have tasted is the 1978, still rich in fruit, quite full-bodied, complex and, yes, not unlike a smaller-scaled Hermitage.

DOMAINE PRADELLE ***

In 1978, brothers Jacques and Jean Louis Pradelle left the cooperative, Union des Propriétaires in Tain L'Hermitage, so that they could estate bottle their own red and white Crozes-Hermitage. Their cellars are located in the eastern part of the appellation in Chanos-Curson. They own 22 acres of Syrah and another 8 acres of Marsanne, all of which lie in the stony, sandy soil of Mercurol. Over two-thirds of their vines are on the plateau rather than the hillsides. The Pradelles are a good source for red Crozes, but their white wine, despite their modern winemaking philosophy, seems to lack character and tastes very tart and thin. For all of the white wine's one-dimensional quality, the red wine here is a brawny, fruit-filled, rustic style of Crozes that offers a dramatic contrast to the innocuous white. It is aged in casks and foudres for one year prior to bottling.

VINTAGES

1985—*Crozes-Hermitage (red)*—A plump, deeply colored, chunky spec-
·   imen, the 1985 is tannic, has good concentration, quite a bit of
82   body, and seems to need cellaring. Anticipated maturity: 1988–
       1992. Last tasted 6/86.

1985—*Crozes-Hermitage (white)*—Dull, tart, lacking fruit, this clean
·   yet neutral-tasting wine has no character. Last tasted 1/87.
60

1984—*Crozes-Hermitage (red)*—Rustic, full-bodied, surprisingly big
·   and tannic for a 1984, this wine tastes a trifle coarse, but for
79   quaffing with a good stew, it would serve adequately. Drink over
       the next 3–4 years. Last tasted 12/86.

1984—*Crozes-Hermitage (white)*—Where's the fruit? All I can taste is
·   acidity and alcohol. Last tasted 1/87.
65

1983—*Crozes-Hermitage (red)*—Very tannic and hard, the 1983 is
·   closed, well colored, but is there enough fruit to outlast the
?   tannins? Judgment reserved. Last tasted 1/87.

RAYMOND ROURE***

Raymond Roure has a 16-acre estate located in the best area of the appellation, on the hilly slopes of Gervans. His wine has one of the best reputations in Crozes, as his vines produce what is the appellation's smallest yield per acre. The trade name for his red wine is Les Picau-dières, a wine that spends two years in old wooden casks. Despite the obvious risk of oxidation and fruit loss, Roure's rich, intense, red Crozes seems to benefit from such a long sojourn in oak casks in top vintages such as 1978 and 1983. However, his inflexibility in altering this formula in light years like 1980 and 1981 is detrimental to the overall quality of the wines produced in those years. My advice is not to miss an opportunity to try Roure's red Crozes in the top vintages, but approach it with caution in lighter, less obviously successful ones. Roure's wines seem to need three to four years to develop.

VINTAGES

1983—*Crozes-Hermitage Les Picaudières (red)*—Medium to dark ruby,
·   this is a typical 1983 in the sense that it is quite concentrated,
84   but also very tannic and hard. The underlying fruit seems to be
       there to support 2–4 years of aging. Last tasted 1/87.

1981—*Crozes-Hermitage Les Picaudières (red)*—Dried out wood flavors
·   are hard and deficient in ripe fruit. Last tasted 6/86.
62

1978—*Crozes-Hermitage Les Picaudières (red)*—A complex bouquet of
·   ripe cherry fruit and saddle leather suggests a fine burgundy.
82   On the palate, the wine is less charming, but pleasant and fully
       mature. Last tasted 1/85.

GAEC DE LA SYRAH (TARDY AND ANGE)***

In 1979, Charles Tardy and Mrs. Bernard Ange left the cooperative in Tain L'Hermitage to begin their own domaine, called Gaec de la Syrah. Like the aforementioned Pradelle brothers, they have their cellars in Chanos-Curson. They own almost 40 acres of vines from which they produce 4,500 cases of red and white Crozes-Hermitage that I have seen under two labels, Domaine des Entrefaux and Domaine les Pier-relles. I am told these labels are for marketing purposes and there is no difference in the wines. Both Tardy and Ange exhibit great flexibility and seem to have a thorough knowledge of what they want to do and how they want to do it. Their white wine, which is 100% Marsanne, is fermented at very cool temperatures to preserve its freshness and fruit, then bottled after four to six months. It is a lighter-styled Crozes but very fresh, aromatic, and most important, delicious. The red wine is made in a very supple, lush style with plenty of clean, pure Syrah fruit quite well displayed. Its freshness and accessibility belie the fact that Tardy and Ange keep it 16–18 months in wood foudres.

VINTAGES

1985—*Crozes-Hermitage Pierrelles (red)*—A delicious, plump, deep-colored wine loaded with smoky, cassis-scented Syrah fruit.
• Full-bodied, rich and long, this is what fine Crozes is all about.
85 Anticipated maturity: now–1992. Last tasted 6/86.

1985—*Crozes-Hermitage Pierrelles (white)*—Quite fruity and stylish with a great deal of elegance, the 1985 shows very clean wine-making and a good, dry, snappy finish. Drink over the next 2
84 years. Last tasted 1/87.

1984—*Crozes-Hermitage Pierrelles (red)*—Soft, simple, one-dimensional, fruity flavors are clean, but rather boring. Drink up. Last
78 tasted 10/86.

1983—*Crozes-Hermitage Pierrelles (red)*—Rich, wild berry aromas interlaced with gamelike, earthy scents as well as smoked meat
84 create quite a complex wine. On the palate, the wine is fat and long, delicious now but will keep. Drink over the next 4 years.
Last tasted 10/86.

1982—*Crozes-Hermitage Pierrelles (red)*—Round, fruity, soft, and lush, this wine has good body, a satisfying plumpness, an elevated
82 degree of alcohol, and low acidity. Last tasted 10/86.

Other Crozes-Hermitage Producers

Delas—This négociant does a fine job with most northern Rhônes. Their red Crozes is somewhat dull but the 1985 showed delicious fruit. However, don't ignore their white Crozes-Hermitage made from 100% Marsanne. The 1985 is excellent, 1984 good, and the 1983 a rich, creamy, surprisingly big and fresh wine.

Jaboulet-Vercherre—This large négociant in Beaune produces Crozes-Hermitage of marginal quality.

Robert Michelas—This grower has 30 acres of well-placed vineyards. I have only tasted one of his wines, a red 1982 Crozes-Hermitage to which I gave good marks. He has an emerging reputation and may be a name to follow.

Moillard—This négociant in Burgundy produces a surprisingly good and faithful example of red Crozes-Hermitage. The 1985 is especially good.

Père Anselme—This négociant in Châteauneuf-du-Pape should not stray out of the southern Rhône. Their Crozes-Hermitage tastes sharp and angular, often having a cooked, cardboard character. It is below average in quality.

Domaine des Remezières—Alphonse Desmeure has 35 acres in Crozes-Hermitage. The white Crozes is rather dull, lifeless wine that appears to be made in an old, heavy, oxidized style. The red Crozes is much better. The 1983 and 1985 exhibited good, ripe, peppery, Syrah fruit. The 1984 tasted compact and short.

L. Revol—Very dull, bland, often neutral-tasting wines that rarely reflect their appellation are produced by this négociant in Tain L'Hermitage.

Robert Rousset—The young, dark-haired Rousset has 14.8 acres of vineyards divided equally between Syrah for his red wine and Marsanne for his white. I have tasted only two vintages of his red, a 1984 and 1983, both of which were certainly good. Locally, he is well respected.

de Vallouit—Madam de Vallouit produces 1,700 cases of red and white Crozes-Hermitage from 8.4 acres of vines. It is usually a soundly made, serviceable wine, although the 1983 red was quite rich and impressive.

Union des Propriétaires à Tain L'Hermitage—This large cooperative produces very cleanly made, correct red and white Crozes-Hermitages that lack flair and personality but are consistently well made. The red seems a better bet than the straightforward white wine. Their 1985s look to represent a new and more exciting level of quality.

ST.-JOSEPH

Better Than Most Crozes-Hermitages
and a Good Value

ST.-JOSEPH AT A GLANCE

Type of wine produced:	Red and white wine
Grape varieties planted:	Marsanne and Roussanne for the white wine; Syrah for the red wine
Acres currently under vine:	800
Quality level:	Good to excellent
Aging potential:	White wine: 1–5 years
	Red wine: 1–6 years
General characteristics:	The red wines are the lightest, fruitiest, and most feminine of the northern Rhône. The white wines are perfumed and fleshy with scents of apricots and pears
Greatest recent vintages:	1985, 1983, 1978
Price range:	$6–$10

This is one of my favorite appellations. The red wines, despite their deep color, are the lightest and most overtly fruity wines of the northern Rhône. They do not repay more than five to six years of cellaring. It is their delightful charm and a savory, round, supple character they possess that are the reasons for their appeal. With the exception of a handful of cases, I would opt for a St.-Joseph red or white wine rather than a Crozes-Hermitage.

For one thing, the St.-Joseph appellation is on the western bank of the Rhône, with its best vineyard sites fanning out across the valley behind and above the town of Tournon. The area that is entitled to appellation status is enormous, stretching from just south of Condrieu at Chavannay to Guillerand, directly across the river from Valence. This amounts to virtually the entire length of the northern Rhône viticultural district. All of the appellation is on the western bank of the Rhône, but some portions are not terribly promising for top-quality wine. Nevertheless, there has been a huge increase among the bulging number of new St.-Joseph vineyards. From a tiny appellation of 200 acres in 1970 it has grown to over 800 acres, planted with Syrah, Marsanne, and tiny quantities of Roussanne. However, the top St.-Joseph wines come from only a narrow stretch of hillsides between St.-Jean-de-Muzol (just north of Tournon), south past Mauves, to the picturesque Châteaubourg six miles north of Valence. The vineyards in this area are planted primarily in granite-based soil with some clay and sand. While the exposure here is not quite as ideal as that at Hermitage, Côte Rôtie, or Cornas, it is far superior to other sections of the St.-Joseph appellation. The tragic thing about St.-Joseph is that among the numerous new vineyards being planted, the majority are being placed on flat, high-yielding soils and not on the terraces overlooking the Rhône between Mauves and St.-Jean-de-Muzols. In fact, many of these hillside locations, which produce St.-Joseph's best wines, are facing the same problems that the hillsides of Cornas must confront—the encroachment from residents of Valence who want to build homes on the scenic hillsides overlooking the Rhône and are prepared to pay top dollar for the land. To exacerbate the problem further, the French government has done little to set aside these hillside areas as agricultural zones. Consequently, the long-range prospects are that the quality of St.-Joseph wine will decline as more and more of the wine comes from the high-yielding plateau areas and not from the better hillside vineyards.

Red wine represents 80% of the production in St.-Joseph. The white wine from this appellation, which can be excellent, has become increasingly popular and the amount of it produced has jumped by 10% in the last five years.

St.-Joseph received appellation contrôlée status only in 1956. Although named after a saint, in all likelihood the name St.-Joseph came from several hillside vineyards between Mauves and Tournon that were once owned by a monastery. The monks are said to have frequently referred to their vines as those of St. Joseph. John Livingstone-Learmonth records that the wine was also famous in the era of King Henry II (1519–1559) and that Victor Hugo, in his classic work *Les Misérables*, referred to "the good wine of Mauves." However, Hugo could well have been drinking a red or white Hermitage, not a St.-Joseph, given the fact that Gérard Chave's family, who lived in Mauves at the time, has been producing Hermitage at Mauves since the 1480s. Lastly, it is documented that Louis XII (1462–1515) apparently had a vineyard on the right bank of the Rhône near Tournon, which today is the heart of this appellation.

There are a number of very fine winemakers who produce St.-Joseph. The négociants Paul Jaboulet and Chapoutier also make St.-Joseph, but it is the small growers, all located in Tournon, Mauves, and St.-Jean-de-Muzols, who make this appellation's finest wines.

RECENT VINTAGES

1986—In 1986 a large crop of healthy grapes was harvested that should provide fruity, soft, well-colored wines. Both Jean Louis Grippat and Pierre Coursodon, two of the better growers, liken it to a blend of the fat, supple, deeply fruity, seductive 1985s and the tannic, tougher 1983s—high praise indeed. Optimum maturity: 1988–1993.

1985—Wines that are precocious, densely colored, with vividly developed bouquets, rich, intense fruit, but low acids were produced in 1985. The whites are particularly fat, fruity, and succulent, but must be drunk young. Optimum maturity: now–1991.

1984—Wines with higher acidity than 1983, 1985, and 1986 were made. The best wines have a racy charm, crisp acidity, and good fruit. The worst are lean, angular, and lacking in fruit. Trollat's 1984 is an unqualified success in this vintage. Optimum maturity: now —1991.

1983—A very highly regarded vintage by all the growers, the 1983s are big, full-bodied, surprisingly tannic wines for St.-Joseph. Most of them may lose their fruit before all the tannin melts away, yet the best-balanced examples will be very special. The white wines should have been drunk by now. Optimum maturity: 1988–1995.

1982—Richly fruity, supple, round, low-acid wines similar to 1985 (only less concentrated and colored) were produced. All are fully mature and should be drunk up over the next 2–3 years.

OLDER VINTAGES

I know of no St.-Joseph white wine that will improve beyond two to three years in the bottle. As for the red wines, they are at their best when they have the exuberant raspberry, peppery fruitiness well displayed. This is usually when they are between three and six years old. Despite the close proximity to Hermitage, the wines of St.-Joseph do not evolve well in the bottle once they are over six or seven years of age. The only exception would be a great vintage such as 1978.

A Personal Rating of the St.-Joseph Producers

**** (EXCELLENT PRODUCERS)

J. L. Chave	R. Trollat
J. L. Grippat	

*** (GOOD PRODUCERS)

M. Chapoutier	B. Gripa
Chol	P. Jaboulet
M. Courbis	J. Maisonneuve
Pierre Coursodon	J. Marsanne

** (AVERAGE PRODUCERS)

Cave Coopérative	P. Gonon
Delas Frères	de Valloiut
E. Florentin	Vidal-Fleury

JEAN LOUIS CHAVE ****

The remarkable winemaker and grower Gérard Chave quietly produces 250–300 cases of gorgeously fruity, elegant, supple, medium-bodied, red St.-Joseph. One wishes he had the time to produce more, for his wine is one of the best. The little that is exported goes to his representatives in Great Britain, the Yapp Brothers, who are highly esteemed merchants in Wiltshire, and to the well-known, influential, Berkeley, California, restaurant of Alice Waters, Chez Panisse. It is a wine Chave bottles after ten months' aging in wood, and is best drunk within the first five to six years of life.

VINTAGES

1985—*St.-Joseph*—The 1985 is decadently fruity and ripe. The luscious
·   scents of peppery, raspberry fruit are extremely intense. Quite
86   supple, this lovely wine should be drunk over the next 3–4 years.
      Last tasted 6/86.

CHAPOUTIER ***

This large, well-known firm in Tain L'Hermitage has 13.5 acres of
hillside vineyards in St.-Joseph from which they produce one of the
appellation's very finest white wines, and a good, solid, fruity red wine.
The trade name Max Chapoutier uses for his St.-Joseph is "Deschants." While the white is put through a malolactic fermentation and
bottled after a year, the red spends one to one and a half years in large
wooden foudres. The St.-Josephs of Chapoutier are notable values and
well worth seeking out for their excellent rapport in quality and price.

VINTAGES

1985—*St.-Joseph Deschants (red)*—This is a very elegant, fruity, soft,
·   cherry-and-raspberry-scented wine. The 1985 will provide de-
83   lightful drinking over the next 2–3 years. Last tasted 6/86.
1985—*St.-Joseph Deschants (white)*—Clearly reminiscent of a white
·   Hermitage, the 1985 white St.-Joseph is a wonderfully rich, ripe,
87   deeply fruity, full-bodied wine bursting with fruit and power.
      Quite impressive. Last tasted 6/86.
1984—*St.-Joseph Deschants (red)*—Quite light but fruity and not too
·   acidic, this fresh, vivacious wine should be drunk over the next
82   1–2 years. Last tasted 6/86.
1984—*St.-Joseph Deschants (white)*—One hundred percent Marsanne,
·   as usual, Chapoutier's 1984 St.-Joseph is surprisingly rich, long,
85   deep, and filled with character. Impeccably made. Last tasted
      6/86.
1983—*St.-Joseph Deschants (red)*—Rather burly and intensely spicy,
·   the 1983 also has a surprising measure of tannin and body. Will
82   the fruit outlast the tannin? Drink over the next 4–5 years. Last
      tasted 6/86.

MAURICE COURBIS ***

Courbis has 20 acres of vines spread out in the more prolific-yielding
soils south of Mauves. His cellars are in Châteaubourg as is his best
vineyard, the hillside slope called Les Royes. The white wine from

Courbis is fairly neutral in taste; however, his red offers more excitement.

VINTAGES

1985—*St.-Joseph (red)*—This wine will not age well (few St.-Josephs
· can), but for drinking over the next 2–3 years, it offers spicy,
82 moderately intense, peppery, chewy fruit, medium body, and
low acidity. Last tasted 6/86.

1985—*St.-Joseph (white)*—This is a one-dimensional, chunky, rather
· fat wine that is mouth-filling but neutral. Last tasted 6/86.
78

1983—*St.-Joseph (red)*—A rustic, spicy, earthy nose is acceptable,
· even complex. On the palate, the wine is dry as well as a trifle
76 too tannic. Last tasted 6/86.

PIERRE COURSODON***

Like Courbis, Coursodon has 20 acres of vines from which he produces
2,900 cases of red wine and 400 cases of white. His cellars are in the
tiny, nondescript town of Mauves, a short two-minute walk from those
of Gérard Chave. Pierre, who appears to be in his mid-thirties, is in full
control of the production here since his father Gustave retired several
years ago. The Coursodon vineyards are all located on the steep hillsides just to the rear of the town of Mauves. Pierre says that 85% of the
vines are 60 to 70 years old. From these old vines comes a very special,
luxury cuvée of St.-Joseph red that the Coursodons call "Le Paradis
Saint-Pierre." This is a house whose reds are probably the longest-lived
of any from this appellation and should be sought out. The white wine
is bottled early for freshness. In contrast, the red wine here spends 18
months in very old oak foudres.

VINTAGES

1985—*St.-Joseph (red)*—Despite the low acidity, the 1985 has a deep
· ruby color, a very perfumed bouquet of rich, berry fruit, full
85 body, and a succulent, lush finish. It will be delicious for 2–4
years. Last tasted 6/86.

1985—*St.-Joseph (white)*—Rather full-bodied, this wine has plenty of
· one-dimensional fruit, some real power and palate presence, but
80 no complexity. Last tasted 6/86.

1984—*St.-Joseph (red)*—Hard, austere flavors offer little charm in this
· modestly endowed wine. It will not improve. Last tasted 6/86.
74

1984—*St.-Joseph (white)*—This is a dull, simple, straightforward wine
·   that has as its main attributes tart, clean fruit and decent wine-
72   making. Last tasted 6/86.

1983—*St.-Joseph Le Paradis St.-Pierre (red)*—This was the debut vin-
·   tage for this special cuvée made from Coursodon's old vines.
85   Another will be made in 1985, but I have not tasted it. The 1983
   is deep in color, has good body, and is altogether a richer, more
   serious and more tannic wine. Anticipated maturity: 1988–1994.
   Last tasted 6/86.

1983—*St.-Joseph (white)*—Scents of peaches and hazelnuts are com-
·   bined nicely in this medium- to full-bodied, somewhat alcoholic
81   wine. It has good freshness and seems in no danger of losing its
   fruit. Last tasted 6/86.

1979—*St.-Joseph (red)*—Not unlike a lighter-weight Hermitage, Cour-
·   sodon served me this to prove the aging potential of his wines.
85   Aromatic, spicy, with supple, fat, attractive flavors, this wine
   has 4–6 years of life left in it. Very good. Last tasted 6/86.

EMILE FLORENTIN (CLOS DE L'ARBALESTRIER)**

This estate in Mauves consists of 14 acres of vines of which one-fourth
is devoted to making white wine and the rest red. The style of wines
produced by Florentin is very traditional—to an extreme. The white
wine is heavy and sometimes oxidized, the red very tannic, austere,
and angular.

VINTAGES

1985—*St.-Joseph (red)*—I hope the 1985 signals that Florentin is put-
·   ting more fruit into his wine. Medium ruby with soft, berry aro-
82   mas and flavors, this wine is quite attractive. Anticipated
   maturity: now–1991. Last tasted 10/86.

1984—*St.-Joseph (red)*—This is a compact, lean, unyielding wine, yet
·   surprisingly it has more fruit than his wine from two higher-rated
70   vintages, 1983 and 1982. Last tasted 10/86.

1983—*St.-Joseph (red)*—Thin, astringent flavors give this pale ruby-
·   colored wine very little appeal. Last tasted 10/86.
65

1982—*St.-Joseph (red)*—Old and decrepit with the fruit drying out, all
·   that is left is a tannic toughness and tart acidity. Last tasted
62   10/86.

BERNARD GRIPA***

The balding, yet handsome, enthusiastic Bernard Gripa has 12.3 acres of hillside vineyards in and around Mauves. He produces 4,000 cases of red St.-Joseph, 600 cases of white, as well as a little wine from the neighboring appellation of St.-Péray. His white St.-Joseph is quite good, rather full-bodied, with lovely scents of peaches and apricots in years such as 1985. His red is a richly fruity, densely colored wine that exhibits very fine winemaking. The red never spends more than one year in wooden foudres.

VINTAGES

1985—*St.-Joseph (red)*—This is a vibrant, juicy, very fruity wine with
· good body, decent acidity, and a lush texture. Anticipated ma-
84 turity: now–1990. Last tasted 6/86.

1985—*St.-Joseph (white)*—The 1985 white St.-Joseph is very elegant,
· medium bodied, peach-scented with a great deal of fruit, full
84 body, and adequate acidity. It should be drunk over the next 2
years. Last tasted 6/86.

1984—*St.-Joseph (red)*—While light in color, Gripa's 1984 has charm-
· ing fruit, shows clean winemaking, and medium body. Last
82 tasted 6/86.

1983—*St.-Joseph (red)*—Not a blockbuster, Gripa's 1983 is medium-
· bodied, fruity, and soft for a 1983. Fully mature, it should be
84 drunk over the next year. Last tasted 12/86.

1982—*St.-Joseph (red)*—Ripe, soft, moderately deep fruit gives this
· wine immediate appeal. Low in acidity and showing some orange
82 at the edge, it should be drunk up. Last tasted 11/85.

JEAN-LOUIS GRIPPAT****

The ebullient Grippat, who makes great white Hermitage and dull red Hermitage (see page 112), devotes most of his time and energy to producing white and red St.-Joseph. He owns nine acres of vines superbly situated on the hillside above Tournon (where he maintains his cellars) and in Mauves. In addition, he rents from Tournon's hospital one acre of 100-year-old vines high up the hillside near the medieval tower overlooking Tournon and Tain L'Hermitage. From this plot of vines he produces 75–100 cases of his St.-Joseph Cuvée des Hospices, unquestionably the appellation's greatest red wine. Unfortunately, it is virtually impossible to find in the marketplace.

Grippat's other red St.-Joseph wines are elegant, soft, fairly light wines that one is apt to like for their charm and lightness rather than power or intensity. However, he makes St.-Joseph's best white wine, which is very aromatic with vivid aromas of peaches and apricots. It is a very pleasurable wine to seek out for both its quality and modest price.

VINTAGES

1985—*St.-Joseph (red)*—Extremely soft, this medium ruby-colored wine has an engaging berry fruitiness, silky finish, and no as-
· tringence whatsoever. Drink over the next 2–3 years. Last tasted
82 6/86.

1985—*St.-Joseph Cuvée des Hospices (red)*—This is a marvelously fruity, fat, sumptuous St.-Joseph that is bursting with black
· cherry and raspberry fruit. Plump and unctuous, it will provide
87 a delicious mouthful of wine over the next 3–5 years. Last tasted 6/86.

1985—*St.-Joseph (white)*—Loaded with scents and flavors of tropical fruit, this lush, richly fruity, medium- to full-bodied wine is a
· great joy to drink. It should be consumed before 1989. Last
86 tasted 6/86.

1984—*St.-Joseph (red)*—Light ruby with a faint cherry, strawberry fra-
· grance, this medium-bodied wine is a little diluted, but does
77 have adequate soft Syrah fruit. Last tasted 6/86.

1984—*St.-Joseph (white)*—The 1984 is a very pleasing wine from this appellation's best white winemaker. A flowery, peach-scented
· bouquet is quite pleasant. On the palate, it lacks the richness
84 and fat of the 1985 but has more acidity. Last tasted 6/86.

1983—*St.-Joseph (red)*—Surprisingly evolved, ripe and fruity given the vintage, Grippat's 1983 is deliciously soft, medium-bodied with
· cherryish and plummy fruit flavors. Drink over the next 2–3
81 years. Last tasted 11/86.

PAUL JABOULET AINÉ ***

Consumers looking for a good St.-Joseph are most likely to encounter this fruity, exuberant-styled St.-Joseph from the Jaboulet firm called "Le Grand Pompée" (named after one of Charlemagne's favorite generals). Jaboulet produces nearly 12,000 cases of this modern-styled, cleanly made red wine. Curiously, they make no white wine from this appellation. Like all St.-Josephs, it is a wine to drink within five years of the vintage for its freshness and fruit.

VINTAGES

1985—*St.-Joseph Le Grand Pompée*—Gobs of super-ripe fruit seem to
· gush from the glass. On the palate, this wine is fat, plummy,
84 seductive, and already quite delicious. Consume it over the next
2–3 years. Last tasted 12/86.

1984—*St.-Joseph Le Grand Pompée*—Dull, short, thin flavors leave lit-
· tle to get excited about. Last tasted 6/86.
72

1983—*St.-Joseph Le Grand Pompée*—Bottle variation is a problem
· here. Some bottles show chewy, fleshy, berry fruit, a soft tex-
? ture, and good finish. Other bottles seem pruny, overripe, and
out of balance. Judgment reserved.

1982—*St.-Joseph Le Grand Pompée*—Quite rich in color, the 1982 is
· somewhat similar to the 1985, with a rich raspberry-scented
84 bouquet, soft, voluptuous flavors, and a good finish. Drink over
the next 2–3 years. Last tasted 11/86.

JEAN MARSANNE***

Marsanne, who resides above his wine cellars in Mauves, produces very
small quantities of red St.-Joseph from his five acres of vines. He earns
most of his living from his fruit tree orchards. Marsanne's red wine is
quite traditionally made and aged 18 months or more in large foudres.
It is one of the biggest St.-Joseph reds, yet is always loaded with fruit.
Its style reminds me of the beefy, more full-bodied red St.-Joseph
produced by Pierre Coursodon, a neighbor of Jean Marsanne.

VINTAGES

1985—*St.-Joseph (red)*—This is a different and unique style of St.-
· Joseph. Wild gamelike, smoky, untamed Syrah aromas predom-
84 inate. On the palate, the wine is quite full-bodied, spicy, and
has at least 5–8 years' cellaring potential. Anticipated maturity:
1988–1994. Last tasted 6/86.

1983—*St.-Joseph (red)*—Very tannic, spicy, less fruity and concen-
· trated than the 1985, the 1983 is smoky, full-bodied, with a
82 bacon fat character to the wine's aroma and flavor. Anticipated
maturity: now–1993. Last tasted 6/86.

RAYMOND TROLLAT****

Although the minuscule quantities of Grippat's Cuvée des Hospices red
St.-Joseph may well qualify as the appellation's single best wine, it is
exceedingly difficult to find. For year in and year out consistency and

excellence in St.-Joseph, no one is better than the fit-looking Raymond Trollat. His white St.-Joseph is almost the equal of Grippat's, and his red wine is deliciously fruity and always consistent. Trollat has his cellars in the hilly hamlet of St.-Jean-de-Muzols. His eight-acre vineyard occupies one of the top two or three vineyard sites of the appellation. It has a magnificent view of Tain L'Hermitage and the forbidding Hermitage hill, making it a prime spot for real estate developers who have already swallowed up some of the vineyards of Trollat's neighbors. Trollat believes his St.-Joseph should be drunk within five years of the vintage, except for those who like the taste of "old wine." He says one can keep his red wine for up to ten years. Trollat is a very skilled winemaker who, I have no doubt, would have greater fame and fortune were he working in a more prestigious appellation. I cannot recommend his very reasonably priced wines highly enough.

VINTAGES

1985—*St.-Joseph (red)*—As St.-Josephs go, this is an opulent, ripe, broadly flavored, intensely fruity wine. Deep ruby in color with
·
87 fruit oozing from within, this wine will provide great hedonistic enjoyment over the next 5–6 years. Last tasted 6/86.

1985—*St.-Joseph (white)*—Despite low acidity, this floral, peach-scented, medium- to full-bodied wine is fleshy, very cleanly
·
85 made, very, very fruity, and soft and velvety on the palate. Drink over the next 2 years. Last tasted 6/86.

1984—*St.-Joseph (red)*—Surprisingly intense peppery, raspberry aromas jump from the glass. On the palate, the wine tastes more
·
85 like a 1983 than a 1984. Deep in color with vibrant, fresh berry fruit flavors, this wine is very successful for the vintage. Drink over the next 3 years. Last tasted 1/87.

1983—*St.-Joseph (red)*—A gorgeously seductive bouquet of peppery, raspberry fruit is disarming. On the palate, the wine has excel-
·
86 lent depth and a surprisingly long finish. Some tannin in the finish may warrant limited cellaring, but I would opt to drink this wine over the next 5–6 years. Last tasted 11/86.

Other St.-Joseph Producers

Cave Coopérative de St.-Désirat-Champagne—Over two-thirds of the St.-Joseph production is made by this growers' cooperative. To date, I have not found the wine of this cooperative to be anywhere near the quality of the wine produced by the cooperative in Tain L'Hermitage, the Union des Propriétaires.

A. Cuilleron—Cuilleron produces small amounts of good white wine from Condrieu, so perhaps it is not surprising to find both his 1984 and 1985 white St.-Joseph superior in quality to his dull, rustic red St.-Joseph. Cuilleron's cellars are in Chavannay.

B. Faurie—Young Faurie, who lives and has his cellars in Tournon, is generally considered one of the emerging stars for both white and red Hermitage. What is not so well known is that he makes a little St.-Joseph too. I have never tasted it, but he is a high-quality, meticulous winemaker.

Chol-Domaine de Boisseyt—I have only tasted two vintages of Chol's red St.-Joseph, the 1982 and 1983. Both were very good, rich, dense, well-made wines with considerable character. Chol has 15 acres of vines at St.-Joseph and ages the wine in their cellars at Chavannay for two years in wooden foudres. This is a name to consider when looking for red St.-Joseph.

Pierre Gonon—Both white and red St.-Joseph are produced from Gonon's five acres of vines situated between Tournon and Mauves. Neither wine is exciting.

Jean Maisonneuve—I have never seen a bottle of wine from Maisonneuve. He is respected by Gérard Chave, who says he makes good traditional St.-Joseph red wine from his three-acre vineyard in Mauves (where his cellars are also located).

de Vallouit—Solid red St.-Joseph is made by this firm that appears to be making great strides in increasing the quality of their range of Rhône wines.

Vidal-Fleury—Numerous changes are underfoot at this famous Ampuis firm now that the Guigal family is in control. They have traditionally made a sound St.-Joseph—light, but fruity and satisfying. Marcel Guigal claims they will continue to produce this wine.

CORNAS

Anachronism of the Twentieth
Century

CORNAS AT A GLANCE

Type of wine produced:	Red wine only
Grape varieties planted:	Syrah only
Acres currently under vine:	240
Quality level:	Very good to exceptional
Aging potential:	5–20 years
General characteristics:	Black/ruby in color, very tannic, full-bodied, virile, robust wines with a powerful aroma
Greatest recent vintages:	1985, 1983, 1979, 1978, 1976, 1969
Price range:	$9–$16

The impenetrable black/ruby color, the brutal, even savage tannins in its youth, the massive structure and muddy sediment in the bottle are all characteristics of a wine that tastes as if it were still made in the nineteenth century. Yet for the adventurous, these wines, kept cellared for seven to twelve years, reveal remarkable aromas of cassis and raspberries, chestnuts and truffles. The tiny appellation of Cornas continues to survive against all odds. The best of these primitive wines are made from grapes grown on the steep hillsides just south of Hermitage that must be tilled by hand. The suburban housing boom outside the large commercial city of Valence continues to jeopardize more and more of the appellation. The wines themselves, so complex and stunning after a decade of cellaring, are forbiddingly raw and unapproachable in their youth. Yet the league of Cornas followers continues to grow and grow, and the top producers seem to sell out their entire crop in vintages such as 1985 and 1983 with little trouble. There are 408 acres in the Cornas appellation, of which 240 are in vines. The best wines all come from the steep *coteaux* (or hillsides) behind the town. The grape here is the Syrah, and, as in Côte Rôtie, no white wine is made here. Unlike Côte Rôtie, no white wine Viognier grapes are even permitted to be grown here. Given the increasing demand for Cornas, 70% of each year's crop is now exported, with the Dutch, English, Swiss, and Americans clamoring for the "real wine" of Cornas.

While the inhabitants of Valence who desire a hillside building location with a fabulous view of the Rhône Valley are encroaching upon this tiny appellation, the expansion of vineyards on the valley floor beneath the steep slopes may in the long run diminish the blossoming reputation of Cornas more than French yuppies looking for a second home in the country. Wine from these valley vineyards clearly lacks the character and strength of that produced from the hillside sites.

The entire appellation of Cornas, like Côte Rôtie, lies on the western bank of the Rhône. However, Cornas has an even more privileged situation. The sun-drenched vineyards sit in an amphitheater-like setting with a southerly exposure, but the configuration of the surrounding hills gives Cornas protection from the severe, turbulent winds that can buffet the vineyards of Côte Rôtie and Hermitage. The lack of wind here also serves to exacerbate the effect of the summer's heat, and usually means that the Syrah of Cornas bakes in the hot sun at much higher temperatures than in Hermitage only seven miles farther north. Interestingly, the word "Cornas" is believed to originate from the ancient Celtic vocabulary and loosely translated means "burnt" or

ST-JOSEPH, CORNAS, AND ST-PÉRAY

Toward VIENNE

N7

A7

St-Pierre de Boeuf

RHÔNE

Chavanay

Malleval

D79

D503

Toward BOURG-ARGENTAL

N86

Limony

Chanas

Félines

Serrières

Peyraud

Champagne

St-Désirat

St-Etienne de Valoux

Talencieux

Ardoix

Sarras

Andance

A7

N7

N86

Toward ANNONAY

St-Joseph

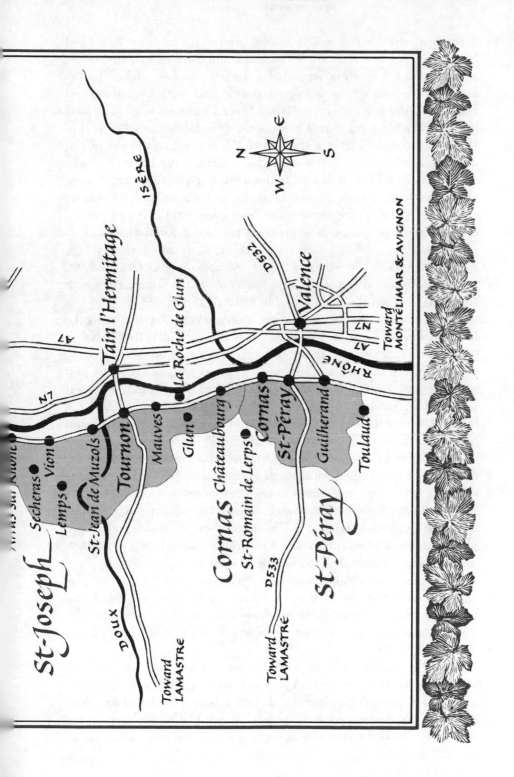

"scorched earth." The soil is mostly granite, as in Côte Rôtie and Hermitage, but one finds more limestone and clay, and as one moves south toward the St.-Péray appellation the soil becomes sandier, particularly on the valley floor and lower slopes. Like both Côte Rôtie and Hermitage, the hillside vineyards are braced by stone walls that form terraces which zig-zag across the slopes. The slopes reach 800 feet in height in places and have a gradient of 45°, preventing the use of machines for cultivation. This special microclimate, the absence of any white wine in the blend to mollify the intense, powerful color, flavors, and tannin of the Syrah, as well as the ancient winemaking techniques employed by the village growers has resulted in what is truly France's most robust, enormously structured and blackest-colored wine.

Cornas is believed to be among the oldest vineyard sites in France, with references to the wines of this region appearing as long as 2,000 years ago. Local Cornas historians proudly recite the fact that Emperor Charlemagne paid the town a visit in 840 A.D. and tipped his goblet to the local growers. Despite its past and its remarkable location along the Rhône, as recently as a decade ago many growers felt there was no future in making Cornas. There were two reasons for this feeling.

First, the backbreaking labor served as an impediment to many prospective growers. Second, the prices fetched for Cornas were extremely low, forcing most growers to seek employment in the large factories across the river in Valence, or to plant fruit orchards to supplement their income. However, in the mid-seventies more and more interest began to develop in these unique wines, and the greater demand meant that higher prices could be established. Today, interest is so strong in the top wines that Cornas's best growers, such as Auguste Clape and Noel Verset, must now allocate each year's crop to guarantee that their customers receive a fair share. New vineyards have been planted and old vineyard sites left uncultivated are being reclaimed. Several large négociants with excellent reputations, particularly Paul Jaboulet Ainé, have taken aggressive positions with respect to purchases of new vintages of Cornas, adding evidence to the belief that Cornas is an appellation whose wines are about to become fashionable. Yet, despite surging consumer interest, Cornas is still a remarkably undervalued wine.

A word of caution is appropriate for readers who are ready to rush off to their merchant to seek a bottle of Cornas. Cornas is a broodingly dark, rustic, massively proportioned, very muscular wine that can obliterate one's senses if modern, industrial, vapid, technically flawless red wines are the usual frame of reference. It is doubtful that Cornas tastes much different today than when the Romans guzzled it down 2,000 years ago. But, if one has the patience to wait seven, nine, or ten years for its aggressive coarseness to mellow out, and for the huge, tarlike, peppery, cassis bouquet to develop nuances of truffles and saddle leather, one will be treated to a stunning, great gustatory treasure. It is convenient to compare Cornas to Hermitage, but in truth they are very different despite the fact that they share the same grape and are grown in much the same type of soil. Cornas is a bigger, more structured wine, yet it does not generally seem to keep its fruit past 10–15 years as a great red Hermitage will do. Why this occurs is bewildering to me, for the wine seems initially to have just as much concentrated fruit as a Hermitage. Perhaps the nineteenth-century rustic winemaking philosophy employed by virtually all the growers in Cornas precludes great longevity for the wines largely because the fruit dries out after a decade and a half. Therefore it is unable to support the huge tannins of these wines. Whatever the reason, the top vintages of Cornas need seven to eight years to shed their tannins, but most should then be consumed before they turn 15 years of age.

Few growers in Cornas ever fine or filter their wines, so expect a five- or ten-year-old Cornas to have a tremendous amount of sediment, not only in the bottom of the bottle, but caked around the sides like a vintage port. This is one wine that demands decanting. Modern centrifuges and micropore filters that make life easy for the winemaker but can eviscerate the character and flavor of a wine with a switch of a button are unknown in the bucolic appellation of Cornas.

The overall quality of winemaking in Cornas is extremely high, surprisingly so in view of the antiquated winemaking techniques, ancient barrels, and dilapidated wine cellars in which most growers work. In spite of this high quality, and unlike other French wine villages, one could pass through Cornas without ever being aware that wine was made there. The drab village does little to promote its wines. But every grower here does sell his wine directly to the consumer, and as a result shrewd Europeans can often be seen loading their car trunks with cases of the black wine of Cornas.

RECENT VINTAGES

1986—Cornas could turn out to be one of the most favored appellations in the northern Rhône. The yield was above normal, and the grapes healthy and ripe with thick skins. This should be a very good year. Optimum maturity: 1990–2000.

1985—An excellent year for the growers of Cornas, 1985 produced a great deal of wine that is black/ruby in color, very fleshy, ripe, quite perfumed, tannic, but lower in acidity. Heat during the harvest did not cause any problems. The wines are fruitier than the tough 1983s. This could prove to be the best vintage for Cornas since 1978. Optimum maturity: 1988–1998.

1984—Lighter, more elegant wines were produced in Cornas in 1984. However, the wines have good fruit, are well balanced, and for a change are not terribly rustic and aggressive. Verset and Clape made very good wines that can be drunk now. This is somewhat of an underrated vintage in Cornas. Optimum maturity: now–1994.

1983—Initially considered a classic year for the growers, one now hears grumblings about the level of astringence and high tannin content in the 1983s. For Clape, Verset, and Delas, it was an exceptional year in which one sees the requisite fruit necessary to balance out the tannins. The other wines are all quite hard and may, in some cases, dry out before they soften. This is certainly a *vin de garde* year, and one can expect the revisionist writers to have fun with these wines in several years. Optimum maturity: 1990–2000.

1982—This might have been a special year, but none of the growers in Cornas was equipped to cool down the fermentations. Torrid heat caused numerous problems for the growers, from overheated fermentations to total shutdowns due to excessively high temperatures. Many wines have color stability problems as well as volatile acidity. The négociants Jaboulet and Delas did better than many of the growers. However, Verset made a fine 1982. This is a dangerous year and selection is very critical. Optimum maturity: now—1990.

1981—Nineteen eighty-one was much better in Cornas than in Hermitage and Côte Rôtie. The warmer microclimate gave a bit more maturity to the Syrah than elsewhere in the northern Rhône. The wines are overall more successful than the 1982s, medium weight, with a great deal of tannin as well as color. A few wines tend to be a little austere and angular. Optimum maturity: 1988–1995.

1980—This is a very attractive vintage of relatively supple, fruity, lighter-styled wines with good color, more charm and finesse than usual, but good, clean flavors. Most of the wines have just entered their plateau of maturity. Optimum maturity: now–1992.

1979—An excellent vintage, 1979 was underrated at first; however, very deeply colored, rich, intense, full-bodied wines were produced that have evolved very well. The vintage is not dissimilar from 1978, a year considered great in the entire Rhône Valley. Clape, Voge, and Michel made stunning wines in 1979. Optimum maturity: now–1994.

1978—As the 1978s have evolved, they appear to be slightly superior to the 1979s. They will be very long-lived since few have reached full maturity. The wines are quite rich, dense in extract, still very tannic, and enormously long. Jaboulet produced an exceptional Cornas, as did Clape, Voge, Verset, and Juge. In overall brilliance, 1978 is the best vintage in Cornas between 1976 and 1985. Optimum maturity: now–1996.

OLDER VINTAGES

Old vintages of Cornas rarely appear in the marketplace. The top vintages according to Clape were 1976, 1972, and 1969, and I wholeheartedly agree. Michel and Voge claim 1969 and 1971 were tops. Barjac likes 1970. So what does all this prove? Vintages in Cornas, perhaps more than anywhere else in France, depend on the individual skills of the winemaker and his flexibility in dealing with the different climatic factors that shape each vintage.

A Personal Rating of the Cornas Producers

*****(OUTSTANDING PRODUCERS)*

Auguste Clape	Noel Verset

****(EXCELLENT PRODUCERS)*

Guy de Barjac	Marcel Juge (Coteaux Cuvée)
Delas Frères	Robert Michel
Paul Jaboulet Ainé	Alain Voge

***(GOOD PRODUCERS)*

René Balthazar	Jean Lionnet

**(AVERAGE PRODUCERS)*

H. Dumien	Jean Teysseire
André Fumat	

GUY DE BARJAC****

The deep, baritone voice seems to go quite well with the handsome face of Guy de Barjac, a look-alike of Yves Montand. When I last saw him in the summer of 1986, I found him with a beer in one hand and a cigarette in the other, after what he called "a hot morning in the vines." De Barjac produces excellent Cornas wines that typify the best of the appellation. They are black/ruby in color, quite intense and robust, and capable of throwing as much sediment as a vintage port. De Barjac has deep, old cellars in the town of Cornas, and ages his wine in these cool, neatly kept cellars in very old oak barrels for 18 months prior to bottling. He is proud of his five acres of vines that average 50 years of age, with over two acres of vines that are almost eighty years old. All of them are on the steep hillsides. His wines are made very traditionally. There is neither fining nor filtration; only winter's cold weather is necessary, says Barjac, to cause his wine to fall brilliant and be cold-stabilized naturally and gradually. He likes to drink his Cornas old, after five to ten years, and says it is ideal with game, meat, and strong cheeses.

VINTAGES

1985—*Cornas*—As young Cornas wines go, the 1985 is quite flattering
·   due to the lower than normal acidity and ripe, soft tannins. It
87   has very broad, velvety flavors, a big, forward bouquet of pep-
        pery, blackberry fruit, and a sweet, long finish. It is quite seduc-
        tive. Anticipated maturity: now–1995. Last tasted 6/86.

1984—*Cornas*—Surprisingly burgundy-like, the 1984 is light by de Bar-
·   jac's standards, but has a vivid ruby color, lively black cherry
84   fruitiness, medium body, and light tannins. It will mature rap-
        idly. Anticipated maturity: now–1991. Last tasted 6/86.

1983—*Cornas*—Black/purple in color with a rustic, leather-and-spice-
·   scented bouquet, the 1983 is quite a tannic, powerful wine with
87   deep, concentrated fruit and mouth-shattering tannins. I would
        not touch this behemoth before 1990. Anticipated maturity:
        1990–2000. Last tasted 12/86.

1982—*Cornas*—Tasted only twice, the 1982 seems awkward and a bit
·   out of balance. It is rather light in color for a Barjac Cornas,
78   with soft, somewhat diluted flavors and fragile balance. It should
        be drunk up. Last tasted 10/85.

1981—*Cornas*—Quite a textbook Cornas, the 1981 is a fiercely tannic,
·   full-bodied, savage wine loaded with Syrah fruit, peppery, black-
86   currant flavors, and abrasive tannins. Anticipated maturity:
        1989–1998. Last tasted 12/85.

1980—*Cornas*—Rather one-dimensional, this wine still offers a great
·   deal of chunky Syrah fruit, a peppery, full-bodied constitution,
84   and good yet coarse finish. Perhaps it will show more dimension

with cellaring. Anticipated maturity: now–1992. Last tasted 12/85.

AUGUSTE CLAPE *****

The scholarly looking Clape, who must now be in his fifties, has his cellars directly on the Route National that passes through Cornas. Like Marcel Guigal in Côte Rôtie, Gérard Chave in Hermitage, François and Jean Pierre Perrin in Châteauneuf-du-Pape, and E. Durrbach in the Coteaux Baux, Clape is the rare winemaker who is not only the consummate craftsman but the passionate guardian of a tradition that in many ways he defined and for which he established the standards. Everyone agrees that Clape's Cornas is the best, but it is also true that it was his success with Cornas that aroused significant worldwide interest in the wines of this appellation.

Clape himself now has a problem. Everyone wants his wine. Great French restaurants, for example the nearby Pic, but also Alain Chapel and Vrinat's Taillevent in Paris, eagerly buy as much of every vintage of his Cornas as he permits them to have. His foreign buyers have been put on allocation and he can no longer take new clients, for even in generous vintages such as 1985 there is simply not enough wine to satisfy the demand.

Not that he has not tried. Clape has increased his vineyards to 13 acres, of which 90% is located on the steep hillsides. His vines average 30 years of age, and produce an average of 2,000 cases of Cornas each year. His wines spend 18 months in old wooden barrels and are fined once with the whites of eggs, but never filtered. Clape's wines, better than any other save Verset's, consistently marry the robust, aggressive tannins and enormous structure of a Cornas with a tremendous extraction of peppery, jammy fruit. This characteristic, plus the success of Clape in less spectacular vintages such as 1980 and 1981, has added to his impeccable reputation. In most vintages, Clape's wines need a full six to eight years of cellaring, and in the great years for Cornas, such as 1972, 1976, 1978, 1983, and 1985, will age harmoniously for ten to fifteen years. Clape's 35-year-old son is interested in carrying on in his father's footsteps, a fact that Clape is obviously overjoyed about. Asked what he eats with his Cornas, Clape responds unequivocally, venison, rabbit, and Roquefort cheese.

The gentlemanly, articulate Auguste Clape is, more than any one person, responsible for the renewed interest in the wines of Cornas. It would be a shame for any serious wine enthusiast to pass up the opportunity to experience this man's outstanding wine. (Clape also produces around 1,000 bottles of white St.-Péray from the Marsanne grape. It is generally only sold to good friends.)

VINTAGES

1985—*Cornas*—Clape seems to prefer his 1983 to the 1985, but for me they are equal in quality if different in style. The 1985 has all
· the great depth and length of the 1983, but it is fatter, softer,
90 and more lush with an explosive richness. There are plenty of tannins, but they are ripe and round. This is an unctuous, gorgeous Cornas that will provide tantalizing drinking while young, but will keep well too. Anticipated maturity: 1988–1998. Last tasted 6/86.

1984—*Cornas*—An exceptionally elegant Cornas, Clape's 1984 has a
· full-intensity bouquet of berry fruit, good ripeness and length,
87 medium to full body, and enough backbone to guarantee a fine evolution. Anticipated maturity: 1988–1996. Last tasted 6/86.

1983—*Cornas*—Another titan of a wine, the 1983 from Clape could well
· turn out to be the finest Cornas he has made and the longest-
90 lived. Opaque ruby/black in color, with a bouquet of crushed blackcurrant fruit, pepper, and licorice, this enormously structured wine has stunning depth and enough tannin to keep most tasters at bay for another 5–7 years. Anticipated maturity: 1992–2005. Last tasted 12/86.

1982—*Cornas*—From the cask and from initial tastings out of the bot-
· tle, I was unimpressed with this wine, which tasted soft, low in
83? acidity, and a trifle shallow. Tasted with Clape in his cellar, it showed much better, with good (not great) color, a smoky, plummy nose, and mature, round flavors. Anticipated maturity: now–1990. Last tasted 6/86.

1981—*Cornas*—I prefer the 1981 to both Clape's 1982 and 1980. Deep
· ruby/purple in color, medium-bodied, peppery and robust to
86 smell, this aggressive wine still exhibits a great deal of tannic toughness, but also very fine fruit and length. Anticipated maturity: 1989–1996. Last tasted 6/86.

1980—*Cornas*—Beginning to reach full maturity, the 1980 Cornas has
· good deep ruby color with some amber at the edge, medium to
84 full body, spicy, tar-scented, smoky fruit, a relatively soft texture, and decent finish. Not sublime, the 1980 is however quite good. Anticipated maturity: now–1992. Last tasted 5/84.

1979—*Cornas*—A very good vintage for Clape, the 1979 has the ruby/
·   purple opaque color Cornas is famous for, a gamelike, plummy,
87   spicy bouquet, full body, layers of flavor, and yes, layers of
       tannin as well. It still needs time. Anticipated maturity: 1989–
       1995. Last tasted 1/87.
1978—*Cornas*—Now approaching its apogee, the 1978 is still wonder-
·   fully deep in color, has an intense bouquet of smoky, berry fruit,
90   superb concentration, a very long finish, and still a good tannic
       clout. Anticipated maturity: now–1998. Last tasted 6/86.

OLDER VINTAGES

Clape's 1976 is outstanding. Among his top years, it is the only recent
great vintage that is close to full maturity. He also made a superb 1972,
which exhibits a multidimensional bouquet of cedarwood, smoked
meat, and oodles of jammy blackcurrant fruit.

DELAS FRÈRES ****

This firm, which produces an entire range of wines from both its own
vineyards in the northern Rhône and from purchased wine and grapes
from growers throughout the region, has a small vineyard of 2.5 acres
in Cornas. The production of Cornas is augmented by purchases from
other growers. The Cornas is excellent, especially the recent vintages.
Though its trade name is "Chante-Perdrix," which means "the singing partridge," I suspect most Frenchmen would envision a bottle of
Cornas with a supine partridge on their plate rather than one singing its
song. After Delas's exceptional red Hermitage Cuvée Marquise de la
Tourette, I would rate this firm's Cornas as their next best red wine. It
is also very fairly priced. The gamelike, smoky, intense, rich fruit is
emphasized in their style of Cornas, with a more supple, velvety character in its youth than other wines of this appellation. It can be quite
exciting to taste.

VINTAGES

1985—*Cornas Chante-Perdrix*—This is one of the most tannic and
·   backward wines of Cornas in 1985. Very dark ruby with an
87   earthy, almost truffle-scented bouquet, this full-bodied, chewy
       wine has heaps of both tannin and fruit, but will require pa-
       tience. It may ultimately merit a higher score. Anticipated ma-
       turity: 1992–2000. Last tasted 6/86.

1984—*Cornas Chante-Perdrix*—One-dimensional, light-intensity, black
· cherry flavors are pleasant but uninspiring. The wine is light for
78 a Cornas with a soft, sweet, smoky aroma. Anticipated maturity:
now–1990. Last tasted 6/86.

1983—*Cornas Chante-Perdrix*—Unlike the other wines of the 1983 vin-
· tage, this Cornas is much more accessible. A very complex bou-
90 quet of roasted chestnuts, plums, and truffles is top-rank. In the
mouth, the wine in unctuous, very concentrated, still loaded
with tannins, but accessible. It is a superb Cornas. Anticipated
maturity: 1989–1999. Last tasted 12/86.

1982—*Cornas Chante-Perdrix*—Approaching maturity, this broadly fla-
· vored, rich, deep wine has relatively soft tannins and low acidity,
86 but full body and plenty of length. Drink over the next 4–6 years.
Last tasted 6/86.

1978—*Cornas Chante-Perdrix*—Now fully mature, the 1978 has an in-
· tense bouquet of roasted curranty fruit and, I believe, coffee.
84 Full-bodied, still a little coarse and rustic, this is a good wine
that has dropped its tannin but has not gained any refinement or
finesse. Drink over the next 5–6 years. Last tasted 1/87.

PAUL JABOULET AINÉ ****

This famous firm has increased its purchases of wine from Cornas (it
owns no vineyards there) significantly in the decade of the eighties. For
example, 75% of the appellation's production in the bountiful year of
1985 was reportedly bought by Jaboulet since they believe fervently in
the potential there. Certainly Jaboulet has made some fine Cornas
wines over the years that have proven their ability to age and improve
in the bottle. The style of Cornas made at Jaboulet is a muscular, full-
bodied, rather old style with enormous structure and plenty of hard
tannins. Despite the "lightening up" of some of Jaboulet's other Rhône
wines, especially their Châteauneuf-du-Pape "Les Cèdres" and Gigondas, this firm seems totally content with the size, style, and structure
of their big, brawny, beefy Cornas.

VINTAGES

1985—*Cornas*—A charming and flattering wine for a young Cornas, the
· 1985 is marked by the low acidity of this vintage as well as a
86 lush, rich, black cherry fruitiness. Full-bodied yet supple, this
wine will develop quickly. Anticipated maturity: 1988–1995.
Last tasted 6/86.

1984—*Cornas*—Quite spicy and again attractively fruity, the 1984 does
·   not have the body or concentration of the 1985, but can stand on
84   its own merits. The acidity is a bit higher, the finish less lush
      and rich, but this wine has turned out well. Anticipated matu-
      rity: 1988–1994. Last tasted 6/86.

1983—*Cornas*—The 1983 was remarkably impressive from the cask, so
·   much so that I ordered a case of it for my cellar. After a half-
87?   dozen tastes out of the bottle, I have found the wine stubbornly
      backward and very sturdy, and consequently have lowered my
      confidence in it. Still terribly closed, very tannic and hard, this
      immensely proportioned wine seems to need at least another
      decade of cellaring. Will the fruit hold? Anticipated maturity:
      1996–2005? Last tasted 12/86.

1982—*Cornas*—Jaboulet turned out one of the better wines of Cornas
·   in 1982, no doubt because he was better equipped to deal with
84   the torrid heat of the harvest than the majority of Cornas's grow-
      ers who labor in primitive wine cellars. Jaboulet's wine is a
      beefy, very tannic, robust, virile Cornas with full body and
      mouth-zapping tannins. Anticipated maturity: 1990–2000. Last
      tasted 6/85.

1981—*Cornas*—Light and lacking generosity, this lean, medium-bod-
·   ied Cornas may improve, but I have to believe there is too much
78   tannin for the moderate level of fruit. Drink up. Last tasted
      6/85.

1980—*Cornas*—This wine has evolved well. Smoky, spicy, blackberry
·   and gamey flavors are attractive. Medium- to full-bodied with
83   good fruit and plenty of stuffing, this wine's only shortcoming is
      a lack of length. Drink over the next 4–5 years. Last tasted
      10/85.

1979—*Cornas*—The 1979 is turning out to be a very fine Cornas. It has
·   still not reached its plateau of maturity, but the dense, rather
86   opaque color, ripe, wild berry aroma intertwined with tar and
      roasted nuts, the full body and deep, rich fruit and tannins all
      portend something special. Anticipated maturity: 1988–1996.
      Last tasted 3/84.

1978—*Cornas*—This is the best Cornas I have tasted from Jaboulet.
·   Opaque ruby with a profound bouquet of truffles, earthy black-
89   berry fruit, and smoked meat, this very concentrated, full-bod-
      ied wine is just hitting its apogee where it will no doubt remain
      for another 6–10 years. Quite impressive. Anticipated maturity:
      now–1996. Last tasted 11/85.

OLDER VINTAGES

From the seventies, the 1972 is fully mature and, after the aforementioned 1978, the next best Cornas of the decade. I still have a few bottles of the hard, tough 1970 in my cellar. It is good but lacks some charm and has always had too much muscle. A half-bottle of the 1962, drunk at the tiny Grappe d'Or restaurant in Tain L'Hermitage in June 1985, was one-third sediment, but still exuberantly fruity, aggressive, and powerful.

MARCEL JUGE ****

The diminutive, implike Marcel Juge is certainly the free spirit of Cornas. His cellars lie below his modern home, right next to a school playground, in the town of Cornas. He appears to be in his early fifties, but his devilish grin and playful personality make him seem younger. One unforgettable part of a visit here is Nino, the seven-year-old (in 1987) mutt. This dog is an inveterate Cornas drinker, and for several years running I have been amazed at how much young Cornas Nino is capable of consuming from Juge's "wine thief" or pipette.

Juge owns 7.5 acres of vineyards of which one-half is on the hillsides and one-half on the valley floor. The average age of his vines is 35–40 years old, but he has a tiny parcel of seven-year-old vines, as well as one parcel of 80-year-old vines. Consequently, he makes and sells two separate cuvées of Cornas. In some vintages the label is identical, making it impossible to determine which is the richer, more interesting cuvée. He claims that he will be using the designated Cuvée Spéciale or Coteaux Sélection to prevent confusion in the future.

With respect to the style of Juge's Cornas, he is a less consistent winemaker than either Clape or Verset, but when he succeeds, which is most of the time, his wines are the most elegant and burgundy-like made in Cornas. Obviously, his cuvée of wine from the hillside vineyards is his best wine. Juge keeps his wine in both barrels and foudres for a minimum of 16–18 months. It is neither fined nor filtered. His wines tend to drink well at a much younger age than other wines from Cornas.

VINTAGES

1985—*Cornas Cuvée Spéciale*—This is certainly one of the most spectacular young wines of Cornas I have ever tasted. Only 150 cases
·
92   were made, and Juge intends to fetch a high price for it. Black/ruby in color, stunningly concentrated and perfumed, it is enor-

mous on the palate with staggering length. Anticipated maturity: 1991–2005. Last tasted 6/86.

1985—*Cornas Demi-Coteaux*—A totally different wine, this 1985 is a

·

84   blend of younger vines on the hillside with Juge's valley vineyard. It is a very pretty, medium-bodied, finesse-styled wine with good, soft fruit. Anticipated maturity: now–1992. Last tasted 6/86.

1984—*Cornas*—What this wine lacks in sheer power and size it com-

·

85   pensates for with wonderfully elegant, raspberry fruit that recalls a fine Volnay. Round and supple with medium body, this precocious Cornas offers considerable value and delightful charm. Anticipated maturity: now–1992. Last tasted 6/86.

1983—*Cornas*—Juge has two separate cuvées on the market, neither

·

72–86 label of which indicates whether it is a hillside or a valley cuvée. The wine from his hillside vineyards is deeper in color, has more fruit, but is extremely tannic and hard, and must be kept for at least another 6–7 years. The regular 1983 is dusty, very astringent in the nose, medium-bodied, and excessively tannic. Last tasted 6/86.

1981—*Cornas*—The 1981 is quite an elegant, medium-bodied wine that

·

86   expresses quite perfectly the Juge style. Medium ruby, with a spicy, raspberry, ripe bouquet, this wine has reached its apogee, and offers very delicious fruit and total harmony on the palate. Drink over the next 5–6 years. Last tasted 9/86.

1980—*Cornas*—A heftier wine than the 1981, Juge's 1980 is more typi-

·

85   cal of the style of Cornas seen elsewhere in this tiny village. Dark ruby with a plummy and gamey aroma, still tannic and a trifle coarse, this full-bodied wine needs several more years. Anticipated maturity: now–1994. Last tasted 3/84.

*ROBERT MICHEL*****

Robert Michel, only in his late thirties, is a tall, balding, red-haired man, and one of the youngest growers in Cornas. He is also one of the most forward-thinking. Believing that few wine enthusiasts know what a properly mature Cornas tastes like, he is in the process of building a new cellar in which he will set aside 1,000 bottles of each vintage for aging and conservation. Michel's cellars are right in the middle of the village, and are exceptionally damp and cold, even in the summer. He owns 14.8 acres of vineyards of which 13 acres are located on the steeply terraced hillsides. His vines average an impressive 40 years in age, one tiny parcel being almost 100 years old. Michel is adamantly against filtering his black-colored, robust Cornas, but does believe in fining it to take out some of the coarse tannins. Nevertheless, I find Michel's Cornas the most robust and savagely raw and intense wine of the appellation. In fact, his wines are unapproachable and excruciatingly tannic to taste when young. Michel keeps his wine two full years in two- and three-year-old burgundy barrels and has no intention of using new oak. Two cuvées of Cornas are made, a single vineyard (planted in 1910) called Le Geynale and a regular cuvée.

VINTAGES

1985—*Cornas Le Geynale*—Deep ruby/purple in color, very dense and
· peppery, this full-bodied wine has considerable tannin, and is at
87 least a decade away from maturity. Anticipated maturity: 1996–
2005. Last tasted 6/86.

1985—*Cornas*—Quite hard and closed, but showing ripe, decent fruit
· underneath, this tough, aggressive wine seems to be so hard that
82 I must wonder about its balance. Anticipated maturity: 1992–
1996? Last tasted 6/86.

1984—*Cornas Le Geynale*—Incredibly tannic and backward, I confess
· it seems impossible to find the fruit. Deep in color with a prom-
? ising bouquet, this wine tastes too severe, and may take 15 years
of cellaring to come around. Judgment reserved. Last tasted
6/86.

1984—*Cornas*—Quite elevated acidity gives this wine a tart, angular
· palate impression. It has a typically opaque black/ruby color,
78 but is so, so closed. Am I being too conservative? Last tasted
6/86.

1983—*Cornas*—This wine seems to be drying out despite its enormous
· structure and gigantic tannin level. There is an astringent bitter-
62 ness and very coarse texture that obliterates the fruit. This is a
gamble. Last tasted 11/86.

1982—*Cornas*—A very old-style wine, the 1982 has a touch of volatile
· acidity, a big, smoky, peppery aroma, a fleshy, chewy texture,
75 and still gobs of tannin. Anticipated maturity: 1988–1995. Last
tasted 6/86.

1981—*Cornas*—One of the best of Michel's Cornas in the eighties.
· Dense in color with a smoky, plummy, grilled-meat bouquet, this
86 full-bodied wine has good fruit, moderate tannins, and a harmonious feel on the palate. Anticipated maturity: now–1993. Last
tasted 11/85.

1979—*Cornas*—Quite successful, the 1979 remains a very young ex-
·   ample of a big, virile, brawny Cornas that has the fruit and flesh
86   to balance out its huge tannic clout. Quite substantial on the
       palate, with very good length, this beefy wine still needs time.
       Anticipated maturity: 1988–1996. Last tasted 12/86.

OLDER VINTAGES
The two older vintages of Michel's I have tasted were both very impressive. The opulent, lush, fully mature 1971 resembled a smoky, rich,
multidimensional Hermitage. It was loaded with fruit when tasted in
1985. The 1969, tasted with Michel in 1986, was showing some dryness
and coarseness in the finish, but had a stunningly complex bouquet of
exotic spices, wild berry fruit, and immense body.

NOEL VERSET *****
The bald, elderly, squeaky voiced Noel Verset has 6.2 acres of vines
that other growers consider the most superbly situated of the appellation. These gnarled old vines range in age from 40 to 90 years old, and
consistently produce one of the two best Cornas of the village. The
enthusiastic and animated Verset complains that his wife only gave him
two daughters, no sons, and so at his age, which appears to be in the
late sixties, he has only "20 more years" of winemaking to look forward
to. He says his father, Emanuel, who is 98, was active in the winery
until three years ago. Verset's production is the smallest per acre,
which no doubt accounts for the great concentration of fruit in his
splendid Cornas. His cellar, which looks like a seventeenth-century
antique, is filled with ancient barrels and the larger oak foudres where
he stores his precious wine for 18 months. He does one fining with egg
whites and bottles his wines unfiltered. He claims he adores his Cornas
with a venison or rabbit stew or a hard, strong cheese. Verset's production of 800 cases is minuscule, but he proudly sells his wine to America,
Great Britain, Holland, Switzerland, and Australia. His Cornas, which
gives every indication of lasting and improving in the bottle for 10–15
years, is indeed very special and well worth searching out.

VINTAGES
1985—*Cornas*—A blockbuster wine, Verset's 1985 has aromas of vi-
·   olets, jammy blackberry fruit, licorice, and exotic spices. On the
91   palate, it is unbelievably concentrated, with layers of flavor that
       persist and persist. The extraordinary level of ripe fruit actually

conceals a very high level of ripe tannins. Anticipated maturity: 1990–2003. Last tasted 6/86.

1984—*Cornas*—One of the finest wines of the appellation, the 1984
· Cornas is a broadly flavored, plummy, typically black/ruby-col-
86 ored wine that has loads of fruit, a supple, succulent texture, and good fruit. Anticipated maturity: now–1995. Last tasted 8/86.

1983—*Cornas*—More obviously tannic than the 1985, the 1983 is dark
· ruby/purple, quite full-bodied with heaps of cassis fruit, and an
90 extremely long finish, but is 5–7 years away from maturity. Anticipated maturity: 1990–2000. Last tasted 12/86.

1982—*Cornas*—This is the best wine produced in Cornas in 1982, very
· deep in color with a truffle-scented, tarry, smoky bouquet that
88 is also filled with ripe fruit. Quite rich and lush on the palate with a full-bodied, soft texture, this wine should be drunk over the next 5–7 years. Last tasted 11/85.

1981—*Cornas*—Beginning to soften and hit its apogee, the 1981 is still
· impressively deep in color, shows a fennel-and-tar-scented bou-
85 quet, full body, and good ripeness. It is only slightly less concentrated than other recent vintages. Nevertheless, it is a good wine that will offer delicious drinking over the next 5–6 years. Last tasted 6/84.

OLDER VINTAGES

Verset's spectacular 1971 was velvety, supple, and still filled with ripe, jammy fruit in 1986. It was fully mature then and a wondrous wine to drink. The 1976 is youthfully deep in color, peppery, and full-bodied, but spicy and still relatively tannic and unevolved.

ALAIN VOGE ****

Two of the greatest Cornas I have tasted were the 1978 and 1979 from Alain Voge. His wines, more than any other grower's of this appellation, do indeed resemble fine Hermitages. Voge, a bullish-looking, serious man, owns 12.4 acres situated entirely on the hillsides behind the town of Cornas. He keeps his opulent, unctuous wines in stainless steel tanks for a year. Then he places the wine in wooden barrels and foudres for another year. Like most of the other growers, he fines his wines but never filters them. Because of their intense, plump, succulent character, Voge's wines tend to show well three to five years after the vintage and keep for at least a decade. In the early eighties I thought I detected a change in style and direction, but it must have been just those vintages because both the 1983 and 1985 are excellent.

VINTAGES

1985—*Cornas*—A splendid 1985 Cornas, this deep-colored, full-bodied
· wine is loaded with exotic spices and jammy, lush fruit. How-
88 ever, it has plenty of tannin in the finish. It should mature
quickly but offer sumptuous drinking for at least another 7–8
years. Anticipated maturity: 1988–1995. Last tasted 6/87.

1984—*Cornas*—Less opulent and full-bodied than the 1985, the lighter,
· less forthright 1984 has charm, a supple texture, and round,
84 pleasant finish. Anticipated maturity: now–1992. Last tasted
12/86.

1983—*Cornas*—A big, hickory-scented, smoky, bacon fat, ripe,
· plummy bouquet seems to gush from the glass. More open and
88 advanced than other wines from this vintage, Voge's Cornas
shows plenty of ripe fruit, full body, excellent concentration, and
at least a decade of cellaring potential. Anticipated maturity:
now–1996. Last tasted 12/86.

1982—*Cornas*—A little diffuse and flabby with soft, one-dimensional
· flavors, the 1982 is an adequate but not a good example of this
80 man's winemaking talents. Drink up. Last tasted 11/85.

1980—*Cornas*—The 1980 seems rather light with a vegetal aroma. Two
· bottles tasted were totally different in color and intensity of fruit,
72 and both had a leafy, vegetal character. It is not a very interesting wine. Last tasted 6/84.

1979—*Cornas*—The rich, smoky, bacon fat aromas and opulent, deep
· fruit of this wine are breathtaking. Full-bodied, velvety, intense,
90 and extremely long, this hedonistic, decadently rich Cornas offers superlative drinking over the next 6–8 years. Last tasted
1/87.

1978—*Cornas*—Even richer and more concentrated than the 1979, the
· 1978 is very port-like, has an unctuous texture with layers of
92 toasty, jammy fruit, as well as a creamy, very lingering finish.
An unbelievable Cornas. Last tasted 1/84.

Other Cornas Producers

Thierry Allemand—The youngest grower in Cornas (23), Allemand is
just beginning to plant his vineyards. Quite serious, his should be a
name to follow in the future.

René Balthazar—Balthazar is a grower with an emerging reputation. His 1983 was very good and his 1984 quite respectable.

Roger Catalon—I was unable to get an appointment with Catalon and am therefore unable to comment on his wines.

Henri Dumien—I have only tasted a 1980 and 1981 from Dumien. Both examples were unimpressive.

André Fumat—I have only tasted two vintages of Fumat's wines, a 1980 and 1981. Both were disappointing.

Jean Lionnet—A respected grower, Lionnet produces typically hard, blackish-colored wines that seem to be dry and very tough. Lionnet owns 25 acres of vines that produce 1,500 cases of Cornas and a small quantity of St.-Péray white wine. I thought his 1985, 1983, and 1979 were better than other recent wines.

Jean Teysseire—This producer, based in St.-Péray where he makes white wine, made one-dimensional, dull Cornas wines in 1981 and 1983.

ST.-PÉRAY

Dull White Still and Sparkling Wines
from a Forgotten Appellation

ST.-PÉRAY AT A GLANCE

Type of wine produced:	White still and sparkling wines
Grape varieties planted:	Marsanne and Roussanne
Acres currently under vine:	150
Quality level:	Below average to average
Aging potential:	1–4 years
General characteristics:	Dull, somewhat odd, uninteresting wines that are heavy and diffuse
Greatest recent vintages:	None
Price range:	$8–$15

St.-Péray is situated across from Valence on the west bank of the Rhône, just south of but contiguous to Cornas. The wine here offers little to get excited about. The town itself is undistinguished, yet a hike or drive to the ruins of the Château de Crussol, which sits on a craggy outcropping of granite that dominates the town, will provide an exhilarating view of Valence and the Rhône River basin. If the pollution from Valence is not too bad, you can also see the Alps. Also not to be missed is a drive west up the perilous, twisting D287 in the direction of St.-Romain-de-Lerps, which offers splendid views of the Rhône Valley. Further, one will encounter a gorgeous, tranquil countryside after crossing onto the plateau above St.-Péray. In spite of these tourist diversions, it is the wine that has made St.-Péray famous. There is plenty of historical documentation giving credit to the monks of the tenth century for planting the vines on the steep, terraced slopes behind the town. The local growers all seem to be in agreement that in 1795 Napoleon, who was a cadet stationed in Valence, developed a taste for the wines of St.-Péray. But this story pales in comparison with the other widely quoted tale that the famous German composer Richard Wagner, while in the midst of composing *Parsifal*, ordered 100 bottles of St.-Péray be sent to him in Bayreuth.

Only white wine is made at St.-Péray. It comes in two types, dull still wines and dull sparkling wines. The two white grape varietals used are the Marsanne and the Roussanne. Over 80% of the wine made here is sparkling. It is produced in the traditional manner and is naturally fermented in the bottle. To say it is adequate would be disingenuous. Heavy, prone to oxidation, and never, in my experience, lively or interesting, sparkling St.-Péray is a curiosity piece that seems doomed in the highly competitive, quality-conscious wine world of today. The still wines are marginally better, but they too have little commercial viability since they tend to be heavy and very low in acidity.

In my opinion, there is no future for this appellation in either of these wines. The granite slopes above the town would no doubt prove much more desirable for Syrah, which is grown with great success on these same slopes only one mile north in Cornas. However, it is unlikely that Syrah will get a foothold here because housing developers have begun to aggressively develop the scenic hillsides.

The middle-aged, bald Jean-François Chaboud is this appellation's most famous producer, and even he seems to recognize that the end is near. His fears are based not so much on the lack of appeal of St.-Péray's wines but on the increasing competition in France from lower-priced sparkling wines produced in greater and greater amounts in areas such as Alsace, the Loire Valley, and Burgundy. The growth of the sparkling wine business from these areas will do more to put producers out of business than will any inherent deficiencies in these wines. Chaboud readily acknowledges that good money is also to be made by any grower who wants to sell his vineyards to the eagerly awaiting housing developers.

St.-Péray is the only dinosaur of the Rhône Valley viticultural districts. Because of its unique sparkling wines and historic tradition, one would like to see this tiny appellation of 150 acres survive. But the intrinsic quality of the wines made here does not merit anything more than curiosity.

For the adventurous, most of St.-Péray's wines are not inexpensive. They cost a little less than a good non-vintage champagne, but more than a better sparkling wine from Alsace, the Loire, or Burgundy. They are wines that require drinking up within two to three years of the vintage. Whether it is the primitive winemaking technique or the use of Marsanne and Roussanne to make the wine, many of the wines taste bizarre and sometimes oxidized upon release. They are not wines that can be recommended.

RECENT VINTAGES

1985—Because of the very ripe character of the grapes and their consequent low acidity, this is not considered a good vintage for the producers of St.-Péray. The wines are very alcoholic and clumsy.

1984—Just the opposite of 1985, this vintage gave the producers underripe, high-acid grapes that should turn out decent sparkling wine but austere still wines.

1983—Of the recent vintages, 1983 is considered by the growers to be their best vintage. The best sparkling wines I tasted from St.-Péray included Chaboud's and Darona's 1983 wines.

A PERSONAL RATING OF ST.-PÉRAY PRODUCERS

Given the fact that the white wines are at best no more than adequate, rating the growers seems pointless. Certainly, Jean-François Chaboud has the finest reputation, but other noted producers include Jean-Louis Thiers, Jean Teysseire, and Pierre Darona. Some of the Cornas producers make tiny quantities of St.-Péray. Clape, Voge, and Juge in Cornas produce decent, rather heavy, old-style white wines from St.-Péray.

JEAN-FRANÇOIS CHABOUD

From Chaboud's 20 acres of vines, he produces both sparkling and still wine, but mostly the former (80%). His family has been making wine in St.-Péray since 1715. His underground cellars are impressive and he claims to have a very bustling direct-sale business to tourists who pass through the area. Chaboud is very skeptical of the future of St.-Péray's wines, but claims he has no problem selling any of his wine. His sparkling wine is always made from 100% Marsanne; his still wine is 80% Marsanne and 20% Roussanne.

VINTAGES

1985—*St.-Péray (still)*—My tasting notes simply said, "curious wine,
·   little fruit, strange and alcoholic"—which is how I generally feel
60   about the wines of St.-Péray. Last tasted 6/86.

1983—*St.-Péray (sparkling)*—Chaboud's 1983 was the best sparkling
·   St.-Péray I tasted. Flowery scents and unusual flavors that are
82   hard to define characterize this medium-bodied, decent spar-
       kling wine. Last tasted 6/86.

N.V.—*St.-Péray (sparkling)*—Fishy, gluelike smells take one's senses
·   away from any frame of reference. Big, clumsy bubbles and flat,
62   odd flavors are at the very least quite bizarre. Last tasted 6/86.

PIERRE DARONA

Darona has a modest-sized vineyard of 22 acres, and like Chaboud, 80% of his production (3,800 cases) is in sparkling wine. His sparkling wines are less identifiable as textbook St.-Pérays, and for that reason seem to be less bizarre and unusual to taste. Nevertheless, Darona's sparkling wines, which are cleanly made, lack a focal point in flavor interest and fall into the bland, one-dimensional category. I prefer the still wine here to the sparkling.

VINTAGES

1983—*St.-Péray (still)*—Light golden with an apple/cider bouquet, this
·   one-dimensional wine is palatable but unusual. Last tasted 6/86.
70

N.V.—*St.-Péray (sparkling)*—Good acidity, but rather austere, green,
·   thin, and chalky, this medium-bodied wine seems to have no
67   length or flavor intensity. Last tasted 6/86.

JEAN TEYSSEIRE

Teysseire, who also makes Cornas, has 8.6 acres of vines in St.-Péray. I prefer his still to his sparkling wine, but that is hardly a compliment.

VINTAGES

1983—*St.-Péray (still)*—Light straw-colored with a greenish hue, this one-dimensional wine has decent fruit, no eccentricities, and decent acidity. Last tasted 6/86.

72

N.V.—*St.-Péray (sparkling)*—Oxidized aromas and fishy smells make this wine totally unacceptable. Last tasted 10/86.

56

Other St.-Péray Producers

Cave des Vignerons de St.-Péray—Situated in the back of the town in attractive quarters, the cooperative produces over 75% of the appellation's wine. The quality is acceptable, but quite variable.

Auguste Clape Cornas's greatest winemaker produces almost 100 cases of good, chunky still wine from St.-Péray each year. His impeccable winemaking skills extract as much character from the wine as is available.

Gilles Père—This négociant markets barely acceptable St.-Péray wine.

Jean-Louis Thiers—Thiers produces tiny amounts of decent sparkling wine that, if lacking in character, is however cleanly made, crisp, and fresh.

Eugène Verilhac—I have had no luck with this négociant's stale, oafish bottles of St.-Péray wine.

Alain Voge—Like Clape, Voge's strength is his excellent Cornas. However, he dabbles a bit in St.-Péray, producing a foursquare, chunky wine.

II

THE

SOUTHERN

RHÔNE

Gigondas, Châteauneuf-du-Pape, Tavel,
Lirac, the Côtes du Rhône-Villages, and
Côtes du Rhônes

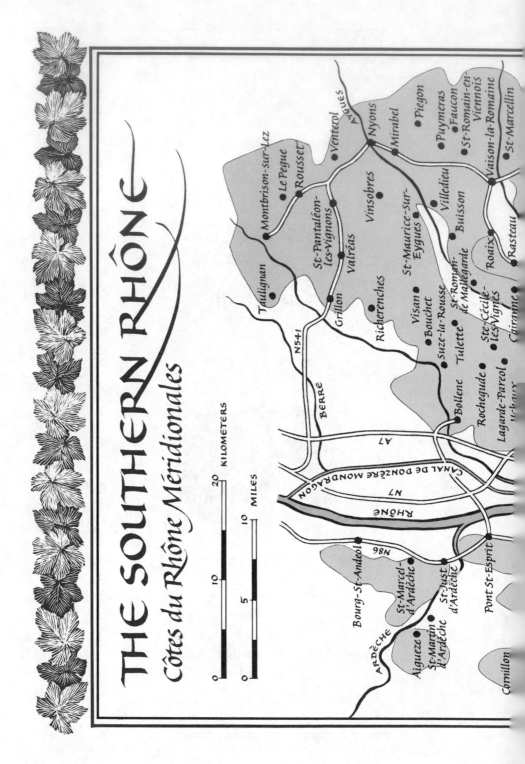

THE SOUTHERN RHÔNE
Côtes du Rhône Méridionales

KILOMETERS
0   10   20

MILES
0   5   10

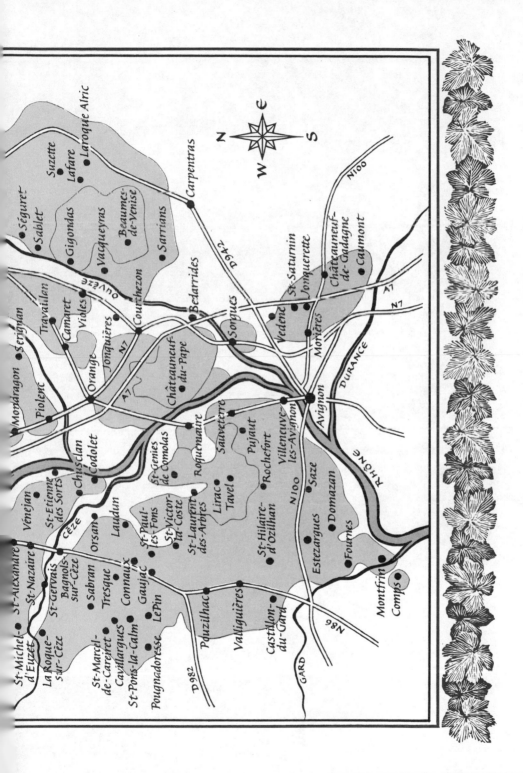

INTRODUCTION

The northern Rhône's viticultural region (often referred to by the French as the Côtes du Rhône Septentrionales) ends after the appellation of St.-Péray, located just west of the large commercial city of Valence. For all intents and purposes, the viticultural region of the southern Rhône Valley (referred to by the French as the Côtes du Rhône Meridionales) does not begin until one reaches the old Roman city of Orange, 58 miles south of Valence.

While the distance between Valance and Orange is not great, the differences in climate and geography are striking and vividly divergent, regardless of how many times one travels between the two cities. Aside from the huge, rather forbidding nuclear power plants that dominate the landscape between Montélimar and Orange, the vegetation becomes notably less lush, and the topography reflects the windswept and sun-drenched climate of the southern Rhône. In climatic terms, the southern Rhône has a much drier, hotter, breezier Mediterranean-influenced climate than the north. The aromas of Provençal herbs, which grow wild, are more than just imaginary flights of olfactory fancy —one can smell them virtually everywhere. It has never surprised me that these same aromas often end up in some of the wines of the southern Rhône.

In the northern Rhône, nearly every vineyard is in view of or within a mile of the Rhône River, and all the best growing sites are on the steep, terraced hillsides that flank the river. In the south, there are no steep, terraced vineyards in the top appellation of Châteauneuf-du-Pape, and few vineyards are within view of the Rhône. In the Côtes du Rhône-Villages and Gigondas, there are hillside vineyards, but the hills have nothing like the steep gradient that exists in northern appellations such as Côte Rôtie, Hermitage, or Cornas.

The one major characteristic of many southern Rhône vineyards is the stones. In Châteauneuf-du-Pape particularly, the carpet of stones, many as big and as rounded as a softball or a football, are a remnant of the Ice Age glaciers that once covered this area. Although very destructive to mechanical equipment, this stony soil does provide excellent drainage, and stores as well as reflects the intense heat and light of the sun common to this area.

While the Rhône River passes through the region, the vast viticultural areas composing the southern Rhône fan out both east and west for many miles. On the right bank is Lirac, a promising appellation that has yet to fulfill its potential, Tavel, the home of France's most expensive and occasionally its best rosé wines, and a handful of Côtes du Rhône-Villages, the best of which is St.-Gervais.

The bulk of the southern Rhône wines are made on the left bank or eastern side of the Rhône. This area is also among the most scenic and most traveled in France. Coexisting with the charming medieval hill towns filled with artists and artisans and spectacular scenery is Châteauneuf-du-Pape, the most famous appellation of the entire Rhône Valley. Near Châteauneuf-du-Pape is another famous appellation, Gigondas, which produces very high-quality, chewy, full-bodied wines. Within view of Gigondas is Beaumes de Venise, known for its opulent, fortified dessert wines. With few exceptions, this eastern sector has a monopoly on the finest Côtes du Rhônes-Villages. Quaint towns such as Vaison-la-Romaine, Séguret, Cairanne, Rasteau, Vacqueyras, and Carpentras, to name a few, sit scenically and strategically amidst an ocean of vineyards. This area of sun-scorched, lazy hill towns is fertile territory not only for the frequent tourist or amateur photographer but also the shrewd wine enthusiast either looking for a bargain or on a chase for something great.

One of the most complicating aspects and stumbling blocks to understanding the wines of the southern Rhône is the number of grape varieties utilized by the growers. As in the northern Rhône, there is Syrah, but it is far less important in the south, where many growers feel it overripens and raisins in the intense heat and sun of this region. Grenache is the dominant red wine grape in the south. It produces fleshy, ripe, alcoholic wines without much character when its yield is not controlled. When pruned severely to curtail the yield, the Grenache is capable of producing magnificent wines. Only a few wines made in the southern Rhône are 100% Grenache; most reds are the result of a blend of at least four varietals. Other grape varieties used for these blends are the Mourvèdre, which has the disadvantage of ripening very late but offers superb color, structure, and complexity to any blend, and Cinsault, which is widely planted in the Rhône since it is easy to grow, is relatively prolific, and adds aromatic complexity and acidity. In addition, the permitted red wine varietals that are less commonly encountered include the Counoise, Muscardin, Terret, and Vaccarèse, the last of which is increasingly believed to have immense potential for high-quality wines.

For the white wines made in the south, three grapes found in the north, the ubiquitous Marsanne, the fickle Roussanne, and the fascinating Viognier, are also planted in the southern Rhône, but to a much lesser extent. The workhorse white wine varietals in the south are the Grenache Blanc, Clairette, and Bourboulenc, followed by the Picardin and Picpoul.

With such an assortment of grape varietals, it is no wonder that the type and style of each producer's wine in the southern Rhône can vary enormously depending on the percentage of a particular grape used in the blend. To facilitate your comprehension, the major grape varietals used in the southern Rhône are listed below with their telltale personality traits.

White Wine Varietals

Bourboulenc—This grape offers plenty of body. The local cognoscenti also attribute the scent of roses to Bourboulenc, though I cannot yet claim the same experience.

Clairette Blanc—Until the advent of cold fermentations and modern equipment to minimize the risk of oxidation, the Clairette produced heavy, alcoholic, often deep yellow wines that were thick and ponderous. Given the benefit of state-of-the-art technology, it now produces soft, floral, fruity wine that must be drunk young. The superb white Châteauneuf-du-Pape of Vieux Télégraphe has 35% Clairette in it.

Grenache Blanc—Deeply fruity, highly alcoholic yet low-acid wines are produced from Grenache Blanc. When fermented at cool temperatures and the malolactic fermentation blocked, it can be a vibrant, delicious wine capable of providing wonderful near-term pleasure. The exquisite white Châteauneuf-du-Pape from Henri Brunier's, Vieux Télégraphe, contains 25% Grenache Blanc; that of the Gonnet Brothers' Font de Michelle, 50%. In a few examples such as this, I find the floral scent of paper white narcissus and a character vaguely resembling that of Condrieu.

Marsanne—The Marsanne planted in the south produces rather chunky wines that must receive help from other varieties because it cannot stand alone. Jancis Robinson often claims it smells "not unpleasantly reminiscent of glue."

Picardin—This grape has fallen out of favor largely because the growers felt it added nothing to their blends. Apparently its neutral character was its undoing.

Picpoul—Frankly, I have no idea what this grape tastes like. I have never seen it isolated or represented in sufficiently hefty a percentage as to be identifiable. Today it is seen very rarely in the southern Rhône.

Roussanne—For centuries, this grape was the essence of white Hermitage in the northern Rhône, but its small yields and proclivity to disease led to its being largely replaced by Marsanne. It is making something of a comeback in the southern Rhône. It has the most character of any of the white wine varietals—aromas of honey, coffee, flowers, and nuts, and produces a wine that can be very long-lived, an anomaly for a white wine in the southern Rhône. The famous Châteauneuf-du-Pape estate Beaucastel uses 80% Roussanne in their wine, which not surprisingly is the longest-lived white wine of the appellation.

Viognier—As has already been stated, Viognier produces a great and unique white wine. It is synonymous with Condrieu and Château Grillet in the northern Rhône. In the south, there is little of it, but the experimental plantings that have been put in have exhibited immense potential. The finest example in the southern Rhône is the Domaine Ste.-Anne in the Côtes du Rhône *village* of Gervais. Saint-Estève is another domaine in the Côtes du Rhône that produces a good Viognier.

Red Wine Varietals

Cinsault—All the growers seem to use a small amount of Cinsault. It ripens very early, gives good yields, and produces wines that offer a great deal of fruit. It seems to offset the high alcohol of the Grenache and the tannins of the Syrah and Mourvèdre. Despite its value, it seems to have lost some appeal in favor of Syrah or Mourvèdre, but it is a valuable asset to the blend of a southern Rhône wine.

Counoise—Very little of this grape exists in the south because of its capricious growing habits. However, I have tasted it separately at Château Beaucastel in Châteauneuf-du-Pape where the Perrin family is augmenting its use. It had great finesse and seemed to provide deep, richly fruity flavors and a complex perfume of smoked meat, flowers, and berry fruit. The Perrins feel Counoise has at least as much potential as a high-quality ingredient in their blend as Mourvèdre.

Grenache—A classic hot climate grape varietal, Grenache is for better or worse the dominant grape of the southern Rhône. The quality of the wines it produces ranges from hot, alcoholic, unbalanced, coarse wines to rich, majestic, very long-lived, sumptuous wines. The differences are largely caused by the yield of juice per acre. Where Grenache is pruned back and not overly fertilized, it can do wondrous things. The sensational Châteauneuf-du-Pape, Château Rayas, is a poignant example of that. At its best, it offers aromas of kirsch, blackcurrants, pepper, licorice, and roasted peanuts.

Mourvèdre—Everyone seems to agree on the virtues of the Mourvèdre, but few people want to take the risk and grow it. It flourishes in the Mediterranean appellation of Bandol, but only Château Beaucastel in Châteauneuf-du-Pape has made it an important part (one-third) of their blend. It gives great color, a complex aroma, superb structure, and is very resistant to oxidation. However, it ripens very late and unlike other grape varietals has no value until it is perfectly mature. When it lacks maturity, the growers say it gives them nothing, as it is colorless and acidic. Given the eccentricities of this grape, it is unlikely that anyone other than the adventurous or passionately obsessed growers will make use of it. Its telltale aromas are those of leather, truffles, fresh mushrooms, and tree bark.

Muscardin—More common than Terret Noir, Muscardin provides a great deal of perfume while imparting a solidarity and a good measure of alcohol and strength to a wine. Beaucastel uses Muscardin, but by far the most important plantings of Muscardin at a serious winemaking estate is at Chante-Perdrix in Châteauneuf-du-Pape. And the Nicolet family uses 20% in their excellent Châteauneuf-du-Pape.

Syrah—Syrah, the only game in town in the northern Rhône, is relegated to an accessory role in the south. However, its role in providing needed structure, backbone, and tannin to the fleshy Grenache is incontestable. Some growers believe it ripens too fast in the hotter south, but it is, in my opinion, a very strong addition to many southern Rhône wines. More and more of the Côtes du Rhône estates are producing special bottlings of 100% Syrah wines that show immense potential. The finest Syrah made in the southern Rhône is the Cuvée Syrah from the Château de Fonsalette, a wine that can last and evolve for 10–15 years. Its aromas are those of berry fruit, coffee, smoky tar, and hickory wood.

Terret Noir—Little of this grape is now found in the southern Rhône, though it remains one of the permitted varieties. It was used to give

acidity to a wine and mollify the strong character provided by the Grenache and Syrah. None of the best estates employs it any longer.
Vaccarèse—It is again at Beaucastel where I tasted the wine produced from this grape, which the Perrins vinify separately. It is not as powerful or as deep as Syrah, nor as alcoholic as Grenache, but has its own unique character that I would describe as giving aromas of pepper, hot tar, tobacco, and licorice.

There are exceptionally great wines made in the southern Rhône, and the potential for high quality is enormous. The climate is the most consistent and favorable of all France's viticultural regions (save for Provence). The dry heat and persistent gusty winds (called the *mistral*) inhibit the dreaded rot that causes so many problems in Burgundy. The legally permitted yields of juice per acre remain very conservative, and lead routinely to a production per acre that is less than half of that now produced in Burgundy or Bordeaux. Machine harvesters are prohibited in appellations such as Châteauneuf-du-Pape and Gigondas. Unlike the tiny amounts of wine produced in the northern Rhône, quantities of the top wines from the south are far more plentiful and easier to find. The prices for these wines qualify them as among the greatest bargains in serious red wine in the world. Furthermore, most of the wines have the virtue of being drinkable, or are at least accessible, when released. However, the top Châteauneuf-du-Papes can last and evolve 15–20 years, the best Gigondas 8–12 years, and even a good Côtes du Rhône 2–5 years.

There is a vast amount of enjoyment to be discovered in the southern Rhône for only a modest amount of money, for these are some of the most sumptuous and pleasure-giving wines produced in the world.

GIGONDAS

Hearty, Robust Wines for a Cold
Winter's Night

GIGONDAS AT A GLANCE

Type of wine produced:	Red wine and a small quantity of rosé
Grape varieties planted:	Grenache, Syrah, Mourvèdre, and Cinsault are the dominant varietals
Acres currently under vine:	3,000
Quality level:	Good to exceptional
Aging potential:	5–15 years
General characteristics:	A robust, chewy, full-bodied, rich, generous red wine; light, vibrant, fresh, underrated rosé
Greatest recent vintages:	1985, 1979, 1978
Price range:	$7–$11

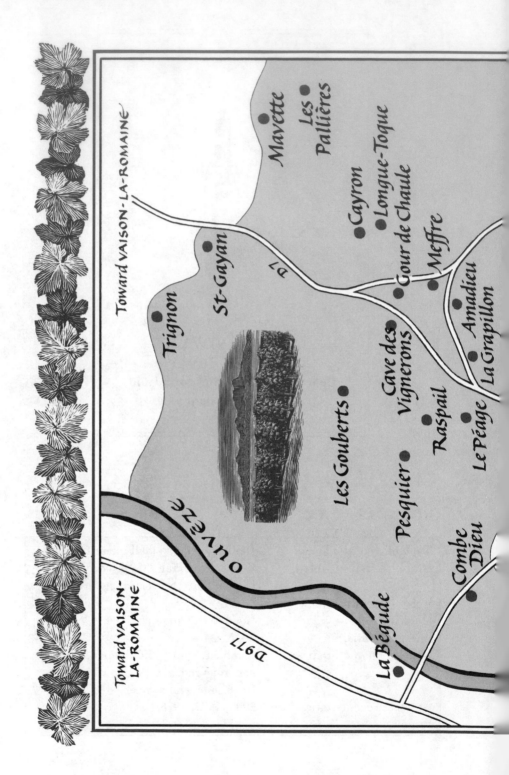

Toward VAISON-LA-ROMAINE

OUVÈZE

D977

Toward VAISON-LA-ROMAINE

La Bégude

Combe Dieu

Les Gouberts

Pesquier

Raspail

Le Péage

La Grapillon

Amadieu

Cave des Vignerons

Trignon

St-Gayan

D7

Meffre

Gour de Chaule

Longue-Toque

Cayron

Mavette

Les Pallières

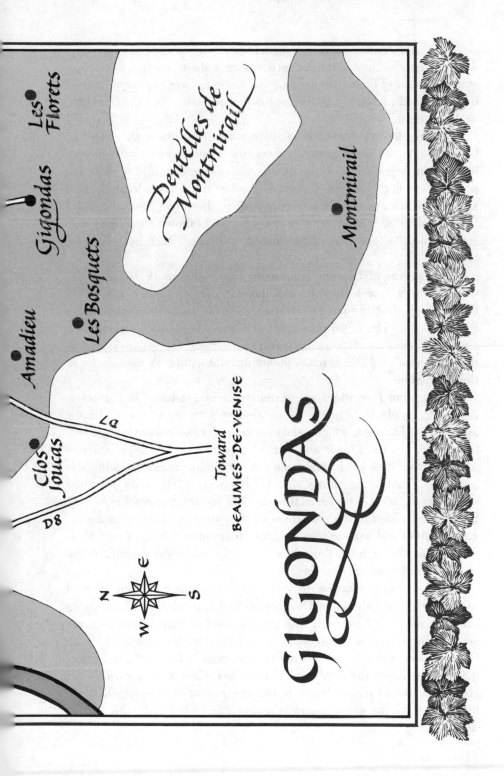

GIGONDAS

Les Florets

Gigondas

Amadieu

Les Bosquets

Clos Joucas

D8

La

Dentelles de Montmirail

Montmirail

Toward
BEAUMES-DE-VENISE

N
W E
S

The sleepy village of Gigondas, which seems to have as many dogs and cats as human inhabitants, sits on a sheltered spot at the foot of a craggy set of limestone needles that seem to have exploded upward from the earth, hovering above the town. They are called the Dentelles de Montmirail.

There are several things immediately apparent about the wines of Gigondas. At the small grower's level, the quality is consistently very high; at the négociant level the quality varies considerably, so selection is as always extremely important. Gigondas offers considerable value since its wines are indeed a worthy rival to those of Châteauneuf-du-Pape—only a 20-minute drive to the west, and in most cases they cost at least 15–20% less than a Châteauneuf-du-Pape, which itself is a fine bargain.

Gigondas was given appellation contrôlée status in 1971, being elevated from a Côtes du Rhône-Villages. The wines are similar to Châteauneuf-du-Pape but are more robust, and sometimes much more rustic in style. The 3,000-plus acres of vineyards produce a significant amount of wine, and there is considerable room for expansion since there are another 3,705 acres of plantable land within the boundaries of the appellation.

Only red and rosé wines are permitted to be produced in Gigondas. Any white made in Gigondas is entitled only to the Côtes du Rhône appellation. The rosé, which used to account for the bulk of the production, has fallen from favor and little of it is now seen. This is unfortunate, for the rosé made here can be very fine. Today, Gigondas is justifiably famous for chewy, heady, red wines. The laws permit a maximum of 80% Grenache in the wine but require a minimum of 15% Syrah to be added to the red wine. Most producers also use an assortment of other red wine grapes such as Mourvèdre, Cinsault, and Muscardin. But Grenache, followed by Syrah, far and away dominates the aromas and flavors of Gigondas.

Gigondas does not have a distinguished history, and is often referred to as merely a booster wine. The growers and négociants (without giving precise names) all can recall with great detail big Burgundy négociants sending their trucks to Gigondas over past decades to load up with Gigondas in order to give their burgundies more color, flesh, and stamina. This is hardly the same type of fame that Châteauneuf-du-Pape or Hermitage would claim, but it is the one aspect of this appellation's history that all the growers and négociants seem to relish with a great deal of pride.

The vineyards are spread out over a series of hills as well as the plateau that fans out below the old village of Gigondas. The soil varies, but at the best locations it is composed of limestone, clay, and small stones, and as elsewhere, the best vineyards always seem to be those that are on higher ground. Gigondas derives its sturdiness, strength, and often dizzying degree of alcohol (13.5% to 14.5% is not rare in the hot years) from the Grenache that is planted in these soils. Most growers' Gigondas is at least 65% Grenache, so it is not surprising to hear its admirers describe a fine Gigondas as a wine with a heady perfume of coffee, tobacco, grilled toast, raspberry, black pepper, and leather, as well as round, generous flavors with a good alcoholic kick. These are all personality traits of the Grenache grape that thrives at Gigondas. When some Syrah is added to give structure and acidity, the ingredients for a sumptuous, ageworthy wine are present.

Much of the appeal of Gigondas is that it can be drunk when released by the producers, but it will also keep well in the right vintages for up to a decade, providing a great deal of flexibility to the consumer. Once past ten years of age, even the best wines of Gigondas tend to lose their fruit as the walloping degree of alcohol becomes more and more apparent. One will no doubt encounter a great many styles of Gigondas, ranging from a few wines made by the carbonic maceration method to big, strapping, black/ruby-colored wines oozing with fruit, body, and tannin. (These styles are described in detail with the portrait of each producer.)

Gigondas is never a shy or subtle wine. Its appeal is its robust, frank, generous character, and the value it represents in the world's marketplace.

RECENT VINTAGES

1986—For those growers able to harvest prior to the heavy rains that began to fall on October 12 and who continued virtually uninterrupted for 2 weeks, the vintage should be quite successful, with deep-colored, tannic, rather alcoholic wine being produced. For those that got caught with unharvested grapes, they will either have to make very strict selections or turn out mediocre, diluted wine. This will be a very irregular year. Optimum maturity: 1990–1997.

1985—Early-maturing wines with low acidity but excellent concentration, full body, and a good dosage of tannin were produced in this bountiful vintage. The wines are wonderfully rich, fragrant, supple, and a joy to drink young. Only a few growers produced long-lived wines, but this is the most consistent and delicious Gigondas vintage since 1979. Optimum maturity: now–1995.

1984—Somewhat less successful in Gigondas than Châteauneuf-du-Pape, 1984 was certainly a decent vintage that produced less fleshy, more tannic and firm wines. While the wines do not have the initial attack and chewy texture of Gigondas, there are a number of good wines. Optimum maturity: now–1994.

1983—A small crop of wines was produced due to the problems with the Grenache crop during the summer. While the vintage has an excellent reputation, I believe it to be somewhat overrated, though there are some outstanding successes in this year. The wines tend toward the rustic, tannic, very full-bodied style. Certain wines lack fruit. Optimum maturity: now–1995.

1982—Overripeness and torrid heat during the harvest created significant problems. Many wines have color stability problems as well as exaggerated degrees of alcohol (14.5% and up). The successes are fat, jammy, very soft, and very alcoholic. This is a vintage to buy carefully and drink up over the short term. In general, Gigondas was more successful than its neighbor, Châteauneuf-du-Pape. Optimum maturity: now–1992.

1981—Quite an irregular vintage, ranging in quality from average to excellent, the 1981s have a rustic, full-bodied, rather coarse style. Where there is good ripe fruit to balance out the tannin and body, the wines can be very good. Almost all the wines are fully mature, but will keep. Optimum maturity: now—1992.

1980—Rather elegant wines were produced in 1980 in Gigondas. They have good color, are not excessively alcoholic or chewy, and show a good, ripe, charming fruitiness. All of the 1980s are fully mature and should be drunk over the next 4–5 years.

1979—Originally thought to be inferior to the 1978s, the 1979 wines of Gigondas have proved to be a match for the 1978s. Quite deeply colored, rich in fruit, body, and tannin, this is a year for keeping. There are a lot of top successes in Gigondas in this very consistent vintage. Optimum maturity: now–1992.

1978—Truly a great year throughout the Rhône, the 1978s in Gigondas are full-bodied, intense, sometimes overblown wines that are now reaching their apogee. They are a bit fuller and more alcoholic than the 1979s, but will also be very long-lived by Gigondas standards. Optimum maturity: now–1994.

OLDER VINTAGES

Few Gigondas made prior to 1978 would still be in fine form today. The best older vintages in the seventies have been 1971 and 1970. In the sixties, 1967 was superb, as was 1964. Should you run across any old Gigondas from these vintages, your best bets would be from such producers as Domaine Raspail, Domaine les Pallières, Domaine St.-Gayan, and Domaine Georges Faraud, since these growers usually produce the longest-lived wines of Gigondas.

A Personal Rating of the Gigondas Producers

***** *(OUTSTANDING PRODUCERS)*

Domaine Les Goubert   Domaine Raspail
Domaine Les Pallières

**** *(EXCELLENT PRODUCERS)*

Domaine de Cayron   Domaine de Longue-Toque
Clos des Cazeaux   Domaine Saint-Gayan
Domaine du Gour de Chaule

*** *(GOOD PRODUCERS)*

Robert Cuillerat   Château de Montmirail
Domaine du Grapillon d'Or   Domaine l'Oustau Fauquet
E. Guigal   Domaine des Pradets
Mas des Collines

** *(AVERAGE PRODUCERS)*

P. Amadieu   Domaine de la Mavette
Domaine des Bousquets   Domaine du Pesquier
Caves des Vignerons   Château Raspail (G. Meffre)
P. Jaboulet   Château du Trignon
Clos de Joncuas (F. Chastan)

DOMAINE DE CAYRON ****

As one enters the sleepy town of Gigondas, the first cellar on the left is that of the family of Georges Faraud. Mr. Faraud, a gray-haired, very elderly man, is now aided by his handsome, athletic son, Michel. Faraud's family has been making one wine, an extremely concentrated, intense Gigondas, for over 150 years. He has 34 acres of vines that average 30 years of age at the foot of the "Dentelles" that loom over the town.

Faraud's wines are the richest, most exotic, and often the most dramatic of the appellation. On occasion, their explosive richness and rustic set of aromas can be a bit overwhelming. I still do not know what to make of the full-throttle, behemoth-styled wine Faraud made in 1978. His wines, made in one of the few underground cellars in Gigondas, are never fined or filtered but are allowed to settle naturally by virtue of a two- to three-year sojourn in ancient wooden foudres. He uses the minimum amount of Grenache permitted under the appellation laws (65%) and incorporates with that 20% Syrah and 15% Cinsault. His wines do not lack for power; they normally reach 14% alcohol naturally. The squeaky-voiced Faraud recommends that people give his wines one to two hours' breathing because of their size and style. Stating that there is no need to rush to drink them, he says they will improve for 10–15 years. I might add that they should also be decanted, given their enormous amount of sediment.

Faraud's wines are such forceful examples of Gigondas that they, more than any other wine of this appellation, require rich stews, cassoulets, and game to absorb their strong personalities. Properly served and matched up with the right culinary offering, they are memorable wines that can take one on a pleasant trip to the nineteenth century.

VINTAGES

1985—*Gigondas*—Faraud thinks this is one of the finest wines he has
· ever made. With a whopping 14.4% natural alcohol, there is no
89 doubting its ability to grab your attention. Black/ruby with an intense chocolatey, spicy bouquet, heaps of flavor, great depth and length, this should prove to be a propitious effort. Anticipated maturity: 1989–2000. Last tasted 6/86.

1984—*Gigondas*—Very deep in color, the 1984 also has a peppery,
· blackcurrant bouquet, rich, spicy flavors, very good depth and
86 balance, and "only" 13.3% alcohol. This is a top success for the vintage. Anticipated maturity: now–1994. Last tasted 6/86.

1983—*Gigondas*—The stunningly complex bouquet of cedar, pepper,
· olives, berry fruit, and truffles is top-rank. On the palate, a trace
87 of coarseness keeps the rating down as does the 14.8% alcohol level. Extremely full-bodied, this is a brawny, muscular wine, the likes of which one rarely sees today. Anticipated maturity: now–1994. Last tasted 6/86.

1982—*Gigondas*—Another blockbuster, the 1982, with 14.5% alcohol,
· has a full-intensity bouquet of fruitcake, pepper, and herbs.
87 Port-like and lush with a trace of sweetness, this is a large-

scaled, very lush, generously flavored wine that offers a big mouthful of wine. It should be drunk over the next 5–7 years. Last tasted 6/86.

1981—*Gigondas*—This is a very good Gigondas, spicy, earthy, and

· Provençal herb-scented. Deep in color, quite concentrated, full-

86 bodied, and well made, this is a gutsy, powerful Gigondas oozing with character. Anticipated maturity: now–1993. Last tasted 1/87.

OLDER VINTAGES

Faraud produced a very good, supple 1980, an excellent, still youthful 1979, and an incredibly concentrated, blockbuster but bizarre-smelling and -tasting 1978. The only other vintage my notes show was a tired, out of balance, strange-tasting 1974.

DOMAINE LES GOUBERT *****

In certain vintages I have felt that Jean-Pierre Cartier produces the single best Gigondas of the appellation. He is a balding man in his early forties who is often seen sporting a baseball hat rather than the traditional béret. His 1985, 1981, and 1979 Gigondas are, in my book, *hors classé* for their respective vintages. Cartier's obvious winemaking talent has yet to become widely known. This estate was founded in 1973 and until the eighties was content to sell all of its wine within Europe. Cartier owns 37 acres of vineyards of which 19 are in Gigondas. One of Cartier's best-kept secrets is an excellent red Beaumes de Venise he makes that tastes very much like his Gigondas. He also produces a little Gigondas rosé that is vibrant and quite refreshing, a worthy competitor to the more expensive and more reputed rosés of Tavel. His white wines are from Sablet, a Côtes du Rhône-Village, and although he started making a white wine only in 1983, he has won two first prizes for his 1983 and 1985 at the big French wine festival in Mâcon. Influenced by Marcel Guigal of Côte Rôtie fame, in 1985 Cartier implemented a luxury cuvée of his Gigondas called Cuvée Florence. He made only 330 cases of this wine, which is the first wine of Gigondas to be aged in new oak casks from the Vosges Mountains.

Cartier's emergence as a potential superstar in the southern Rhône has caused increased interest in his wines. As of 1986, 40% of his wine is exported, primarily to Great Britain, Belgium, Denmark, and the United States. His winemaking abilities are profound, and I enthusiastically recommend his wines.

VINTAGES

1985—*Gigondas Cuvée Florence*—This is the single greatest Gigondas
· I have tasted. The blend of 88% Grenache, 10% Syrah, and 2%
92 Mourvèdre seems to have benefited immensely from the sojourn
in new oak barrels. Very fragrant and complex, rich and full-
bodied, and not lacking acidity and structure as are many 1985s,
this is a profound effort. Anticipated maturity: 1988–1998. Last
tasted 6/86.

1985—*Gigondas*—Oozing with wonderfully ripe raspberry fruit, spicy
· pepper, and some floral aromas, the regular 1985 has great con-
90 centration, exceptional length and depth, and good aging potential notwithstanding its precocious appeal. Anticipated maturity:
1989–1990. Last tasted 6/86.

1984—*Gigondas*—The best 1984 Gigondas I tasted, Cartier's 1984 is
· without question lighter this year than in 1981 or 1985, yet it has
87 a close similarity to a very good burgundy. Voluptuous cherry
and raspberry fruit flavors are concentrated, but harmonious and
elegant. The bouquet would fool most burgundy experts. Anticipated maturity: now–1992. Last tasted 6/86.

1983—*Gigondas*—Like other reds in 1983, the 1983 Gigondas from
· Cartier lacks some color and fleshy fruit. Otherwise, this is a
83 good, robust wine with character and a rustic personality. In
1983, Cartier's red Beaumes de Venise is better and, of course,
cheaper. Anticipated maturity: now–1990. Last tasted 6/86.

1981—*Gigondas*—Fully mature but clearly capable of lasting 5–7
· years, the 1981 has a full-intensity aroma of saddle leather,
90 smoked meat, and ripe berry fruit. Dense in color, quite rich
and full-bodied, with marvelous length, there are not many
wines I could enjoy more than this. Drink over the next 5–7
years. Last tasted 12/86.

1979—*Gigondas*—If the 1985 is the glorious epitome of power and rich-
· ness, Cartier's 1979 is Gigondas at its elegant and stylish best.
88 Deep ruby color with a beautiful floral, berry fruit bouquet, voluptuous, velvety flavor and fine length personify this disarming,
seductive wine. Drink over the next 3–4 years. Last tasted 6/86.

DOMAINE DU GOUR DE CHAULE ****

This estate keeps a very low profile yet makes very delicious, velvety,
richly fruity Gigondas. The estate is 25 acres in size and the blend used
for their well-bred Gigondas is 80% Grenache and 20% Syrah and Mour-

vèdre. The wine is aged one year in cement tanks, then 14–16 months in large wooden foudres. This is quite a serious domaine, impeccably looked after by Madame Bonfils. I find it a mystery why the wines are not better known.

VINTAGES

1985—*Gigondas*—This is a luscious wine, black/ruby in color, very full-bodied, loaded with peppery blackberry fruit, very lush and fat, but it has good ripe tannins in the finish. Anticipated maturity: 1988–1994. Last tasted 10/86.
·
88

1983—*Gigondas*—Less well colored than the 1985 with a leathery, smoked meat scent to the bouquet, the 1983 has harsh tannins, a rich berry fruitiness, good body, a mid-term aging potential. Anticipated maturity: now–1993. Last tasted 6/86.
·
86

1982—*Gigondas*—Madame Bonfils feels this wine is too alcoholic, but there is no denying its round, sumptuous style, deep silky texture, and immediate gratification. Drink over the next 4–5 years. Last tasted 6/86.
·
85

1981—*Gigondas*—One of the best 1981 Gigondas tasted, this wine is fully mature, has a deep, velvety, berry fruitiness, a toasty, vanillin character, and plump texture. Drink over the next 5 years. Last tasted 6/86.
·
86

1979—*Gigondas*—The 1979 produced here is an outstanding Gigondas. Very deep ruby/purple, it has a full-intensity bouquet of peppery fruit, lush, velvety flavors that show dazzling concentration, impeccably clean winemaking, and a fine mouth-filling finish. Drink over the next 4–5 years. Last tasted 12/85.
·
89

ETIENNE GUIGAL ***

This northern Rhône vineyard owner and négociant reaches into the southern Rhône to purchase grape juice for its good, sometimes excellent Gigondas. Marcel Guigal says he spends considerable time tasting in the growers' cellars, believing that if one is willing to pay cash on the spot for certain good lots, a fine Gigondas can be made from the component parts. There is no doubt that Guigal has increased the quality of his Gigondas, with the 1982 and 1983 representing the two best wines he has made to date from this appellation. The style of Gigondas produced at Guigal is powerful, jammy, and authoritative. It is best drunk within five to ten years of the vintage.

VINTAGES

1983—*Gigondas*—Guigal feels 1983 was a mediocre year for Gigondas, but he also admits that his Gigondas in this vintage is his best
87   yet, due to the larger quantity of Syrah and Mourvèdre in the blend. This is a rich, full-bodied, powerful Gigondas with loads of peppery, cassis-scented fruit. Drink over the next 5–7 years. Last tasted 1/87.

1982—*Gigondas*—Along with the Domaine les Pallières, Domaine Cayron, and Domaine St.-Gayan, Guigal's 1982 Gigondas is one of
86   the best of the vintage. Peppery, raspberry, jammy aromas are followed by a wine that has luscious, even unctuous flavors with full body, a hefty dose of alcohol, and low acidity. Quite delicious. Drink over the next 2–5 years. Last tasted 6/86.

1981—*Gigondas*—More austere than either the flamboyant 1982 or powerful 1983, the 1981 is, nevertheless, a full-bodied, spicy,
85   quite well-made wine with a good deal of fruit and character. Drink over the next 3–4 years. Last tasted 1/87.

OLDER VINTAGES

The 1976, 1978, and 1979 are still holding up, but one would be tempting the hands of fate by not consuming these wines over the next 1–3 years. The 1969 and 1971 are no longer very pleasurable.

PAUL JABOULET AINÉ **

The famous Jaboulet firm of Tain L'Hermitage has always made very good Gigondas. In fact, until 1980 it was usually one of the top five or six wines of the appellation. It also had superb aging potential. Bottles of the 1964, 1967, 1969, and 1970 are still in very good condition. However, since 1980 the style has clearly changed since the Jaboulets apparently have decided to produce a more modern-style, very clean, filtered and polished commercial wine that, at most, has a shelf life of four to six years. This is all rather regrettable, but even worse, their heretofore sublime Châteauneuf-du-Pape, Les Cèdres (also called La Grappe des Papes), has suffered the same ignominious fate. Their Gigondas now tastes vapid, and in a blind tasting would be impossible even to identify. Fortunately, the price is reasonable.

VINTAGES

1985—*Gigondas*—Nearly 100% Grenache, the 1985 Gigondas is a generously fruity, straightforward wine with plenty of body and al-
83   cohol. Anticipated maturity: now–1991. Last tasted 12/86.

1984—*Gigondas*—Light, fruity, medium-bodied, and soft, this wine is
·   fully mature but rather insipid and short on the palate. Drink
74   over the next 2–3 years. Last tasted 6/86.

1983—*Gigondas*—Light to medium ruby in color, slightly spicy, the
·   1983 Jaboulet Gigondas has a fleeting bouquet of watery cherry
78   fruit, medium body, and a short finish. There is not much to it.
      Drink over the next 2–3 years. Last tasted 1/87.

1982—*Gigondas*—More alcoholic and fleshier than the other recent
·   Gigondas wines from Jaboulet, the 1982 is fruity but one-dimen-
81   sional. It should be drunk up. Last tasted 6/85.

OLDER VINTAGES

Neither the 1981 nor the 1980 offers much in the way of flavor interest
or concentration. Both vintages should be drunk up. One has to go back
to 1979 and 1978 to find full-flavored, authoritative examples of Gigondas from Paul Jaboulet. Both vintages offer loads of peppery, spicy,
rich fruit, interesting mouth-filling flavors, and five to eight more years
of drinkability. The 1979 may actually turn out to be better than the
1978. Both wines are a far cry from the vapid Gigondas Jaboulet is now
producing. Older vintages that are still drinking well, and thus proving
the cellaring potential of a well-made Gigondas, include a very good
1969, good 1970 and 1971, delicious, rich 1967, and slightly fading 1964.
(All of these older wines were tasted in December 1986.)

DOMAINE DE LONGUE-TOQUE****

The diminutive, nearly bald, soft-spoken Serge Chapalain produces the
most elegant and stylish wine of Gigondas. He is a philosophical individual who appears to be in his late thirties, with the emaciated, radical
look of a late-sixties American hippy. The domaine was founded by his
father in 1962. They have 57 acres and produce only one wine—a
supple, expressive, rather opulently fruity, silky Gigondas that merits
serious attention.

Chapalain's father originated the idea of using the carbonic maceration for 50% of his grapes, and blending that soft, fruity wine with the
other 50%, which is vinified traditionally and given a moderately long
maceration of 15 days with the skins. The results have been wines that
have the flesh and body of Gigondas but an open and charming fruitiness as well as elegance. The wines spend 10–15 months in wooden
foudres, and since 1984 have been given a light filtration prior to bottling, a procedure that Chapalain abhors but says is necessary because
"the restaurants think sediment in a wine is bad." Chapalain's Gigon-

das is a blend of 65% Grenache, 20% Syrah, 10% Cinsault, and 5% Mourvèdre. I worry, as does Chapalain, that his recent introduction of filtration has robbed this wine of some of its richness and style. But, as Chapalain sadly laments, "that is the commercial reality producers face." Longue-Toque's wines are best drunk within their first five or six years of life. Even the proprietor agrees with that and says that only magnums from vintages such as 1979 and 1983 are worth drinking at ten years of age.

VINTAGES

1985—*Gigondas*—A heady, quite enjoyable wine, the 1985 Gigondas
 ·   has good dark ruby color, a soft, very fruity, lush texture, low
 85   acidity, but good length and an obvious alcoholic kick. Drink it
       over the next 4–5 years. Last tasted 11/86.

1984—*Gigondas*—Medium-bodied, rather straightforward in style, this
 ·   ripe fruity wine is pleasant enough, but lacks concentration,
 79   body, and length. Last tasted 11/86.

1983—*Gigondas*—Surprisingly light to medium ruby in color, yet very
 ·   fragrant with a similarity to a fine Volnay or Pommard, this
 87   spicy, velvety, elegant wine has quite a lot of concentrated fruit,
       medium body, and a generous, solid finish. Quite charming.
       Drink over the next 3–4 years. Last tasted 11/86.

1981—*Gigondas*—The first bottle I tasted was bizarre, but two recent
 ·   bottles I evaluated have been fully mature, rich in fruit, velvety,
 85   and quite attractive, but they should be drunk up. Last tasted
       12/86.

CHÂTEAU DE MONTMIRAIL ***·

This moderate-sized estate has its cellars in the quaint Côtes du Rhône-Villages Vacqueyras, and is run with obvious enthusiasm by Maurice Archimbaud and Monique Bouteiller. They own 79 acres in Gigondas with the vineyards well situated on the sun-drenched terraces. The Gigondas, which is made from 75% Grenache, 15% Syrah, and 10% Mourvèdre and Cinsault, spends 16–18 months aging in wooden foudres and cement cuves prior to bottling. Archimbaud does not want to risk any oxidation and is a great believer in early bottling to effect this end. His wines are not fined, but given a light filtration prior to bottling. The Gigondas called Cuvée Beauchamp is one of only four red wines made at Montmirail. They also make three different cuvées of Vacqueyras. Their Gigondas is, however, the firm's best wine and is always rather deep in color and jammy, with plenty of fruit; it lacks the complexity and power of the top Gigondas, but it has broad commercial appeal because it is so easy to understand and drink. It is a wine that usually requires drinking young, normally before it attains seven or eight years of age.

VINTAGES

1985—*Gigondas Cuvée Beauchamp*—Very jammy and scented with
· blackberries, the 1985 is quite low in acidity, very fruity and fat,
83 with its exuberant fruitiness disguising a good level of tannin. I believe this precocious wine should be drunk over the next 5 years; the staff at Montmirail claims it will last 10–15 years. Last tasted 11/86.

1984—*Gigondas Cuvée Beauchamp*—I prefer the 1984 to the 1985. It is
· a firmer structured wine with just as much rich blackcurrant
85 fruit, a ripe, lush palate texture, and good finish. It is quite seductive. Drink over the next 5 years. Last tasted 11/86.

1983—*Gigondas Cuvée Beauchamp*—Deep in color with a richly fruity,
· berry-scented bouquet, this medium- to full-bodied wine has
84 lush, easy to like flavors, not much tannin, but a round, straight-forward finish. Last tasted 1/87.

1981—*Gigondas Cuvée Beauchamp*—I sense raspberries and pepper in
· the 1981, whereas the more recent vintages seemed to possess
82 jammy currant fruit. On the palate, the 1981 is a larger-scaled wine with tannins still present and a rather chewy texture. Drink over the next 4–5 years. Last tasted 1/87.

1980—*Gigondas Cuvée Beauchamp*—Beginning to fade, the 1980 has
· an amber edge, soft, earthy, somewhat dull flavors, and a fleet-
76 ing bouquet. Drink up. Last tasted 11/86.

DOMAINE L'OUSTAU FAUQUET***

Roger Combe, whose cellars lie midway between the ancient village of Gigondas and the prettier town of Vacqueyras (a Côtes du Rhône-Villages), produces only red wine from both appellations. Combe and his family own 59 acres of which 20 are in Gigondas. The wine produced here is quite traditionally made. Produced from 80% Grenache and the rest of a field blend of Syrah, Mourvèdre, and Cinsault, it is a wine that is never filtered or fined, and spends 8–12 months in cement tanks and wooden foudres before being bottled. All of the Gigondas vineyards are on the hillsides of Mt. Montmirail. The Combes claim the best recent vintages for Gigondas have been 1978 and 1979, followed by 1985. This is a good source for reliable, rarely exciting but soundly made, very reasonably priced Gigondas. Not surprisingly, their three separate wines of Vacqueyras often resemble their Gigondas, but at an even lower price.

VINTAGES

1985—*Gigondas*—Quite fat and fruity with a very deep color, this suc-
· culent, plump wine lacks acidity but makes a delicious mouthful
84 of wine. Anticipated maturity: 1987–1991. Last tasted 11/86.

· 1984—*Gigondas*—A much firmer, probably more ageworthy wine than
· the 1985, Combe's 1984 has medium body, good fruit, fine bal-
83 ance, and zesty acidity that is not excessive. The finish could be
longer. Drink over the next 2–4 years. Last tasted 11/86.

1983—*Gigondas*—Ready to drink, the 1983 is quite rich and fruity with
· the pronounced aroma of raspberries, oak, and pepper. On the
85 palate, the wine has a great deal of jammy fruit and alcohol.
Drink over the next 4–5 years. Last tasted 11/86.

1982—*Gigondas*—One of the most successful 1982s I tasted in Gigon-
· das, Combe's offering from this vintage is a very alcoholic
85 (14.5%), but rich, jammy, almost port-like wine with stunningly
rich fruit but low acidity. Drink over the next 3–4 years for its
fiery display of power and muscle. Last tasted 11/86.

DOMAINE LES PALLIÈRES *****

No one in Gigondas has more exacting standards than Pierre and Christian Roux, the two brothers who manage the most splendidly situated property in all of Gigondas. They are the sons of the late Hilarion Roux, the first person to estate bottle Gigondas in the late nineteenth century and the founder of the growers' association headed now by Roger Meffre of St.-Gayan. The ruddy-faced, unusually shy Pierre Roux runs the 62 acres of vineyards that are strategically located on the slopes of the Dentelles. He also looks after Lilly, a pet dog that in 1986 was 25 years old and, according to Roux, the oldest dog in France. Pierre and Christian are both bachelors and have no children, so local gossip is filled with rumors about who will take over this great estate when they are unable to manage it.

Roux produces a very traditional, flavorful, and long-lived wine from a blend of 60% Grenache, 27% Mourvèdre, and 13% Syrah and Cinsault. Approximately three-quarters of the vines are 70 years old and the balance only 12 years of age. His Gigondas spends two to three years in concrete vats and old wooden foudres, prior to being given a light filtration and then bottled. This makes Les Pallières the last to be bottled in a given vintage. Roux, by his own admission, wants a robust, full-flavored Gigondas that will last up to ten years. There is no doubt that he excels in producing exactly this style of wine. It is a vivid example of impeccable winemaking, and is filled with flavor and personality. Among the most robust wines of the appellation, it requires full-flavored dishes to do it justice.

VINTAGES

1985—*Gigondas*—There is no doubt that the 1985 Les Pallières is a
· super wine, and one of the great successes of the southern
91 Rhône in this vintage. Black/ruby in color with an exceptionally intense fragrance of black pepper, raspberry fruit, and violets, this full-bodied, powerful yet harmonious wine should provide superb drinking when released in 1989. Anticipated maturity: 1989–1999. Last tasted 6/86.

1983—*Gigondas*—Roux used more Mourvèdre and Syrah in 1983 be-
· cause of problems with the Grenache crop. One can hardly com-
90 plain about the results. A sweet, rich bouquet of cedary, smoky fruit is stunning. On the palate, the wine has vast length, rich layers of lush fruit, huge body, and quite a future ahead of it. A quintessential Gigondas. Anticipated maturity: now–1996. Last tasted 6/86.

1982—*Gigondas*—The heady bouquet of berry fruit and spice is lovely.
· On the palate, this wine has quite an alcoholic clout (14.5%),
89 rich, ripe fruit, full body, and a round, lush, long finish. It is quite a success for the vintage. Drink over the next 6–8 years. Last tasted 1/86.

1981—*Gigondas*—Different from the three most recent vintages, the
· 1981 has a bouquet of fresh saddle leather, earthy, meaty aro-
86 mas, a spicy, rustic texture, and a long, supple finish with some tannin to lose. Drink over the next 4–5 years. Last tasted 1/87.

1979—*Gigondas*—Just now approaching its apogee, the 1979 has a very
· dense ruby/purple color, a rich, chewy, tarry, smoky, berry-
88 scented bouquet and flavors, full body, and an unctuous texture. Drink over the next 5 years. Last tasted 6/86.

1978—*Gigondas*—The exotic bouquet of black pepper, gamelike,
· meaty smells, and grilled nuts is first class. On the palate, the
90 wine is loaded with fruit and alcohol, and has a good measure of tannin left. Quite pleasurable for robust drinking now, this big, weighty wine is a classic, old-style Gigondas. Drink over the next 5–8 years. Last tasted 6/86.

DOMAINE RASPAIL *****

For sheer consistency the Gigondas produced by the Domaine Raspail of Francois Ay, now managed by his articulate, serious-minded son, Dominique, is one of the leading wines of the appellation. This is an impeccably made wine that can age for up to 20 years, the only Gigondas I find to have that kind of longevity. (The Raspail estate was divided several years ago and the wine of this 44.5-acre property should not be confused with that of Château Raspail, owned by one of the largest négociants in France, Gabriel Meffre.)

The deeply colored, rich, fragrant wine produced by Monsieur Ay is vinified in temperature-controlled, stainless steel tanks, given a long maceration lasting three weeks, and then aged 18–24 months in large wood foudres. It settles naturally and is neither fined nor filtered, so a heavy sediment will precipitate in the highly concentrated vintages. Ay uses a blend of 65–70% Grenache, 15% Syrah, with the rest a mixture of Cinsault and Mourvèdre. The average age of his vines is 25 years. Ay's Raspail is undoubtedly a textbook Gigondas. If I were trying to teach the personality characteristics of Gigondas, I would use his wine as the prototype. The deep color, the peppery, raspberry-scented bouquet, full-bodied, fleshy texture, and heady alcoholic punch defines what Gigondas at its best is all about. Dominique Ay, who looks like the older brother of international tennis star Vitas Gerulaitis, is a big believer in the Gigondas appellation, which he says "produces higher quality wine than Châteauneuf-du-Pape, and sells it for less."

VINTAGES

1985—*Gigondas*—This looks to be the finest vintage for Raspail since
·   the glorious 1978. Ruby/purple in color with a fabulous crushed
90   raspberry, peppery, even violet bouquet, this full-bodied, very
        concentrated, very rich wine has layers of flavors and a sensa-
        tional finish. The natural alcohol is 14%. Anticipated maturity:
        1988–1997. Last tasted 10/86.

1984—*Gigondas*—Somewhat light and high in acidity, without much
·   body or fruit for the ideal balance, this is a pleasant, straightfor-
76   ward wine that should be drunk over the next 3–4 years. Last
        tasted 10/86.

1983—*Gigondas*—Medium to deep ruby with a moderately intense
·   raspberry, peppery, and earthy bouquet, this full-bodied wine
83   has soft flavors, exhibits good ripeness, but has only a so-so
        finish. Quite good, it is, however, not special. Anticipated ma-
        turity: now–1992. Last tasted 1/87.

1982—*Gigondas*—Undeniably a success for the vintage, the 1982 Ras-
·   pail has very soft, somewhat diffuse flavors, but good color and
84   concentration, a solid, heady lashing of alcohol, and a lush fin-
       ish. Drink over the next 2–3 years. Last tasted 10/86.

1981—*Gigondas*—Of recent Raspails, the 1981 is the most rustic in
·   style with tarry, gamelike, almost smoky aromas and flavors,
86   heaps of fruit as well as body, and a good deal of tannin. This is
       a big, old-style Gigondas with character. Drink over the next 5–
       6 years. Last tasted 1/87.

1979—*Gigondas*—This wine may suffer in comparison with the 1978,
·   but it is an elegantly wrought, very attractive wine with a youth-
85   ful deep ruby color, medium to full body, and richly fruity, sup-
       ple texture. It should be drunk over the next 2–4 years. Last
       tasted 6/85.

1978—*Gigondas*—The 1978 is a blockbuster Gigondas that is just now
·   entering its period of full maturity. Very deep in color with a
90   complex bouquet of berry fruit and spicy pepper, this full-bodied
       wine is rich in color and extract, and seems capable of lasting
       for at least 6–10 more years. Quite impressive. Last tasted 1/86.

OLDER VINTAGES

I have been a keen buyer of Ay's Gigondas since college, when its full-
bodied warmth and low price provided much pleasure. Not much has
changed regarding his wines. In top vintages, they tend to peak when
around seven or eight years old, but will keep another ten. The 1964,
drunk in 1985, was just slightly on the downside. The 1967 is still
wonderful, as are the 1970 and 1971. The 1976 is a harder-styled, somewhat coarse wine with a great deal of tannin as well as concentration.
Perhaps it will blossom with more cellaring.

DOMAINE SAINT-GAYAN****

Roger Meffre is a warm, friendly, extremely confident and optimistic
man in his early fifties. He has been the active president of the Gigondas growers' association for a good many years. His family has been
making wine at Saint-Gayan since 1400, so along with Gérard Chave in
Mauves (whose family of winemakers dates from 1481) he has winemaking genetically programmed into his blood. Meffre has an exuberance when talking about the potential for Gigondas that is infectious.
He points out that mechanical harvesters are forbidden, and that the
yield of juice per acre is restricted to one-third that of what growers in
Burgundy and châteaux in Bordeaux are routinely producing today. He

claims the local cooperative has just hired a new team and will be concentrating more on quality, and that finally Gigondas is getting some respect for their wines. With quality such as is produced at Saint-Gayan, Gigondas deserves to get much more attention and respect.

Meffre, who now has his son Jean-Pierre to assist him, has 47 acres of vineyards, 35 of which are in Gigondas, lined with rows of very old vines that average 50–60 years. The cépage, or blend of grapes he uses to produce his Gigondas, is 80% Grenache, 15% Syrah, 4% Mourvèdre, and 1% Cinsault. His wines, which are consistently rich and full-bodied, spend one year in cement cuves, followed by one year in wood foudres. He fines his wines prior to bottling but never filters them, saying, "To make a great wine one must take risks." Meffre's Gigondas, which seem to peak at about six or seven years and begin to fade around age twelve, are among the richest wines of the appellation. They are characterized by an intense, almost port-like, jammy, berry fruit that Meffre attributes to his very old vines. With respect to Gigondas vintages, the gregarious Meffre ranks them as follows, beginning with the best: 1978, 1979, 1985, 1976, 1971, 1981, 1980, and 1983.

This is an excellent estate dedicated to making as natural and as fine a wine as that appellation can produce.

VINTAGES

1985—*Gigondas*—This wine should show very well young (as most · 1985s will no doubt do). Deep ruby/purple with a full-intensity, 87 port-like bouquet of jammy, berry fruit, the 1985 is quite full-bodied, lush, and long with oodles of fruit. Anticipated maturity: 1989–1993. Last tasted 6/86.

1984—*Gigondas*—The 1984 has nowhere near the depth of the 1985, · but shows very good ripe berry fruit, medium to full body, a 85 spicy, peppery nose, and good finish. Anticipated maturity: 1988–1993. Last tasted 6/86.

1983—*Gigondas*—Not as dark as the 1984 or 1985, the 1983 is drier, · more tannic, rather rustic in style with less fleshy fruit and suc-83 culence. It is good, but for me it seems to be missing something. Anticipated maturity: 1988–1996. Last tasted 6/86.

1982—*Gigondas*—Roger Meffre produced a very successful 1982 Gi-· gondas that is ready now. Intense, ripe black cherry fruit mixes 86 nicely with scents of leather. On the palate, the wine is fat, quite alcoholic, deep, and lush. This is a hedonistic, opulently fruity wine. Drink over the next 4–6 years. Last tasted 6/86.

1981—*Gigondas*—Just beginning to open up, the tannic, firmly struc-
·   tured 1981 has a bouquet of berry fruit, medium to full body,
85   good length, but should get even better with 1–2 more years of
     cellaring. Anticipated maturity: now–1991. Last tasted 1/87.

1980—*Gigondas*—Very deeply colored with a bouquet that suggests
·   jammy, berry fruit and Provençal herbs, quite full-bodied, deli-
86   ciously deep, fruity, supple, and long, this is a big wine with all
     the component parts in harmony. Drink over the next 4–5 years.
     Last tasted 1/87.

1979—*Gigondas*—Still evolving, the 1979 is a chewy Gigondas, loaded
·   with a peppery, cassis and raspberry, chocolatey-scented bou-
87   quet. Quite concentrated, full-bodied, and long, this wine seems
     now to be at its apogee. It is an excellent Gigondas. Last tasted
     6/86.

1978—*Gigondas*—The finest Saint-Gayan I have tasted, the 1978 has a
·   big, truffle-scented, chocolatey, berry-dominated bouquet, and
88   splendidly rich, supple, full-bodied flavors that have finally
     thrown off their cloak of tannin. This is an impressive Gigondas.
     It should be drunk over the next 4–5 years. Last tasted 11/85.

CHÂTEAU DU TRIGNON * *

The round, friendly, welcoming face of André Roux is enough to put
even the most foul-dispositioned visitor in a good mood. Enthusiastic,
genteel, and extremely kind, André Roux runs the Château du Trignon
in Sablet, a Côtes du Rhône-Villages. Roux produces a number of
Rhône wines, but his best is his Gigondas. Roux is one of the Rhône
Valley's most vocal exponents of the carbonic maceration method of
fermentation (see page 224). He worked under the famous Dr. Nalys of
the Domaine Nalys, a well-known estate in Châteauneuf-du-Pape that
practices this method of making red wine. Wines made by the carbonic
maceration method are usually delightfully fresh, fruity wines that must
be consumed when young. Roux disagrees that the wines cannot age
well, and has bottles of Nalys's superior 1967 Châteauneuf-du-Pape,
made in this manner, to prove his point. However, despite isolated
examples such as this, I have never found that the Trignon Gigondas
improves much or even lasts beyond three to five years. It has heretofore been a wine to consume in its exuberant youth. Roux thinks that
the answer is to add more and more Syrah and Mourvèdre to the blend,
and his 1985 Gigondas is an example of the direction in which Roux is
moving. The 1985, which has one-third each of Grenache, Mourvèdre,

and Syrah, contrasts sharply with his previous efforts, which were 60% Grenache, 25% Cinsault, and 15% Syrah and Mourvèdre.

Roux owns 23 acres in Gigondas (he also has 104 acres in the Côtes du Rhône-Villages), and ages his wines in tanks and wooden foudres prior to bottling. His wines are straightforward, fruity, and supple, never thrilling, but always fairly priced. They should be drunk young, within the first 3–5 years of life.

VINTAGES

1985—*Gigondas*—This is Roux's best wine to date. Very sound, bursting with fruit, this rich, supple wine will be delicious to drink · over the next 2–3 years. Last tasted 10/86.
85

1984—*Gigondas*—High acidity, a fleeting fruitiness, and moderate extract give this palatable wine a meagerly endowed feeling. Last · tasted 6/86.
75

1983—*Gigondas*—Medium ruby with good fruit, this spicy, chunky wine is quite one-dimensional, but adequately fruity, soft, and · pleasant. Last tasted 6/86.
80

Other Gigondas Producers

Pierre Amadieu—Amadieu is the largest producer of Gigondas. The firm owns 296 acres and offers its wines under a host of different labels. Its two most important Gigondas vineyards are Le Ramane and La Machotte. The Gigondas produced here is made in a very rustic, chunky style with plenty of peppery fruit, body, and tannin. It is also fairly priced. The 1981 and 1983 are superior to the 1982 and 1984. For tourists, his aging cellars are worth a stop.

M. Archimbaud and Vache—My experience with the wines from this domaine (called Clos des Cazeaux) has been quite good. I only wish I saw the wines more frequently. Their very good Gigondas (called Cuvée de la Tour Sarrazine), in the vintages I have seen, 1981, 1982, and 1983, was very well colored, brimming with fruit, and extremely well made. It represents a synthesis between the commercial, fruity style and the huge-bodied, tannic, chewy style. The production averages 4,500 cases.

Raymond Boutière—Boutière's Domaine du Pesquier comprises 37 acres from which a very muscular, rather heavy, tannic style of Gigondas emerges. His blend is 65% Grenache, 25% Syrah, and the rest Mourvèdre and Cinsault. It is a wine with a rustic appeal, but I find it lacking charm and flesh. The 1985 looks to be better than either the 1983 or 1982.

Cave des Vignerons—Without realizing it, many visitors to the southern Rhône have probably drunk this fruity product of the carbonic maceration method of winemaking. The Gigondas made by this cooperative is the house wine of the legendary restaurant L'Oustau de Baumanière in Les Baux. The other trade name used with great success by the cooperative is Cuvée du Président. The wines here are cheap, fruity, soundly made, and if never exhilarating or thrilling, certainly pleasant and round. The cooperative produces an average of 83,000 cases of Gigondas.

Fernand Chastan—This is a unique cellar, for Chastan is the only grower in Gigondas to stock 10 vintages of Gigondas for sale. He is also the only grower to produce Gigondas from Grenache and Cinsault. No Syrah or Mourvèdre are employed. His wines, called Clos de Joncuas after his 25-acre vineyard, are robust, sound, sturdy, and heady, lacking distinction, but concentrated and chunky.

Bernaud Chauvet—Chauvet, a cold, impersonal individual who seems to discourage visitors, produces Gigondas from his 34-acre estate called the Domaine du Grapillon d'Or. His wines have more charm, warmth, and personality than he does. In fact, he makes a big Gigondas—well colored, spicy, full-bodied but with fruit and character. The 1983 and 1985 are particular successes here.

Robert Cuillerat—With 20 acres of very old Grenache vines planted on the hillside, the youthful, bearded Robert Cuillerat seems to be gaining a reputation as one of the better young growers in Gigondas. His wines, which are at least 85% Grenache, are very intense and powerful. The 1985 is excellent, the 1984 better than the dull 1983.

A. Faravel—Both 1983 and 1984, the only vintages I have tasted of Faravel's Gigondas, called Domaine la Bouissière, have been very disappointing.

Jean Gorecki—Gorecki's Gigondas, called Mas des Collines after his 50-acre vineyard, has a very good reputation. The 1982 and 1983 are intense, old-style wines that lack finesse but offer robustness and power. Both wines seem to require some cellaring.

André Gras—Gras produces sound, beefy, well-colored Gigondas from his estate called Domaine Santa Duc. It is very reasonably priced and considering the good wines he made in 1983, 1984, and 1985, merits more recognition.

Pierre Lambert—Lambert and another man, Roland Gaudin, manage the Domaine de la Mavette, a 15-acre estate that produces very good, fresh, modern-styled Gigondas Rosé, and an equally fresh, vibrant, fruity Gigondas. These are commercial, straightforward wines, but are attractive and well made. The 1983, 1984, and 1985 are all quite nice. I give an edge to the 1985. They require drinking within 3–5 years of the vintage.

Gabriel Meffre—The largest négociant in the southern Rhône, Meffre is also a very important vineyard holder, owning 2,340 acres of which 135 acres represent his Gigondas estate, Château Raspail. He also has another 140 acres in Gigondas and produces two wines called Domaines des Bosquets and La Chapelle. All three of these Gigondas wines are at best mediocre as well as devoid of character. Lighter in color than what one should expect, they also have cooked bouquets that suggest pasteurization to this taster. Despite the fact that they are not unfairly priced, they do not represent an especially good value (as the wines of Gigondas often do).

Pierre Quiot—Quiot's estate, the Domaine Pradets, produces very modern-styled, impeccably clean, very fruity, supple wines with excellent color. The 1984 is among the best wines of that year; the 1985 is gloriously fruity. These are Gigondas to drink within their first 4–5 years.

CHÂTEAUNEUF-DU-PAPE

The Bordeaux of the Rhône

CHÂTEAUNEUF-DU-PAPE AT A GLANCE

Type of wine produced:	Red: 97%; white: 3%
Grape varieties planted:	Thirteen (actually 14 if the white clone of Grenache is counted) varieties are permitted; for red wines, Grenache, Syrah, Mourvèdre, Cinsault, Muscardin, Counoise, Vaccarèse, and Terret Noir; for white wines, Grenache Blanc, Clairette, Bourboulenc, Roussanne, Picpoul, and Picardin
Acres currently under vine:	7,900

Quality level:	Red wine: at the estate-bottled level, very good to exceptional; at the négociant level, poor to very good
	White wine: mediocre to exceptional
Aging potential:	Red wine: 5–20 years
	White wine: 1–3 years
General characteristics:	Red wine: from full-bodied, generous, rich, round, alcoholic, and long-lived to soft, fruity, and reminiscent of Beaujolais; there is a multitude of styles
	White wine: floral, fruity, straightforward and fresh if drunk within 2 years of the vintage
Greatest recent vintages:	1985, 1981, 1979, 1978, 1970, 1967
Price range:	$10–$25

The name Châteauneuf-du-Pape is certainly as well known in the global wine market as France's three most glamorous viticultural regions, Bordeaux, Burgundy, and Champagne. However, little is really known about the leading estates, called both domaines and châteaux. There are at least fifty major estates in Châteauneuf-du-Pape, yet none of them is studied as meticulously or has been written about as often as the sixty-three châteaux of Bordeaux's famous 1855 classification of the wines of the Médoc. In addition, there has never been an attempt to classify the quality of the Châteauneuf-du-Pape estates. Given the multitude of styles of wine produced here, buying a Châteauneuf-du-Pape can be confusing and fraught with uncertainty about what type of wine one is getting. Before the individual estates and their wines are examined, there are several significant things one should first know about Châteauneuf-du-Pape.

It is one of France's most privileged appellations. First of all, Châteauneuf rarely suffers from the problems that can spell doom for other French wine regions. Constant sunshine, dry heat, and strong winds virtually guarantee that rot and pourriture, so dreaded in Burgundy, Bordeaux, and elsewhere in France, are rarely a problem. The legal limitation that only 35 hectoliters per hectare can be produced ensures a decent concentration of flavor and discourages the type of overproduction one now sees with increasing regularity in Bordeaux and Burgundy, where 60 to 80 hectoliters a hectare at many top properties was attained in vintages such as 1986 and 1985. Finally, no machine harvesters (which can only operate on the thin, small trunks of young vines) are permitted at Châteauneuf-du-Pape, so vines are encouraged to grow old and yield richer and more concentrated juice.

Châteauneuf-du-Pape has the potential to consistently produce some of the finest and longest-lived red wines in the world, but sadly not enough of the domaines or châteaux of this appellation desire to achieve something special. In spite of the appellation's enormous potential, there are numerous problems to overcome. Despite a recent trend to diminish the percentage of the ubiquitous Grenache grape in their wines, this grape is still too heavily represented in the blend of many Châteauneuf-du-Papes. In addition, the increasing trend to satisfy consumer demand (primarily in the Benelux countries, Switzerland, and Germany) with fat, fruity, precocious wines has caused some estates to produce less distinctive wines, bottling them very quickly, and, in essence, giving the consumer nothing more than a glamorous and more expensive rendition of a Côtes du Rhône. Châteauneuf-du-Pape, with its fabulous climate, high percentage of old vines, and impressive number of estates, could as an appellation, if it wanted, produce as high quality wines as the finest Bordeaux Crus Classés or Grand Cru burgundies. But as of today, no more than several dozen estates seem to have such high aspirations. However, those that do achieve something special produce remarkably long-lived, multidimensional wines that offer splendid value. Châteauneuf-du-Pape has the potential to become the Bordeaux of the Rhône—but will its producers enable this to happen?

Châteauneuf-du-Pape produces in excess of one million cases of wine from a vast area covering 7,900 acres. The entire appellation sits on the left bank of the Rhône River. The appellation begins less than twelve miles north of the hallowed, historic walled city of Avignon. It ends about eight miles further north, at the bustling, ancient village of Orange. In between is a slightly hilly region blanketed with large, smooth, cream-colored stones and a gently rising plateau just behind the actual village of Châteauneuf-du-Pape. All of the domaines are sprinkled about this area and are well marked by road signs. Additionally, most domaines maintain small tasting booths in the tiny village of Châteauneuf-du-Pape. Given the strength of this heady wine, and the enormous number of tourists that descend on the village, I have always considered driving in these parts among the most risky in France.

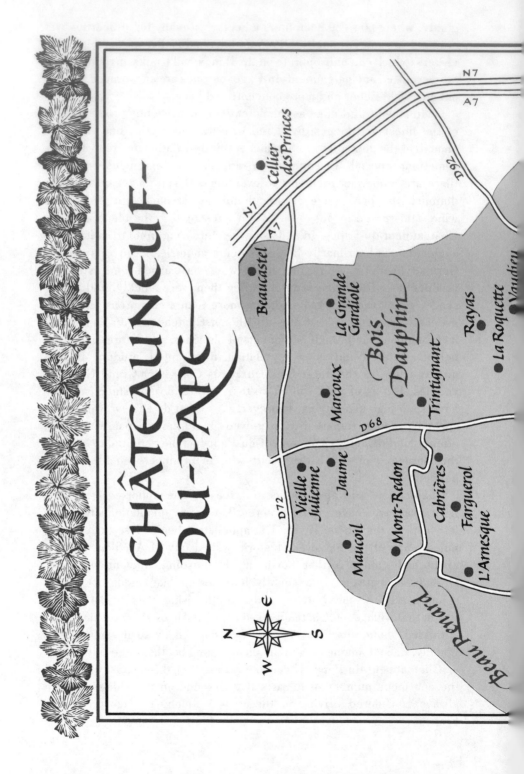

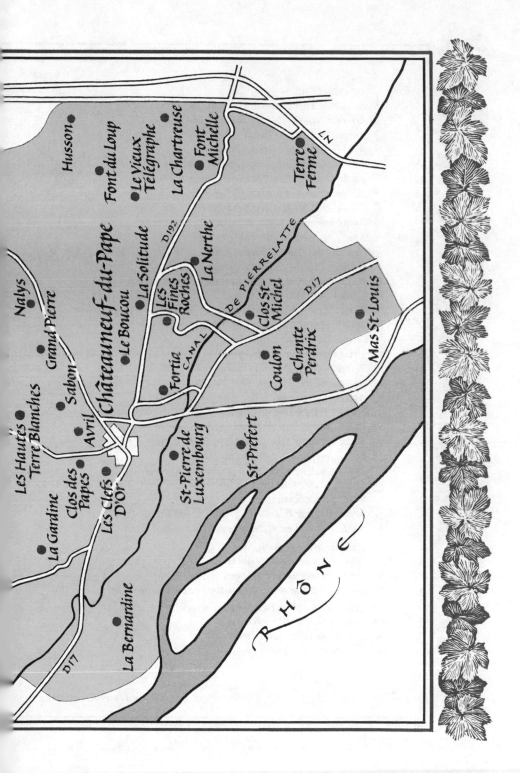

Husson

Font du Loup

Le Vieux Télégraphe

La Chartreuse

Font Michelle

Terre Ferme

N7

Nalys

Grand Pierre

Sabon

Châteauneuf-du-Pape

La Solitude

D192

La Nerthe

Les Fines Roches

DE PIERRELATTE

D17

Mas St-Louis

Clos St-Michel

Le Boucou

Les Hautes
Terre Blanches

Avril

Fortia

CANAL

Coulon

Chante Perdrix

La Gardine

Clos des Papes

Les Clefs D'or

St-Pierre de Luxembourg

St-Préfert

La Bernardine

D17

R H Ô N E

PRODUCERS

1. Amouroux Léonce - Clos de l'Oratoire des Papes
2. Armenier/G.A.E.C. Philippe & Elie - Dne de Marcoux
3. Arnaud Louis & Fils - Dne de Cabrières
4. Avril Paul & Régis - Clos des Papes
5. Baron LeRoy de Boiseaumarié Henri - Château Fortia
6. Barrot Lucien & Fils - Dne Lucien Barrot & Fils
7. Boiron Maurice - Bosquets des Papes
8. Bouachon P. & Fils - Caves Saint Pierre
9. Brotte Jean-Pierre - Père Anselme
    Musée des Vieux Outils de Vignerons
10. Coulon Paul - Dne de Beaurenard
11. Diffonty Félicien - Cuvée du Vatican
12. Diffonty Rémy & Fils - Dne du Haut des Terres Blanches
13. Durieu Paul - Dne Paul Durieu
14. Geniest Louis - Mas Saint Louis
15. Jean Paul Mme Vve - Dne Jean Trintignant
16. Jeune Elie - Dne de Grand Tinel
17. Laget Pierre - Dne de l'Arnesque
18. Brunier Henri - Dne de la Roquette
19. Marchand Jean - Dne de Bois Dauphin
20. Mestre Jean-Claude - Dne Jean-Claude Mestre
21. Nicolet Frères - Dne de Chante Perdrix
22. Quiot Jérome - Dne du Vieux Lazaret
23. Riche Claude & Fils - G.A.E.C. Dne Riche Claude & Fils
24. Sabon Joseph - G.A.E.C. Du Clos Mont Olivet
    Les Fils de Joseph Sabon
25. Sabon Nöel & Fils - G.A.E.C. Sabon/Favier
    Dne Chante Cigale
26. Sabon Roger & Fils - G.A.E.C. Roger Sabon & Fils - Les Olivet
27. S.C.E.A. Domaine des Sénéchaux/Raynaud Pierre

UNION DE VIGNERONS

X Cave de la Cuvée des Hospices
Y Caves Reflets - Union de Vignerons
Z Caveau Prestige & Tradition - Union de Vignerons

HOTEL/RESTAURANTS (HR/R)

HR La Mère Germaine - 6 Rooms
R La Mule du Pape - Rue République
R Le Pistou - Rue J. Ducos

H·L·M· Bois de

21
X

Aven
D17
to SORGUES-AVIGNON
8 4

to
Fines Roches
Hostellerie Château Fines Roches (HR)

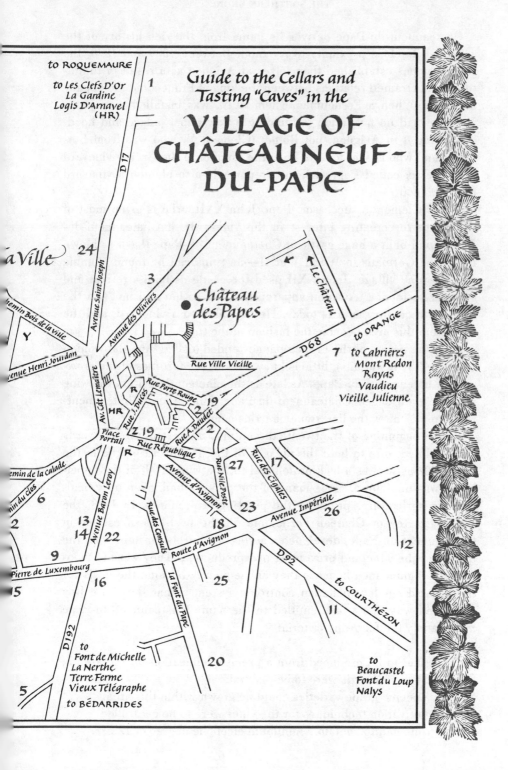

Guide to the Cellars and
Tasting "Caves" in the

VILLAGE OF
CHÂTEAUNEUF-
DU-PAPE

to ROQUEMAURE

to Les Clefs D'Or
La Gardine
Logis D'Arnavel
(HR)

1

D 17

la Ville

24

3

Avenue Saint-Joseph

Avenue des Oliviers

Chemin Bois de la Ville

Y

Avenue Henri Jourdan

Château
des Papes

Le Château

to ORANGE

D 68

7 to Cabrières
Mont Redon
Rayas
Vaudieu
Vieille Julienne

Rue Ville Vieille

R

Rue Porte Rouge

Av. Cdt Lemaître

HR

Rue J. Ducos

19

Rue A. Daudet

2

19

Z

Place
Portail

Rue République

2

R

Chemin de la calade

Chemin du clos

6

2

13
14

22

Avenue Baron Leroy

Rue des Consuls

Avenue d'Avignon

Rue Nte Poste

27

Rue des Cigales

17

23

Avenue Impériale

26

12

18

Route d'Avignon

D 92

to COURTHÉZON

9

Pierre de Luxembourg

15

16

La Font du Pape

25

11

D 192

to
Font de Michelle
La Nerthe
Terre Ferme
Vieux Télégraphe

20

to
Beaucastel
Font du Loup
Nalys

to BÉDARRIDES

5

Châteauneuf-du-Pape derives its name from the rich history of the area and its close proximity to Avignon. Between 1309 and 1378, the Roman popes established themselves at Avignon as a result of tumultuous and strained relations between the king of France and the papacy of Rome. When a Frenchman, Clement V, was installed as pope in 1309, he had no hesitation in building a new papal palace and headquartering it in Avignon, not Rome. (Clement V, who was from Bordeaux and who is said to have been the founder of the Graves vineyard in Bordeaux called Pape-Clément, reportedly also planted a vineyard near Avignon.)

It was Clement's successor, Pope John XXII, who is given most of the credit for creating interest in the vineyards of Châteauneuf-du-Pape. John built a huge castle at Châteauneuf-du-Pape that was blown up by the Germans in World War II—its ruins can be found looming over the tiny village. John XXII used the castle as both a retreat and summer residence, Avignon apparently being as hot and noisy in the fourteenth century as it is today. He also planted a vineyard, and the wine from this area became the fashion of the times.

After the period of the French papacy ended (called "the Babylonian captivity" by historians), little is known about the fortunes of the growers at Châteauneuf-du-Pape. As late as the nineteenth century the wine was not even called Châteauneuf-du-Pape, but rather "Châteauneuf-Calcernier," after the limestone quarries nearby.

By the beginning of the twentieth century, interest in the vineyards had declined, due to both the ravages of the phylloxera plague in the late 1800s as well as a lack of demand for the wine. Half of the appellation was unplanted, since many of the growers had given up viticulture for agriculture, primarily the planting of orchards. In 1923, the Baron Le Roy of Château Fortia, one of the best-known estates in Châteauneuf-du-Pape, developed a series of controls for improving the quality of the wine and preventing overproduction. They were of monumental significance because they subsequently became the basis for the entire French appellation contrôlée system. What Baron Le Roy stipulated was that wines entitled to the name Châteauneuf-du-Pape must satisfy the following criteria:

1. They had to be produced from a precise delineation for the area in which the vineyards were to be planted.
2. Only specific grape varieties could be grown within this area.
3. The cultivation techniques for the vines were to be controlled.
4. The wine had to contain a minimum alcoholic degree of 12.5%.

5. At harvest time, 5% of the crop had to be discarded, regardless of quality—a sort of mandatory selection process.
6. No rosé wine could be made, and all wines were to be submitted to a tasting panel before they were allowed to bear the name Châteauneuf-du-Pape.

Whether it was these laws or just increased awareness and interest in the generous and sumptuous joys that the wines of Châteauneuf-du-Pape can provide, the acreage under vine has doubled in the last 50 years to the point where the entire appellation is completely under vine. In addition, over 70% of the wine is now exported, and the top domaines have so much interest in their products that allocation systems have been set up. Yet a great deal of bad Châteauneuf-du-Pape is still produced. Most of it seems confined to several industrial-sized négociants in the dreary town of Sorgues that turn out enormous quantities of excessively alcoholic, unbalanced wines that are a travesty when compared to the majestic wines made by the committed owners at the top estates. As tragic as this is, it appears that a few gigantic producers of Châteauneuf-du-Pape have prejudiced many about Châteauneuf-du-Pape.

The best wines of Châteauneuf-du-Pape achieve their complexity and generosity from various blends of the 13 different grape varieties permitted. The type of soil varies, but not nearly to the extent that it does in Bordeaux or Burgundy. The large stones that blanket this appellation are, at their best or worst (depending on your point of view), in the north and northwest sectors of the appellation. A visit to the vineyards of Mont-Redon or Les Cabrières will offer a spectacular vista of vineyards where not a speck of soil is to be seen, just layers of round rocks and stones. This area north of the town is the plateau of Châteauneuf-du-Pape, and it is said that the finest vineyards are in this region. South and east of the village in the direction of Avignon, the plateau drops off and the density of stones and rocks is less severe. The wines from these lighter soils tend to be slightly lower in alcohol. In the north and northeasterly sector, in the direction of Courthézon and Bédarrides respectively, there is more clay and sand in the subsoil below the rocky surface. Throughout all of these sectors, one cannot help but notice the very old average age of the vines, and the fact that they are pruned very low to the ground. The reason for this severe pruning is the fierce *mistral* wind that blows (usually 25–45 m.p.h.) in this area on an average of 300 days a year. There are top estates in all of these sectors.

In reality, what probably influences the style of wine produced in

Châteauneuf-du-Pape as much as the soil and choice of grape varieties is the type of vinification employed by the growers. There are three basic approaches to vinification in Châteauneuf-du-Pape. In brief, they are as follows.

1. *The classic vinification*—This type of vinification produces very tannic, densely colored, robust wines. All of the grapes are crushed, not destemmed, assembled in the fermentation tanks, fermented at hot temperatures, then given a long, three-week maceration period. Famous estates that generally practice this type of vinification include Clos des Papes, Les Clefs d'Or, Beaucastel, Clos du Mont Olivet.

2. *The vinification by carbonic maceration*—This type of vinification tends to produce fruity, jammy, very soft wines that drink well young but rarely last. It is a method of vinification used in Beaujolais wherein the grapes are not crushed but put in the fermentation tanks whole; the tanks are then flooded with carbonic gas. Well-known domaines that utilize this form of vinification include Nalys and Domaine de la Solitude.

3. *The modern or modified whole-berry vinification*—Today, this is far and away the prevailing philosophy of vinification used in Châteauneuf-du-Pape: about 50% of the whole grapes (usually the Grenache and Cinsault) are vinified uncrushed and sometimes by the carbonic maceration method. The other 50% (the remaining Grenache, but usually Syrah and Mourvèdre) are crushed, not destemmed, and vinified in the classic manner. There are many variations on this approach—sometimes the Syrah is given the carbonic maceration and all of the Grenache is traditionally vinified. Frequently the percentage of grapes vinified whole or crushed, as well as destemmed, will vary widely. The advantage of this vinification is that the fruit and precocious appeal of the whole berry fermentation—perhaps complemented by a few lots being given a carbonic maceration method—is preserved, but the wines are capable of aging and developing for up to 10–12 years because at least 50% of the grapes are crushed and vinified classically. Mont-Redon, Chante-Perdrix, Chante-Cigale, La Gardine, Vieux Télégraphe and Fines-Roches are well-known practitioners of this style of vinification, which is the most popular approach to making Châteauneuf-du-Pape. However, there are significant variations on this approach since many properties follow the whole-berry (*raisin entier*) method of vinification but will not use carbonic gas as part of this process.

Keeping in mind that there are numerous variations to these vinifications, the result of these different vinification philosophies is that the
wines produced generally present the taster with very different sets of
aromas and flavors.

Wines vinified in the carbonic maceration (or modern) method are
distinguished by their aromas of ripe berry fruit—blackcurrants, raspberries, and blackberries. Those vinified in the classic manner often
have the berry fruit character as well, but added to that are aromas of
saddle leather, fennel, licorice, black truffles, irises, pepper, nutmeg,
and smoked meats.

Châteauneuf-du-Pape is a rich, full-bodied wine that drinks well
young but can easily age for one to two decades. It does not have a reputation for great longevity, but the wines of the top producers will certainly keep. In the course of the research and tastings for this book I have
drunk great old Châteauneuf-du-Papes, such as the 1949, 1955, and 1961
Mont-Redon; 1954, 1962, 1964, 1966, and 1967 Beaucastel; 1961, 1962,
and 1964 Rayas; 1961, 1962, 1967, and 1969 Paul Jaboulet Les Cèdres.
All had great depth of fruit and vitality and offered as much complexity and pleasure as any great Bordeaux or burgundy I have ever
consumed. The price for a top Châteauneuf-du-Pape seems modest given
the degree of majesty the wine can provide when fully mature.

While no rosé can be made in Châteauneuf-du-Pape unless it is
called Côtes du Rhône, a tiny quantity of white wine (about 3% of the
total production) is made. With the single exception of that made by
Beaucastel, the white Châteauneuf-du-Pape is a wine to drink within
its first two or three years of life since it does not age well. It can, in
the hands of producers such as Nalys, Vieux Télégraphe, Clefs d'Or,
Font de Michelle, and several other domaines, offer delicious drinking,
but it can also be dull and neutral tasting.

According to the growers' association, only 25% of the thirteen million bottles produced in a given vintage are estate-bottled wines. All
the estate-bottled Châteauneuf-du-Papes are distinguished by their
own bottle, which is burgundy-shaped. However, below the neck it has
an embossed papal coat of arms with the words "Châteauneuf-du-
Pape" surrounding it. This bottle, instituted by the growers in 1939 just
before the Second World War, is a good guarantee of authenticity. The
only two estates not to use this bottle are the great Château Rayas run
by the eccentric and reclusive Jacques Reynaud, and Château La Gardine, who prefer to use their own specially designed bottle.

There is no cooperative in Châteauneuf-du-Pape, somewhat unusual
given the number of growers and enormous amount of wine produced

there. There are two growers' associations that one should know about because of the high quality of the wines produced by their members. One, founded in 1954, is called Les Reflets and its best members are such estates as Les Cailloux, Chante-Perdrix, Clos du Mont-Olivet, and Cuvée du Belvedere. The other is Prestige et Tradition, and includes excellent estates such as Cuvée du Tastevin, Bosquet des Papes, Vieux Donjon, and Domaine de la Solitude. Both of these groups were formed to give them the advantage of marketing their wines and being able to pool their resources to purchase bottles and a modern bottling facility. Each grower's wine is distinctly different from the others, and many of these wines are among the very best in Châteauneuf-du-Pape.

Fortunately for the consumer, the best estates of Châteauneuf-du-Pape are more widely represented in the export markets than ever before. Given their quality, value, and diversity of style, there is a considerable amount of exceptionally interesting wine at modest prices just for the asking. It is beyond question that the top estate-bottled Châteauneuf-du-Papes compete with the finest burgundies and Bordeaux, yet cost significantly less.

RECENT VINTAGES

1986—Over 90% of the grapes were harvested under textbook conditions. For that reason, 1986 should be a good, sometimes exceptional vintage, although those who had not harvested by October
12 were inundated with rain that fell for the subsequent two
weeks. The wines are well colored, less opulent than the 1985s,
and the tannins are harder. The size of the crop was much
smaller than in 1985. Optimum maturity: 1992–2000.

1985—The potential of the wine from some estates looked excellent,
possibly exceptional. However, there is a wide range in quality
due to the tremendous heat and drought that put considerable
stress on both the vines and winemakers. At best, the wines will
be quite special, densely colored, quite full-bodied, very ripe,
rich, and loaded with flavor, though low in acidity. At worst, the
wines will be good, but loosely knit and flabby. This should turn
out to be quite an exciting year, but also uneven due to the heat
and drought. Optimum maturity: 1988–1998.

1984—France's most successful viticultural region in this difficult year
was Châteauneuf-du-Pape. The wines are surprisingly good,
firmly structured, well colored, and while more austere than
usual, they are not ungenerous. Prices are quite reasonable and

the 1984s should age well for the next 5–8 years. For many of the wines, it is a much better vintage than 1983, a year rated much more highly. Optimum maturity: 1988–1994.

1983—I had initially thought this to be a top vintage since my judgment was colored by the great success had by Beaucastel, Vieux Télégraphe, Bosquet des Papes, Fortia, and several other producers. However, after tasting virtually all the wines produced, I was surprised to see that it was not a consistent vintage. While some wines are quite outstanding, others seem to be lacking color and their fruit seems to be drying out at an accelerated pace. It is certainly a very good vintage with some great wines produced, but it is also irregular, no doubt due to the problems with both the flowering and ripening of the Grenache grape. It is a tricky vintage for which to predict maturity. Optimum maturity: now–2000.

1982—Very soft, very alcoholic, somewhat fragile wines were produced in 1982. The yield was enormous and many wines lack color and concentration. The good examples are perfect for drinking now, although the overripening that took place this year has left them with a tremendous alcoholic kick of 14.5% and higher (regardless of what the label says). Optimum maturity: now–1990.

1981—I initially thought 1983 was better than 1981. Now, having had the opportunity to taste across the entire appellation, I have no doubt that 1981 is a superior year. The wines are powerful, rich, big, ripe, complex wines with excellent balance. The classic examples of this vintage will last for another 10–15 years, although most of the 1981 Châteauneuf-du-Papes should be drunk between 1986 and 1995. Overall, this vintage has more consistency than 1983. Optimum maturity: now–2001.

1980—A rather overlooked vintage, Châteauneuf-du-Pape produced France's best wines in this year. All the 1980s are fully mature (even the stubbornly slow evolving Beaucastel) and are among the most flattering wines of this appellation for current drinking. Not big wines, they are rather elegant, fruity, supple wines that should be drunk over the next 2–3 years.

1979—An underrated vintage, 1979, following in the footsteps of the great 1978 vintage, seemed at first less exciting. However, the wines have aged very well and are now in the full bloom of maturity. Well-colored, ripe, richly fruity wines were produced that will, at the top levels, continue to hold for 4 to as long as

10–15 years in the cases of Beaucastel, Rayas, Cuvée du Taste-vin, and Vieux Télégraphe. Optimum maturity: now–2000.

1978—Along with 1961 and 1967, this is the greatest vintage for Châteauneuf-du-Pape in the last 25 years. Unfortunately, there has been no vintage since 1978 that equals the overall success of so many wines. The myth that Châteauneuf-du-Pape ages quickly is dispelled by a vintage such as this. At 9 years of age, the top wines of 1978 are just beginning to open up and display their remarkable richness, power, and symmetry. Great classic wines were produced by Vieux Télégraphe, Rayas, Beaucastel, Clos des Papes, Bosquet des Papes, Fortia, Les Cailloux, La Nerthe, Chante-Perdrix, Grand Tinel, Marcoux, Les Clefs d'Or, and Mont-Olivet; they will last and in most cases improve for another decade. It is an extraordinary vintage. Optimum maturity: now–2005.

1977—What was a terrible year for most of France turned out to be an adequate year in Châteauneuf-du-Pape. The wines have matured nicely, and many have even dropped their annoyingly high acidity and green character. Drink them over the next 4–6 years. Vieux Télégraphe is an especially appealing wine in this vintage.

1976—I have never agreed with those who have held this vintage in high regard. The wines have from the beginning shown a toughness and lack of charm, combined with a lack of color. Rain during the harvest apparently was much more deleterious than many believed. There are, however, some successes, Fortia, Grand Tinel, Clos du Mont-Olivet, but overall this is a mediocre year. Optimum maturity: now–1992.

OLDER VINTAGES

While 1975 is quite poor, 1974 and 1973 were good years that produced amiable wines that should now be drunk up. The 1972s are still quite good. They tend to be quite robust, powerful, and alcoholic. The 1971s matured quickly and were quite delicious, but suffered because of the accolades bestowed on the 1970s (an excellent vintage across-the-board). The 1970s are drinking beautifully today, but will not get any better. In the sixties, there were many top vintages in Châteauneuf-du-Pape. The finest two years were 1961 and 1967, and well-preserved examples from these vintages exhibit the majestic richness and balance Châteauneuf-du-Pape can attain. Almost as good were years such as 1964, 1966, and 1962. Well-cellared examples of classically made Châteauneuf-du-Pape can provide memorable drinking today.

A Personal Rating of the Producers of Châteauneuf-du-Pape —Red Wine

*****(OUTSTANDING PRODUCERS)

Beaucastel (Perrin)

Clos des Papes (Avril)

Fortia (Baron Le Roy)

Rayas (Reynaud)

Vieux Télégraphe (Brunier)

****(EXCELLENT PRODUCERS)

Henri Bonneau (H. Bonneau)

Bosquet des Papes (M. Boiron)

Les Cailloux (Brunel)

Chante-Perdrix (Nicolet)

Les Clefs d'Or (Deydier)

Clos du Mont-Olivet (Sabon)

Cuvée du Belvedere (Girard)

Cuvée du Tastevin (Barrot)

Cuvée du Vatican (Diffonty)

Durieu (Durieu)

Font du Loup (Melia)

Grand Tinel (Jeune)

Marcoux (Armenier)

Mont-Redon (Fabre/Abeille)

La Nerthe (Société Civile)

Sénéchaux (Raynaud)

Vieux Donjon (Michel)

***(GOOD PRODUCERS)

Beaurenard (Coulon)

La Bernadine (Chapoutier)

Domaine de Cabrières (Arnaud)

Les Cèdres (P. Jaboulet)

Chante-Cigale (Favier-Sabon)

Clos St.-Jean (G. Maurel)

Delas Frères (Delas)

Fines-Roches (Mousset)

Font de Michelle (Gonnet)

La Gardine (Brunel)

Guigal (Guigal)

Haut des Terres Blanches (Diffonty)

Maucoil (P. Quiot)

Nalys (DuFays)

Père Anselme (Brotte)

Père Caboche (Boisson)

Relagnes (Boiron)

R. Sabon (Sabon)

La Solitude (Lancon)

Terre Ferme (Societé Civile)

Jean Trintignant

Vaudieu (Meffre)

Vieille Julienne (Daumen)

Vieux Lazaret (J. Quiot)

A Personal Rating of the Producers of Châteauneuf-du-Pape —White Wine

*****(OUTSTANDING PRODUCERS)

Beaucastel (Perrin)

Nalys (DuFays)

Vieux Télégraphe (Brunier)

Beaurenard (Coulon)	Font de Michelle (Gonnet)
Les Cailloux (Brunel)	La Gardine (Brunel)
Les Clefs d'Or (Deydier)	Marcoux (Armenier)
Font du Loup (Melia)	La Nerthe (Société Civile)

CHÂTEAU BEAUCASTEL (PERRIN)*****

The fact that Beaucastel produces the longest-lived red wine of the southern Rhône is irrefutable. However, this estate also produces one of the Rhône Valley's greatest and most distinctive wines. The wine is one of the few made by totally organic methods. No chemicals are used in the vast 272-acre vineyard located in the northernmost sector of Châteauneuf-du-Pape near the town of Courthézon. Over 500 tons of manure are dumped on these vineyards whose vines, through a meticulously planned rotational replanting formula, maintain an average age of 50 years. The late Jacques Perrin, considered by many to be one of the Rhône Valley's most brilliant and philosophical winemakers, believed adamantly in three principles: (1) a wine must be made naturally, (2) the percentage of Mourvèdre in the blend must be significant, and (3) the wine's character and intrinsic qualities could not be compromised by concessions to modern technology. Jacques Perrin died in 1978, but his two sons, François and Jean-Pierre, were well indoctrinated with their father's beliefs, and have not only carried on his methodology, but have further increased the quality of Beaucastel.

The vineyards of Beaucastel are one of three major estates to have all 13 permitted varieties planted. The others are Mont-Redon and Domaine Nalys. For their red wines, Beaucastel is marked by the high percentage of Mourvèdre. The preferred blend here is 30% Grenache, 30% Mourvèdre, 10% Syrah, 5% Cinsault, and the rest Counoise, Muscardin, and Vaccarèse. They are augmenting the percentage of Mourvèdre and Counoise in their new plantings. For their white wine, they remain unique as well, using an unusually high percentage of 80% Roussanne, and the rest Bourboulenc, Clairette, and Grenache. No other estate in this appellation uses this much Mourvèdre for its red or Roussanne for its white.

The results are stunning. The red wine is usually a black/ruby or purple color, loaded with layers of fruit, tannin, and a multitude of fascinating scents and aromas. Except in lightweight vintages such as 1973, 1980, and 1984, it is rarely a flattering or enjoyable wine to drink young, but like a great thoroughbred, age, usually a minimum of six to ten years, brings forth its majestic richness and compelling array of aromas. Most top vintages of Beaucastel improve and last in the bottle for a minimum of 20 years. Much of this has to do with the fact that the high percentage of grapes such as Mourvèdre, Syrah, and Counoise gives the wine a certain protection from oxidation. Unique at Beaucastel is a controversial *"vinification à chaud."* It is a process of heating the incoming grapes to very high temperatures and then immediately cooling them down as they go into the fermentation tanks. The Perrins believe this process achieves two critical results: It halts any oxidation in the grapes and it extracts tremendous color and flavor from the skins of the grapes. Its critics call it a flash pasteurization. After the fermentation, the red wine of Beaucastel spends 18–22 months in huge 5,500-liter oak casks. It is fined only with the whites of eggs and never filtered unless it fails to fall brilliant naturally. François Perrin, a youthful-looking, trim, very serious individual, experimented with filtration in one vintage and was shocked at the effect it had on the wine's bouquet and richness. He realizes fully that an unfiltered wine is alive, and if abused by hot storage will go bad very quickly. A filtered wine is more stable, but he says he prefers to put the essence of what his vineyards can produce into the bottle and hope that consumers will be intelligent enough to treat the wine as a fragile, evolving, living thing. Beaucastel, after only two or three years in the bottle, will throw a heavy sediment, making decantation absolutely essential.

To make wine in the manner that Beaucastel does requires a great effort. There are only a handful of growers who are as committed to making quality wine and preserving the tradition of natural wine as François and Jean-Pierre Perrin. In 1980 they constructed a new underground cellar that allows them to bottle the entire crop at the very same time. Previously, Beaucastel was bottled as it was sold. Since this estate produces up to 25,000 cases of wine, some vintages remained in cask four or five years after the initial bottling. This procedure, which is still a common practice at many estates in Châteauneuf-du-Pape, led to severe bottle variation. The Perrins realized this and since 1980 do only one *mise en bouteille*.

The white wine produced at Beaucastel amounts to only about 1,000 cases per year. It is the only white Châteauneuf-du-Pape that can age well; it can last and evolve in the bottle for 10–15 years, whereas the other white wines must be drunk within their first two or three years of life. Curiously, it drinks well young for four or five years, then closes up and seems to have nothing to it for three to five years, but then bursts forth with smoky, buttery, hazelnut aromas and tremendous fruit. The Perrins age 15% of the white wine in new oak barrels for several months and then blend it back with the remaining 85%.

Beaucastel represents more than just a great wine from Châteauneuf-du-Pape. François and Jean-Pierre Perrin, like Gérard Chave in Hermitage, Marcel Guigal in Côte Rôtie, and E. Durrbach in the Coteaux Baux, are the consummate craftsmen of their profession, committed to preserving the tradition and grandeur of naturally made, expressive wine without any concession to the commercial wine world's demand for polished, ready to drink, zealously filtered wines incapable of any evolution and lacking the character of their place of origin.

VINTAGES

1985—*Beaucastel (white)*—Somewhat reminiscent of the 1982, this
· full-bodied, rich wine has scents of nuts and pineapples, is very
90 concentrated, extremely long, and should keep for at least a
decade. Anticipated maturity: 1990–2000. Last tasted 1/87.

1985—*Beaucastel (red)*—The Perrins believe this wine is too soft to be
· a classic Beaucastel. It is more open and accessible, but very
91 opaque ruby/black in color. It has an exciting melange of flavors,
from blackberry to chestnuts. Extremely full-bodied, chewy,
dense, opulent and rich, this wine will drink well young but also
keep. Anticipated maturity: 1989–2001. Last tasted 6/87.

1984—*Beaucastel (white)*—Much lighter in style than normal, the 1984
· has a scent of herbs, wet stones, and fruit. On the palate, it is
84 medium-bodied, crisp, fresh, and ready to drink. It will keep for
4–6 years. Last tasted 6/86.

1984—*Beaucastel (red)*—This wine has turned out very well. Deep in
· color, although by standards here it is not opaque. A rich, fra-
87 grant bouquet of spring flowers and broad cherry fruit is intense.
Full-bodied, surprisingly concentrated with some tannin to lose,
this is an elegantly wrought Beaucastel. Anticipated maturity:
1988–1995. Last tasted 1/87.

1983—*Beaucastel (red)*—Only 12,000 cases, compared to the normal
· 24,000 cases, of wine were made at Beaucastel in 1983. Jean-
93 Pierre Perrin says this is the finest Beaucastel since 1978. His
younger brother, François, prefers the 1981. The 1983 is a great
wine with a huge aroma of crushed raspberries, leather, and
truffles. Enormously concentrated and tannic, it has perfect balance and great length. Anticipated maturity: 1990–2005. Last
tasted 1/87.

1982—*Beaucastel (red)*—The Perrins sold 50% of their crop to négo-
·   ciants in 1982. From the cask, this wine seemed to lack equilib-
85   rium, but it has come together in the bottle. It is very alcoholic
      (14.5%), but heady, fat, soft, and ideal for drinking over the next
      5–6 years. Last tasted 1/87.

1981—*Beaucastel (red)*—This is a real blockbuster, very classic Beau-
·   castel. The complex bouquet of leather, truffles, cedarwood,
93   licorice, and blackberry fruit is superb. On the palate, the wine
      is very concentrated, quite powerful, dense, with layers of ex-
      tract and tannin. It might turn out to be the best Beaucastel
      since the 1970. Anticipated maturity: 1991–2010. Last tasted
      1/87.

1980—*Beaucastel (red)*—Now reaching full maturity, the 1980 Beau-
·   castel is not terribly concentrated or powerful, but has a soft,
85   fruity, well-developed character, good length, and no tannins or
      astringence in the finish. Drink over the next 3–5 years. Last
      tasted 10/86.

1979—*Beaucastel (red)*—This is an excellent Beaucastel, initially over-
·   shadowed by the 1978, but now showing more suppleness and
89   current appeal than the tannic 1978. Dense in color with a tarry,
      peppery, raspberry-scented, damp woodsy aroma (truffles?), this
      rich, full-bodied, multidimensional wine is a few years short of
      its plateau of maturity. Anticipated maturity: 1989–2005. Last
      tasted 10/86.

1978—*Beaucastel (red)*—The rating is based more on potential than
·   current appeal. This is an enormous wine that I have followed
94   closely from its days in cask. It appeared to be a monumental
      sort of wine in 1978–82, but has since gone into a tannic shell
      and seems dumb, and a decade away from maturity. It is ex-
      tremely concentrated, still ruby/purple in color, but so so tannic.
      Anticipated maturity: 1993–2020. Last tasted 1/87.

1976—*Beaucastel (red)*—The Perrins have never quite been as critical
·   of this wine as I have. I have consistently found it to be hard,
72   lacking fruit and charm, a little hollow, and for Beaucastel, light
      in color. I believe it has no future. Last tasted 6/85.

1973—*Beaucastel (red)*—This soft, fragrant, fruity wine drank ex-
·   tremely well in 1975–76, so well that I never dreamed it would
84   last. Now it shows a great deal of orange at the rim, but still has
      a good measure of soft, smoky fruit. Drink it up. Last tasted
      6/85.

1972—*Beaucastel (red)*—Aside from the few bad bottles I had of this
· wine, which I suspect came from bad storage, the 1972 is a
87 burly, alcoholic, heavyweight Châteauneuf with a rustic, robust
texture and aggressive aromas of smoked meats and game. Fully
mature, it requires an intense dish to absorb its extroverted
personality. Drink over the next 4–6 years. Last tasted 12/86.

1970—*Beaucastel (red)*—This was a fabulous year for Beaucastel. The
· wine is approaching full maturity with a huge bouquet of exotic
94 spices, fruitcake, coffee, and cedar. On the palate, it is impeccably balanced, very long, complex, and totally a joy and privilege to drink. Anticipated maturity: now–2000. Last tasted 2/87.

1967—*Beaucastel (red)*—This wine peaked several years ago and now
· seems to be on the decline. It is still immensely pleasing, with a
88 big, exotic, rich nose of toasty, smoky fruit, and soft, full-bodied,
deep flavors, but the alcohol is beginning to show up in the
finish. Drink it up. Last tasted 10/86.

1966—*Beaucastel (red)*—Not quite the powerhouse style of 1970 or
· 1981, the 1966 is rich yet elegant, and deftly balances brute force
92 with grace and charm. Absolutely delicious, sweet, lush, and
long, this wine requires drinking up. Last tasted 6/85.

1964—*Beaucastel (red)*—Fully mature, with an orange edge to its color,
· the 1964 is quite spicy with aromas of toast, oak, jammy fruit,
86 herbs, and grilled meat. On the palate, it is slightly out of balance, with the alcohol poking its head through. Drink it up. Last
tasted 1/87.

OLDER VINTAGES

One of the greatest vertical tastings I have ever attended was one of
red Beaucastel stretching from 1942 to 1978, and white Beaucastel from
1962 to 1978. The wines all came from the Perrin cellars. The white
wine seems to take on a buttery richness as it gets older, with the scent
of grilled or smoked nuts not unlike that of a white Hermitage. Some
great vintages for the white Châteauneuf-du-Pape made here are 1982,
1980, 1978, and 1971. The old red Châteauneuf-du-Papes seem capable
of going on and on. Both the 1942 and 1948 are much more alive than
the 1954. This is a wine for the serious collector to cellar, for it rarely
fails to provide great pleasure.

DOMAINE DE LA BERNADINE (CHAPOUTIER)***

The famous négociant Chapoutier, of Tain L'Hermitage, owns a 67-
acre estate in the sandy, lighter soils of the western sector of Château-

neuf-du-Pape. Chapoutier's Châteauneuf-du-Pape is made from a blend of 70% Grenache and 30% Syrah, Mourvèdre, Counoise, and Cinsault. The wine spends two to three years in oak casks and is offered commercially in three styles. Two of these styles are the vintage-dated "La Bernadine" and a blend of three vintages called the "Grande Cuvée La Bernadine." Once every decade, Chapoutier makes a luxury cuvée of Châteauneuf-du-Pape that is non-vintage and represents various blends from his best lots from different years. This luxury cuvée is called "Cuvée Barbe-Rac." He released a Barbe-Rac in 1954 and in 1986. The 1986 release consisted of 550 cases.

With the exception of this rare, luxury cuvée of Barbe-Rac, Chapoutier's Châteauneuf-du-Pape is a fruity, full-bodied, rather soft wine that is always agreeable but rarely exciting. It is usually at its best between four and eight years after the vintage.

VINTAGES

1985—*La Bernadine*—Relatively one-dimensional, the 1985 exhibits
·   plenty of ripe, chunky fruit, a soft, lush texture, low acidity, and
84   good near-term drinking potential. Anticipated maturity: now–1992. Last tasted 6/86.

1984—*La Bernadine*—Light in color, with a rather feeble, diluted
·   aroma, and thin, unsubstantial flavors, this wine is a disappoint-
74   ment. Anticipated maturity: now–1990. Last tasted 6/86.

1983—*La Bernadine*—Fruity, solid, and foursquare, this full-bodied
·   wine has good fruit, a spicy aroma, and good flavor depth. It
80   lacks excitement, but offers pleasant, uncritical drinking. Antic-ipated maturity: now–1990. Last tasted 6/86.

1982—*La Bernadine*—The 1982 has light to medium ruby color, with a
·   fruity yet simple nose, and soft, medium-bodied yet alcoholic
73   flavors. Somewhat out of balance, this wine should be drunk over the next 3–4 years. Last tasted 6/86.

N.V.—*Cuvée Barbe-Rac*—Compared to Chapoutier's somewhat dull
·   and commercial La Bernadine offerings, this special bottling is
88   a totally different animal. Very deeply colored with a huge bou-quet of smoky, jammy, licorice-and-cedar-scented fruit, this full-bodied wine has quite a large amount of power and depth, and should continue to drink well and evolve for 5–10 years. Last tasted 6/86.

DOMAINE DE BEAURENARD (PAUL COULON)***

Proprietor Paul Coulon is a busy man. He and his enthusiastic son, Daniel, run this 77-acre estate that produces just over 10,000 cases of wine. In addition, Paul Coulon has a large tasting room in the village of Châteauneuf-du-Pape, plus a wonderful wine museum in the Côtes du Rhônes village of Rasteau. Managing all of this keeps him on the run.

Beaurenard is clearly a wine made from the modern school of wine-making. Coulon ferments 50% of his grapes uncrushed via the carbonic maceration method. The other 50% are given a classical vinification and the resulting wines are then blended together. His wines are effusively fruity, soft, delicious, and quite ready to drink when released. The blend of grapes the Coulons use is 68% Grenache, 10% Syrah, 10% Mourvèdre, 10% Cinsault, and 2% Clairette. Coulon's wines do, however, age well, which has always amazed me given their undeniable fruity charm when young. He began to vinify his wine in the above manner in 1966; his 1967 is still in top form.

Coulon is very proud of his wines and is not shy about displaying the gold medals his Châteauneuf-du-Pape have won all over the walls of his office. He also adds, "Paul Bocuse is a great admirer of my wine." Coulon produces an excellent white Châteauneuf from a blend of 90% Clairette and 10% Bourboulenc. Unfortunately, its quality will never be widely known since the production rarely exceeds 300 cases.

Beaurenard is hardly ever an outstanding Châteauneuf-du-Pape, but it is consistently good, and more important, always quite fruity and delicious to drink.

VINTAGES

1985—*Beaurenard (white)*—A deliciously fruity, fragrant, amazingly
·   fresh and vibrant wine that goes down far too easily given its
86   13% alcohol. It should be drunk within the first two years of the
      vintage. Last tasted 6/86.

1985—*Beaurenard (red)*—Coulon believes this is his finest wine since
·   the 1967. I tend to agree. Very deep in color with an intense
87   bouquet of ripe berry aromas, this voluptuous, lush wine is
      bursting with fruit. Full-bodied and soft, it should drink well for
      the next 6–7 years. Last tasted 6/86.

1984—*Beaurenard (red)*—The 1984 lacks the explosive fruitiness of the
·   1985; however, it offers a straightforward, medium-bodied, soft
82   berry fruitiness. Drink it over the next 2–3 years. Last tasted
      6/86.

1983—*Beaurenard (red)*—A big, peppery, spicy, fruity nose is quite
·   appealing. Medium dark ruby with good body and depth, this
86   wine has more tannin in the finish than one normally finds from
      this estate. Anticipated maturity: now–1991. Last tasted 6/86.

1982—*Beaurenard (red)*—Very woody, the 1982 lacks delineation,
·   tastes too alcoholic, but shows a decent ripe berry fruitiness.
78   Drink up. Last tasted 6/86.

1981—*Beaurenard (red)*—A spicy, austere nose seems to lack fruit. On
·   the palate, the wine is full-bodied, a little austere, but very spicy
82   and flavorful, and has a soft finish. Drink it over the next 1–3
      years. Last tasted 4/85.

1980—*Beaurenard (red)*—The nose has a cardboard filter pad smell.
·   On the palate, there is the perception of ripe black cherries and
74   a burnt sugar quality. Something seems awry here. Last tasted
      6/86.

1978—*Beaurenard (red)*—This wine, which was so fruity, easy to drink,
·   and seemingly fully mature in 1980, has remained the same.
86   Richly fruity, plump, full-bodied, with very good color, it offers
      a round, generous mouthful of wine. Drink it over the next 5–6
      years. Last tasted 6/86.

1974—*Beaurenard (red)*—Coulon produced a top-rank 1974. A beauti-
·   ful bouquet of berry fruit and pepper is intense. In the mouth,
86   the wine is opulently fruity, full-bodied, very supple, and alto
      gether a joy to drink. Anticipated maturity: now–1991. Last
      tasted 6/86.

1967—*Beaurenard (red)*—I find it hard to accept that all of Beau-
·   renard's vintages could hold up this well. However, this was the
90   first vintage vinified in the modified carbonic maceration man-
      ner, and the wine has aged extremely well. There are still the
      rich berry fruit flavors in the nose and on the palate, but exotic
      spices, pepper, and leather notes have entered the picture. De-
      licious, fat, succulent fruit flavors persist and persist on the
      palate—this wine is very fresh and vibrant. Drink it over the
      next 5–6 years. Last tasted 6/86.

DOMAINE HENRI BONNEAU ****

Bonneau, a reclusive man who seems to desire to avoid attention from
writers and the public, is one of the finest growers in Châteauneuf-du-
Pape. I have tasted only three of his vintages because I have never
seen the wine in the export markets, and he simply would not allow me
to purchase any bottles or continue the tasting. Tucked away at the top
of the village of Châteauneuf-du-Pape, Bonneau produces 1,600 cases
of a stunningly rich, multidimensional wine with a concentration I have
only seen from such estates as Beaucastel and Rayas. He has ten acres
of vines that are dominated by the Grenache (more than 80%). His

vinification is the classic or traditional method of crushing all the grapes, giving them a hot and lengthy maceration, and then aging them in small barrels. Bonneau has an obvious horror of publicity, but if the three vintages I saw are representative of his talents, this is a spectacular, amazingly undervalued and unknown estate. If Monsieur Bonneau has his way, it will stay that way.

VINTAGES

1981—*Bonneau*—Lush and intense aromas of raspberry fruit, choco-
· late, sweet oak, and smoke swell in the glass. On the palate, this
89 full-bodied, still youthful wine has loads of extract, tremendous depth and persistence, and 10–12 years of evolution. Anticipated maturity: 1990–2000. Last tasted 10/86.

1979—*Bonneau*—An extraordinary wine, black/ruby in color with an
· explosive bouquet of ripe blackberry fruit, subtle herbs, and
91 oriental spices, velvety, rich, even unctuous on the palate, this impressively concentrated wine has heaps of flavor. Anticipated maturity: now–1994. Last tasted 10/86.

1978—*Bonneau*—Again, the huge nose of jammy berry fruit, cedar,
· herbs, and roasted nuts is superb. Fabulously concentrated,
93 very deep and full-bodied, this statuesque wine is a privilege to drink. Anticipated maturity: now–1995. Last tasted 10/86.

LE BOSQUET DES PAPES (MAURICE BOIRON)****

This modest-sized estate of 57 acres is located just behind the village of Châteauneuf-du-Pape on the road to the ruins of Pope John's castle. Bosquet des Papes is a member of the growers' association called Prestige et Tradition. The estate produces both red and white wine. The white wine is adequate but a little dull. The red wine is one of the finest of the appellation, possessing a breadth of flavor and depth that is quite profound. The wine is made from a blend of 70% Grenache, with the rest equal parts of Syrah, Mourvèdre, and Cinsault. The wine is vinified in the classic manner and aged 18 months in large oak casks. Madame Boiron, who seems to know all the goings-on in Châteauneuf-du-Pape, and her shy husband run this family-owned estate with a great deal of care. I have no experience with any vintages older than 1978, but I see no reason not to expect Bosquet des Papes to last at least a decade in the top vintages. The wine has also demonstrated excellent consistency in so-called off years.

Bosquet des Papes has become quite fashionable in wine circles in Paris, so prices and demand will no doubt increase.

VINTAGES

1985—*Bosquet des Papes (white)*—This is rather typical of the rank-
· and-file white Châteauneufs, a neutral, slightly dull bouquet,
78 and chunky flavors. It requires drinking before the end of 1988.
Last tasted 2/87.

1985—*Bosquet des Papes (red)*—This appears to be one of the top dozen
· or so red wines of the appellation in 1985. Very deep in color,
89 this wine has a big, black cherry-scented bouquet, robust, rich,
deep flavors, plenty of length and depth, as well as 8–10 years
of aging potential. Anticipated maturity: 1989–1997. Last tasted
6/86.

1984—*Bosquet des Papes (red)*—A very fine 1984, Bosquet des Papes
· has surprisingly deep color for this vintage, a fragrant cherry
86 and olive scented aroma, lush, full-bodied flavors, and shows
impeccable winemaking. Anticipated maturity: now–1993. Last
tasted 12/86.

1983—*Bosquet des Papes (red)*—Dark ruby in color with a gorgeous
· fragrance of blackcurrants, tobacco, Provençal herbs and
90 spices, this finely crafted wine is rich on the palate, soft enough
to be accessible now, but long, deep, and ageworthy. Anticipated maturity: now–1995. Last tasted 2/87.

1982—*Bosquet des Papes (red)*—Quite soft with an elevated degree of
· alcohol, this medium-bodied, richly colored wine has a hot fin-
84 ish, but plenty of berry fruit in its bouquet and flavors. Drink it
over the next 3–4 years. Last tasted 12/85.

1981—*Bosquet des Papes (red)*—A bouquet of leather, herbs, and
· jammy fruit is first-class. On the palate, the wine shows less
87 elegance than the 1983, but more robustness and brute strength.
This is a big, spicy, extroverted wine. Anticipated maturity:
now–1991. Last tasted 6/86.

1978—*Bosquet des Papes (red)*—A superb Châteauneuf-du-Pape, the
· huge, well-developed bouquet of cedar, ripe plums, thyme, and
90 fruitcake persists and swells in the glass. Rich and full-bodied,
the tannins have melted away, and the wine is opulent and very
long. Drink it over the next 5–6 years. Last tasted 10/86.

DOMAINE DE CABRIÈRES (LOUIS ARNAUD) ***

The Domaine de Cabrières is situated on the plateau near Mont-Redon.
Virtually everyone agrees that this area has the most potential for producing great Châteauneuf-du-Pape. It is an especially stony area, and

the vineyards adjacent to Cabrières are among the most forbidding looking yet fascinating in the entire appellation.

This estate is meticulously looked after by the Arnaud family, and is quite large, comprising 161 acres of superbly situated vines. Both a red and white wine are made. The red is 55% Grenache, 10% Syrah, 10% Mourvèdre, 10% Cinsault, and the balance Counoise and Muscardin. The white is made from Clairette, Grenache Blanc, and Bourboulenc.

The winemaking philosophy at Cabrières is clearly inspired by state-of-the-art technology. Both the winery and the wines have that California feel of being the products of technical razzle-dazzle where statistics and stability are the primary ends sought. The results are, of course, wines where the vintage differences are muted and much of the character and flavor eviscerated by too much filtration. After filtering the wines twice at Cabrières, M. Arnaud says proudly, "We guarantee that all the germs and microbes harmful to the wine are removed." Yet tasting the current wines proves that this is not all that has been exorcised from the wine—it has lost its soul as well. This is all rather sad; old vintages of Cabrières such as the 1961, 1966, and 1967 are still splendidly rich and complex, hardly examples of bad wine ruined by a few microbes or germs.

The red wines being produced today are very cleanly made with moderately intense aromas and flavors of cherry fruit and spices. They are good wines that exhibit consistency from vintage to vintage. Yet given the potential of their vineyards and the fact that their Châteauneuf tastes much like many others produced in this style, it is for winelovers a tragedy. Cabrières spends 12 to 18 months in oak foudres. The Arnauds have begun to employ some new oak barrels for aging part of their red wine.

The wines here are good, but the older vintages of Cabrières, produced before the advent of dual filtration and the centrifuge, are indeed remarkable wines with character and majestic flavors. The same cannot be said for the likes of the contemporary vintages.

VINTAGES

1985—*Cabrières (white)*—This is a very lean, crisp, pleasant, cleanly made wine with high acidity. Cabrières blocks the malolactic fermentation to get the high acidity. Last tasted 6/86.

82

1985—*Cabrières (red)*—The Arnauds believe this is among the best five vintages of the last three decades. It is a medium-bodied, very fruity wine, extremely clean, not that deep, but round and charming. Anticipated maturity: now–1993. Last tasted 6/86.

84

1984—*Cabrières (red)*—A much firmer, more tannic wine than the
· 1985, the 1984 has some pleasant, clean, peppery, berry fruit
82 flavors, medium body and a sculptured feel to it. Anticipated
maturity: now–1990. Last tasted 6/86.

1983—*Cabrières (red)*—An earthier, more spicy, tannic, and alcoholic
· wine, the 1983 has good fruit, full body, a very spicy taste, and
84 noticeable tannin in the finish. Anticipated maturity: now–1995.
Last tasted 6/86.

1982—*Cabrières (red)*—Weedy, oaky, very hot flavors are out of bal-
· ance in this wine that seems to be starting to fall apart. Last
72 tasted 6/86.

1978—*Cabrières (red)*—Scents of caramel, raspberry and cherry fruit,
· oak, and fruitcake are very attractive. On the palate, the wine is
85 not as broadly flavored as the nose suggests, as there is a narrow
focus to the wine's structure. Now fully mature, it should be
drunk over the next 5–6 years. Last tasted 12/85.

1977—*Cabrières (red)*—Rather light, the 1977 is, however, a success
· for the vintage. Straightforward cherry fruit flavors and medium
78 body offer decent drinking. Anticipated maturity: 1988–1992.
Last tasted 6/86.

1974—*Cabrières (red)*—The 1974 has a big, spicy, cigar box nose, me-
· dium ruby color, and soft, pleasant, fruity flavors that could use
82 more depth and length. Drink up. Last tasted 6/86.

1967—*Cabrières (red)*—A full-intensity bouquet of rich, sweet, jammy
· fruit is very alluring. On the palate, the wine shows a depth and
87 richness that recent vintages lack. Full-bodied and long, this is
a delicious Châteauneuf-du-Pape. Drink it over the next 5–6
years. Last tasted 6/86.

1966—*Cabrières (red)*—A huge perfume of flowers, smoky meat, berry
· fruit, and exotic spices is excellent. Full-bodied, sweet, opulent,
88 with quite a fine finish, this wine has reached its peak and should
be drunk up. Last tasted 1/85.

1961—*Cabrières (red)*—Why would anyone forsake this style of Châ-
· teauneuf-du-Pape? Still rich, full of fruit, with an exceptional
91 bouquet of sweet oak, flowers, tar, and smoke, this complex,
full-bodied wine has layers of fruit and will hold for 3–4 years.
It is absolutely superb. Last tasted 6/85.

LES CAILLOUX (ANDRÉ BRUNEL)****

Young, articulate, and serious, André Brunel, who resembles the movie
actor William Hurt, produces noteworthy Châteauneuf-du-Pape from

44 acres of vineyards. Brunel, who is a member of one of the two very fine growers' associations, Les Reflets, has one of his two vineyards on the plateau near Mont-Redon, and the other on sandier, lighter soil near the dreary industrial town of Sorgues. His red wine is a blend of 70% Grenache, 10% Syrah, 5% Cinsault, and 15% Mourvèdre. He is planning to augment the amount of Mourvèdre and Syrah to the detriment of the Grenache.

His winemaking is an amalgam of styles. For two-thirds of his grapes he follows a classic vinification, crushing them and giving them a long maceration. For the other third he follows the modified whole-berry vinification method. His wines are neither fined nor filtered, and stay in cement tanks until bottling, which normally occurs within two years of the vintage.

Brunel believes that Châteauneuf-du-Pape has a privileged situation that should allow it to produce great wine. As he points out, the yield permitted by law is very low, the average age of the vines is quite high, and no mechanical harvesters are permitted. Yet he laments that far too many growers simply rely too heavily on the Grenache to give them fruity, alcoholic wines that with modern technology can be bottled early and sold to the endless number of customers who want a fat, fruity wine.

While Brunel admits that his wines lacked consistency in the seventies, he is excited about his wines in the eighties, and feels that he is now making the style of wine he wants. He also produces about 500 cases of good white Châteauneuf that is made from 60% Clairette, 30% Roussanne, and 10% Bourboulenc.

VINTAGES

1985—*Les Cailloux (white)*—This is the best white Châteauneuf-du-
· Pape I have tasted from Brunel. Scents of tropical fruit, candy,
86 and herbs combine nicely. On the palate, the wine is full-bodied, soft, and should be drunk over the next year. Last tasted 12/86.

1985—*Les Cailloux (red)*—This deeply colored wine is quite rich and
· chewy with heaps of fruit and length. It is full-bodied, slightly
87 low in acidity, but appealing and forward. Anticipated maturity: 1988–1995. Last tasted 6/86.

1984—*Les Cailloux (red)*—This is another example of how good 1984
· was for many growers in Châteauneuf. Deep in color, classically
86 structured, firmly tannic, this wine has fine depth and aging potential. Anticipated maturity: 1988–1996. Last tasted 6/86.

1983—*Les Cailloux (red)*—This wine is developing very well. Undoubt-
·   edly a success for the vintage, the wine has a good, deep color,
87   a spicy, black cherry-scented bouquet, some subtle herbaceous-
       ness, full body, and considerable length. Anticipated maturity:
       1990–2004. Last tasted 6/86.

1981—*Les Cailloux (red)*—Drinking well, now, the 1981 has good rich-
·   ness, a moderately intense, peppery, spicy bouquet, medium to
84   full body, and a decent finish. It is good but not exciting. Drink
       it over the next 3–4 years. Last tasted 7/86.

1980—*Les Cailloux (red)*—A medium ruby-colored wine with a spicy,
·   quite herbaceous, peppery bouquet, the 1980 Les Cailloux is
80   austere and lean. It is now fully mature. Last tasted 6/85.

1979—*Les Cailloux (red)*—I have experienced severe bottle variation
·   with this wine ranging from a washed-out color and weedy, green
?   character, to wine with good fruit, ripeness, and body. Judgment
       reserved. Last tasted 6/84.

1978—*Les Cailloux (red)*—Just now reaching its peak of maturity, this
·   is, to date, the finest Les Cailloux I have drunk. Smoky, cedary,
89   tobacco-scented, ripe berry aromas create a very complex bou-
       quet. On the palate, the wine is very deep, well structured for
       aging, with considerable length. Anticipated maturity: now–
       1995. Last tasted 12/86.

LES CÈDRES (PAUL JABOULET AINÉ) ***

I have sought out, drunk with great pleasure, and cellared as many
cases of Paul Jaboulet's exquisite 1961, 1962, 1967, and 1969 Châteauneuf-du-Pape called Les Cèdres as I could find and afford. These wines
were and continue to be quintessential examples of full-bodied, sumptuous, magnificently perfumed wines. However, vintages since the seventies have become lighter and lighter, and in the eighties the wines
are nothing more than vapid, characterless, commercial specimens.

The Jaboulets own no vineyards in Châteauneuf-du-Pape and buy
their juice from selected growers for making their wine. Whether they
have lost access to the juice from some of the best growers, or have just
decided to change the style of their wine, it is a decision that any wine
enthusiast should regret with the deepest sorrow, for this firm was
capable of producing great Châteauneuf-du-Pape.

The wine is usually dominated by the Grenache grape. Until 1985 the
blend over recent vintages has been 85% Grenache and 15% Syrah. In
1985 they doubled the Syrah to 30%, added 5% Cinsault, and dropped

the Grenache to 65%. Perhaps there is a move underfoot to put some character and aging potential back into this wine. Jaboulet ages his wine in cask for 12–18 months prior to bottling after a filtration. (In certain countries his wines are marketed under another name, "La Grappe de Pape." It is the identical wine to Les Cèdres.)

Formerly one of my favorite three or four Châteauneufs, it is now just simple and innocuous; Les Cèdres could use a facelift. Hopefully, the proud Jaboulets, a family that has done so much for the image of high-quality Rhône wines, will put some "pop" back into their Châteauneuf-du-Pape.

VINTAGES

1985—*Les Cèdres*—This is better than some of the one-dimensional
  ·   wines recently produced, but it is still a far cry from the wines
 84   made in the decade of the sixties. Medium deep ruby, with a grapy, straight-forward bouquet, this wine is fat, soft, quite pleasant and full-bodied. Anticipated maturity: 1988–1992. Last tasted 6/86.

1984—*Les Cèdres*—Medium ruby with a good bouquet of cherry fruit
  ·   and vanillin, the 1984 is leaner and more tannic than the 1985,
 81   but could use some more flesh on its bones. Anticipated maturity: 1988–1993. Last tasted 6/86.

1983—*Les Cèdres*—A modest cherry fruit character and engaging ripe-
  ·   ness in the nose suggest a good Côtes du Rhône. On the palate,
 82   the wine is medium- to full-bodied, spicy, and offers good drinking. Anticipated maturity: now–1991. Last tasted 5/86.

1982—*Les Cèdres*—Fat, rather alcoholic, the 1982 has good color, a
  ·   soft, loosely knit texture, and an elevated degree of alcohol. It is
 80   drinking nicely, but must be drunk up within the next 2–3 years since its balance is fragile. Last tasted 6/85.

1981—*Les Cèdres*—A narrow-focused, compact wine without a great
  ·   deal of charm or flesh, the 1981 is tannic and lean. I cannot
 75   imagine that it will improve. Last tasted 9/84.

1980—*Les Cèdres*—Among recent vintages, the 1980 has turned out to
  ·   be quite good. A moderately intense peppery, raspberry-domi-
 84   nated bouquet is attractive. On the palate, the wine has solid, rich fruit, and a good spicy, soft finish. Drink it over the next 4–5 years. Last tasted 11/84.

1978—*Les Cèdres*—For the greatness of the vintage, this is less exhila-
  ·   rating than other wines of this appellation. Yet the 1978 Les
 85   Cèdres shows good richness, a full-bodied texture, plenty of

ripeness, and a more complex character than the wines in the post–1978 era. Drink it over the next 5–6 years. Last tasted 11/84.

1969—*Les Cèdres*—Medium dark garnet with an amber edge, the 1969
• has a big, hickory-scented, tarry, rich, sweet fruitcake sort of
87 bouquet, full body, deep flavors, and a soft finish. It is fully mature, but will keep for 4 to 6 years. Last tasted 2/87.

1967—*Les Cèdres*—This is a fabulous vintage for Châteauneuf-du-
• Pape, and Les Cèdres is one of the top two or three wines of the
96 vintage. Deep garnet with an amber edge, the bouquet bursts from the glass with exotic scents of oriental spices, layers of plummy fruit, and smoky, cedary aromas. On the palate, there is a breadth and depth of fruit that is remarkable. The sweet, long finish lingers on and on. This glorious wine is now at its apogee. It should keep 4–5 more years. Last tasted 2/87.

1962—*Les Cèdres*—A rich, complex, almost port-like, sweetish, choc-
• olatey, plummy bouquet offers great pleasure. In the mouth, the
90 wine is not as concentrated as the 1961 or 1967, but still very deep, full-bodied, sweet, and quite special. It should be drunk up over the next 2–3 years. Last tasted 2/87.

1961—*Les Cèdres*—A magnificent wine, the 1961, which has thrown a
• deep, murky sediment, is quite similar to the 1967, only slightly
95 less sweet, but profound. The huge bouquet of smoky, ripe fruit, the great richness, length, and immense presence of this wine on the palate are the stuff of which wine legends are made. The color suggests full maturity, so don't tempt fate and cellar this splendid wine any longer. Last tasted 2/87.

DOMAINE CHANTE-CIGALE (FAVIER-SABON) ***

The charmingly named Domaine Chante-Cigale (the singing grasshop-per) is run by Christian Favier, the son-in-law of Noel Sabon, who has fathered many a winemaker in Châteauneuf-du-Pape. This is a good-sized estate of 99 acres planted with 80% Grenache, 10% Syrah, 5% Mourvèdre, and 5% Cinsault for the red wine. These vines are an impressive 40 years of age. A small quantity of white wine (about 2,000 bottles) is made from 30% Grenache Blanc, 30% Bourboulenc, and 40% Clairette.

The style of vinification here is the classic method in which the grapes are crushed and the juice given a long maceration period with the skins. The wine is never filtered, only fined by egg whites, and spends up to two years in old, giant wooden foudres.

This estate has made some excellent wines, but the decade of the eighties, for whatever reason, has not rendered as many successful wines as one might suspect after tasting what the property produced in the seventies. Favier, an incredibly voluble and animated man, acknowledges that he is at a loss to explain why the recent vintages of 1985, 1984, and 1983 are less exciting than their predecessors. Nevertheless, this is a very good estate that produces traditional, interesting wines that can age for 10–15 years in the successful vintages. I find the wine possesses a bouquet of cured smoky olives, saddle leather, and bing cherries.

VINTAGES

1985—*Chante-Cigale (white)*—While this is not in the top league of
· white Châteauneufs, it is far better than many of them. Crisp,
83 fruity, full-bodied, with some character, it should be drunk over
the next year. Last tasted 6/86.

1985—*Chante-Cigale (red)*—Herbaceous earthy aromas dominate this
· chunky, robust wine that seems a bit unstructured and diffuse.
83 Favier says he is in the minority, but he believes 1985 is a
mediocre year. Anticipated maturity: 1988–1994. Last tasted
6/86.

1984—*Chante-Cigale (red)*—The 1984 lacks generosity, is hard, rather
· lean, and has a dry, astringent aspect in the finish. Anticipated
75 maturity: 1988–1992. Last tasted 6/86.

1983—*Chante-Cigale (red)*—Lacking color, the 1983 Chante-Cigale is
· dry, medium-bodied, and missing the fat flesh and body one
78 normally associates with Châteauneuf-du-Pape. Favier admits
he fermented the wine at too low a temperature this year. Anticipated maturity: now–1990. Last tasted 6/86.

1982—*Chante-Cigale (red)*—This was certainly the most difficult recent year for the vignerons of Châteauneuf. In spite of such
· obstacles posed by 1982, this is the most successful Chante-
86 Cigale in the period 1982–86. A big bouquet of cherries and
leather is intense. Fully mature, deep in color, this wine has a
broad, sweet, very oaky character not dissimilar from a Spanish
Rioja. Drink over the next 5 years. Last tasted 6/86.

1981—*Chante-Cigale (red)*—To date, this is the best Chante-Cigale in
· the eighties. The 1981 has this estate's telltale aroma of olives,
87 cherry fruit, and leather. In the mouth, the wine is quite deep,
full-bodied, very spicy, and filled with character. Drink it over
the next 5–7 years. Last tasted 6/86.

1980—*Chante-Cigale (red)*—The 1980 has good color, an open-knit,
·   smoked meat and smoky fruit bouquet. On the palate, the wine
84   is spicy, fully mature, well made, lighter than normal, but pleas-
     ant. Drink over the next 3–4 years. Last tasted 6/86.

1979—*Chante-Cigale (red)*—After tasting two very pruny, overripe bot-
·   tles of this wine, I have had a succession of very fine examples
87   of the 1979. The honest Favier likes his 1979 better than the
     1978. There is no doubt that he made a rich, spicy, deep, well-
     colored, big wine in 1979. The bouquet of herbs, olives, and fruit
     is captivating. Softer and more velvety than the 1978, this is a
     delicious Châteauneuf for drinking over the next 5–6 years. Last
     tasted 6/86.

1978—*Chante-Cigale (red)*—The deep, black ruby color shows no sign
·   of age. The intense set of aromas suggestive of tobacco, olives,
88   plums, and tar are very persistent. This is a full-bodied, rich,
     very deep, broadly flavored wine that is just reaching its apogee.
     Anticipated maturity: now–1995. Last tasted 1/87.

1976—*Chante-Cigale (red)*—Another very fine wine, the 1976 has a
·   full-intensity bouquet of olives, truffles, cherries, and vanillin.
88   Very deep, intense, and full-bodied, this wine has reached ma-
     turity, but can be kept for at least 5–6 years. It is one of the top
     successes from this overrated vintage. Last tasted 6/86.

DOMAINE DE CHANTE-PERDRIX (NICOLET FRÈRES) ****

The domaine of the "singing partridge," Chante-Perdrix, produces one
of the blockbuster wines of Châteauneuf-du-Pape. Here one gets Châteauneuf at its most flamboyant and dramatic. The estate is not large,
only 50 acres, and while the amount of Grenache used is not unusual,
80%, the relatively high percentage of Muscardin, 20%, is. Nicolet's
vineyards, which average 20–25 year in age, are situated on the plain
south of the village of Châteauneuf-du-Pape in the direction of Sorgues.
M. Nicolet is a quiet and unassuming man, diminutive in stature and
seems totally (from a physical perspective) incapable of producing
wines that are enormous in size, voluptuous in texture, and among the
most decadently rich produced in this appellation. Wines are rarely
described as having sex appeal, but the Chante-Perdrix of Nicolet is a
seductive, disarming, amply endowed wine. His vinification is the modern method wherein half the grapes remain uncrushed but destemmed
and the other half crushed, not destemmed, and given a classically
long, very hot fermentation and maceration. He ages his wine two years

in wooden foudres and gives it a slight filtration at bottling if required. The wines of Chante-Perdrix are especially successful in off years such as 1984 and 1980.

Despite the power and sheer magnitude of the red wines made here, they age quite well. This is a full-bodied, full-throttle Châteauneuf for wintertime drinking.

Nicolet also makes a little bit of reliable white wine from 50% Grenache Blanc and 50% Clairette.

VINTAGES

1985—*Chante-Perdrix (white)*—This is a fresh, straightforward, decent
· wine that is a trifle neutral in character, but otherwise accept-
80 ably made. Anticipated maturity: now–1988. Last tasted 6/86.

1985—*Chante-Perdrix (red)*—Black/ruby in color, this intense, opulent
· wine is bursting with blackberry fruit, and aromas of sweet
89 candy and flowers. Quite concentrated as well as alcoholic, this
velvety textured wine will provide delicious drinking. Anticipated maturity: 1988–1995. Last tasted 6/86.

1984—*Chante-Perdrix (red)*—This is unquestionably one of the vin-
· tage's great successes. Black/ruby in color with a stunning bou-
89 quet of sweet, smoky, blackberry fruit, this luxuriously rich wine
is oozing with fruit. It has remarkable dimension and length.
Anticipated maturity: 1988–1995. Last tasted 6/86.

1983—*Chante-Perdrix (red)*—The voluptuous style of Chante-Perdrix
· is again admirably displayed in this densely colored, powerful,
90 loaded wine. A super bouquet of jammy black cherry fruit is
quite enticing. In the mouth, the wine is full-bodied, very
broadly flavored, utterly delicious and deep, with enough tannin
and depth to carry it for a decade. Anticipated maturity: now–
1997. Last tasted 6/86.

1981—*Chante-Perdrix (red)*—Deep ruby with a tarry, smoky, slightly
· herbal bouquet, the 1981 is full-bodied, not as overtly fruity and
87 deep as usual, but firm, quite concentrated, weighty, alcoholic,
and still a little tough. Anticipated maturity: now–1996. Last
tasted 10/86.

1979—*Chante-Perdrix (red)*—Now approaching full maturity, the 1979
· has a dense, opaque color and has thrown a good bit of sediment.
87 It has a chewy, unctuous texture, very open bouquet, and seems
to have just reached full maturity. Anticipated maturity: now–
1992. Last tasted 3/84.

1978—*Chante-Perdrix (red)*—A blockbuster wine, dense in color with
a huge, multidimensional bouquet of smoky, herbal, tarry,
90   plummy scents. Very powerful, full-bodied, and deep, the port-
like texture and richness almost overwhelm the palate. This
behemoth-styled wine should be served with stews, cassoulets,
or strong cheeses. Drink it over the next 5–7 years. Last tasted
2/87.

DOMAINE LES CLEFS D'OR (JEAN DEYDIER)****

At the foot of the ruins of the old papal château, on the tiny, twisting
back streets of the village of Châteauneuf-du-Pape, are the home and
cellars of Jean Deydier. This is a highy regarded Châteauneuf-du-Pape.
The elderly Deydier, who missed two scheduled appointments and refused to come to the telephone when I called, was finally "trapped" at
the end of his working day when I decided to simply go unannounced.
I found him to be a remarkably provincial man with an obvious distrust
of wine writers. The latter characteristic seems surprising in view of
the high marks his wines have gotten not only from me but from the
European press as well. He owns 62 acres of vineyards planted with
80% Grenache, and the rest a field blend of Syrah, Mourvèdre, Vaccarèse, and Muscardin. His vines average 30 years in age, and Deydier
rarely filters his wines. He makes 8,000 bottles of very good white wine
from equal proportions of Bourboulenc, Grenache Blanc, and Clairette.
His vines are admirably situated on the plateau, one parcel near Mont-
Redon, another further east toward Vieux Télégraphe. His wine can
last 10, 15, even 20 years in great vintages such as 1978. These are
traditionally-styled wines, but also seem to have an elegance and breed
that sets them apart.

The vinification combines the traditional, classic method with the
newer, modern, whole-berry style. Two-thirds of the grapes are crushed
and given the classic long, hot vinification. The other one-third are
destemmed and put in the tank whole. Jean Deydier's son, Pierre, is
assuming more control and has no intention of changing a thing about
this very well-made, popular Châteauneuf-du-Pape. Seventy percent of
Deydier's production is exported because he says "the foreigners know
more about fine wine than the French."

VINTAGES

1985—*Clefs d'Or (white)*—The white wine made here is normally
among the top half-dozen whites of the appellation. Crisp, fruity
86   with style and flavor, it is a medium- to full-bodied wine that
must be consumed when very young. Last tasted 6/86.

1985—*Clefs d'Or (red)*—Very dense in color, the 1985 has a rich pep-
· pery, raspberry, and black cherry bouquet, lush, intensely con-
88 centrated flavors, and a sweetness and length on the palate that
is very attractive. While not quite as profound as the 1978, this
still will make a fine bottle. Anticipated maturity: 1988–1996.
Last tasted 6/86.

1984—*Clefs d'Or (red)*—With very good deep ruby color, the 1984 is
· rather hard and closed on the palate, but shows good ripeness,
84 body, structure, and acidity. Anticipated maturity: 1989–1996.
Last tasted 6/86.

1983—*Clefs d'Or (red)*—Medium to slightly dark ruby in color, the 1983
· has a well-developed berry fruit, peppery, vanillin-scented bou-
87 quet. Sweet, rich, very round, generous flavors are exciting and
show maturity. For a 1983, this is elegant and velvety. Drink
over the next 5–7 years. Last tasted 6/86.

1982—*Clefs d'Or (red)*—This is a pleasant, fully mature, medium-
· bodied wine that exhibits an elevated degree of alcohol, but has
82 charm, flesh, and a supple texture. Drink it over the next 2–3
years. Last tasted 6/86.

1981—*Clefs d'Or (red)*—Dark ruby with a bouquet of ripe cherries,
· some floral scents, and black pepper, this full-bodied wine has
86 good length, a more rustic, tough finish than the 1983, but plenty
of extract and character. Anticipated maturity: now–1994. Last
tasted 11/85.

1979—*Clefs d'Or (red)*—Perhaps I expected too much, but Deydier's
· 1979 is not as concentrated or as deep as I would have thought.
84 Fairly elegant and lighter in weight than normal, this wine offers
good, ripe cherry fruit, a soft, silky texture, and adequate finish.
Drink it over the next 3–4 years. Last tasted 6/85.

1978—*Clefs d'Or (red)*—This is great Châteauneuf-du-Pape. The color
· is still ruby/purple, though the wine has deposited a great deal
91 of sediment. The bouquet of violets, ripe plum and raspberry
fruit plus some pepper, the deeply concentrated yet still tannic
impression on the palate, the superb length and balance, all
characterize an outstanding wine. It has not yet reached maturity. Anticipated maturity: 1988–2004. Last tasted 2/87.

CLOS DU MONT-OLIVET (JOSEPH SABON)****

One of the very best Châteauneuf-du-Papes, Mont-Olivet is made by
the three sons of the legendary Joseph Sabon. They produce a splen-

didly rich, old-style Châteauneuf-du-Pape from ancient vines (an average age of 60 years) from 55 acres of vineyards. Another 20 acres is also farmed by the Sabon brothers. The blend of cépages is 80% Grenache, 5% Cinsault, 10% Syrah, and 5% of assorted varietals. As superb as the red wine can be, the white wine produced here has been green, acidic, and mediocre. As for the red, my only criticism of the Sabons is their practice of "bottling upon ordering," meaning that the same vintages may spend different amounts of time in the large oak foudres. For example, some of the fine 1978 that I purchased in London five years ago was still resting in a wooden foudre at the property in 1986 awaiting a purchaser. It cannot taste the same as the 1978 I possess which has eight years of bottle age. Nevertheless, I believe if you purchase the early bottlings here you can get truly remarkable wine in Sabon's great years such as 1967, 1970, 1971, 1976, 1978, 1979, and 1985. The wines of this estate will keep a good 10–15 years in the top vintages, and they are worth searching for.

The vinification practiced by the Sabons is totally traditional or classic. All the incoming grapes are crushed and given a hot, lengthy fermentation and maceration. The wine is not fined, but given a light filtration at the time of bottling. Except for their practice of different bottling dates (mis en bouteille) for their wines, Clos du Mont-Olivet is a wine to look for, for it seems to deftly marry the robustness of an old-style Châteauneuf-du-Pape with a measure of finesse and elegance. In addition, the Sabons, who are also members of the growers' association Les Reflets, charge very modest prices for their wine.

VINTAGES

1985—*Mont-Olivet (white)*—Sabon's white Châteauneuf-du-Pape is
·   made from early-harvested grapes, and seems to always be ex-
73   cessively green, lean, neutral tasting, and highly acidic. The
       1985 possesses this same character. Last tasted 6/86.

1985—*Mont-Olivet (red)*—This is a fabulous wine, black/ruby in color
·   with an intense fragrance of berry fruit, floral scents, and exotic
92   spices. Extremely dense and rich, very full-bodied, this is a
       sensational wine that will age for two decades. Anticipated ma-
       turity: 1990–2005. Last tasted 6/86.

1984—*Mont-Olivet (red)*—Deep ruby in color with a moderately intense
·   plummy, spicy bouquet, the 1984 lacks the extra dimension of a
85   1983 or 1985, but is unquestionably a success for the vintage.
       Anticipated maturity: now–1991. Last tasted 6/86.

1983—*Mont-Olivet (red)*—The aromas of *"sur-maturité"*—peaches,
·   apricots, as well as berry fruit—are wonderfully present in this
87   wine. On the palate, it is almost burgundy-like with supple,
      broad, velvety flavors, full body, and a delicious, long finish.
      Anticipated maturity: now–1993. Last tasted 6/86.

1982—*Mont-Olivet (red)*—The color shows a watery edge, the bouquet
·   has some pleasant berry fruit, but also the hotness of high alco-
76   hol. Somewhat disjointed, this is a palatable wine that is precar-
      iously balanced. Drink it up. Last tasted 6/86.

1981—*Mont-Olivet (red)*—A spicy, almost buttery aroma combines
·   with scents of cherry fruit and leather. On the palate, the wine
84   is medium- to full-bodied, somewhat dry in the finish, but cor-
      pulent and interesting. Anticipated maturity: now–1991. Last
      tasted 6/86.

1979—*Mont-Olivet (red)*—More opulent and charming than the 1981,
·   the 1979 has reached its peak. It has a bouquet of spicy, black
86   cherry fruit, is full-bodied, and quite fruity with the tannins
      completely melted. It should be drunk over the next 4–5 years.
      Last tasted 11/85.

1978—*Mont-Olivet (red)*—A top wine, even for the vintage, it, like so
·   many of the 1978 Châteauneuf-du-Papes, has an extra layer of
90   fruit, is wonderfully fragrant, full-bodied, loaded with extract,
      and while quite drinkable now will keep for at least another 5–7
      years. Last tasted 1/87.

1976—*Mont-Olivet (red)*—A bouquet of roasted nuts and plummy fruit
·   is intertwined with leather and exotic spices. Surprisingly fleshy
88   and succulent, particularly for a 1976, this is a classic Château-
      neuf-du-Pape at the bloom of maturity. Drink it now. Last tasted
      6/86.

1967—*Mont-Olivet (red)*—Amber at the edges suggests full maturity.
·   Soft, ripe, broad flavors are creamy and delicious. This is an
89   excellent wine that is just beginning to show signs of fading.
      Drink it up. Last tasted 6/86.

CLOS DE L'ORATOIRE (MADAME AMOUROUX)**

This large estate of 123 acres used to be one of the best examples of
Châteauneuf-du-Pape, but since the early seventies the wine has increasingly taken on the character of a fruity, soft, rather one-dimensional wine. Recent vintages have shown little character of
Châteauneuf-du-Pape, and this is all very unfortunate. The wine remains pleasant and fruity, but you can obtain the same character in a

good Côtes du Rhône at one-third the price. When I visited the domaine in June, 1986, the 1985 had been bottled in April—shockingly early even by most modernists' standards.

. Certainly, the wine can be better. The old vintages from the sixties can still be excellent. The vinification is by the modified carbonic maceration method, but the wine tastes as if all of it was vinified in the carbonic manner. Despite my disappointment at the compromises that have been made here, the wine is very cleanly made and its character is one with a forceful, one-dimensional, berry fruitiness and powerful alcoholic kick. It is a wine that should now be drunk young, usually within 5–8 years of the vintage.

VINTAGES

1985—*Clos de L'Oratoire*—Deep ruby in color with a jammy, straight-
· forward bouquet of berry fruit, but flabby, fat, and low in acidity,
83 this chunky wine will offer good, uncomplicated drinking for 5–
7 years. Last tasted 6/86.

1984—*Clos de L'Oratoire*—Not dissimilar from the 1985, fat, jammy,
· very fruity, but showing no complexity or finesse, this wine
82 should be drunk over the next 3–4 years. Last tasted 6/86.

1983—*Clos de L'Oratoire*—Less dense in color than either the 1984 or
· 1985, the 1983 is harder, seems less concentrated, too one-
75 dimensional and simple. Drink it up. Last tasted 6/86.

1982—*Clos de L'Oratoire*—A hot, baked character to the bouquet is
· off-putting. Alcoholic, very flabby flavors show little concentra-
70 tion or balance. This wine is precariously balanced. Last tasted
6/86.

1981—*Clos de L'Oratoire*—This plump, deep ruby-colored wine has a
· chewy, unctuous texture, intrusive alcohol, full body, and little
82 charm or complexity. Drink it over the next 1–3 years. Last
tasted 6/86.

1978—*Clos de L'Oratoire*—This was totally ready to drink when re-
· leased in 1980. It has not changed. Deep in color with a jammy,
83 berry fruit bouquet, it is plump, fat, quite tasty, and offers no
complexity. Last tasted 6/86.

CLOS DES PAPES (PAUL AVRIL) *****

One wishes there were more winemakers/proprietors such as Paul Avril. A forward-thinking, very optimistic man in his early forties, the tall, articulate Avril realizes fully that as great a wine as Châteauneuf-du-Pape can be, not enough producers desire to make the effort to produce something special. Demand for Avril's wines makes them hard to find. The 15 three-star French restaurants he sells his wine to, and Switzerland, his biggest export market, see that most of his rich, multidimensional, classic wine is taken. For his red wine he has 70 acres of vineyards planted with 70% Grenache, 20% Mourvèdre, 8% Syrah and the rest Vaccarèse and Muscardin. From another ten acres of vines, he makes an elegant, fresh white Châteauneuf-du-Pape that is produced from a blend of 30% Clairette, 10% Grenache Blanc, 20% Picpoul, 20% Roussanne, and 20% Bourboulenc. The average age of the vines is 30 years, and the only clarification of the wine is a coarse gravity filtration prior to bottling. The vinification here is totally classic; 100% of the grapes are crushed and no destemming takes place. Avril's red wines are fermented at hot temperatures, macerated for three weeks, and then put in large wooden foudres for 12–18 months. Avril believes that the fierce, hot, dry *mistral* wind causes more problems than just the shot nerves of the local inhabitants. He claims the wind, which is usually accompanied by extremely low humidity, dries out the wine cellars, causing excessive evaporation within the large foudres, resulting in an increased risk of oxidation. To combat this problem he has installed a "fogging" machine (the only one I have ever seen) that emits a dense layer of cool moisture-laden fog throughout his cellar to keep his barrels moist and prevent excessive oxidation. The fog is so thick that visibility in the cellars is restricted to about 10–15 feet— such is the dedication of Avril.

Avril says the greatest vintages for Châteauneuf-du-Pape have been 1961, 1970, and 1978, followed by 1967, and for his wines, 1983 and 1985. In the top vintages, his wines keep and improve for 10–15 years. For the sumptuous Clos des Papes 1966 and 1970 I drank in 1986 I would unhesitatingly exchange some clarets I have from those two vintages. Avril is one of the last to harvest, always seeking the extra ripeness that gives his wines flesh and rich fruit. Avril's Châteauneuf is one of the finest and longest-lived of the appellation.

VINTAGES

1985—*Clos des Papes (white)*—Avril's white wine is a rather perfumed
· wine with a candylike nose, crisp acidity, good body, but a neu-
83 tral character to its flavors. It must be drunk young. Last tasted
1/86.

1985—*Clos des Papes (red)*—This is a very rich wine with a huge berry-
scented bouquet, very unctuous, fat flavors, heaps of fruit, full
88   body, and excellent length. Avril believes it is too low in acidity
to age more than 10–15 years, but he thinks it is among the best
wines he has made. Anticipated maturity: 1988–1996. Last
tasted 6/86.

1984—*Clos des Papes (red)*—This is a top success for the vintage and
another reason why this appellation should be considered in
86   1984. Moderately deep ruby with an intense fragrance of berry
fruit, this elegantly wrought wine has ripe black cherry flavors
and a good finish. Anticipated maturity: 1988–1993. Last tasted
6/86.

1983—*Clos des Papes (red)*—The complex bouquet of vanillin, berry
fruit, and fennel is very attractive. On the palate the wine is still
87   a bit hard and closed but shows a great deal of depth and length.
Anticipated maturity: 1991–2001. Last tasted 6/86.

1982—*Clos des Papes (red)*—I have had severe bottle variation with the
1982. The best examples do not provide inspirational drinking,
?   but are round and generous, though too alcoholic. Judgment
reserved. Last tasted 6/86.

1981—*Clos des Papes (red)*—The 1981 Clos des Papes is one of the
exceptional successes of the vintage. More concentrated and
89   powerful than the 1983, it is indeed a rich, multifaceted wine
with plenty of extract and body. It is quite impressive in a big
manner, but ideally needs more time. Anticipated maturity:
1990–2005. Last tasted 6/86.

1980—*Clos des Papes (red)*—Fully mature, nicely colored with only a
hint of amber, the 1980 is plump, fruity, soft, not terribly com-
83   plex, but satisfying. Drink it over the next 2–4 years. Last tasted
6/86.

1979—*Clos des Papes (red)*—Very dark in color, the 1979 has the wild,
gamelike, smoky character I associate with Mourvèdre and
88   Syrah. Very full-bodied, rich and powerful on the palate, the
1979 is just beginning to show some signs of reaching maturity.
It has thrown a great deal of sediment. Anticipated maturity:
now–2002. Last tasted 6/86.

1978—*Clos des Papes (red)*—Avril believes this is his finest Clos des
Papes since the 1961. It is still a baby. Deep ruby in color with
93   an emerging yet restrained bouquet, tremendous ripeness, peppery, berry scents, great depth of fruit, a superb finish, and

exceptional balance—all point to a rich future for this monumental Châteauneuf. Anticipated maturity: 1990–2002. Last tasted 6/86.

1970—*Clos des Papes (red)*—Avril used more Grenache and less Mourvèdre in his 1970. It is fully mature and has a super, complex
·
90 bouquet of oriental spices, truffles, pepper, and sweet fruit. Opulent and lush, it begs to be drunk now, though I suspect it will keep for 3–4 years. Last tasted 6/86.

1966—*Clos des Papes (red)*—Avril prefers his 1970, I his 1966. The
· remarkably intense, sublime bouquet of melted, smoky caramel,
94 jammy, sweet berry fruit, and cedar is exciting. Fabulously rich, almost honeyed and nectarlike on the palate, this wine comes close to resembling a fine port. Very rich, very lush, and fully mature, I cannot demand much more pleasure from a wine than this. Last tasted 6/86.

CLOS ST.-JEAN (G. MAUREL)***

It was only recently that I tasted through a series of vintages from this producer that had been released onto the market. Except for the old vintages from the fifties and early sixties that were quite maderized, I was pleased with the big, robust, slightly coarse but distinctive style of these wines. The estate is large, just under 80 acres, most of which is in the eastern sector of the appellation, south of Beaucastel and near Vieux Télégraphe. The blend used consists of 70% Grenache, 15% Syrah, and the rest an assorted mixed field blend of Cinsault and Mourvèdre. The wines here are kept an inordinately long time in foudres prior to bottling, which probably contributes to their tannic, tough texture. This is a big, chunky wine with character and an aggressive personality, but it is not a style that seems to gain much harmony with age.

VINTAGES

1981—*Clos St.-Jean*—A very dense opaque color renders aromas of
· smoked meat, aggressive spicy scents, tar, damp earth, and
84 fennel. This intense, very robust and rustic wine needs time in the bottle. Anticipated maturity: 1990–1996. Last tasted 11/86.

1979—*Clos St.-Jean*—A smoky, tobacco aroma leads to a wine that is
· coarse yet powerful, very concentrated, heavy, and alcoholic,
85 but nevertheless very interesting. It is more impressive than enjoyable. Anticipated maturity: 1988–1994. Last tasted 11/86.

1977—*Clos St.-Jean*—This vintage was not nearly as bad in Châteauneuf-du-Pape as elsewhere in France. The 1977 from Clos St.-
·
81 Jean is intensely spicy, fat, rich, heavy, and coarse, but paired

with the right food can be a good match. Anticipated maturity: now–1990. Last tasted 11/86.

1974—*Clos St.-Jean*—Fully mature, this old-style, very weighty wine

·

82   has a bouquet that smells of tar, resin, pepper, tobacco, and (I believe) iodine. Intense and full-bodied, with no finesse, this full-throttle wine is not recommended for the shy or light-hearted. Drink it over the next 4–5 years. Last tasted 11/86.

CUVÉE DU BELVEDERE (ROBERT GIRARD)****

Proprietor Robert Girard, a wiry, inquisitive man, owns only ten acres of vines from a vineyard called Le Boucou. His vineyards are primarily Grenache (80%), but they also contain an unusually high amount of Counoise (15%), and 5% Syrah. Interestingly, he uses no Mourvèdre or Cinsault. Though not well known, he is a very fine winemaker. (He says that he makes wine only for his pleasure, and only enough for himself or to share with friends.) I have tasted only four vintages of his wine, but what an impressive quartet of wines they were. He uses the classic, old-time vinification, keeping his wines two years in wooden foudres. The style of his wine is one of a deep, rich color, an intense cherry, chocolatey bouquet, and rich, full-bodied, supple flavors. From what I have tasted, Girard's wines are exceptional—it is sad he does not produce more of it.

VINTAGES

1985—*Cuvée du Belvedere*—More like a Côte Rôtie than Châteauneuf-

·

90   du-Pape, the dense, dark ruby color, the bouquet of roasted raspberry fruit, and the opulent texture bursting with flavor of this seductive wine will offer great drinking at an early age. Anticipated maturity: 1989–1996. Last tasted 6/86.

1983—*Cuvée du Belvedere*—Girard's 1983 is another winner, yet again

·

89   its personality seems unlike a Châteauneuf-du-Pape. The black cherry, chocolatey, intense bouquet reminds one of a fine Pomerol. On the palate, the wine is creamy, lush, sweet, and very long with melted tannins. Anticipated maturity: now–1995. Last tasted 6/86.

1981—*Cuvée du Belvedere*—This is a very good, fully mature wine that

·

86   suffers only in comparison with the proprietor's other wines. His telltale winemaking style is again displayed—Pomerol-like crushed berry fruit and a soft, unctuous texture. Drink it over the next 2–4 years. Last tasted 6/86.

1978—*Cuvée du Belvedere*—A stunning wine with a persistent, smoky,
· crushed berry fruit aroma, this very deep, very expansive, ripe,
91 richly fruity wine has superb depth and complexity. It is a total
joy to drink. Anticipated maturity: now–1992. Last tasted 6/86.

CUVÉE DU TASTEVIN (LUCIEN BARROT)****

The elderly, crusty Lucien Barrot is another member of the excellent
growers' association called Prestige et Tradition, whose ten members
joined forces to share in the cost of a modern bottling facility. Barrot's
wines first came to my attention through the irrepressible Rhône wine
enthusiast Mark Williamson, of Willi's Wine Bar in Paris. The wines
made by Barrot are very rich and quite traditional, dense and loaded
with extract. I have no experience with anything older than 1978, but
his wines give every indication of being able to support 10–12 years of
cellaring. This is a very seriously run domaine with very high standards.
Unfortunately, less than 2,000 cases of red wine only are produced.

VINTAGES

1984—*Cuvée du Tastevin*—Moderately dark ruby in color, the 1984 has
· very supple, ripe, broad, easy to appreciate flavors of berry fruit
83 and subtle herbs. The finish is a little short, but this wine offers
uncritical drinking for the next 3–4 years. Last tasted 6/86.
1983—*Cuvée du Tastevin*—A big bouquet of cedar, chocolate, and
· plummy fruit is quite intense. Deep in color as well as deep and
86 broad on the palate with a powerful alcoholic clout, this full-
bodied wine needs a few more years to reach its peak. Anticipated maturity: 1988–1996. Last tasted 6/86.
1981—*Cuvée du Tastevin*—A complex cedary, rich, intense bouquet
· shows signs of full maturity. Full-bodied with a leathery, spicy,
86 robust texture, this old-style Châteauneuf-du-Pape will provide
very good drinking for at least 5–7 more years. Last tasted 6/86.
1979—*Cuvée du Tastevin*—Among recent vintages, this is the best ex-
· ample I have seen from Barrot. Very deep in color, rich in ex-
87 tract, and more concentrated than either the 1981 or 1983, this
is an ideal wine to serve with stews, meat, or game. Anticipated
maturity: now–1992. Last tasted 1/87.

CUVÉE DU VATICAN (FELICIEN DIFFONTY)****

The Diffonty family, like the Sabon family, is quite a famous name in
Châteauneuf-du-Pape. Diffonty's brother, Rémy, runs another estate in
Châteauneuf, Domaine du Haut des Terres Blanches. For various rea-

sons they are difficult men, and for some inexplicable reason seem to have a hostile view of America. Felicien Diffonty, the mayor of Châteauneuf-du-Pape, now refuses to sell his wine in America, and refuses to say why. That's a shame, because I remember old vintages such as the 1966, 1967, and 1970 Cuvée du Vatican that were delicious. The recent vintages augur well too, so hopefully Diffonty will see the folly of his narrowmindedness. The vineyard is 42 acres in size and dominated by the Grenache (90%). The remaining 10% consists of Cinsault, Syrah, and Mourvèdre. The wine is for drinking within its first 12 years of life—a fat, succulent, alcoholic, rather hedonistic, strongly flavored wine that is fleshy and plump.

The vinification practiced by Diffonty is very traditional. All the grapes are crushed and the wine fermented at very hot temperatures and macerated for an exceptionally long time, usually 21–25 days. The wine spends two full years in the oak foudres and is rarely filtered. It is one of the most forceful and powerful wines of Châteauneuf du Pape, and I enjoy its intensity and full-flavored character. It is sad that Diffonty will not, for the moment, sell his wine to America.

VINTAGES

1983—*Cuvée du Vatican*—While some 1983s are lacking in color and
• are tough wines, this wine has oodles of rich, intense, ripe fruit,
87 a powerful, voluptuous palate impression, a walloping alcoholic clout, and long finish. Drink it over the next 5–7 years. Last tasted 7/86.

1982—*Cuvée du Vatican*—There are few Châteauneufs this good in
• 1982. A rich bouquet of jammy, berry fruit and exotic spices is
87 first-class. On the palate, the wine has layers of fruit, an almost port-like unctuousness and sweetness, as well as a very long finish. It should be drunk over the next several years. Last tasted 7/86.

1981—*Cuvée du Vatican*—The jammy, berry fruit appears to be a dom-
• inant character, but in the 1981 one also finds scents of herbs
86 and leather. Dense, ripe, and quite alcoholic, this wine is fully mature and will continue to drink well for 5–6 years. Last tasted 7/86.

1980—*Cuvée du Vatican*—Most 1980s are lighter-styled wines, but Dif-
• fonty's Cuvée du Vatican is very alcoholic, generously flavored,
85 plump, and succulent. Drink it over the next 3–4 years. Last tasted 7/86.

1978—*Cuvée du Vatican*—A very good, possibly excellent wine, the
· smoky, berry fruit aromas swell and persist in the glass. In the
87 mouth, the wine shows the depth and structure of this great
vintage, has fine extract, and a long finish. It is just reaching its
apogee, where it should remain for 5–7 more years. Last tasted
7/86.

1976—*Cuvée du Vatican*—Browning at the edge and losing its fruit,
· this wine is just beginning to become unknit and the high alcohol
76 is beginning to become very noticeable. Drink it up. Last tasted
10/84.

1970—*Cuvée du Vatican*—The 1970 was better several years ago as it
· has now begun to fade. Nevertheless, it has a well-aged bouquet
86 of truffles, bacon fat, and warm, candied fruit. Soft, mellow and
generous on the palate, this full-bodied wine requires drinking
up. Last tasted 2/87.

1966—*Cuvée du Vatican*—Still holding together, this wine has been
· fully mature for over a decade, and proves that these wines,
87 after hitting their peaks, can last quite well if properly cellared.
A bouquet of smoky fruit and hazelnuts is attractive. Creamy,
round, very soft flavors still possess a great deal of opulent fruit.
The finish is long and alcoholic. Last tasted 10/85.

DELAS FRÈRES (DELAS) ***

This northern Rhône négociant reaches into the southern Rhône to buy
juice for its range of wines from Châteauneuf-du-Pape and Côtes du
Rhône. They own vineyards in the north and produce a bevy of exceptional wines, particularly their Hermitage, Condrieu, and Cornas, but
their southern wines are not of the same level of quality. I find their red
Châteauneuf-du-Pape sound, but straightforward and slightly dull. The
white Châteauneuf-du-Pape is a better wine and can be counted on for
its freshness and lively character. However, it is a wine to drink very
young.

DOMAINE DURIEU (PAUL DURIEU) ****

The "caves," and that is exactly what they appear to be, of the Domaine
Durieu are in the middle of the busy little wind-beaten village of
Châteauneuf-du-Pape. The tasting room here is reached after descend-
ing underground via some steep steps. Durieu's cellars stretch into the
bowels of the earth, where one is amazed to find the huge wooden
foudres and large fermentation tanks that had to be brought into these

caves piece by piece and then assembled. The handsome, black-haired Paul Durieu has 52 acres of vines ranging in age from 10 to 75 years old. His blend is 70% Grenache, 10% Syrah, and 20% Mourvèdre and Counoise. He is as critical of the light Beaujolais-styled wines of Châteauneuf-du-Pape as he is of the heavy, oxidized, overly muscular style that was widely practiced 30–40 years ago. He tries to strike a balance between these two extremes and, I believe, succeeds. He wins a lot of medals for his wines at the Mâcon fair each year. As vintages go, he likes 1978 the best, then 1983, 1981, and lastly 1985, a year that he says the press overrated.

Durieu, who believes in putting 50% of his grapes into the tanks uncrushed and the balance crushed, does not believe in the usefulness of the carbonic maceration method for making Châteauneuf-du-Pape. He has steadily augmented the percentage of Mourvèdre and Syrah in his wines, for it is these two varietals that he believes give a Châteauneuf-du-Pape the structure and stamina to last beyond ten years. He believes in only a limited use of wood for aging his wine. Normally his Châteauneuf is bottled early, after 12–14 months in wooden foudres. (Durieu also produces a decent Côtes du Rhône from a small vineyard near Vaison-la-Romaine.)

This is a good estate that produces a generously flavored, agreeable Châteauneuf-du-Pape with moderate aging potential.

VINTAGES

1985—*Durieu*—Durieu's 1985 is less successful than many other wines from this vintage. Quite low in acidity, it comes across on the palate as intensely fruity and cleanly made, but heavy and alcoholic. Anticipated maturity: now–1993. Last tasted 6/86.
· 82

1984—*Durieu*—This is another very good 1984, exhibiting broad, sweet, plummy fruit, lush, deep flavors, a soft texture, and undeniable appeal and charm for at least 2–3 years. Last tasted 6/86.
· 85

1983—*Durieu*—I agree with Durieu that this is one of the best wines of the vintage. A chocolatey, cedary, richly fruity bouquet is followed by a wine with voluptuous, concentrated flavors and a smashingly long finish. It should keep for at least a decade. Last tasted 6/86.
· 90

1982—*Durieu*—This vintage shows the alcoholic hotness that is often seen in this copious vintage. It has a heady, powerful bouquet, but the balance is fragile, and the wine's alcohol content of 15% clearly shows through. Drink it up. Last tasted 6/86.
· 80

1981—*Durieu*—The bouquet of ripe plums and leather is moderately
·   intense. On the palate, the wine is less deep than both the 1983
84   and 1984. It is a good wine, but should be drunk over the next
       2–4 years. Last tasted 6/86.

1978—*Durieu*—Fully mature, this big, intense, concentrated wine has
·   a multidimensional bouquet of chocolate, cedar, and smoky
88   fruit. Full-bodied, soft, and velvety, the 1978 offers very gener-
       ous flavors. Drink it over the next 4–6 years. Last tasted 6/86.

FONT DU LOUP (CHARLES MELIA)****

The Domaine Font du Loup is located in the northeastern sector of the
appellation of Châteauneuf-du-Pape. It is run by the handsome, young,
serious Charles Melia and his artist wife. The soil in this area is very
sandy, certain parcels being covered with the blanket of smooth, large
stones that are so common in Châteauneuf-du-Pape. This domaine was
purchased by Melia's grandparents in 1942, and since 1977 has been
run by Charles. He is a very dedicated winemaker who makes it clear
that since his time is spent in the vineyard and wine cellars, he has
little time for visitors. His vineyard has many old vines (the average age
is 45 years) and the blend he uses is 70% Grenache, 10% Syrah, 10%
Cinsault, and 10% Mourvèdre. He intends to incorporate Muscardin
into this formula as his acre of Muscardin comes into production. His
white wine is one of the best of the appellation, but he only makes 250
cases of it from 60% Grenache Blanc with the balance equally split
between Bourboulenc, Roussanne, and Clairette.

Melia argues that a strict selection is essential to get the highest
quality. Each vintage he claims his yield is among the lowest, and he
sells off to négociants those lots of wine he does not want. He complains
that few of his clients seem to care about this when they argue that his
Châteauneuf-du-Pape is more expensive than many others.

The wines of Font du Loup are very good and filled with character. I
predict many good things for this estate in the future.

VINTAGES

1985—*Font du Loup (white)*—This wine has a lovely rich fruitiness,
·   full body, yet delightful freshness and charm. It should be drunk
85   over the next 1–2 years. Last tasted 10/86.

1985—*Font du Loup (red)*—The 1985 red Châteauneuf-du-Pape from
·   Melia has exceptional depth, great color, a long, persistent pal-
88   ate impression, loads of black cherry fruit, and quite a future
       ahead of it. Anticipated maturity: 1988–1996. Last tasted 10/86.

1984—*Font du Loup (red)*—An unqualified success in the vintage, the
·   1984 is surprisingly dense in color, has a spicy, blackcurrant
86   bouquet and lush, round, generous flavors. Anticipated matu-
       rity: now–1996. Last tasted 10/86.

1983—*Font du Loup (red)*—Lighter in color than the other vintages,
·   the 1983 is fruity yet lacks flesh and depth, and seems very one-
75   dimensional. Drink it over the next 1–3 years. Last tasted 10/86.

1981—*Font du Loup (red)*—Almost a blockbuster, this is a deep, pro-
·   found, rich, densely packed wine with excellent color, plenty of
89   velvety, deep fruit, full body, and quite an alcoholic kick to it. It
       should drink well for 5–7 years. Last tasted 10/86.

1980—*Font du Loup (red)*—Deep ruby with some amber at the edge,
·   the 1980 has a ripe, straightforward bouquet, a fat, rather dull
83   palate, and lacks grip and acidity in the finish. Drink it up. Last
       tasted 10/86.

*FONT DE MICHELLE (GONNET FRÈRES)****

The youthful Gonnet brothers, inspired by their mentor and uncle, Henri Brunier of Vieux Télégraphe, have quickly built a reputation for a modern style, interesting, distinctive white (one of the appellation's best) and red Châteauneuf-du-Pape. The estate is of good size, 75 acres, and has a fairly typical blend of grapes for its red wine—70% Grenache, 10% Syrah, 10% Mourvèdre, and 10% Cinsault. Over three-fourths of the production is exported, primarily to England. The vines have a 30–35 year average age, and much of the vineyard is near the famous Vieux Télégraphe. Unfortunately, given its excellent quality, only 750 cases of white wine are made from a blend of 50% Grenache Blanc, 25% Clairette, and 25% Bourboulenc. Like some of the more quality-conscious growers, the Gonnets plan to augment the percentage of Mourvèdre in their wine to give it more structure and aging potential.

The vinification here is the modern style but with a twist. Only the Syrah is vinified by the carbonic maceration method; the other grape varieties are crushed and fermented in the classic manner. The wine spends no more than 6–12 months in large wooden foudres. Despite the similarities between the Gonnets' wine and Brunier's Vieux Télégraphe (even the equipment in each *chai* is the same), their wine is lighter and usually not as powerful or as alcoholic as Brunier's. I find Font de Michelle's red wine to be among the most elegant and stylish of the appellation. It is impeccably made, consistent from year to year, and very reasonably priced.

VINTAGES

1985—*Font de Michelle (white)*—Richly aromatic with the scent of
· tropical fruit, this crisp, luscious wine has enough acidity for
86 balance, and a very fragrant bouquet. It must be drunk very
young. Last tasted 10/86.

1985—*Font de Michelle (red)*—Plummy, fat, low in acidity, but deeply
· colored, round, and generous, this will make a fine bottle for
86 drinking early on. Anticipated maturity: 1988–1993. Last tasted
10/86.

1984—*Font de Michelle (red)*—Quite peppery and spicy in its bouquet,
· the 1984 Font de Michelle has good fruit, some firm tannins in
84 the finish, and an attractively elegant framework. Anticipated
maturity: 1988–1994. Last tasted 10/86.

1983—*Font de Michelle (red)*—Font de Michelle was very successful
· in 1983. More powerful and tannic than usual, this peppery, full-
87 bodied wine has plenty of depth and at least 5–7 years of aging
potential. Last tasted 10/86.

1982—*Font de Michelle (red)*—Soft and fully mature, this grapy, alco-
· holic wine has medium ruby color, decent flavor extract, and a
80 hot finish. Last tasted 10/86.

1981—*Font de Michelle (red)*—Fully mature, the 1981 smells of plum
· jam, has ample, round flavors, and a soft, pleasing finish. It
85 should be drunk over the next 2–3 years. Last tasted 10/86.

1978—*Font de Michelle (red)*—A big, smoky, tobacco-scented bouquet
· is followed on the palate by a wine that has broad layers of sweet,
89 ripe berry flavors. Quite delicious, this big, well-structured wine
will keep another 8–10 years. Very impressive—the best Font
de Michelle I have tasted. Last tasted 10/86.

CHÂTEAU FORTIA
(BARON LE ROY DE BOISEAUMARIE)*****

Historically, the ivy-covered, impressive, turreted Château Fortia is the
most important property of Châteauneuf-du-Pape. The late Baron Le
Roy developed in 1923 a set of stringent wine-producing regulations
that in 1936 became the basis for all of France's appellation contrôlée
laws. His son, also called Baron Le Roy, now runs this property with
his sister and brother-in-law. Despite the quality of the wine here (the
red is one of the finest of the appellation), three recent visits to Fortia
left me with the vivid impression that Baron Le Roy is not at all content
with either the wine of Fortia or the wine of Châteauneuf-du-Pape, an
appellation that he says "is going to hell." Seemingly tired of working

and feuding with the other owners, he castigates their expensive new destemmer-crusher (it does not crush the grapes enough), says there is still too much Grenache in the wine (he wants to add more Mourvèdre and Counoise to the vineyards), and says if he doesn't get his way he is going to retire. All of this notwithstanding, Fortia still produces a very fine, very ageworthy wine.

The vineyards are situated just to the east of the village. There are nearly 70 acres planted with 80% Grenache, 10% Syrah, 8% Mourvèdre, and 2% Counoise. If the baron gets his way, the percentage of the last two groups will increase. They also make a small amount (about 1,000 cases) of white wine from 70% Clairette, 15% Roussanne, and 15% Grenache Blanc. The vinification is classic, with the grapes crushed and then kept two years in large oak foudres in the impressive underground cellars.

At the time of writing this book (1987), I detected a lack of direction in the affairs of Fortia. I hope I have misread the situation because this estate is one of the leaders of Châteauneuf-du-Pape, and I would hate to see the wine suffer from a period of inattention and internal bickering among family members.

VINTAGES

1985—*Fortia (white)*—This is rather dull and neutral-tasting wine with plenty of acidity but no real focal point to its flavor. Last tasted 74 10/86.

1985—*Fortia (red)*—Richly fruity, deep in color, but dangerously low in acidity, if this wine develops more structure to go along with 85 the excellent concentration, it will merit a better review. Anticipated maturity: 1988–1994. Last tasted 10/86.

1984—*Fortia (red)*—Moderately deep color with chunky, fruity, fat textures, the 1984 has good fruit, but a straightforward, one-84 dimensional quality. Anticipated maturity: now–1991. Last tasted 10/86.

1983—*Fortia (red)*—Quite soft, but opulently rich and fruity, the 1983 Fortia has a very deep color, full body, plenty of jammy, sweet 87 berry fruit, melted tannins, and a long, supple finish. Anticipated maturity: now–1993. Last tasted 6/86.

1982—*Fortia (red)*—Delicious to drink in an uncritical way, the 1982 has average color, a fat, alcoholic, heady fruitiness that swells 84 in the glass, low acidity, and a short finish. Drink it up. Last tasted 10/86.

1981—*Fortia (red)*—I ran across some disappointing bottles of this
· wine in France, but tasted here the wine is deep in color, has a
87 full-intensity bouquet of jammy fruit and oriental spices, full
body, good harmony, and 5–7 more years of life. Last tasted
10/86.

1980—*Fortia (red)*—A notable success for the vintage, this wine is fully
· mature, has a flattering, seductive, open bouquet of peppery,
86 raspberry fruit, soft, round, generous flavors, and a good finish.
Drink it over the next 2–3 years. Last tasted 12/85.

1979—*Fortia (red)*—This is certainly a good wine; however, given the
· vintage, I would have expected more concentration. A moder-
84 ately intense peppery, raspberry-scented bouquet is pleasant.
Soft and well developed, this medium- to full-bodied wine is
good, but falls off in the mouth. Drink it up. Last tasted 11/84.

1978—*Fortia (red)*—This is the finest Fortia in the last decade. It has
· developed beautifully in the bottle, displaying classic raspberry,
90 peppery, and floral aromas. Still youthfully deep ruby/purple,
this full-bodied wine has layers of fruit and finishes long and
harmoniously. Anticipated maturity: now–1992. Last tasted
1/87.

1976—*Fortia (red)*—Fully mature, the 1976 Fortia is one of the stars of
· this generally overrated vintage. Showing some brown at the
87 edge, it has a well-developed oriental spice, leathery, smoked-
meat bouquet, robust, dusty flavors with a good deal of fruit and
body. Drink over the next 2–5 years. Last tasted 6/86.

1974—*Fortia (red)*—Soft and intensely spicy, this ample wine has a
· creamy richness and earthy, rustic style that give it appeal.
84 Drink it up. Last tasted 6/86.

1964—*Fortia (red)*—Quite brown at the edge, the 1964 Fortia has a big,
· mushroomy nose of candied, smoky, but faded fruit. On the
84 palate, it is soft, sweet, a little tired, but still full-bodied and a
pleasure to drink. I suspect it was a much better, more intense
wine 4–5 years ago. Last tasted 6/86.

CHÂTEAU DE LA GARDINE (GASTON BRUNEL)***

The late Gaston Brunel, who acquired this estate that lies in the western
sector of the appellation not far from the Rhône River, was one of
Châteauneuf-du-Pape's great champions. The soil is lighter and shal-
lower here, and not as highly regarded as the other sections of the
Châteauneuf-du-Pape. In hot drought years this soil often causes se-

vere stress to the vineyards. However, Brunel, through an extensive rehabilitation program, enlarged this domaine to 131 acres, planted it with an interesting blend of 60% Grenache, a very significant portion of Syrah (23%), and the rest Mourvèdre, Muscardin, and Cinsault. There are plans to increase the percentage of Mourvèdre while decreasing the amount of Grenache. The vines average 32 years of age.

Gaston Brunel, the author of a major book on the region published in 1980, died tragically in the summer of 1986 in a fishing accident, the first time in his life he had ever gone fishing. His two sons, Maxime and Patrick, now run the property and were well prepared by their father.

Although approximately 700 cases of good white wine are made here from a blend of one-third each of Roussanne, Bourboulenc, and Grenache Blanc, the pride of this house is their red wine. While La Gardine could use the special embossed bottle approved for the growers of Châteauneuf-du-Pape, they utilize their own bottle, a brown-colored, squat, somewhat crooked-looking bottle that I find aesthetically unpleasing as well as eccentric. Certainly the red wine, though not one of the blockbuster Châteauneuf-du-Papes, is quite good and very consistent in mediocre vintages. It is made largely in the traditional manner, with 70% of the grapes crushed and 30% uncrushed. The wine is kept one year in tanks and two years in oak foudres. The cellars here are very impressive (fully air conditioned, a luxury in France) and kept meticulously clean. The wine style they search for is one of "harmony and balance without excessive alcohol."

La Gardine's red wine ages very well. If not among the most exciting of wines, it is very good, and quite an elegant, very different style of Châteauneuf-du-Pape that is extremely consistent from vintage to vintage. In certain vintages, a special luxury cuvée, called Cuvée de la Génération, is made. This is normally only produced in the vintages that La Gardine considers the finest (e.g., 1985, 1978, 1961, 1959, and 1952). It is rarely sold on the market, but reserved for family drinking.

VINTAGES

1985—*La Gardine (white)*—La Gardine's very fruity, crisp, fresh white
· wine would appear to be somewhat of a secret. It is quite good
85 and like most of the others made here requires drinking within
1–2 years of the vintage. Last tasted 7/86.

1985—*La Gardine (red)*—Brunel is quite high on this vintage. Interest-
· ingly, their 1985 is more restrained and less obviously opulent
86 than other wines. It still has a good measure of ripe black cherry

fruit, full body, and 5–10 years of further evolution. Anticipated maturity: 1989–1998. Last tasted 6/86.

1984—*La Gardine (red)*—A lighter style of Châteauneuf, the 1984 has medium ruby color, medium body, moderately intense cherry fruit, and an adequate finish. Anticipated maturity: now–1991. Last tasted 6/86.

• 82

1983—*La Gardine (red)*—More powerful than the 1984 or 1985, the 1983 is rather closed and tannic, but has a good spicy, leather-and-tar-scented bouquet, and dry, full-bodied finish. It needs time in the bottle. Anticipated maturity: 1990–1997. Last tasted 6/86.

• 84

1982—*La Gardine (red)*—Slightly hot in the finish, with a soft, fruity character, the 1982 requires drinking up over the next 2–4 years. Last tasted 6/86.

• 82

1981—*La Gardine (red)*—Quite good, the 1981 La Gardine has reached full maturity, has a rich open-knit, fruity, floral bouquet, full body, good depth, and soft, melted tannins. Drink over the next 5–6 years. Last tasted 6/86.

• 85

1980—*La Gardine (red)*—An excellent year for La Gardine, the 1980 has a peppery, raspberry, intense bouquet, seductive, creamy, rich flavors, an elegant framework, and very soft, enjoyable finish. Anticipated maturity: now–1992. Last tasted 6/86.

• 86

1979—*La Gardine (red)*—Typically very elegant, as many vintages of La Gardine are, the 1979 is ready to drink but will keep for 5–6 years. It is quite similar to a good Premier Cru burgundy. Last tasted 6/86.

• 85

1978—*La Gardine (red)*—Still not mature, the big, earthy, leathery, oaky nose is followed by a wine that is full-bodied, not as powerful as other Châteauneuf-du-Papes, but mouth-filling and still filled with promise. Anticipated maturity: 1988–1996. Last tasted 6/86.

• 87

1969—*La Gardine (red)*—The bouquet of roasted prunes, fennel, and leather is complex. The color is showing age and the impression on the palate is one of leanness and austerity. It is not my style of Châteauneuf-du-Pape. Last tasted 6/86.

• 72

1952—*La Gardine (red)*—This is in much better shape than the 1969. An intense bouquet of roasted hazelnuts and rich, jammy fruit is followed by a wine filled with sweet, ripe layers of extract. The tremendous expansion and breadth on the palate is much like that of a very fine burgundy. This is a delicious, fully mature wine. Last tasted 6/86, from a magnum.

• 90

CHÂTEAUNEUF-DU-PAPE

DOMAINE DU GRAND TINEL (ELIE JEUNE)****

This large estate of 185 acres, planted with 80% Grenache and the rest Syrah, Mourvèdre, Counoise, and Muscardin, produces a very traditional Châteauneuf-du-Pape that emphasizes power, body, leathery, spicy, exotic scents over the pure berry fruit found in the wines from the more modern school of Châteauneuf producers. The average age of the vines is quite old (50 years—there is one parcel of 90-year-old vines). Most of its vineyards are located in the eastern half of the appellation, one near Courthézon and the other superbly placed near La Nerthe. Jeune is a fine winemaker, but he, like some other estates in Châteauneuf, continues the ridiculous practice of bottling only when the wine is sold. Today one can find vintages back to 1976 still in foudres. This practice saves space and money initially, but wines kept too long in the large wooden foudres and then bottled lack the freshness and fruit of earlier bottlings. Jeune makes excellent, often outstanding, wine, but I wish he would do his entire *mise en bouteille* at the same time, as is done at the very best domaines serious about putting approximately the same wine in all the bottles. (Jeune also uses a secondary label for his Châteauneuf-du-Pape, Les Caves St.-Paul.)

The wine of Grand Tinel, very classically made, extremely powerful, and aged in oak foudres for two to three years before bottling, is one of the most forceful and distinctive of the appellation, but I would advise buying the first releases of a given vintage (normally three years after the vintage) and staying away from the old vintages that have just been bottled and put on the market.

VINTAGES

1985—*Grand Tinel*—Tasted from several foudres, this is a monster Châteauneuf-du-Pape with the alcohol tipping the scales at
· 90   14.7%. An intense bouquet of roasted nuts and peppery raspberry fruit is followed by a huge, very concentrated wine of immense size, weight, and clout. It is not for the shy. Anticipated maturity: 1990–2001. Last tasted 6/86.

1983—*Grand Tinel*—This is a densely colored, rather opaque wine with a big, chocolatey, cedar box, spicy, smoked-meat nose, power-
· 87   ful, bold flavors, and plenty of tannin in the strong finish. Anticipated maturity: 1988–1996. Last tasted 6/86.

1982—*Grand Tinel*—The 1982 Grand Tinel is out of balance, with excessive alcohol that scorches the palate. The color also shows a
· 74   great deal of orange at the rim. This wine is on the edge. Drink it up. Last tasted 6/86.

· 269 ·

1981—*Grand Tinel*—The 1981 has a huge, cedary, peppery, plummy
· bouquet, is quite full-bodied, very long, chewy, and reminiscent
90 of the huge, massive Châteauneufs of yesteryear. Anticipated
maturity: now–1998. Last tasted 6/86.

1979—*Grand Tinel*—Peppery, raspberry fruit oozes from the glass. On
· the palate the wine is more elegant and less extroverted than
86 most Grand Tinels. Quite fruity and lush, this is an attractive
wine for drinking over the next 4–5 years. Last tasted 9/84.

1978—*Grand Tinel*—The 1978, from the first *mise en bouteille*, not the
· oxidized, tired bottling done in 1986, is a robust, full-throttle,
90 chewy, intense, highly concentrated wine with tremendous palate presence and, I am sure, a whopping degree of alcohol.
Anticipated maturity: now–2000. Last tasted 11/86.

E. GUIGAL (E. GUIGAL)***

This superb producer and vineyard owner from Ampuis in the northern
Rhône purchases juice from growers in Châteauneuf-du-Pape for his
bottlings from that appellation. With the decline of Paul Jaboulet's Les
Cèdres Châteauneuf-du-Pape in the seventies and eighties, Guigal's
wine is clearly the best among the négociants. In fact, it is very good
and capable of at least ten years of cellaring. Guigal refuses to reveal
his sources for juice, but he keeps the wine in tank and barrel for two
to three years before its release. He has been trying to get more Syrah
and Mourvèdre in the blend to give the wine more aromatic complexity
as well as structure.

With all the fine Châteauneufs from the top growers, it is tempting to
overlook the quality of Guigal's Châteauneuf. Don't make that mistake.
His 1982 and 1979 competed with the best of the appellation.

VINTAGES

1982—*Guigal*—This is an example of why one does not pass up Gui-
· gal's Châteauneuf. It may be the finest wine of the appellation
87 in 1982. It is loaded with black cherry fruit, has a deep color,
full body, excellent depth, and shocking length. Anticipated maturity: now–1993. Last tasted 12/86.

1981—*Guigal*—The 1981 is a good, chunky, full-bodied, straightfor-
· ward-styled wine that will provide agreeable drinking over the
84 next 5–7 years. Last tasted 12/86.

1980—*Guigal*—Well colored, deep in extract, but fairly simple and
· even dull, this wine should be drunk over the next 3–4 years.
83 Last tasted 3/85.

1979—*Guigal*—A noteworthy success, the 1979 has a black/ruby color,
a spicy, smoked-meat bouquet, tremendous richness, ripeness
87 and length, and a very generous finish. Anticipated maturity:
now–1992. Last tasted 11/84.

1978—*Guigal*—Dense in color, but somewhat dull and flat on the palate, I have seen much better bottles of Guigal's 1978 Château-
? neuf. Judgment reserved. Last tasted 11/86.

DOMAINE HAUT DES TERRES BLANCHES
(RÉMY DIFFONTY)***

High up on a hill to the east of the village of Châteauneuf-du-Pape are
the home and cellars of Rémy Diffonty. From this spot is undoubtedly
one of the best vistas in the environs of Châteauneuf. Diffonty owns 80
acres of vines planted with 70% Grenache, and the rest Syrah, Mourvèdre, and Cinsault. His wine tends to fall in between the very intense,
concentrated, old style of properties such as Grand Tinel and the floral,
berry fruit-scented, more modern-styled wines such as Vieux Lazaret.
It is never very dark in color or especially concentrated, yet it always
seems to have broad, expansive flavors and a certain amount of charm.

Diffonty, who failed to show up for two scheduled appointments,
would not permit tasting of recent vintages; no explanation was given.
The notes below are from several years ago. Suffice it to say I found
him difficult, if not openly hostile.

No white wine is produced here.

VINTAGES

1981—*Haut des Terres Blanches*—Rather light in color, moderately rich
and fruity, this full-bodied wine has plenty of peppery, berry
84 fruit, and a well-developed bouquet of caramel and spices. Anticipated maturity: now–1989. Last tasted 12/84.

1979—*Haut des Terres Blanches*—This is the best vintage of Diffonty's
Châteauneuf that I have tasted. Fleshy, rich, and generously
86 flavored, its velvety texture offers great appeal. It should be
drunk up. Last tasted 10/84.

1978—*Haut des Terres Blanches*—Given the vintage, the 1978 is disappointing. Straightforward, jammy berry aromas interplay with
82 scents of thyme. On the palate, the wine is light, round, and
fully mature. Last tasted 10/84.

1976—*Haut des Terres Blanches*—Browning at the edge, this wine
lacks flesh and length. The finish exhibits plenty of tannin and
76 alcoholic hotness. Last tasted 4/83.

DOMAINE DE MARCOUX (ELIE ARMENIER)****

There are not many Frenchmen who tower above six feet, five inches in height, but the young Armenier, who runs Domaine de Marcoux's 57 acres of vineyards in the northernmost end of the appellation, certainly exceeds this. An imposing figure, he uses only three grapes for making his red wine—70% Grenache, 15% Cinsault, and 15% Mourvèdre. His white wine is, along with Vieux Télégraphe's, the finest in the non-malolactic modern school of white Châteauneufs. It is a blend of 60% Clairette and 40% Bourboulenc. The red wines, stylistically, are very much as Armenier describes them—"not too tannic, not too heavy, but rich and fruity."

The fermentation used at Marcoux is typical of many estates at Châteauneuf-du-Pape. Seventy-five percent of the grapes are crushed and vinified traditionally, the balance put in the tanks whole. The juice usually macerates with the skins for at least 12–15 days.

This is a very good estate that seems to garner a lot of top awards at Châteauneuf-du-Pape's annual wine judging, the Festival of St. Marc. Most of the local cognoscenti think Marcoux's white wine is one of the two or three best of the appellation, and the red clearly among the top two dozen.

VINTAGES

1985—*Marcoux (white)*—This is a good concentrated, gloriously fruity, fragrant, ripe, sensual wine loaded with character. Drink it over the next year. Last tasted 12/86.
· 87

1985—*Marcoux (red)*—Very deeply colored, the 1985 Marcoux has a powerful, rich, jammy bouquet of cassis, fat, low acid flavors, full body, and a soft, generous finish. Anticipated maturity: 1988–1994. Last tasted 10/86.
· 86

1983—*Marcoux (red)*—Differently styled than the above wine, the 1983 has more of a spicy, leather-scented, beefy aroma, a drier, leaner, more tannic impression, but has good fruit in the finish. Anticipated maturity: 1990–1998. Last tasted 10/86.
· 85

1982—*Marcoux (red)*—Surprisingly more successful than the property's 1981, the 1982 has a gutsy, rich, full-bodied, corpulent style, rich, chunky, berry fruit, and if not much finesse, plenty of flavor. Drink it over the next 3–4 years. Last tasted 10/86.
· 83

1981—*Marcoux (red)*—This is an awkward wine that may turn out better than the rating suggests. The color is deep, but the wine is closed and unyielding and has considerable tannin; however,
· 82

there are signs of fine underlying depth. Anticipated maturity: 1989–1996. Last tasted 10/86.

1978—*Marcoux (red)*—Very deep in color, the 1978 is a very big, ripe,
· rich wine with an amazingly high level of tannin still present.
87 Surprisingly, there are no signs of maturity in this robust, very unevolved, intense wine. Anticipated maturity: 1990–2000. Last tasted 10/86.

1970—*Marcoux (red)*—A great wine, the 1970 has a full-intensity bou-
· quet of cedarwood, blackcurrants, (a Lynch-Bages imitator?),
90 rich, broad layers of flesh and fruit, a super finish and at least a decade of life ahead of it. This is very impressive wine. Antici-pated maturity: now–2000. Last tasted 10/86.

1969—*Marcoux (red)*—A washed-out bouquet of tobacco, herbs, and
· faded fruit signals that this wine is in decline. On the palate, the
74 wine is very spicy, but a little dry and severe. It is past its prime. Last tasted 10/86.

1967—*Marcoux (red)*—The 1967 lacks the complexity and finesse of
· the 1970, but for sheer power, an extroverted, powerful bouquet,
88 and robust, concentrated, alcoholic flavors, this big, burly wine provides immense pleasure. Drink it up. Last tasted 10/86.

CHÂTEAU MAUCOIL (PIERRE QUIOT)***

Château Maucoil is in the very northwestern section of the appellation. Its 55 acres of vineyards adjoin those of Mont-Redon. The family of Pierre Quiot manages this estate and produces nearly 12,000 cases of Châteauneuf-du-Pape from a blend of 60% Grenache, 10% Cinsault, and the rest Mourvèdre and Counoise. The style of wine is very modern. Rich, ripe, rather uncomplicated, berry fruit flavors, and soft, easy to drink, grapy fruit are preferred over something a bit more serious and cerebral. The Quiots also own another small estate in Châteauneuf-du-Pape called Quiot Saint-Pierre that produces the same style of wine. The Gigondas estate of Les Pradets is also part of this family's holdings.

This is certainly a good wine, cleanly made and bottled very early to preserve its freshness and fruit. It requires drinking young, preferably within five to eight years of the vintage.

No white wine is produced here.

VINTAGES

1985—*Maucoil*—Medium deep ruby color, intense cherry fruit aromas,
· soft, quite alcoholic, ripe, chewy, but not complex, this wine will
84 provide uncomplicated drinking early on. Anticipated maturity: now–1992. Last tasted 10/86.

1984—*Maucoil*—Deep in color, with a light-intensity berry fruit nose,
· the 1984 has some hard, tough tannins in the finish, but good
75 ripeness and a fleshy texture. Anticipated maturity: 1988–1992.
Last tasted 10/86.
1983—*Maucoil*—This offering has a leathery, spicy, beefy character in
· the nose, good length, more power and tannin than either the
84 1984 or 1985, but seems less fruity, albeit more interesting. Anticipated maturity: now–1993. Last tasted 10/86.

DOMAINE DE MONT-REDON (FABRE/ABEILLE)****

Mont-Redon is one of the historic old names in Châteauneuf-du-Pape,
with perhaps the most splendidly situated vineyard of any domaine,
directly on the stony plateau north of the bustling village. A very large
property, Mont-Redon has 208 acres of vines. For the red wine, the
vineyards are planted with 65% Grenache, 15% Syrah, 15% Cinsault,
and 5% Mourvèdre. The domaine also has experimental plantings of
the other permitted varieties of this appellation. This is an impeccable
property, run with great enthusiasm by Jean Abeille and Didier Fabre,
the grandsons of the late Henri Plantin who purchased this estate in
1921. For several years I was critical of the "lightening up" of Mont-
Redon, preferring to remember with great joy the pleasures of the
extraordinary 1947, 1949, 1955, and 1961. (The last two vintages were
on the wine list at the famous Paris restaurant Taillevent until several
years ago at shockingly low prices.) The flirtation with this lighter,
rather insipid style appears to have ended. Mont-Redon seems, since
1981, to be putting more flesh and muscle back into the wine. Interestingly, Abeille and Fabre vigorously deny any change in the style of the
wine other than the purchasing of new equipment for making the wine.
They also intend to increase the percentage of Mourvèdre to 15% to
give their wine more character and structure. They think 1985 is, along
with 1978, 1970, 1967, and 1961, among the five greatest vintages in the
last 25 years, and clearly the best in the eighties for Mont-Redon. The
current style of winemaking here is one that seems to capture the
proper marriage between the unbridled power and hefty weight of an
old-style Châteauneuf-du-Pape and the unexciting, simple, fruity, commercial style of some of the most modern practitioners.

Their white wine is not nearly as good as that made at such domaines
as Nalys, Beaucastel, Vieux Télégraphe, Font du Loup, Marcoux, or
Fond du Michelle, and improvements could be made. They are the

largest producers (about 4,500 cases) of white Châteauneuf-du-Pape (made from a blend of 40% Grenache Blanc, 25% Bourboulenc, 25% Picpoul, and the rest Terret Blanc).

The red wine here is vinified in the traditional or classic manner. The grapes are all crushed and fermented at temperatures of 31–32° centigrade. The maceration period lasts three weeks. The wine is then passed through a filtration prior to being placed for 14–16 months in large oak foudres, and again filtered prior to bottling. Everything here is run with great attention to detail. To keep the average age of the vines at an impressive 40 years old, there is a detailed rotational replanting system. Each year 100 tons of cow manure are spread on the vineyards. The innovative Abeille and Fabre have even begun to experiment with new oak casks for aging their red wine.

To suggest that the current wines at Mont-Redon are as profound, concentrated, and as long-lived as their wines of the forties, fifties, and sixties would be foolish and, of course, untrue. However, the red wines are of a very high level of quality. I hope that Abeille and Fabre will come to realize that the intense filtration they give their wine is more dangerous to its richness and character than they are now willing to admit. It is these flavor-eviscerating filtrations more than anything else that I feel are retaining some of this wine's potentially great character in the cellulose filter pads through which the wine must pass.

VINTAGES

1985—*Mont-Redon (white)*—Tart, high acid, fruity flavors offer little of
· the generosity or multitude of tropical fruit and floral aromas
78 that a top white Châteauneuf can provide. Last tasted 6/86.

1985—*Mont-Redon (red)*—Regarded as the best vintage for Mont-
· Redon since 1978, the 1985 is dense in color, very ripe, quite
87 full-bodied, soft, and lush, with a fine finish. This wine will
provide great appeal early on. Anticipated maturity: 1988–1996.
Last tasted 6/86.

1984—*Mont-Redon (red)*—Not bad, but compact, narrowly focused fla-
· vors and medium body appear to lack the flesh and substance of
77 the better wines of this vintage. Anticipated maturity: now–
1991. Last tasted 6/86.

1983—*Mont-Redon (red)*—A full-intensity bouquet of very ripe fruit
· and scents of apricots, peaches, and berry jam are followed by
85 a wine that has medium ruby color, round, generous flavors, and

a very forward appeal. Anticipated maturity: now–1993. Last tasted 6/86.

1982—*Mont-Redon (red)*—Somewhat watery in color, the 1982 tastes
·   very alcoholic, unstructured, and lacks focus or depth. Drink it
78   up. Last tasted 6/86.

1981—*Mont-Redon (red)*—Marginally deeper than the 1983, the 1981
·   has more power, body, depth, and a more complex bouquet and
86   set of flavors. Full-bodied yet elegant, this wine has the requisite
     muscle to age nicely for 5–7 years. Last tasted 6/86.

1980—*Mont-Redon (red)*—Deep ruby color, surprisingly more closed
·   and tannic than the 1981, Mont-Redon's 1980 is quite fruity,
85   medium- to full-bodied, and 1–2 years away from maturity. Last
     tasted 6/86.

1979—*Mont-Redon (red)*—Straightforward, moderately intense aromas
·   of cherries and leather are pleasant enough. On the palate, the
83   wine is one-dimensional and ready to drink, but more like a
     Côtes du Rhône than a famous Châteauneuf-du-Pape. Last
     tasted 6/86.

1978—*Mont-Redon (red)*—The new double filtration system as well as
·   new equipment was installed in time for this vintage. This is a
86   very good wine, but I believe the filtering has taken a good
     amount of fruit and body out of it. Medium- to full-bodied, still
     young, this wine should last well. Anticipated maturity: now–
     1994. Last tasted 6/86.

1977—*Mont-Redon (red)*—Simple yet charming, clean cherry fruit fla-
·   vors offer uncritical quaffing from this medium-bodied wine.
78   Drink it up. Last tasted 6/86.

1976—*Mont-Redon (red)*—After the complex, plummy, fruitcake nose,
·   the palate of the 1976 delivers a dry, severe, tannic jolt to the
?   senses. There seems to be some good fruit underneath the tan-
     nin, but this is a hard wine to figure out. Judgment reserved.
     Last tasted 6/86.

1973—*Mont-Redon (red)*—Well-developed, fully mature aromas of to-
·   bacco, berry fruit, herbs, and flowers are quite appealing. In the
85   mouth, the wine is soft, fat, and showing full maturity. Drink it
     up. Last tasted 6/86.

1972—*Mont-Redon (red)*—This is a big, burly, rich, exotic wine, the
·   likes of which one does not see anymore from Mont-Redon.
88   Smoky, truffle, and beeflike aromas lead to a full-bodied, very
     concentrated wine with quite a bit of mouth-filling extract. Drink
     it up. Last tasted 6/86.

1971—*Mont-Redon (red)*—A gloriously rich bouquet of toffee, coffee,
• sweet, jammy fruit is complex and persistent. Very long, deep,
89 velvety, sweet flavors are at their peak. This is a beautiful, very
tasty glass of Châteauneuf. Drink it up. Last tasted 6/86.

1970—*Mont-Redon (red)*—Not as advanced as the 1971, the 1970 may,
• when it reaches full maturity, prove to be a finer wine. Deep
89 ruby with some amber at the edge, this smoky, chewy, dense,
full-bodied wine offers plenty of unctuous, sweet fruit. Anticipated maturity: now–1992. Last tasted 6/86.

1967—*Mont-Redon (red)*—Abeille thinks 1985 and 1981 are this good.
• That seems optimistic to me. A fabulous nose of candied fruit,
90 oriental spices, and smoked meat is of full intensity. Broad,
creamy flavors, full body, and a sweet, almost port-like finish
are superb. Drink it up. Last tasted 6/86.

1964—*Mont-Redon (red)*—Very rustic, earthy aromas in the nose and
• washed-out, faded, leafy fruit flavors suggest senility for this
67 very old, decrepit wine. Last tasted 6/86.

1961—*Mont-Redon (red)*—This is a magnificent Châteauneuf-du-Pape.
• At its apogee but in full form, this fragrant, ripe, decadently
92 rich, velvety, complex wine offers a smorgasbord of earthly de-
lights. It will keep for 4–6 more years. Last tasted 6/86, from a
magnum.

1955—*Mont-Redon (red)*—Just beginning to lose some of its sweet, ripe
• fruit, this wine still has plenty of body, vibrancy, ripeness, and
86 length. Do not tempt fate—it should be drunk up without hesitation. Last tasted 12/84.

1949—*Mont-Redon (red)*—Two bottles of this drunk in 1984 were out-
• standing and very much alive. Practically 20% of the old bottle
92 was sediment, but the balance was loaded with smoky, jammy,
very spicy fruit, very broad, multidimensional flavors, and heaps
of flavor in the exceptionally long finish. Why don't more estates
in this appellation try and achieve something of this magnitude?

*DOMAINES MOUSSET (LOUIS MOUSSET)****

The cellars of the Domaines Mousset are adjacent to the restaurant and
hotel they own just southeast of the village. It is called the Hostellerie
Château des Fines-Roches, and offers the best rooms, food, and wine
list in the small village of Châteauneuf-du-Pape.

The Mousset family, now represented by the tall, handsome, gray
haired Louis, does an enormous business in Rhône wine. They have
four domaines in Châteauneuf-du-Pape, the most famous of which is

Château des Fines-Roches, but also Domaine de Clos du Roi, Domaine de la Font du Roi, and Clos Saint-Michel. From these estates, they produce approximately 40,000 cases of wine. Their négociant business is, however, staggering. Led by their generic wine called Le P'Tit Bistro, they sell 700,000 cases of wine in an average year. There have been some tremendous swings in the quality and style of their wines, but most observers today feel that Mousset is trying very hard to resurrect the reputation of the flagship wine of his empire, the once highly respected Fines-Roches. All of the wines are made in one of the most modern cellars of the region. Temperature-controlled, stainless steel tanks and computer terminals are everywhere. However, the wines are given a relatively traditional, hot, lengthy vinification. While they practice the carbonic maceration method for their generic wines and Côtes du Rhônes, they do not use it for Châteauneuf-du-Pape. The wines are aged 12–16 months in tank and foudre, and given a light filtration prior to bottling.

Among the four estates, Fines-Roches is certainly the best wine, but I must speak highly of the Clos Saint-Michel, which has an unusually high percentage of Syrah (35%) in its makeup. Here are the sizes of the vineyards and the grape percentages used in making the wine.

Fines-Roches: 111 acres, 66% Grenache, 16% Syrah, the balance Mourvèdre, Cinsault, and Counoise

Clos du Roi: 62 acres, 90% Grenache, 10% Cinsault

Font du Roi: 59 acres, 70% Grenache, 10% Syrah, 10% Cinsault, 10% Muscardin

Clos Saint-Michel: 25 acres, 65% Grenache, 35% Syrah

The style of wine here has changed over the last decade. In tasting the 1983s, 1984s, and 1985s, several prominent stylistic similarities stuck out. The wines are very deeply colored, have heaps of ripe fruit and full body, show very clean winemaking, but in many cases seemed to lack backbone and acidity. Delicious as many of them are, they seem to require drinking up before they reach 8–10 years of age.

VINTAGES

1985—*Fines-Roches*—This is a densely colored, very rich wine with loads of peppery, cassis-scented fruit. Quite supple, full-bodied, and low in acidity, the 1985 Fines-Roches will drink splendidly well young. Anticipated maturity: 1988–1994. Last tasted 6/86.
·
87

1984—*Fines-Roches*—Very good for the vintage, the 1984 has a deep, healthy color, plump, richly fruity taste, good acidity, body, and aftertaste. Drink over the next 4–5 years. Last tasted 6/86.
·
85

1983—*Fines-Roches*—Many 1983s tend to be hard and tough; the
· Fines-Roches, however, is very fruity, somewhat loosely knit,
86 but broadly flavored, chunky, and quite appealing, if lacking a
bit of backbone for longevity. Anticipated maturity: now–1991.
Last tasted 6/86.

1985—*Clos Saint-Michel*—The opaque color and fragrant blackberry,
· smoky character of the Syrah comes out immediately. Full-bod-
87 ied, very opulent and unctuous, this wine lacks acidity but offers
a tremendous mouthful of corpulent Châteauneuf-du-Pape. Anticipated maturity: now–1992. Last tasted 6/86.

1984—*Clos Saint-Michel*—Very deeply colored, more oaky on the
· nose, this wine has plenty of extract but seems to lack complex-
83 ity and some character. Drink over the next 2–4 years.

1983—*Clos Saint-Michel*—The very opaque color is again present. The
· bouquet exhibits a little more spice, smoky bacon fat aromas,
86 berry fruit and oak. On the palate, the wine is again a trifle soupy
and unfocused but very meaty and pleasurable. Drink over the
next 4–5 years. Last tasted 6/86.

1985—*Clos du Roi*—Very chunky, fruity, but extremely low in acidity
· and structure, this loosely knit wine will offer enjoyable yet un-
82 complicated drinking for the next 3–5 years. Last tasted 6/86.

1984—*Clos du Roi*—Again the similarity in style, apparently regardless
· of vintage differences, is amazing. Very fruity, quite soft, and
83 low in acidity, this wine has oodles of fruit and requires consumption over the next 3–4 years. Last tasted 6/86.

1985—*Font du Roi*—Deep in color, very ripe, with a jammy, berrylike
· nose, this wine has heaps of fruit, full body, and a velvety finish.
85 Anticipated maturity: now–1993. Last tasted 6/86.

1984—*Font du Roi*—Straightforward scents of fruit swell in the glass.
· Medium- to full-bodied, with some tannin in the finish, this wine
82 shows less concentration than some of the other Mousset wines.
Anticipated maturity: now–1990. Last tasted 6/86.

1983—*Font du Roi*—Quite good, fully mature, this medium-bodied,
· intensely fruity wine offers little in the way of finesse or ele-
84 gance, but so typical of the style here are the loads of ripe,
creamy fruit. Drink it over the next 3–4 years. Last tasted 6/86.

DOMAINE DE NALYS (DUFAYS)***

The late Dr. Philippe DuFays was the southern Rhône's most ardent
proponent of the carbonic maceration method for producing red wines.
DuFays died in 1978 and his beloved domaine was sold to a syndicate.

The winemaking has not changed, however, and at Nalys all 13 of the permitted grape varieties are planted. The current size of the estate is 124 acres; the ages of the vines range from 20 to 81 years. The red wine is a result of a blend that features 60% Grenache, 12% Syrah, 6% Cinsault, and the remainder the other varietals. The white wine, which is excellent and which along with Vieux Télégraphe represents the finest of the modern, fruity, perfumed style, is made from 30% Clairette, 30% Grenache Blanc, 30% Bourboulenc, and 10% Roussanne. It is a delicious wine to drink in its first two to four years and keeps better than the others made in this style.

The controversial carbonic maceration method of vinification is said to sacrifice the wine's depth and potential for longevity in favor of youthful, exuberant fruitiness. Virtually all my experience with red Châteauneuf-du-Papes made in this manner is that they are delicious, charming, round, fruity wines to drink between four to six years, after which period they decline rapidly. There is one exception that sticks in my mind. The 1967 Nalys, drunk with one of the late Dr. DuFay's disciples, André Roux of the Château de Trignon, was sheer hedonistic pleasure when drunk in 1986. Was this an isolated example or is there some merit to Dr. DuFay's belief that these wines do age?

In summary, the white wine here is sure to provide shockingly fine drinking and I cannot recommend it enthusiastically enough. The red wine is also disarmingly lush and seductive, and except for a few freakish vintages, 1967 for example, it is a wine to drink within four to six years of the vintage.

VINTAGES

1986—*Nalys (white)*—A very fruity, quite powerful wine, the 1986
· Nalys is rich in fruit, full-bodied, very ripe, and very concen-
87 trated. It will drink well for 2–4 years. Last tasted 1/87.

1985—*Nalys (white)*—A top class white Châteauneuf-du-Pape. Splen-
· didly fruity and fragrant with intense aromas of tropical fruit and
87 wet stones. It is long and fresh in the mouth. Last tasted 10/85.

1984—*Nalys (white)*—The 1984 has higher acidity than either the 1985
· or 1986, but not nearly the opulently rich fruit. Last tasted
85 10/86.

1978—*Nalys (white)*—A revelation, the 1978 has retained its rich fruit,
· the nose suggests a buttery white burgundy, and the finish is
85 long, ripe, and a little hot. Last tasted 10/86.

1985—*Nalys (red)*—Nalys red hit 14.5% natural alcohol in 1985. Richly
· fruity, ripe, and deep in color, this generously fruity, lush wine
85 will offer delicious drinking for the next 4–5 years. Last tasted
10/86.

1984—*Nalys (red)*—Effusively fruity to smell, the aromas of ripe cher-
· ries are quite persistent. This is a very straightforward style of
84 wine that offers little complexity but sound drinking. Anticipated
maturity: now–1990. Last tasted 10/86.

1983—*Nalys (red)*—More tannic than the 1984, the 1983 has good color,
· some dry, hard tannin in the finish, and a coarse texture. I prefer
82 the 1984. Anticipated maturity: now–1990. Last tasted 10/86.

1982—*Nalys (red)*—Very alcoholic (14.8%), but round, generously
· fruity, velvety, and ideal for drinking over the next 1–3 years.
84 Last tasted 11/86.

1981—*Nalys (red)*—The finest Nalys of this decade, the 1981 has a
· plump, richly fruity style, some surprising stuffing and length,
86 and may be a candidate for further cellaring beyond 5–6 years.
One would never guess this particular wine is the product of
carbonic maceration vinification. Anticipated maturity: now–
1992. Last tasted 10/86.

1978—*Nalys (red)*—Light ruby color with a candylike nose, this wine
· has excessive tannin for the meager amount of fruit I find on the
72 palate. Last tasted 10/86.

1967—*Nalys (red)*—A carbonic maceration product, the 1967 Nalys is
· loaded with clean, jammy, ripe berry fruit, is quite sweet and
88 lush on the palate, and finishes powerfully with a good dosage of
alcohol. Fully mature, one could keep it 4–5 years more. Last
tasted 6/86.

CHÂTEAU DE LA NERTHE (SOCIÉTÉ CIVILE) ****

Historically, this is the most renowned property of the appellation. The
vineyards and château sit on the southeastern side of the village, well
marked from the road, but hidden by a large outcropping of trees. Wine
has been made here continuously since the sixteenth century. Records
show that a merchant in Boston, Massachusetts, actually ordered barrels of La Nerthe in the late eighteenth century. The famous French
poet, Frédéric Mistral, who gave his name to the fierce, persistent
winds of the region, called the wine of La Nerthe "un vin royal impérial
et pontifical." During World War II, the German air force used La

Nerthe as its command control and the property was badly damaged in the subsequent liberation of the area by the British. Until 1985, the estate was owned by the Derreumaud family and the wine was highly prized for its immense size and enormous palate-pleasing pleasure. In 1985 this famous property was purchased by a Rhône négociant firm, David and Foillard. Extensive renovations have already been made at La Nerthe and this will no doubt become one of the showpiece châteaux in the southern Rhône Valley. At present there are 110 acres under vine and another 50 being planted. The current blend for the red wine is 60% Grenache and 30% Mourvèdre, with the remainder consisting of primarily Syrah, Muscardin, Cinsault, and Counoise. As perceptive readers may have noticed, the new regime has also decided to spell the name of the property La Nerthe, not La Nerte (as formerly). The white wine is now being made from 55% Clairette, 17% Grenache Blanc, 17% Bourboulenc, and the rest Roussanne. La Nerthe's red has always been considered one of the blockbuster Châteauneuf-du-Papes—very alcoholic, very rich, often heavy, and occasionally inconsistent from vintage to vintage, but always an interesting, unique mouthful of wine. I hope that with all the new technology introduced and the manager's insistence on making an "elegant, modern style" of wine, La Nerthe will not become another bland, commercial wine designed to offend the least number of tasters. The famous cuvée of "vieilles vignes," Les Cadettes, will be resurrected. It will take several years to see what the new owners turn out, but given their enormous investment in this famous property, the commitment is certainly there. There are even new oak barrels being brought in, a development that will no doubt shake up the cognoscenti of the area. Tremendous changes are underfoot at La Nerthe. Not only the renovated château, but also the wine will have a new look and feel. I am sure the wine will be good, but only when the new team has three or four vintages behind them will it be possible to evaluate their wines and the style of winemaking that will emerge. They seem to be fully cognizant of this property's importance and the reputation of its wines.

VINTAGES

1985—*La Nerthe (white)*—La Nerthe's white wine has traditionally been a flavorful yet very heavy wine of enormous power and alcoholic clout. The new owners want to lighten it up and produce it in a fresher style. Their debut vintage (1985), is still a rich, fat wine with plenty of intensity and fruit. Last tasted 7/86.

·
83

1985—*La Nerthe (red)*—There will be a special "Cuvée des Cadettes"
·   in 1985, but it was not available for tasting. The regular 1985 La
86   Nerthe has a natural alcohol content of 14%, deep, rich, rasp-
      berry fruit, an unctuous texture, low acidity, but gobs of fruit
      and body. It will drink well young. Anticipated maturity: 1988–
      1996. Last tasted 7/86.

1983—*La Nerthe (red)*—This is quite a robust wine that is now reaching
·   full maturity. It is full-bodied with a lot of muscle and flesh, but
85   not a great deal of finesse. Drink it over the next 3–6 years. Last
      tasted 7/86.

1981—*La Nerthe (red)*—A full-blown, almost exaggerated La Nerthe,
·   the bouquet of this wine is filled with deep, peppery, black
87   cherry and raspberry scents. The impression on the palate is of
      tremendous power and weight, and the finish is long and a trifle
      hot. Drink over the next 4–6 years. Last tasted 7/86.

1980—*La Nerthe (red)*—Completely mature, this soft, fruity wine is
·   less robust than usual, but still offers a plump, generous mouth-
84   ful of wine. Drink it up. Last tasted 7/86.

1979—*La Nerthe (red)*—Deep ruby in color with no sign of age, the
·   1979 has the crushed raspberry bouquet interwoven with the
86   smell of flowers and some heat from the high alcohol. Fat and
      tasty, this full-bodied wine should be drunk over the next 2–4
      years, before its excessive alcohol content becomes prominent.
      Last tasted 10/85.

1979—*La Nerthe Cuvée des Cadettes (red)*—The remarkable thing
·   about the Cuvée des Cadettes is that this selection from old
89   vines usually produces wines that naturally reach 15% alcohol.
      However, the immense body and rich fruit disguise the level of
      alcohol, unless one has the bravado to polish off most of the
      bottle. The 1979 is oozing with black cherry and raspberry fruit,
      and seems to have 5–7 years of life left in it. Last tasted 11/86.

1978—*La Nerthe (red)*—This wine has developed exceptionally well.
·   The huge, very intense bouquet of violets and jammy raspberry
90   fruit is excellent. On the palate, the full-bodied size and depth
      of this wine is readily apparent. Quite drinkable now, it can
      benefit from another 5–7 years of cellaring. Last tasted 2/87.

1978—*La Nerthe Cuvée des Cadettes (red)*—Deeper in color and even
·   more perfumed and concentrated than the exceptional regular
92   cuvée, the 1978 Cuvée des Cadettes has a very deep color, more
      noticeable tannin, and an enormous, mouth-filling, viscous rich-

ness. This is an overwhelming wine that in all respects seems to scream out, "Look at me." It has 5–10 years of life ahead of it and should be paired with very robust foods or strong cheeses. Last tasted 6/85.

PÈRE ANSELME (P. BROTTE)***

Just before one enters the village of Châteauneuf-du-Pape are the cellars, wine museum, and offices of Père Anselme, a large négociant. This business specializing in wine from the entire southern Rhône is run by the Brotte family. Their total production is just under 200,000 cases of wine. The Brottes also own the village's well-known restaurant, La Mule du Pape, where the wine list is composed entirely of their wines. Their Châteauneuf-du-Pape is criticized by many, largely I believe because it is a négociant's wine, but it is not at all a bad wine. In fact, the vintages I have tasted, 1978 through 1983, were all sound, deeply colored, burly, chunky wines that offered aggressive, meaty, tarry-scented fruit and a hefty dose of alcohol. If not sublime, they are quite satisfactory. They call their Châteauneuf-du-Pape La Fiole du Pape, and offer it in a funny-looking, misshapen, charcoal-colored bottle covered with fake dust. Their wine deserves better than this gimmicky bottle.

PÈRE CABOCHE (JEAN-PIERRE BOISSON)***

An 80-acre vineyard run with enthusiasm by the portly, loquacious Jean-Pierre Boisson, this estate produces light, fruity, easy to drink red wines and crisp, fresh, fruity white wine. For the red wine, the blend of grapes is 70% Grenache, 15% Syrah, and the rest Mourvèdre and Muscardin. For the white, Bourboulenc represents 50%, Grenache Blanc 25%, and Clairette 25%. Two thousand cases of white wine are made here. In certain top vintages about 1,600 cases of a special cuvée of red wine called Elisabeth Chambellan, their fullest and richest wine, is produced. The Elisabeth Chambellan is given the same type of vinification as the regular wine. The difference is that this special cuvée comes from parcels of Boisson's vineyard where the vines are at least 60 years old. Certainly both wines are vinified in a very modern style. The Syrah here is treated to the carbonic maceration method, the remaining grapes very lightly crushed and fermented in stainless steel at relatively cool temperatures. The red wine is given dual filtrations, through the Kisselguhr system after malolactic and through German micropore filter pads prior to bottling. It is also fined by egg whites. I cannot help but conclude that this excessive degree of clarification robs the red wine here of a significant portion of its color, body, extract, and aroma, for many of the red wines taste eviscerated. This system of vinification was put in place in 1973, and it is interesting that in the vertical tasting I did with Boisson the best two wines were the 1970 and 1972, made before the installation of his state-of-the-art wine cellar. Boisson seems personally to prefer white to red wine, but argues that his red wines will age up to 15 years in top vintages—a point with which I vehemently disagree. Prices for the wines of Père Caboche are quite realistic. Boisson's two favorite recent vintages are 1981 and 1985. Under questioning, he agrees that his 1983 is a disappointment. Given the current style, the red wine of Père Caboche should be drunk before it reaches seven or eight years of age. The special cuvée of Elisabeth Chambellan will keep several years longer. Boisson's obsession with technology means that his wines often fail to show very marked differences between vintages since their character has been muted by the razzle-dazzle of numerous filtrations.

VINTAGES

1985—*Père Caboche (white)*—The white wine made here is crisp, styl-
·   ish, fruity, and among the top dozen or so white wines of the
85   appellation. Last tasted 1/86.

1985—*Père Caboche (red)*—This is a typical 1985 in many respects—
·   fat, fruity, rather alcoholic, and deep colored. It will drink well
84   young. Anticipated maturity: now–1993. Last tasted 6/86.

1985—*Père Caboche Elisabeth Chambellan (red)*—More noticeably
·   tannic than the regular cuvée, with more length, stuffing, and
86   character. Anticipated maturity: 1989–1996. Last tasted 6/86.

1984—*Père Caboche (red)*—Rather dry and astringent in the finish, this
·   is a hard, angular, charmless wine. Anticipated maturity: now–
73   1990. Last tasted 6/86.

1983—*Père Caboche (red)*—Disturbingly light in color, this wine has
·   little fruit, is very dry, and slightly bitter in the finish. It is a
67   disappointment. Last tasted 6/86.

1982—*Père Caboche (red)*—Despite the obviously high alcohol content
·   in the bouquet, the 1982 shows a good measure of ripe cherry
80   fruit, much better color than the 1983, and a round finish. Drink
      it up. Last tasted 6/86.

1981—*Père Caboche (red)*—Scents of cherries and leather provide a
·   bouquet of light intensity. On the palate, this wine is slightly
84   more tannic than the 1982, but has a more balanced, less alco-
      holic finish. Drink it over the next 3–4 years. Last tasted 6/86.

1980—*Père Caboche (red)*—This is a clean, correct wine that has little
· character. Cherry fruit aromas and flavors are pleasant but shal-
78 low. Drink up. Last tasted 6/86.

1979—*Père Caboche (red)*—A fruitier, deeper version of the 1980, the
· 1979 has good color, a polished, measured taste, medium body,
83 and adequate finish. Drink it up. Last tasted 6/86.

1976—*Père Caboche (red)*—This seems to show better than the other
· wines; there is more to it. Full-bodied, deeply fruity, and still a
85 little tannic, this wine has character. Last tasted 6/86.

1974—*Père Caboche (red)*—Brown in color and oxidized in taste, this
· wine is past its prime. Last tasted 6/86.
60

1972—*Père Caboche (red)*—Made before Boisson began to filter the
· wine, the 1972 had a heavy sediment (the other wines had none),
87 a rich, multidimensional bouquet of smoky, jammy fruit and
hazelnuts, full body, a sweet, plump fruitiness, and long, delicious finish. How could M. Boisson think the sterile, clipped
wines of more recent vintages are superior to this? Last tasted
6/86.

1970—*Père Caboche (red)*—Showing less brown than the 1972, this
· rich, full-bodied wine is still loaded with fruit, sweet and round
87 on the palate, with plenty of extract and alcohol in the finish.
Last tasted 6/86.

CHÂTEAU RAYAS (JACQUES REYNAUD)*****

Tucked away off a dirt road just north of the village of Châteauneuf-du-
Pape (there is no sign showing the way) one encounters the reclusive
and eccentric Jacques Reynaud and his modest Château Rayas. A visit
there—amid screaming laborers from North Africa, the pixie-looking,
diminutive Reynaud and a bevy of undisciplined dogs—is quite a cha-
otic experience. At first glance, one would never suspect that one of
France's (and of course the world's) greatest wines is made here. I make
no claims to comprehending Reynaud; for three years he refused to see
me, and more recently failed to show up for a rendezvous when I
arrived. However, I simply waited for him and never regretted a moment of our time together. Rayas is a unique wine in every respect. For
those who say Grenache cannot produce majestic wines on a level with
the Mouton-Rothschilds and Cheval Blancs of the world—taste Rayas.
Produced from 100% Grenache with one major difference—the yield
here is about one-third that produced by Grenache in other vineyards.

The vines are very, very old, averaging 55–70 years, and Reynaud vigorously prunes them back to keep the yield tiny. The Grenache that comes from these old vines has a magical perfume and intensity that alone destroys the myth that this grape varietal is incapable of making splendidly rich and complex wines. The estate is only 32 acres in size and the 2,000 cases of this remarkably intense, compelling wine are quickly gobbled up by shrewd wine enthusiasts. To give you an example of the longevity of Rayas, I have drunk the 1961, 1966, and 1967 at the wonderful La Beaugravière restaurant in Mondragon and could not believe how great these wines were. Reynaud produces Rayas only in the top vintages—there is no 1980 or 1982, as this wine was declassified into his other Châteauneuf-du-Pape, Château Pignan, which is used also as the second label of Rayas but which I find very similar to Rayas. Reynaud also produces the Rhône Valley's finest Côtes du Rhône, Château Fonsalette. About 150 cases of white wine are produced that I find rather heavy-handed, but it has its admirers.

The vinification here is very traditional. All the grapes are crushed and never destemmed. The fermentation is hot and furious, and the maceration period, two to three weeks, not abnormally long. Afterwards, the wine is placed in enamel vats until spring; then it is put into what looks to be ancient filth-covered wooden barrels of many different shapes and sizes. It stays there two years until it is bottled. Unless the wine is hazy, Reynaud will not filter it.

Rayas is Châteauneuf-du-Pape's most expensive wine, yet I have known few to complain about its quality. Rayas, along with Beaucastel (incidentally, neither are fined nor filtered and throw very heavy sediments, making decanting essential) are the longest-lived wines of this appellation. Since Reynaud has no heirs, it is expected that Rayas will be sold and the vineyards torn up and replanted when he dies—a tragedy if such a thing were permitted to happen.

Rayas is a staggeringly rich wine that drinks very well young but can age extremely well for 8–15 years. It should be sought out and tasted by anyone who considers himself to be a connoisseur.

VINTAGES

1985—*Rayas (white)*—I have never been greatly enamored of the white wine of Rayas, but I must admit the 1985 appears to be one of this estate's better efforts. Quite rich, full-bodied, and alcoholic, it is a very big, unctuous wine that should be drunk over the next 3–4 years. Last tasted 6/86.

·

86

1985—*Rayas (red)*—It took this wine almost a year to finish its malo-
· lactic fermentation. Extremely dense and rich with a black/pur-
90 ple color, this wine is slightly low in acidity, but very powerful,
extremely concentrated, with heaps of seductive fruit. It will not
be as long-lived as the 1978 or 1979, but it will be special. Anticipated maturity: 1990–2000. Last tasted 10/86.

1983—*Rayas (red)*—The 1983, deep ruby in color, has layers of
· crushed peppery, raspberry fruit, a particularly lush, intense
91 palate impression, a voluptuous, long finish, and ripe, melted
tannins. Anticipated maturity: 1989–1997. Last tasted 2/87.

1981—*Rayas (red)*—More tannic and perhaps slightly more robust than
· the 1983, the 1981 Rayas is quite full-bodied, fabulously concen-
90 trated, and deep, with an intense cedary, smoky, jammy bouquet and hugely concentrated flavors. Anticipated maturity:
1989–1999. Last tasted 2/87.

1979—*Rayas (red)*—Rayas produced an exceptional wine in 1979. It is
· more flattering to drink now than the monumental but tannic
90 1978. Very deep ruby with a spicy, smoky, very rich bouquet of
fruitcake and raspberry fruit, full-bodied, lush yet tannic in the
finish, this is a very impressive wine. Anticipated maturity:
now–2000. Last tasted 10/86.

1978—*Rayas (red)*—Staggeringly concentrated, this wine that swells in
· the glass, revealing great ripeness and concentration, a roasted
96 chestnut-scented nose, remarkable depth and length, yet still
has plenty of tannins to lose. It has thrown a tremendous amount
of sediment already. Anticipated maturity: 1988–2001. Last
tasted 1/87.

1976—*Rayas (red)*—Fully mature, the 1976 Rayas seems to be declin-
· ing very rapidly. Medium ruby with an orange rim, the rich,
84 roasted, jammy bouquet is losing some fruit. On the palate, the
wine is quite soft, a little fragile, and should be drunk up. Last
tasted 2/87.

1971—*Rayas (red)*—Medium ruby with a great deal of brown at the
· edge, the 1971 Rayas has been fully mature since 1978. Broad,
85 expansive, sweet, plummy fruit is very appealing. Ripe and
round but beginning to fade, this wine was better and more
concentrated 2–3 years ago. It must be drunk up. Last tasted
7/86.

1969—*Rayas (red)*—At its apogee, the 1969 Rayas is in better condition
· than either the 1971 or 1976. A smoky, oriental spice, complex
88 bouquet is followed by an equally intriguing wine with full body,

a broad layer of sweet fruit, full body, and a sumptuous finish. This is a joy to drink. Last tasted 7/86.

1967—*Rayas (red)*—The aromas of roasted nuts, Provençal herbs, smoked meats, and intense candied fruit swell in the glass. On the palate, the unctuous texture from the heaps of fruit, glycerine, and alcohol makes for a wonderfully hedonistic drinking experience. This should be drunk up. Last tasted 6/86.

· 91

1966—*Rayas (red)*—Less expansive and sweet than the 1967, the 1966 is, however, a classic Rayas with a very fragrant, full-intensity bouquet, chewy, port-like flavors, and a long aftertaste. Last tasted 7/86.

· 89

1964—*Rayas (red)*—Like the 1967, this wine cannot get any better or evolve any further and therefore should be drunk up. The telltale bouquet of smoky nuts, oriental spices, and very ripe fruit is all one could ask for. On the palate, the wine is just beginning to lose some fruit and show its hefty alcohol level. Last tasted 6/85.

· 87

1962—*Rayas (red)*—Very light color and washed-out flavors; I drank this bottle in mid-1986 and found the wine in serious decline. Two years earlier I had a splendidly preserved bottle of 1962 Rayas that was as good as the 1967. Storage conditions are extremely important when drinking a wine this old. Last tasted 6/86.

· ?

1961—*Rayas (red)*—Despite the fading color, this wine is still loaded with heaps of ripe, sweet fruit. The palate impression is akin to a 20-year-old Tawny port. This wine is ripe, hedonistic, and a privilege to drink. Last tasted 6/86.

· 92

1983—*Château Pignan (red)*—For one-half, sometimes one-third the price of Rayas, Pignan represents a great value. Very similar to the 1983 Rayas, Pignan is deep in color with vast, sweet berry fruit flavors, a peppery, raspberry fruitiness, and lush finish. Anticipated maturity: 1988–1995. Last tasted 2/87.

· 89

1981—*Château Pignan (red)*—A great Châteauneuf-du-Pape, the 1981 Pignan is deeper in color than the 1983, has a roasted nut and plummy bouquet, intense, very concentrated, full-bodied flavors, and a long, tannic finish. Anticipated maturity: 1989–1998. Last tasted 2/87.

· 90

DOMAINE DES RELAGNES (HENRI BOIRON) ***

This small estate of only 32 acres, of which 87% is planted with Grenache and the rest with Mourvèdre and Syrah, has very old vines that average 50 years in age. While this estate can make rich, deep Châteauneuf-du-Pape, the style has lightened up from the rather robust, full-bodied, chewy-textured wine of the late seventies. Boiron has begun to do two filtrations on his wine because "consumers want their wines without sediment." He does not make a white wine, and his cellar is impeccably kept. He also sells the same wine under the names Cuvée Vigneronne and Cuvée Henri Boiron. He is not a great admirer of the 1985 vintage.

His vinification has become increasingly modern in the eighties. Presently, Boiron puts his grapes in the tanks uncrushed but does not use carbonic gas. His wines after 1981 have become noticeably less intense and powerful. Previous vintages taste richer, fuller-bodied, and potentially longer-lived. Henri Boiron, a handsome man in his early forties, is the cousin of Maurice Boiron, who runs the excellent domaine in Châteauneuf-du-Pape called Bosquet des Papes.

VINTAGES

1985—*Relagnes*—The 1985 here is not unlike Boiron's 1982—very low
·   in acidity with a fat, jammy, effusively fruity character. It is
84   quite tasty, but must be drunk young, within 5–6 years. Last
    tasted 6/86.

1984—*Relagnes*—The 1984 has better structure than the 1985, good
·   ruby color, is quite fruity, medium-bodied, not very powerful as
84   Châteauneufs go, but charming and ready to drink. Last tasted
    6/86.

1983—*Relagnes*—Medium ruby with an expansive fragrance suggestive
·   of very ripe strawberries, this soft, opulently fruity wine is quite
85   enticing, and requires drinking over the next 3–4 years. Last
    tasted 6/86.

1982—*Relagnes*—Despite the 14.5% alcohol, this wine has the fruit to
·   hide the alcoholic heat. A peppery, berrylike bouquet is followed
84   by very soft, round, fruity flavors. Drink up. Last tasted 6/86.

1981—*Relagnes*—This is Boiron's best wine so far in the eighties.
·   Darker in color than other recent vintages, the 1981 has a com-
87   plex, smoky, richly fruity nose, full body, and plenty of length
    and depth. Anticipated maturity: now–1992. Last tasted 6/86.

1979—*Relagnes*—Soft, silky, very fruity and long, this fleshy, alcoholic
·   wine is at its peak and should be drunk up. Last tasted 6/86.
85

1978—*Relagnes*—The most powerful of the Relagnes wines, the 1978
· is still youthfully deep in color with little sign of maturity. Full-
88 bodied, alcoholic, quite concentrated, but still tannic, this wine
needs additional cellaring. Anticipated maturity: 1988–2000.
Last tasted 6/86.

DOMAINE DE LA ROQUETTE (HENRI BRUNIER)**
Until 1986, René Laugier produced both red and white Châteauneuf-
du-Pape from his domaine of 74 acres. Then Laugier sold his estate to
Henri Brunier, the owner of Vieux Télégraphe. Grenache dominates his
plantings with 70%. Production in 1985 was just under 10,000 cases of
wine. This is certainly a decent Châteauneuf-du-Pape, with a fruity,
fairly alcoholic style of wine marked by aging in wooden barrels. In
most years, it seems to be at its best between four and eight years of
age, though I have had no experience with vintages older than 1978.
The vinification is quite traditional, with all the grapes crushed, fermented at hot temperatures, and then aged two to three years in
wooden foudres. The new owner, Brunier, will no doubt modernize the
cellar and upgrade the quality of the wine being made at Roquette.

VINTAGES
1983—*Roquette*—Very spicy, with a rustic, full-bodied, almost coarse
· texture, the 1983 has plenty of body but I would have preferred
80 a bit more fruit. Anticipated maturity: now–1993. Last tasted
10/86.
1982—*Roquette*—Opposite the 1983, this vintage of Roquette is very
· round, fruity, quite alcoholic but surprisingly well structured
84 given the vintage. It should drink well for 3–4 years. Last tasted
10/86.
1980—*Roquette*—Very woody and spicy with some alcohol showing
· through, this wine is big and full but seems to be out of balance,
79 Drink it up. Last tasted 10/86.

DOMAINE ROGER SABON (ROGER SABON)***
The three young Sabon brothers, Jean-Jacques, Denis, and Gilbert, run
this small estate of 32 acres. Like most domaines in Châteauneuf-du-
Pape, Grenache dominates the blend with 85%, Syrah 8%, and the rest
Mourvèdre, Cinsault, and Counoise. The style of wine they aim for is
one that is "relatively agreeable to drink in the first 5–6 years, but
capable of lasting 10–20 years," says Jean-Jacques, the brother who

actually makes the wine. A tiny amount of white wine is also made. This estate produces three separate cuvées of red wine. Their best is called Cuvée Prestige, next is Cuvée Réserve, then their regular cuvée, which represents the bulk of the production here. They claim their best vintages are 1978, 1981, and 1983.

The vinification employed here is to crush 60–80% of the grapes and ferment them in the traditional manner. The maceration period can extend up to 20 days in the case of wine for the Cuvée Prestige. The other grapes are vinified by the carbonic maceration method. Afterwards, the wine goes directly into wooden foudres for 12 to 18 months. In 1985 they employed the Kisselguhr filtration system for the first time. The wine is never fined.

This is a good domaine in which some of the special cuvées can be excellent. However, in tasting through their wines I find an inconsistency in quality.

VINTAGES

1985—*Roger Sabon*—Dark in color, richly fruity with expansive berry
·   fruit flavors, this soft-textured wine has quite an alcoholic clout
85   to it. Anticipated maturity: 1988–1994. Last tasted 6/86.

1984—*Roger Sabon Cuvée Prestige*—Not as supple or as fat as the 1985,
·   the Sabons' top-of-the-line prestige cuvée has a dense, dark ruby
85   color, relatively deep, well-structured flavors, medium to full
         body, and decent aging potential. Anticipated maturity: 1988–
         1996. Last tasted 10/86.

1983—*Roger Sabon Cuvée Réserve*—I find the existence of three sepa-
·   rate cuvées of wine all rather confusing, but the 1983 is a good
83   wine, though dry astringence in the finish detracts from an over-
         all spicy, full-bodied impression. Last tasted 6/86.

1982—*Roger Sabon Cuvée Prestige*—Some brown at the rim suggests
·   full maturity. Quite soft and still fruity, but the wine has no
82   backbone or structure. Drink it up. Last tasted 6/86.

1981—*Roger Sabon*—This is the regular cuvée and it tastes the best of
·   the Sabon wines. A bold bouquet of leather and ripe fruit and a
87   powerful palate impression of cedary, chocolatey fruit is mouth-
         filling and quite satisfying. Drink over the next 4–5 years. Last
         tasted 6/86.

DOMAINE SÉNÉCHAUX (PIERRE RAYNAUD) ****

An ancient domaine—winemaking here can be traced back to the fourteenth century. Sénéchaux, the Provençal word for woods, is a 72-acre

estate with all 13 permitted varieties planted. Grenache is again dominant, accounting for 70% of the blend, with the rest consisting of 10%
Cinsault, 5% Syrah, 5% Mourvèdre, and the remainder a field blend.
The manager, Roland Bensamous, wants to "guard the tradition of
Châteauneuf-du-Pape." His vines are very old (averaging 65 years) and
half his vineyards are located in the eastern portion of the appellation,
contiguous with those of La Nerthe. He is proud of being the last to
bottle a given vintage and thinks 1978 and 1985 are the best two wines
he has ever made. I find his wines to be very good, with their own
pronounced character clearly marked by the long two to three years'
aging in large wooden foudres.

A small amount of fresh, vibrant white Châteauneuf is made here
from equal portions of Grenache Blanc, Clairette, Bourboulenc, and
Roussanne.

The vinification of the red wines is classical, the grapes being
crushed and then given a 15 day maceration with the skins. There are
two filtrations, which I fear may be excessive, but the manager states
that "only a few connoisseurs appreciate unfiltered wines anymore."
Raynaud's wines, apparently in spite of filtration, can age for 10–15
years in specific vintages.

VINTAGES

1985—*Sénéchaux*—This looks to be one of the stars of this vintage.
Very deep in color and stunningly concentrated, this blockbuster
90   wine has 14.5% natural alcohol, makes an immense impression
on the palate, yet finishes with good acidity and tannins. Anticipated maturity: 1989–2000. Last tasted 6/86.

1984—*Sénéchaux*—Very woody and a trifle musty, the 1984 has adequate color and medium body, but lacks generosity and length.
81   Anticipated maturity: now–1991. Last tasted 6/86.

1983—*Sénéchaux*—The 1983 has excellent deep ruby color, quite a bit
of tannin, full body, good extract, but is closed and firm. Antic-
85   ipated maturity: 1989–2000. Last tasted 6/86.

1982—*Sénéchaux*—Aromas of ripe cherries, leather, and wood are
moderately intense. Totally mature and a bit too alcoholic, this
81   wine should be drunk over the next 1–2 years. Last tasted 6/86.

1981—*Sénéchaux*—Deep ruby in color with a full-blown, very spicy,
berry-and-leather-scented bouquet, the 1982 is full-bodied, rich
87   in fruit, still tannic, and has a fine finish. Anticipated maturity:
1988–1995. Last tasted 6/86.

1978—*Sénéchaux*—A full-intensity bouquet of roasted nuts and oaky,
· jammy fruit is quite enticing. On the palate, this wine is ex-
90 tremely full-bodied, dense, and has loads of extract as well as
tannin. Anticipated maturity: now–1998. Last tasted 6/86.

DOMAINE DE LA SOLITUDE (LANÇON) ***
This 197-acre domaine has, for almost 15 years, produced 20,000 cases
of a Beaujolais-styled wine feeble in color and not capable of aging
more than five or six years. The estate also makes 1,500 cases of a
good, light, fruity white wine from 40% Grenache Blanc, 40% Clairette,
and 20% Bourboulenc. For the red wine, the grapes used include 60%
Grenache and 10% each of Mourvèdre, Syrah, and Cinsault. The vinification is the carbonic maceration method. Lançon is now aging part
of the red wine in new small oak barrels that seem to give this wine
more structure. Based on the 1985, 1984, and 1983, I thought them
deeper in color and extract than anything that has been made here for
over a decade. Is Domaine de la Solitude producing wines with more
structure and character, as it appears? I hope so.

VINTAGES
1985—*Solitude (white)*—Very good, the 1985 white Châteauneuf-du-
· Pape is effusively fruity, has good body, and an engaging fresh-
83 ness. Last tasted 6/86.
1985—*Solitude (red)*—Very soft, richly fruity, well colored, this wine
· is quite soft and will provide uncomplicated drinking over the
84 next 3–5 years. Last tasted 6/86.
1984—*Solitude (red)*—Very spicy new wood dominates the bouquet.
· Good ripe, broad, fruity flavors start impressively but fall off on
80 the palate. It has a very short finish. Anticipated maturity: now–
1990. Last tasted 6/86.
1983—*Solitude (red)*—Quite good, the 1983 Domaine de la Solitude is
· the most impressive wine made at this estate in over a decade.
85 Toasty new oak aromas, berry fruit, and supple, expansive flavors are all very attractive. Anticipated maturity: now–1990.
Last tasted 6/86.
1981—*Solitude (red)*—The 1981 here is very diluted in color, with
· washed-out, faded fruit flavors and not much substance on the
67 palate. It is very disappointing. Last tasted 11/85.
1979—*Solitude (red)*—Rosé-colored, this is a very marginal effort from
· Domaine de la Solitude. Light-intensity, cherry flavors fade in
75 the glass. Drink it up. Last tasted 2/84.

1978—*Solitude (red)*—Given the vintage, this wine is very light, one-
·   dimensional, fruity, soft and totally mature. Drink it up. Last
78   tasted 3/83.

1967—*Solitude (red)*—To taste this wine is to learn what a tragedy it is
·   to turn these potentially glorious wines into fruity, soft, commer-
88   cial wines. The 1967 still has an impressive deep ruby color with
      some amber at the edge. Very peppery, spicy with heaps of
      smoky fruit in the nose, this full-bodied wine has an unctuous
      texture and a long, soft finish. It requires drinking up. Last
      tasted 11/86.

DOMAINE TERRE FERME (BÉRARD) ***

I shall never forget a luncheon I had with three dozen of the proprietors of Châteauneuf-du-Pape. Presiding over this group, much like a
godfather, was the boisterous, loud, loquacious Monsieur Bérard,
the owner of Terre Ferme. In 1986 he sold part of his interest in the
estate, but is still active and involved in the day to day affairs. This
is an underrated property in Châteauneuf-du-Pape. The cellars and vineyard of 148 acres are located near that of Vieux Télégraphe in the
eastern sector of the appellation. The blend for their flavorful yet very
elegant red wine is 70% Grenache, 12% Syrah, 15% Mourvèdre, and
3% Cinsault. The Grenache and Cinsault are crushed and vinified classically, the Syrah and Mourvèdre vinified by the carbonic maceration
method. The red wine spends up to 30 months in foudres and is given
a light filtration prior to bottling. The white, also quite good, is made
from 70% Grenache Blanc, 20% Bourboulenc, 3% Roussanne, and 7%
Clairette.

Several vintages of the red Châteauneuf-du-Pape tasted from Terre
Ferme have had an almost Volnay-like fruit and texture to them.

VINTAGES

1985—*Bérard (white)*—A good white Châteauneuf-du-Pape, Bérard's
·   1985 leans a little toward being too heavy, but has plenty of flavor
84   and adequate acidity. Last tasted 10/86.

1985—*Bérard (red)*—Very well structured for a 1985, this richly fruity,
·   full-bodied wine has a floral, berry-scented bouquet, gobs of ripe
86   fruit, good acidity, and a decade of evolution ahead of it. Antic-
      ipated maturity: 1988–1998. Last tasted 10/86.

1984—*Bérard (red)*—Medium ruby, tight, hard, tannic, and closed, I
·   wonder if there is any fruit below the veneer of oak and tannin.
?   Judgment reserved. Last tasted 10/86.

1983—*Bérard (red)*—Quite delicious, with a well-developed bouquet of
· cherry fruit and cedary spices, this moderately ruby-colored
86 wine makes a full-bodied, lush palate impression. Drink over the
next 5 years. Last tasted 6/85.

1982—*Bérard (red)*—Bérard produced a very rich, alcoholic wine in
· 1982 that has the requisite fruit to stand up to the 14.8% alcohol.
86 Decadently rich and even port-like, this wine should be drunk
over the next 2–3 years. Last tasted 10/86.

1981—*Bérard (red)*—Light ruby in color with some orange at the edge,
· the 1981 seems diluted and lacking flesh and fruit. Drink it up,
70 since this wine appears to be fading. Last tasted 10/86.

1978—*Bérard (red)*—The 1978 Châteauneuf-du-Papes are consistently
· excellent to exceptional. Bérard's has now reached its full ma-
89 turity with a long, lush, opulent texture and finish, gobs of leathery and cherry-scented fruit, and good enough balance to last 4–
6 more years. Last tasted 10/86.

DOMAINE JEAN TRINTIGNANT***

This domaine, right near the entrance to the village of Châteauneuf-du-
Pape, produces 11,000 cases of wine from its 86 acres of vines. The
estate is owned and managed by Madame Jean Trintignant. The red
wine is made from a blend of 60% Grenache, 10% Mourvèdre, 15%
Syrah, and 15% Cinsault. The 1,000 cases of white Châteauneuf come
from 50% Grenache Blanc, 20% Clairette, 20% Roussanne, and 10%
Picpoul. The vinification is traditional, although 5–10% of the grapes
each year do receive the carbonic maceration treatment. The wine
produced here is a rather uncomplicated one. It is generously fruity,
chewy, full-bodied, very soft, and usually quite alcoholic. It seems to
be at its best between five and ten years old.

VINTAGES

1985—*Trintignant*—Dense in color with a very rich, intense berry-
· scented bouquet, this wine borders on being too flabby and low
85 in acidity, but it is impressively deep and chewy—not classic,
but fun to drink. Anticipated maturity: now–1993. Last tasted
6/86.

1984—*Trintignant*—This is a one-dimensional, straightforward, fruity
· style that drinks nicely but has no complexity. Last tasted 6/86.
76

1983—*Trintignant*—Very ripe, chunky, alcoholic, deep flavors show
· plenty of ripeness, length, and body. Rather powerful and port-
85 like with some sweetness, this seductive wine will provide good
drinking for 4–6 years. Last tasted 6/86.

CHÂTEAU VAUDIEU (GABRIEL MEFFRE)***

This is a gorgeous estate located next to Rayas. The beautiful château,
one of the most striking in Châteauneuf, was built in 1764. The huge
firm of Gabriel Meffre (based in Gigondas) runs this property of 175
acres, one of the largest in Châteauneuf-du-Pape. The modern-styled
red wine (25,000 cases produced) is made from 75% Grenache, 15%
Syrah, and 10% Cinsault and Mourvèdre. About 5,500 cases of white
wine are made. The wines here have been criticized; I don't doubt that
higher quality could be obtained (given the age of the vines and superb
location of the vineyard), were it so desired, but in all fairness to Vaudieu, the wines are solidly made, richly fruity, supple, and quite fairly
priced. I find Vaudieu's white more one-dimensional than the red.
Meffre regards 1978, 1979, and 1985 as the best vintages, and Clos des
Papes and Vieux Télégraphe as the two best Châteauneufs, a refreshing
response that most proprietors refused to answer.

VINTAGES

1985—*Vaudieu (white)*—This is a one-dimensional, fresh, fairly neu-
· tral-tasting wine that must be consumed when young. Last
78 tasted 10/86.
1985—*Vaudieu (red)*—Deep in color, very fruity, rich, soft, and full-
· bodied, with heaps of extract—I wonder if there is enough spine
85 and backbone. Anticipated maturity: 1988–1995. Last tasted
10/86.
1984—*Vaudieu (red)*—Surprisingly dark with plenty of ripe berry fruit
· in the bouquet, the 1984 has full body, a healthy dose of alcohol,
85 chewy flavors, and is superior to the 1983. Anticipated maturity:
1988–1994. Last tasted 10/86.
1983—*Vaudieu (red)*—The nose lacks the richness and fruit of the
· 1984. On the palate, the wine is tannic, deep in color, but
82 tougher and more unyielding. Anticipated maturity: 1989–1997.
Last tasted 10/86.
1981—*Vaudieu (red)*—Very dark in color with a ripe, plummy, richly
· fruity, even jammy bouquet, the 1981 is lush and full-bodied,
85 fully mature, and will provide fun drinking over the next 3–5
years. Last tasted 10/86.

1980—*Vaudieu (red)*—Medium ruby with a nose similar to the other
· wines, the 1980 is quite fruity, has no apparent tannin remain-
80 ing, and should be drunk up. Last tasted 10/86.
1978—*Vaudieu (red)*—The deepest color of all the wines, the 1978 is
· very full-bodied, has loads of sweet, ripe berry fruit, a long
86 finish, and at least 5–7 more years of drinkability. Last tasted
10/86.

VIEUX DONJON (LOUIS MICHEL)****

This impeccably run estate of 30 acres only produces red wine from a
blend of 80% Grenache, 10% Syrah, and 10% Cinsault and other permitted field varieties. The vines have a very impressive average age of
60–70 years; some are over 100 years old. It is an excellent, traditionally made Châteauneuf that avoids the heavy, high-alcohol style, but
has loads of blackberry fruit. The young Michel family that runs this
estate is a member of the Prestige et Tradition growers' association.
The wines taste like voluptuous, high-class Pomerols, and seem fully
capable of aging for up to a decade. It is the product of a very classical
vinification. No filtration takes place here.

VINTAGES

1985—*Vieux Donjon*—Great color, opaque and dense, the 1985 Vieux
· Donjon is oozing with significant amounts of black cherry,
88 plummy, peppery fruit, has an unctuous, full-bodied texture,
and a powerful finish. The Michels think it is too low in acidity
to last, but for 6–8 years it should be splendid. Anticipated
maturity: 1988–1990. Last tasted 6/86.
1984—*Vieux Donjon*—Very deep color for the vintage, the 1984 has a
· moderately intense, ripe cherry bouquet, deep color, and a
85 charming fruitiness, although less body, alcoholic punch, and
length than the 1985. Anticipated maturity: now–1992. Last
tasted 6/86.
1983—*Vieux Donjon*—Again the hallmark of this wine, like the other
· wines from Vieux Donjon, is a healthy, deep color and heaps of
89 the rich plummy fruitiness that gives a suggestion of Pomerol.
More structured and tannic than either the 1984 or 1985, this
full-bodied wine shows excellent balance and depth. Anticipated
maturity: 1989–1997. Last tasted 6/86.
1981—*Vieux Donjon*—The nose of jammy raspberry fruit explodes from
· the glass. Very deep, concentrated, seductively opulent and lux-
90 uriant flavors fill the mouth. Smooth and velvety, but balanced,

this wine will drink superbly for at least 6–8 years, a really high-class, distinctive wine. Last tasted 6/86.

VIEILLE JULIENNE (ARNAUD-DAUMEN)***

These wines represent the quintessential old, heavy, almost black-colored Châteauneuf-du-Papes. Some are kept up to seven to ten years in large foudres before being bottled. There is a month of maceration used to extract color and tannin. The wines are enormous in body, high in alcohol, quite tannic, and not always the most harmonious examples of winemaking. They are never boring, however. The estate is near Beaucastel and Marcoux in the very northern end of the appellation. Three thousand cases of red wine only are produced. These are wines for the very adventurous. They are unfined and unfiltered, and I recommend decanting them one to two hours before serving.

Vieille Julienne produces true winter weight, burly, full-sized, very tannic Châteauneuf-du-Papes. To me they taste more like old-style Barolos from Piedmont in Italy than a Châteauneuf-du-Pape. They will easily keep ten to twenty years.

VINTAGES

1984—*Vieille Julienne*—Very deep, opaque ruby/purple in color, the
·   1984 is very unevolved and shows a very spicy, deep bouquet,
85   full body, and heaps of extract and tannin. It needs time. Anticipated maturity: 1990–2000. Last tasted 2/87.

1983—*Vieille Julienne*—Much lighter in color than the 1984, the 1983
·   of Vieille Julienne is not a success. Hard, dry, astringent flavors
75   offer little charm or appeal. It is full-bodied and tannic, but the underlying fruit is missing. Last tasted 2/87.

1982—*Vieille Julienne*—Slightly out of balance, with some orange in
·   the color, this wine tastes awkward and hard. It should be drunk
77   up. Last tasted 2/87.

1981—*Vieille Julienne*—Very deep in color, this full-bodied, chewy,
·   very concentrated, potentially promising wine has mouth-
87   shattering tannins, a chewy texture, and seems at least 5–8 years away from maturity. Anticipated maturity: 1993–2000. Last tasted 2/87.

1980—*Vieille Julienne*—Black/ruby in color with a spicy, intense,
·   tarry, chocolatey aroma, this heavy, full-bodied wine has gobs
85   of tannin and extract, but again needs plenty of time. Anticipated maturity: 1992–2000. Last tasted 10/86.

1979—*Vieille Julienne*—Rich in color, this intense wine has a big,
· spicy, cedary, peppery, smoked-meat aroma, very full body,
87 deep flavors, some tough, coarse tannins, but excellent length.
It is just becoming drinkable. Anticipated maturity: 1988–1996.
Last tasted 2/87.

1978—*Vieille Julienne*—Overwhelmingly rich and brutally tannic, but
· loaded with fruit, this wine is an education in how wine was
88 made 50 or 100 years ago. Stubbornly backward, this is a wine
to buy and cellar for your next-of-kin. Anticipated maturity:
1995–2005. Last tasted 10/86.

1977—*Vieille Julienne*—Undeniably a success for the vintage, the
· earthy, smoky, spicy bouquet and Barolo-like texture and tough-
84 ness give this big, aggressive wine plenty of personality. It is not
for the shy. Anticipated maturity: now–1995. Last tasted 10/86.

1976—*Vieille Julienne*—Some orange and brown in the color suggest
· maturity. On the palate the wine is very tannic but seems to be
78 losing its fruit. At present it offers a robust, coarse mouthful of
wine, but it must be drunk without hesitation as the balance
seems suspect. Last tasted 2/87.

1972—*Vieille Julienne*—Another Barolo look-alike, the 1972 has a
· tarry, leather-scented, rich, spicy, deep bouquet that swells in
87 the glass. Full-bodied and unique, I wonder how tasters weaned
on industrially made, vapid wine will respond to wines with this
much character. Anticipated maturity: now–1995. Last tasted
10/86.

VIEUX LAZARET (JÉROME QUIOT)***

One of the strongest proponents of the modern style of Châteauneuf is
Vieux Lazaret, a large property of 198 acres. The average age of the
vines is 18 years and the wine is kept in tank until bottled. The bottling
takes place early. The blend of grapes used in making the red wine is
70% Grenache, 10% Syrah, 10% Mourvèdre and the rest a field blend
of Cinsault and Counoise. Proprietor Quiot, a young, energetic man,
realizes that his red wine is not as concentrated as it should be and
seems inclined to see that it becomes deeper and richer. The white
made here is light and fresh, but like the red is somewhat lacking in
flavor interest.

Quiot is also an important vineyard owner in the Côtes du Ventoux,
as well as the owner of a modern hotel and restaurant just outside the
village of Châteauneuf-du-Pape, Le Logis d'Arnavel.

Quiot argues that while there are enormous variations, there are really only two general styles of red Châteauneuf-du-Pape—the "organic" and "floral" styles. To me, this is somewhat of an over-simplification, but the floral style, to which he subscribes, produces fruity, floral, perfumed wines that are generally from vinifications where a significant portion of the grapes are fermented uncrushed and at lower temperatures. These wines are supple, immediately drinkable, and emphasize aromas of berry fruits and flowers. The traditional or organic style ferments at high temperatures with most of the grapes crushed, and the wine that is produced is more tannic and fuller-bodied, with aromas that are more spicy, peppery, leathery, and truffle-scented. Quiot would also argue that these latter wines are less approachable in their youth and less viable in a commercial world that demands immediate gratification from its red wines.

The wines of Vieux Lazaret are, to my palate, a trifle diluted, boring, and shallow. They should be drunk young, preferably within six to seven years of the vintage.

VINTAGES

1985—*Vieux Lazaret (white)*—This is dull and simple with little flavor interest. Last tasted 6/86.
· 72

1985—*Vieux Lazaret (red)*—One of the better wines from this estate I have tasted, the 1985 has a vibrant ruby color, moderately intense berry fruit aromas, a velvety texture, and some muscle in the finish. Anticipated maturity: 1988–1992. Last tasted 6/86.
· 84

1984—*Vieux Lazaret (red)*—Light ruby color, and very hard and austere, this is not a particularly successful 1984. Last tasted 6/86.
· 70

1983—*Vieux Lazaret (red)*—A light-intensity bouquet of cherries and spicy, berry fruit is simple, but fades in the glass. Medium-bodied with a dry finish and a touch of astringency, this wine lacks the requisite fruit for the proper balance. Last tasted 6/86.
· 74

1982—*Vieux Lazaret (red)*—Surprisingly more successful than the 1983 or 1984, the 1982 is short on the palate and a bit too alcoholic, but has decent color and some charming aromas of cherry fruit. Drink it up. Last tasted 6/86.
· 81

1981—*Vieux Lazaret (red)*—Dry with diluted color, this wine has a cardboard aroma (filter pad smell?), washed-out flavors, and is in full decline. Last tasted 6/86.
· 67

1980—*Vieux Lazaret (red)*—This is clearly one of the most successful
·   Vieux Lazarets made so far this decade. Well colored, the 1980
84   has good concentration, an effusive, berry fruitiness, a generous
      finish, and some muscle and backbone. Anticipated maturity:
      now–1990. Last tasted 6/86.

DOMAINE DU VIEUX TÉLÉGRAPHE (HENRI BRUNIER) *****

The tan and weather-beaten, smiling face of Henri Brunier seems to
invite confidence in his winemaking. Brunier's vineyard of 138 acres,
planted with 70% Grenache, 15% Syrah, 10% Mourvèdre, and 5% Cinsault, is superbly located in the eastern section of the appellation,
which has large stones and a clay and sandy soil base. His vines average
45 years in age, but one parcel of 37 acres averages 80 years. In 1979,
Brunier installed a completely new winery and the style of wine produced here changed dramatically. The old rich, dark, unfiltered, deeply
concentrated, rather profound wine gave way to a well-delineated, fruitier, less intense modern style—still delicious and well made, but a
different animal. To hear Brunier talk, he now has what he wanted,
which is a wine with "equilibrium, without excessive alcohol, without
the taste of wood, without rough tannins—a wine to drink in two to
three years, but which will keep ten years." As good as his wines are
today, I lament the fact that, given the new vinification, nothing as
profound as the 1978, 1972, 1971, or 1967 is likely to ever again be
made here. Nevertheless, I believe Brunier *is the best* at displaying the
modern style of wine. His wines are loaded with hedonistic levels of
ripe fruit and they are joys to drink. Can we expect anything more?

Brunier puts all of his red wine grapes into his gleaming stainless
steel tanks whole. There is a ten to fifteen day maceration period and
then the wine is filtered and put in wooden foudres for eight to twelve
months. His white wine is perhaps the most enjoyable white wine made
in the appellation. Produced from equal parts of Grenache Blanc, Bourboulenc, Roussanne, and Clairette, it is an intensely perfumed wine
with scents of honeysuckle and tropical fruit and a personality much
like that of a Condrieu. Unfortunately, he normally produces only 175
cases, and it must be drunk within one to two years. It is bottled three
months after the harvest, usually in December.

Recently, I asked Henri Brunier and his son Daniel to prepare a blind
tasting of his 1984. I had discussed the filtration issue with Brunier on
each year's visit since his introduction of filtering in 1979. Brunier
believed that filtering caused the wine to close up initially, but he felt

that after one or two years in the bottle no one would be able to tell the difference. He had bottled his 1984 vintage 16 months previously, but one small lot had been bottled unfiltered at the request of one of his importers. In a tasting held with the Bruniers, we were given blind the filtered and unfiltered 1984 Vieux Télégraphe to taste, not knowing which was which. One wine, preferred by the Bruniers as well as this author, was noticeably darker, much more aromatic and richer in fruit —it was the unfiltered wine. I know Brunier was shaken by this tasting, but whether he and his son will change their philosophy about the "commercial necessity" of filtration remains to be seen.

This is an estate that produces exuberant, richly fruity wines that give immense pleasure. Their wines are very worthy additions to anyone's cellar.

VINTAGES

1986—*Vieux Télégraphe (white)*—A splendidly perfumed bouquet of
· tropical fruit and floral scents is gloriously appealing. Lovely,
90 ripe, rich fruit fills the mouth of this unctuous, full-bodied wine.
Last tasted 2/87.

1985—*Vieux Télégraphe (white)*—Now beginning to fade, the 1985 was
· superb in October 1986, but three months later the fruit had
87 begun to come out, proving just how important it is to drink
these wines very, very young. Last tasted 2/87.

1985—*Vieux Télégraphe (red)*—An explosively rich, fruity, deep wine,
· Brunier's 1985 is quite full-bodied, very alcoholic (14.5%), has a
88 sweet, jammy, almost port-like richness and texture, and will
provide hedonistic pleasure for the next 6–7 years. Anticipated
maturity: 1988–1994. Last tasted 6/86.

1984—*Vieux Télégraphe (red)*—A strong effort, the 1984 Vieux Télé-
· graphe is deep in color, loaded with spicy, peppery, berry fruit,
86 quite full-bodied for the vintage, but more elegant and significantly less alcoholic than the full-throttle 1985. Anticipated maturity: now–1993. Last tasted 12/86.

1983—*Vieux Télégraphe (red)*—Among recent vintages, the 1983 is
· (whether intentionally or by chance) the closest wine in stylistic
90 terms to the pre-1979 Vieux Télégraphes. Densely colored, with
a powerful bouquet of pepper, herbs, and jammy, sweet berry
fruit, full-bodied, weighty, and very rich, this hefty, multidimensional wine makes quite an impact on the palate. Anticipated
maturity: now–1994. Last tasted 12/86.

1982—*Vieux Télégraphe (red)*—Fully mature, the 1982 is quite high in
·   alcohol, but manages to deliver enough plump, succulent, ripe
85   fruit to keep the wine from tasting hot and unbalanced. Drink it
     up. Last tasted 10/86.

1981—*Vieux Télégraphe (red)*—I enjoyed this wine much more in 1983–
·   1986 than I do now. It seems to have dropped much of its exu-
85   berant fruitiness. In spite of that, it is still a very good, round,
     generously flavored wine that should be drunk over the next 2–
     4 years. Last tasted 2/87.

1980—*Vieux Télégraphe (red)*—Soft, unctuous, fruity flavors, full body,
·   and an interesting scent of herbs and salty seaweed make for an
84   intriguing concoction of aromas. This is fully mature and should
     be drunk up. Last tasted 6/86.

1979—*Vieux Télégraphe (red)*—Overshadowed by Brunier's monumen-
·   tal 1978, the 1979, the first of his "modern style" wines, has
86   developed well. Still a little tannic, this full-bodied wine has a
     very peppery, spicy bouquet, big, authoritative flavors, and a
     surprising amount of tannin in the finish. Anticipated maturity:
     now–1993. Last tasted 6/86.

1978—*Vieux Télégraphe (red)*—This is the finest Vieux Télégraphe I
·   have ever consumed. It is somewhat of a freak for this property
94   in that it is still not fully mature. Black/ruby and opaque, the
     huge bouquet of smoky, tarry, truffle-scented, herb-tinged fruit
     is very complex. Absolutely enormous and massive on the pal-
     ate, with a staggering depth of fruit, this wine, which has already
     thrown a considerable sediment, will last for at least another 10–
     20 years—it is a blockbuster wine that must be tasted to be
     believed. Anticipated maturity: 1990–2005. Last tasted 1/87.

1977—*Vieux Télégraphe (red)*—Surprisingly good and fully mature, the
·   bouquet has a salty, seawater, almost iodine aroma. On the
82   palate, the wine is fleshy, full-bodied, a bit herbaceous, but solid
     and quite alive. Drink over the next 3–4 years. Last tasted 7/82.

1976—*Vieux Télégraphe (red)*—Approaching full maturity, the 1976 is
·   a very old-style Vieux Télégraphe—a muscular, alcoholic, full-
87   intensity wine with plenty of attention-getting fruit and extract.
     Drink over the next 5–6 years. Last tasted 6/84.

1972—*Vieux Télégraphe (red)*—Brunier made an excellent 1972. It is
·   now in the full bloom of maturity and requires drinking. A sweet,
88   smoky, jammy, nutty bouquet is followed by a wine that is still
     very concentrated, quite soft, alcoholic, and rather viscous.
     Drink it up. Last tasted 6/86.

1971—*Vieux Télégraphe (red)*—More elegant than the robust, powerful
· 1972, the 1971 has the sweet, velvety, smoky, jammy fruit of the
88 1972, but is less heady and heavy on the palate. The color shows
a great deal of orange, and this wine, like the 1972, has dropped
a great deal of sediment. Last tasted 12/85.

Other Châteauneuf-du-Pape Producers

L'Arnesque (P. Laget)—This 44-acre property is run by a member of
the Prestige et Tradition growers' association, Pierre Laget. He produces a dull white wine, and a round, fruity, Grenache-dominated
red wine. His 1983, 1981, and 1980 red wines were standard in quality.

Bois Dauphin (J. Marchand)—Fruity, light-colored, agreeable, soft
wines are produced by the carbonic maceration method. They are
well made, but must be drunk within two to four years of the vintage.

Cellier des Princes—A cooperative of growers from all over the southern Rhône, the Châteauneuf-du-Pape made here is bland, rather
heavy, and does not do justice to the fine wines made by the best
growers.

Domaine de la Chartreuse (André Rey)—This estate is located near
Vieux Télégraphe and Terre Ferme. I have never tasted their wines.

Domaine Le Chêne Vert (Charles Mestre)—This is a tiny estate and I
must confess to never having seen a bottle of this wine in the market.

Cuvée des Hospices—The late Gaston Brunel created this special
cuvée of Châteauneuf-du-Pape in 1973 that is made from wine dona-
tions from all the growers. About 8,000 cases are produced each year
of this good, reliable, but not great example of red Châteauneuf-du-
Pape. The proceeds from the sale of this wine benefit the home for
the elderly in Châteauneuf-du-Pape.

Domaine de Farguerol (J. Revoltier)—Few wines have excited me
from this domaine, but the vineyard is superbly placed and the installation of a new, ambitious, and dedicated proprietor who the
French say is "très sérieux" has everyone watching to see what will
emerge.

Domaine Grande Gardiole (André Rey)—This property sits in the
northern part of the appellation near Courthézon. I have only tasted
one vintage, which was satisfactory.

Domaine de Husson (André Grangets)—The few vintages of red wine
I have tasted from this estate in the eastern sector near Courthézon
have been densely colored, chunky, rather hefty wines. Approxi-

mately 8,000 cases of red wine are produced from the family's 86 acres of vineyards.

Comte de Lauze—These wines, made by the carbonic maceration method, are straightforward, soft, fruity wines that are simple and pleasant, but rather one-dimensional. The blend is dominated by 85% Grenache.

Mas Saint-Louis (Geniest)—Production here averages about 2,500 cases of soft, fruity, straightforward-styled wine that should be drunk within three to five years of the vintage.

Ogier—This large négociant in nearby Sorgues produces terribly alcoholic, thick wines that are very poor examples of Châteauneuf-du-Pape.

Saint-Préfert (Camille Serre)—This is a 50-acre estate that produces lighter-styled, fruity, supple wines that make attractive drinking when young.

Domaine de la Serrière (Michel Bernard)—A domaine of 123 acres that produces a good red Châteauneuf-du-Pape from a blend of 70% Grenache and 15% each of Syrah and Mourvèdre. The 1984 and 1981 are quite good.

Cuvée de Sommeliers (Jacques Mestre)—The quiet Jacques Mestre, a member of Prestige et Tradition, produces very good, ageworthy, classic red Châteauneuf-du-Pape. His 1984 was sound yet unexciting, but his excellent 1983 and equally fine 1981 and 1979 would cause excitement in many wine circles. His red is 85% Grenache, 10% Syrah, and 5% Mourvèdre. I do not recommend his dull white wine.

Jean Versino—Versino is a very highly regarded producer who left unanswered two letters of mine and was unwilling to receive me on several recent visits. The vintages of his wines I have tasted, 1978 and 1981, were dense, powerful, tannic, old-style Châteauneuf-du-Papes with plenty of personality.

Domaine Pierre Usseglio—Both white and red wine are made here. With tasting notes on only two vintages, I hardly know the estate well, but the 1980 and 1981 were round, fruity, full-bodied, easy to drink wines.

Domaine Raymond Usseglio—I wish I had more experience with this estate's wines. The 1979 and 1981 were excellent, deep, full-bodied, rich, and obviously made to last. All of this wine is sold within France or to Belgium.

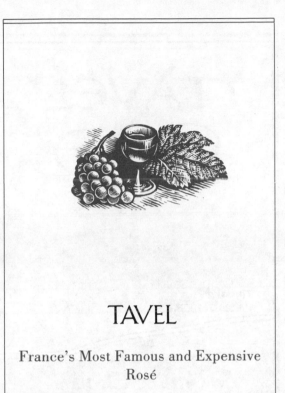

TAVEL

France's Most Famous and Expensive
Rosé

TAVEL AT A GLANCE

Type of wine produced:	Dry rosé wine only
Grape varieties planted:	There are nine authorized varieties; Grenache and Cinsault dominate, followed by Clairette, Syrah, Bourboulenc, Mourvèdre, Picpoul, Carignan, and Calitor
Acres currently under vine:	1,900
Quality level:	Good to exceptional rosé wines; the best are among the finest in the world
Aging potential:	1–4 years
General characteristics:	Tavel is dry and full-bodied; it can be the boldest rosé wine in the world for breadth and depth of flavor
Greatest recent vintages:	1986, 1985
Price range:	$9–$12 (an expensive rosé)

TAVEL

Toward
VALLIGUIÈRES

D4

Roc Epine

La Vau et Clau

Les Joncie

Le Malaven

Forêt de Tavel

N
W E
S

Toward
REMOULINS

A9

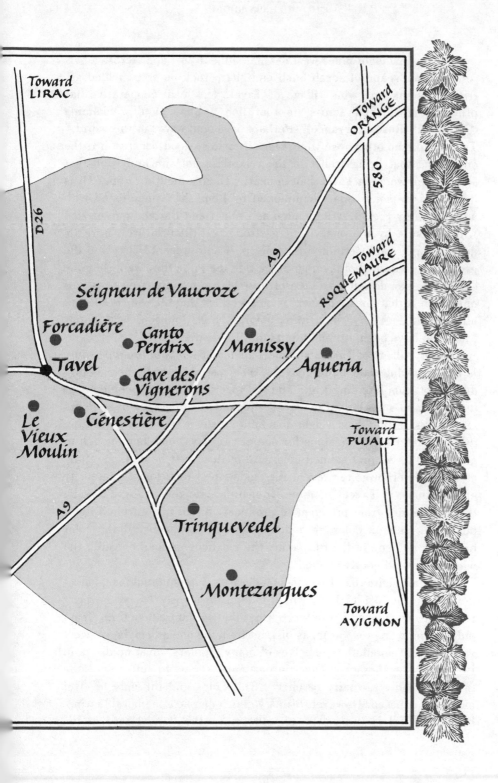

Toward
LIRAC

Toward
ORANGE

D 26

580

A 9

Toward
ROQUEMAURE

Seigneur de Vaucroze

Forcadière

Canto
Perdrix

Manissy

Aqueria

Tavel

Cave des
Vignerons

Le
Vieux
Moulin

Génestière

Toward
PUJAUT

A 9

Trinquevedel

Montezargues

Toward
AVIGNON

Just eight miles west of Châteauneuf-du-Pape, across a barren, dry landscape of scrub bush and sharp rock outcrops called garrigues, is the tiny wine village of Tavel. The local cooperative has proudly embellished across its roof line a huge sign proclaiming "Tavel—1ᵉʳ Rosé de France." Perhaps it should say, "in the world." Tavel is like no other rosé wine. Does it taste so good because it is the only thing that brings relief in the relentless hot sun and wind that seems even worse in Tavel than in nearby Châteauneuf-du-Pape? Or is it that this famous wine, championed by Louis XIV, mentioned with admiration by French writers such as Daudet and Balzac, and guzzled with pleasure by the bon vivant gastronome Brillat-Savarin, is really quite exceptional? Certainly its fame, past and present, has given the growers a great deal of leverage in getting the price they want, but one sometimes wonders if Tavel is worth its high price. Regardless of how one answers that question, there is no argument that the wine is special, although it does have its critics, notably Hugh Johnson, who claims "never to have been attracted to its dry, full-bodied style."

The tiny village of Tavel, which seems to exist only to produce wine, is full of tasting rooms and "caves." The rosé wine made here is produced not from blending white and red together as many people imagine, but from stacking up the freshly picked whole grapes in stainless steel tanks, letting their weight do a light crushing, and then permitting the juice to sit with the skins for one or two days, just long enough to give Tavel its vibrant salmon color. All of this must be done carefully at cool temperatures to prevent the oxidation of the aromatic intensity and freshness of Tavel's bouquet. In tasting through a range of Tavels, the color varies from producer to producer. It can range from a light, pale, pink salmon color, to a deep, vibrant, light ruby. If the color becomes too deep in the ruby tone, the local cognoscenti consider the wine vulgar and poorly vinified.

The locals claim that Tavel has moderate aging potential for its alcohol content of 13% to 14%, which is high for a rosé. I have never, I repeat never, enjoyed one of these wines that was more than three years old. To me, a fine rosé wine, as distinct from the cheap, cloyingly sweet varieties that populate the shelves of many retailers, must be drunk in its youthful exuberance. Tavel in particular seems to suffer once the gush of fresh strawberry or cherry fruit fades and the ugly level of alcohol is exposed. However, drunk young it can be a memorable wine, because Tavel is the only rosé, other than the Bandol rosé of the

Domaine Tempier (see page 393), that has the depth and length of a red wine on the palate, and a dry, often surprisingly long finish.

Tasting notes for rosé always seem a bit absurd. Rosés are prized for their freshness, vibrancy of fruit, crisp acidity, and balance. A fine Tavel adds body and depth to this formula for a great rosé. Tavel when young has tremendous fruit and body, possessing a deep fragrance of flowers and berry fruit. Rather shockingly, it also feels deep and long on the palate, because of its body and alcoholic clout. If the wine does not have freshness and good fruit, it is simply not pleasant to drink.

There are at last eight growers in Tavel who make fine rosé. They sell every bit of it to western Europeans (who seem to have an inexhaustible thirst for this wine), and therefore live very comfortably, charging whatever price the traffic will bear. The town cooperative produces over half of the appellation's wine and sells it under various labels. It is all of good quality.

RECENT VINTAGES*
* Only recent vintages are of any importance since this wine must be drunk young.

1986—While the production was down from 1985, the growers thought the wines were better balanced with more acidity than the boldly flavored, flamboyant yet low-acid 1985s. Optimum maturity: now–1989.

1985—Very big, ripe, fragrant, intense wines were made that take flavor and body to the maximum limit as far as rosé wines are concerned. They are slightly low in acidity and must be drunk before the end of 1988.

OLDER VINTAGES
There is only one rule here: Caveat emptor.

A Personal Rating of the Tavel Producers

****(EXCELLENT PRODUCERS)*

Domaine de la Forcadière (Armand Maby)
Domaine de la Genestière (Mme. Andrée Bernard)

***(GOOD PRODUCERS)*

Caves Coopératives
Château d'Aqueria (Paul DeBez)
Clos Canto-Perdrix (Méjan Taulier)
Domaine Corne-Loup (J. Lafond)
E. Guigal (E. Guigal)
S. Levêque
Château Manissy
Prieuré de Montézargues (Allauzen)
Roc Epine (Lafond)
Château de Trinquevedel (F. Dumoulin)
Le Vieux Moulin (Gabriel Roudil)

CHÂTEAU D'AQUERIA (PAUL DEBEZ)***

Outside of the tiny village of Tavel in the direction of Roquemaure is the beautiful château of d'Aqueria, which sits among 123 acres of vines. The production here is quite large for an independent grower in Tavel, about 19,000–20,000 cases. The cépage or blend used by proprietor Paul DeBez is 45% Grenache, 20% Cinsault, 15% Clairette, 15% Mourvèdre, and the balance Bourboulenc and Picpoul. The property also produces a red Lirac. The rosé here is quite full-bodied, perhaps not as vibrant and exuberantly fruity as some, but still quite good.

CLOS CANTO-PERDRIX (MÉJAN-TAULIER)***

This estate of 80 acres produces a very fruity, rather deep salmon-colored rosé that can be a little too hefty for its own good in vintages such as 1982, 1983, and 1985. The very modern winemaking facility uses a blend of Grenache, Cinsault, Clairette, Carignan, Syrah, and Bourboulenc to produce its Tavel. Like many other Tavel growers, Clos Canto-Perdrix also produces a red Lirac.

DOMAINE CORNE-LOUP (J. LAFOND)***

This estate of 54 acres produces 8,000 cases of Tavel under the meticulous care of Jacques Lafond. The rosé is usually a bright salmon color, very fruity and perfumed. It is quite dry as well as full-bodied. Lafond believes in bottling his Tavel as early as possible to preserve the freshness and fragrance of the fruit. Normally the wine is in the bottle by the end of March following the vintage. This is a good producer who seems to be making better and better Tavel.

DOMAINE DE LA FORCADIÈRE (ARMAND MABY)****

Armand Maby and his son Roger produce one of the two best Tavels of the appellation. The popularity of Maby's Tavel is such that the 18,000 cases of 1985 he produced were completely sold out six months after the vintage, even in the restaurants of the region, as witnessed by the fact that by late summer of 1986, Maby's Tavel was listed as "epuisé" (exhausted) on the wine lists I saw in this area. Maby has 114 acres and his rosé emphasizes the wonderfully fresh, berry fruit aromas of a Tavel, but always tastes crisp and well balanced in spite of its full body and generous alcoholic clout of 13.5%. This is a Tavel to search out, for it never disappoints.

DOMAINE DE LA GENESTIÈRE
(MME. ANDRÉE BERNARD)****

The late George Bernard's Domaine de la Genestière has long been considered one of the two best Tavels. This is a gorgeous estate just outside the town. It is 64 acres in size and is planted with 50% Grenache, 20% Cinsault, and the balance in white wine grapes such as Clairette, Picpoul, and Bourboulenc. The rosé made here is fairly deep in color, exuberantly fruity, and usually less full-bodied and alcoholic than its peers. The estate also sells wine under a secondary label, Domaine Longval.

DOMAINE LEVÊQUE***

The most traditionally made Tavel is produced here. Aged two years in cask prior to bottling, the wine is very full-bodied and alcoholic, with a mature bouquet suggestive of thyme, resin, and spicy oak. It is a very distinctive wine that is an anachronism among the Tavels. The estate is 74 acres in size and produces 8,000 cases of wine.

CHÂTEAU MANISSY***

On the road to Roquemaure, not far from Château d'Aqueria, hidden behind some large trees, is the Château Manissy. This 74-acre estate produces a Tavel marked by its prolonged aging in wood. Their style of Tavel is not one that I like, but those who prefer their rosés very spicy, soft, and well aged will enjoy the Tavel from Manissy more than I do.

PRIEURÉ DE MONTÉZARGUES (ALLAUZEN)***

This property of 74 acres that produces approximately 10,000 cases of wine is a reliable source of good rather than superb Tavel. The attractive priory, which dates from the thirteenth century, is run by the Allauzen family.

DOMAINE DE ROC EPINE (LAFOND) ***
This 74-acre estate produces nearly 11,000 cases of Tavel. It is aged for 10–12 months prior to being bottled. It is a very spicy, dry wine that has quite a bit of body.

CHÂTEAU DE TRINQUEVEDEL (F. DUMOULIN) ***
Outside the village of Tavel, in the direction of Nîmes, is the historic estate of Trinquevedel. The origins of this domaine can be traced back to the French Revolution. François Dumoulin lives here and produces 8,500 cases of Tavel from his 62 acres of vineyards planted with 43% Grenache, 21% Cinsault, 18% Clairette, 7% Carignan, and 4% Syrah. He uses the carbonic maceration for his wine, among the most perfumed and powerful Tavels made. His 1985 and 1986 are outstanding.

LE VIEUX MOULIN (GABRIEL ROUDIL) ***
Run by three brothers, Henri, Aimé, and Maurice Roudil, the 100-acre estate of Le Vieux Moulin produces a very fine, fruity, fresh, vibrant, full-bodied rosé from mainly two grape varieties, the Grenache and Cinsault. The winery is modern and the standard of this Tavel is consistently high.

LIRAC

Unrealized Potential

LIRAC AT A GLANCE

Type of wine produced:	Red, rosé, and white wines
Grape varieties planted:	All permitted southern Rhône varietals; 33% minimum of Clairette for the white wine, 60% maximum of Grenache for the red wine
Acres currently under vine:	1,729 (approximately a quarter of the surface area within the appellation)
Quality level:	Mediocre to good
Aging potential:	1–5 years
General characteristics:	Soft, very fruity, medium-bodied red wines; neutral white wines; exuberantly fresh, fruity rosés
Greatest recent vintages:	1985, 1978
Price range:	$6–$9

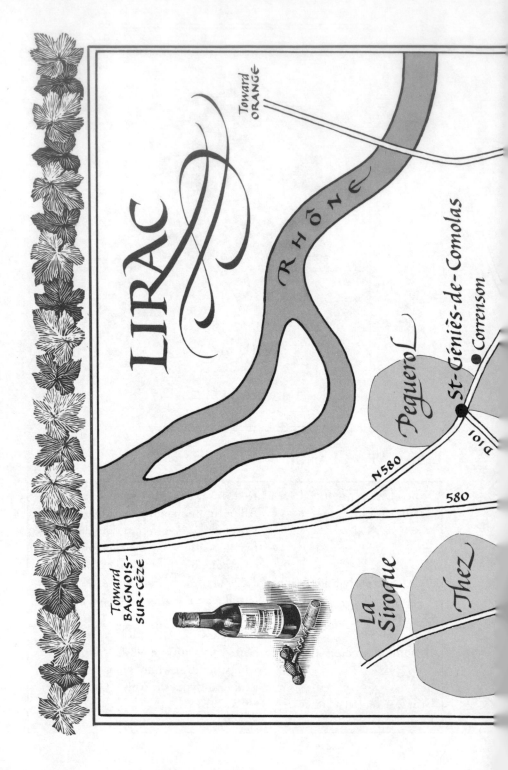

LIRAC

*Toward
ORANGE*

RHÔNE

Peguerol

St-Géniès-de-Comolas

• Correnson

N580

580

*Toward
BAGNOIS-
SUR-CÈZE*

La
Siroque

Thez

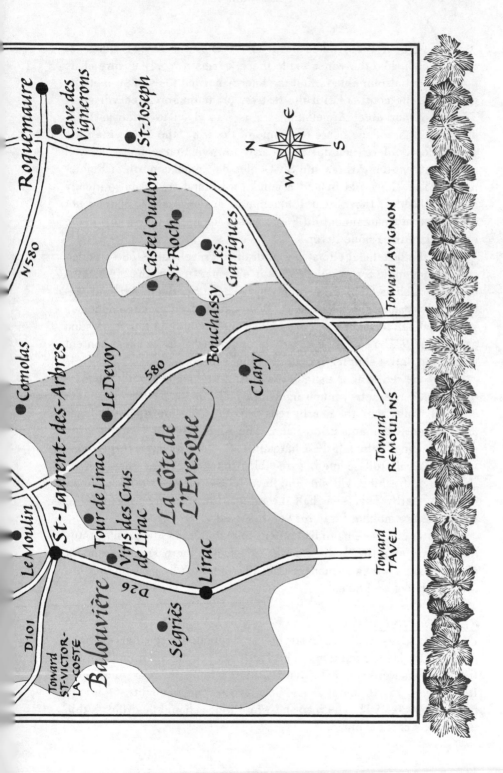

Roquemaure

Cave des Vignerons

St-Joseph

N580

Castel Oualou

St-Roch

Les Garrigues

Bouchassy

Clary

N

E

W

S

Toward AVIGNON

Comolas

St-Laurent-des-Arbres

Le Devoy

580

La Côte de L'Evesque

Toward REMOULINS

Le Moulin

D101

Toward ST-VICTOR-LA-COSTE

Balouvière

Tour de Lirac

Vins des Crus de Lirac

D26

Ségriès

Lirac

Toward TAVEL

About three miles north of Tavel is the sleepy village of Lirac, which, like the wines made there, seems not only unsure of its potential but also unable to find the energy needed to even promote its products. The contrast with the festive, promotion-oriented village of Tavel is remarkable. Appellation status was given to Lirac in 1945, and while that village bears the name of the wine, the area within the appellation borders includes the nearby town of Roquemaure, as well as St.-Laurent-des-Arbres and St.-Genies-de-Comolas north of Roquemaure. The vineyards in and around Lirac tend to be on gradually sloping hillsides; those near Roquemaure are on a stony plateau not unlike that of Châteauneuf-du-Pape, which sits only a mile away on the east bank of the Rhône River.

Given the beneficial climate, well-drained gravel, and stone-studded soil, the potential for excellent wine is obvious. In fact, the top estates of Lirac, such as Château de Ségriès, Château St.-Roch, Armand Maby's La Fermade, and Domaine du Devoy, do indeed produce delicious wines that sell for very low prices given their quality in top years such as 1978 or 1985. Yet the rank and file producers of Lirac seem content to turn out only a simple, one-dimensional wine.

Today the red wine is usually the most attractive of Lirac. It has its own unique character, much lighter in body, more flowery and more obviously fruity than the nearby reds from the Côtes du Rhône-Villages or of course Châteauneuf-du-Pape. The white wine of Lirac is fairly neutral-tasting, although the Château St.-Roch turns out a surprisingly tasty, tropical fruit-scented, agreeable white wine. The rosé can be gloriously refreshing, vibrant, and flavorful as well as a worthy competitor to a nearby Tavel—at half the price. However, only a handful of producers are making Lirac rosé of this quality.

For now, Lirac seems to be content to maintain its low-profile status quo. This is all rather sad, since the prospect of increasing the amount of high-quality wines at modest prices is undoubtedly possible but unfortunately not probable.

RECENT VINTAGES

1986—After several severe storms in September, the harvest took place under ideal conditions. The crop was smaller than in 1985 and the red wines were noticeably harder, more tannic, and less voluptuous. It is too early to call, but it should be above average in quality. Optimum maturity: 1988–1992. The rosé and white wines should be drunk within three years of the vintage.

1985—A very attractive year for the wines of Lirac, 1985 produced deeply colored, sometimes explosively fruity, supple wines that will make ideal drinking over the next four to five years.

OLDER VINTAGES

The 1984s are firm, sometimes austere, the 1983s rather patchy. The 1982s are soft, extremely alcoholic, and the 1981s and 1980s well above average. The last really special vintage for this appellation was 1978. Red wines from 1978, particularly those from Saint-Roch and Château de Ségriès, are still delicious.

A Personal Rating of the Lirac Producers

***(GOOD PRODUCERS)

Château de Clary   Saint-Roch
Domaine Devoy   Château de Ségriès
Domaine Maby

**(AVERAGE PRODUCERS)

Domaines Assemat   Castel Oualou
Château de Bouchassy   Domaine des Joncières

DOMAINES J. C. ASSÉMAT
(LES GARRIGUES AND CHÂTEAU DES CAUSSES) **

This estate of 75 acres produces a bevy of cuvées of Lirac under an assortment of names. The most commonly encountered labels are Les Garrigues and Château des Causses. There are also labels called Lirac Rouge d'Eté (a cuvée of light, fruity wine made by the carbonic maceration method), a Lirac Rouge Classique (more powerful and vinified traditionally), and a Lirac Réserve Syrah (a 100% Syrah wine with five to seven years' aging potential). Jean Claude Assemat, the proprietor, has his attractive cellars in Roquemaure, and regularly wins many awards for his wines at the French wine festivals. The quality here is average to good. The wines are fresh, very soft, easy to drink, light, and fruity. They certainly require drinking within three to four years of the vintage, except for the cuvée of Syrah.

CHÂTEAU DE BOUCHASSY (ROBERT DEGOUL) **

This estate of 89 acres produces only 2,000 cases of red wine from its vineyards near Roquemaure. The white wine is neutral-tasting and one-dimensional; however, the red wine is one of the most powerful and richest of the Liracs, as well as among the longest-lived red wines of the appellation. The 1978 drank well in 1986, and more recently both 1981 and 1982 looked promising. The bulk of the production here is a sound but unexciting rosé wine.

CASTEL OUALOU (MARIE PONS-MURE)**

The proprietor here, like many growers in Lirac, immigrated from Algeria when France gave that country independence in 1961. This estate in Roquemaure owns 126 acres and produces a charming, fairly light rosé, a bland white wine, and a soft, agreeable, raspberry-scented red wine that requires drinking within its first three or four years of life.

CHÂTEAU DE CLARY***

This old, historical property is located in a forest near Tavel. It was here that Roman ruins were found, suggesting that wine was made at this château during that period of history. Only red wine is made here today. Based on the 1985, the only vintage I have ever seen or tasted, it is a deeply fruity, densely colored wine for a Lirac, with a great deal of body and power.

DOMAINE DU DEVOY (JOSEPH LOMBARDO)***

This is one of the most serious estates in Lirac. Two brothers, Marc and Joseph Lombardo, own 86 acres and produce only red and rosé wine. Their cellars are in the interesting village of St.-Laurent-des-Arbres, an old village dominated by a particularly well preserved twelfth-century church. Lombardo, a Frenchman who left Tunisia after his vineyards there were nationalized by the government, produces a deeply colored, beefy, robust Lirac that is distinguished by its dark color and chunky fruit. The rosé is also among the better ones made in Lirac. Prices for the Domaine du Devroy wines are very modest, making this estate's wines a bargain well worth searching out.

DOMAINE DES JONCIÈRES (PIERRE ROUSSEL)**

Most of this domaine's production is in generic Côtes du Rhône, but a tiny amount of decent Lirac rosé and good, well-colored, full-bodied Lirac red wine are made. Both a 1981 and 1982 tasted recently were quite acceptable. The estate covers 79 acres.

DOMAINE MABY (LA FERMADE)***

The Domaine Maby, which also makes one of the best Tavels, makes delicious red, white, and rosé Liracs that sell for very modest prices. The Lirac rosé here is half the price of the domaine's Tavel, and virtually indistinguishable from it. In addition, one of the few good white Liracs is made here, a wine that is fresh, fruity, and has character. However, the best wine of Maby is his serious red Lirac, of which he produces 5,000 cases. Always deep in color with a ripe raspberry-scented bouquet and surprising body, sometimes tannic as well, it has a sense of balance as well as purpose, something many Lirac reds do not possess. The name for his Lirac wines is La Fermade. His 1980, 1981, and 1982 red Liracs are worth looking for. For the white and rosé, make it the last two vintages only (1986 and 1985).

CHÂTEAU SAINT-ROCH (ANTOINE VERDA)***

Located just north of Roquemaure, Chateau Saint-Roch is the most important estate of Lirac. The vineyards of 99 acres are planted with 55% Grenache, 15% Cinsault, 15% Syrah, and 15% Mourvèdre for the red wine and 40% Clairette, 30% Grenache Blanc, and 30% Bourboulenc for the white. The two sons of Antoine Verda, Jean-Jacques and André, manage this property. The red wine spends one year in tanks and two years in foudres prior to bottling. In each vintage about 10% of the best wine is set aside for a special luxury cuvée of red wine called Cuvée Ancienne Vigueria. About 1,000 cases out of the total red wine production of 12,000 cases are made of this wine. The white wine, the best in the appellation, and the rosé, of standard quality, are bottled very early to preserve their freshness and fruit. The 1985 Lirac Blanc was delicious and clearly showed the potential for the production of fine white wines from this appellation.

As for the red wines, they are undoubtedly good, but I believe Verda keeps them aging too long in wooden foudres, thus encouraging a degree of oxidation and lack of freshness, particularly in his special cuvée that spends an extra year in wood. That said, one is not likely to be disappointed by the red wine here—I just think they could be even better. The two best recent vintages for Saint-Roch are 1985 and 1982. The red wines are strong successes in these years. The 1984s and 1983s are surprisingly mediocre.

This estate, run consecutively by three generations of Verdas, is capable of providing delicious bottles of inexpensive wine.

CHÂTEAU DE SÉGRIÈS (J. F. DE RÉGIS)***

The run down Château de Ségriès and its unkempt, scrubby-looking proprietor, Jean-François de Regis, would appear to be unlikely producers of good Lirac wine. The estate has 49 acres of vineyards from which is made a good rosé, adequate white, and good, sometimes very good red wine. The red wine is very important here since it accounts for 90% of the domaine's production. It is made from a blend of 62% Grenache, 12% Cinsault, and 26% Syrah, vinified traditionally, kept 12–18 months in cement tanks, and then bottled unfiltered. It can be long-lived, as Liracs go. The 1978 and 1979 are still drinking well today. Among the more recent vintages, 1982 and 1985 appear the most promising. As so frequently seems the case with tiny growers, one is always shocked by the quality of wine made in a wine cellar as poorly equipped and as shabbily maintained as that of the Château de Ségriès.

Other Lirac Producers

Château Boucarut (Robert Fuget)—A traditional, sturdy, somewhat dull set of wines is made at this 50-acre estate in Roquemaure.

Cave Viticole de Roquemaure—This cooperative, founded in 1922, makes clean, sound, unexciting Liracs that sell for very reasonable prices.

Domaine de la Genestière (Mme. Andrée Bernard)—Bernard has 30 acres at Lirac and is reputed to make a good red Lirac; I have not tasted it.

Domaine du Seigneur (Jean Duseigneur)—Located in the village of Saint-Laurent-des-Arbres, this estate of 42 acres produces mostly red and rosé wine, but also a tiny amount of white.

THE
CÔTES DU
RHÔNE-VILLAGES

Fertile Hunting Ground for
Great Wine Values

THE CÔTES DU RHÔNE-VILLAGES AT A GLANCE

Types of wine produced:	Red, white, rosé
Grape varieties planted:	All legally authorized southern Rhône varieties
Acres currently under vine:	A vast area on both banks of the Rhône and three departments: Vaucluse, Gard, and Drôme, and 17 specific villages; 11,444 acres
Top "Villages" to seek out:	Cairanne, Rasteau, Sablet, Beaume-de-Venise, and Vacqueyras
General characteristics:	White wines are generally dull and neutral; rosé wines can be excellent; red wines vary enormously in quality and style, from innocuous to excellent
Quality level:	Poor to excellent
Aging potential:	1–4 years
Greatest recent vintage:	1985
Price Range:	$4.00–$8.50

Within the gigantic southern Rhône region, the French government, in particular the INAO or National Institute of Appellations of Origin, determined that 17 "villages" or communes had particularly good soil and microclimates and therefore produced superior wine. These 17 "villages" are entitled Côtes du Rhône-Villages, and their wines can be identified by either that appellation on the label or the name of the village preceded by the words "Côtes du Rhône." The 17 "villages" that are recognized by the government to produce wines of special character are Beaumes-de-Venise, Cairanne, Chusclan, Laudun, Rasteau, Roaix, Rochegude, Rousset-les-Vignes, Sablet, St.-Gervais, St.-Maurice-sur-Eygues, St.-Pantaléon-les-Vignes, Séguret, Vacqueyras, Valreas, Vinsobres, and Visan.

The controls governing the vineyard area—permitted yield per acre, grape varieties, and alcohol content—are more strictly limited and regulated for wines called Côtes du Rhône-Villages than Côtes du Rhône. In short, this should ensure that the consumer will get a better wine when purchasing a Côtes du Rhône-Villages rather than a Côtes du Rhône. Ironically, while there are many fine Côtes du Rhône-Villages wines, the two greatest wines made with a Côtes du Rhône appellation are not "Villages" wines. These two wines, the Cru de Coudelet of the Perrin family and Château de Fonsalette of Jacques Reynaud, are obvious exceptions to the rule, but more on them and the generic Côtes du Rhône in the next section.

The appellation Côtes du Rhône-Villages was first granted in 1953 only to Cairanne, Chusclan, Laudun, and Gigondas. (The last, Gigondas, was elevated in 1971 to a full-fledged appellation of its own.) Since 1953, the other 14 villages have asked for and received "Villages" status. It would be foolish to assume that all the village wines are of equal merit. In the course of the vast amount of tasting and visiting of domaines conducted in researching this book, it was apparent to me that certain villages produced better wines than others. Generally, I found the least successful Côtes du Rhône-Villages wines to come from the three villages in the Drôme department. Here in the northeastern quarter of the southern Rhône viticultural area are the official villages of Rochegude, Rousset-les-Vignes, Saint-Maurice-sur-Eygues, Saint-Pantaléon-les-Vignes, and Vinsobres. There is very interesting countryside to see here, but only a few of the wines I tasted from these villages seemed to merit a special "Villages" AOC status. Most of the wines produced in these one-horse towns are made by cooperatives.

On the western bank of the Rhône is the Gard department, which has three official Côtes du Rhône-Villages—Chusclan, Laudun, and Saint-Gervais. To my palate, only the last merits Côtes du Rhône-Villages status, largely because of the fine wine being made at the excellent Domaine Ste.-Anne.

Unquestionably the finest Côtes du Rhône-Villages wines come from the scenic, heavily visited Vaucluse department. Amidst a landscape of vines and hill towns, official Côtes du Rhône-Villages such as Beaumes-de-Venise (also entitled to its own AOC for its sweet, fortified Muscat wine), Cairanne, Rasteau (which has its own AOC, too, for its fortified sweet wine), Roaix, Sablet, Séguret, Valréas, Vacqueyras, and Visan produce vast quantities of very good, full-bodied, honest, sometimes exceptional wine that generally represents a fine value. These Côtes du Rhône-Villages are reviewed in alphabetical order.

BEAUMES-DE-VENISE

BEAUMES-DE-VENISE AT A GLANCE

Type of wine produced:	Sweet fortified wine from the white Muscat grape; dry red wines
Grape varieties planted:	All permitted southern Rhône varieties, and the only legal plantations of Muscat in the Rhône Valley
Acres currently under vine:	600 (Muscat)
Quality level:	Good to exceptional
Aging potential:	Muscat: 1–4 years
General characteristics:	Muscat: sweet, alcoholic, extraordinarily perfumed and exotic, very rich, and ideal as a dessert wine
Greatest recent vintages:	1985, 1983
Price range:	$8–$14

A Personal Rating of the Producers of Muscat

*****(OUTSTANDING PRODUCERS)*

Domaine Durban   Paul Jaboulet Ainé

**** *(EXCELLENT PRODUCERS)*
Domaine de Coyeux

***(GOOD PRODUCERS)

Domaine des Bernardins   Domaine St.-Sauveur
Cave Coopérative   Vidal-Fleury

This sleepy hillside village is largely known for its decadently fragrant and perfumed "vin doux naturel," or Muscat de Beaumes-de-Venise. However, this village is also a very fine source for red Côtes du Rhône. Beaumes-de-Venise is a five-minute drive south of Gigondas, and is tucked up against the Dentelles de Montmirail mountains. It is an ancient village founded by the Romans, who were known to use the sulfur springs nearby. It remains the only area of the Rhône Valley where the Muscat grape is grown.

The Muscat de Beaumes-de-Venise is one of the world's greatest and most underrated sweet dessert wines; I disagree completely with the local cognoscenti who quaff this full-bodied, 17–21% alcohol wine down as an apéritif. Its weakness is its inability to last or improve in the bottle. In short, Muscat de Beaumes-de-Venise must be drunk within three to four years of the vintage. Consumed young, before it loses its freshness and heady fragrance, Muscat de Beaumes-de-Venise inundates the taster with a veritable tidal wave of aromas ranging from scents of apricots, peaches, and coconuts to amaretto, roasted nuts, and oranges. The unctuous, opulent, exotic flavors and staggering level of fruit hide far too easily the hefty alcoholic content. This is a wine to drink as a dessert, or with a very basic food companion—open-face fruit pies and tarts do magnificently. Another virtue of this wine is that the unfinished portion, if refrigerated, can be kept for five to seven days without fear of oxidation.

The acreage planted with Muscat has grown to just under 600 acres. Over 95% (about 67,000 cases per year) of the production of Muscat comes from the huge **Cave Coopérative** that has 330 members. Their wine is quite good, but the foolish-looking bottle they use for it as well as its screw cap present a false impression of the quality inside the bottle.

Two northern wine négociants, **Paul Jaboulet Aîné** and **Vidal-Fleury,** also produce Muscat de Beaumes-de-Venise. That of Vidal-Fleury is good, whereas Paul Jaboulet's is exceptional. The Jaboulets purchase their Muscat grapes from small growers, rush the wine to their facilities in Tain L'Hermitage, give it a long, cool fermentation, and bottle it very early to preserve all of its aromas and flavors. The Jaboulets produce nearly 2,000 cases of Muscat de Beaumes-de-Venise, and it is among the top two wines of the appellation.

Surprisingly, there are only a few growers who estate bottle their Beaumes de Venise. The two finest estates are the Domaine Durban and Domaine de Coyeux.

The 26-acre Muscat vineyard of the **Domaine Durban** produces what most observers would say is the finest Muscat de Beaumes-de-Venise of the appellation. It is certainly the most extroverted and flamboyant. The Domaine Durban, perched on a steep hillside above the village of Beaumes-de-Venise with a spectacular panorama of the countryside, is run by Bernard Leydier. His wine is intense, very concentrated, and viscous, with striking flavors and a haunting fragrance. For years the wine was sold without a vintage, but in 1985 Leydier began to vintage date the wine, a critical and intelligent thing to do given the short shelf life of these wines. Only 2,500 cases of Domaine Durban's nectarlike wine are produced, and it is very enthusiastically recommended.

One of the emerging stars of Muscat de Beaumes-de-Venise is the **Domaine de Coyeux.** The charming, confident, very friendly Yves Nativelle passionately runs this 306-acre estate perched even higher above the Domaine Durban. Nativelle purchased this property in 1978 and produced his first wine only in 1982. The vineyards are still very young, but there is exciting potential here. Nativelle, who has a habit of calling Muscat either the "nectar of the Pope" or "nectar of God," prefers his Muscat, which is less viscous and concentrated than Domaine Durban's, with sorbets or fresh melons. The famous Swiss chef Freddie Girardet, who has Domaine de Coyeux on his wine list, likes to serve it with foie gras, according to Nativelle. Since the debut vintage of 1982, there has been a progression upward in quality, with the 1985 looking to be the best Muscat de Beaumes-de-Venise yet made here. While the style is lighter and less powerful and opulent than that of the Domaine Durban, the quality of the wine is excellent.

Another good estate making Muscat de Beaumes-de-Venise is the **Domaine St.-Sauveur.** The production from owner Guy Rey's 15 acres of vines is never adequate to satisfy the demand. His wine, bottled very early and vintage dated, is closer in style to that of the Domaine de Coyeux. It tends also to be less alcoholic than some of the other wines, usually averaging around 15%.

The other estate that produces the sweet, nectarlike Muscat de Beaumes-de-Venise is Monsieur Maurin's **Domaine des Bernardins.** This 25-acre property produces intensely fruity wines that are straightforward and enjoyable, but slightly below the level of quality of the other domaines.

Finally, it would not be just not to mention the red Côtes du Rhône-

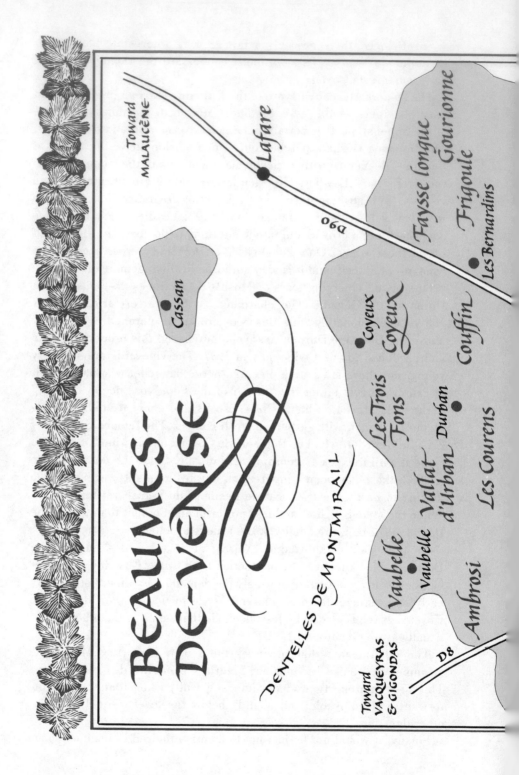

BEAUMES-DE-VENISE

DENTELLES DE MONTMIRAIL

Toward
MALAUCÈNE

Lafare

D90

Cassan

Faysse longue

Gourionne

Frigoule

Les Bernardins

Coyeux

Coyeux

Couffin

Les Trois
Fons

Vallat
d'urban Durban

Les Courens

Vaubelle

vaubelle

Ambrosi

Toward
VACQUEYRAS
& GIGONDAS

D8

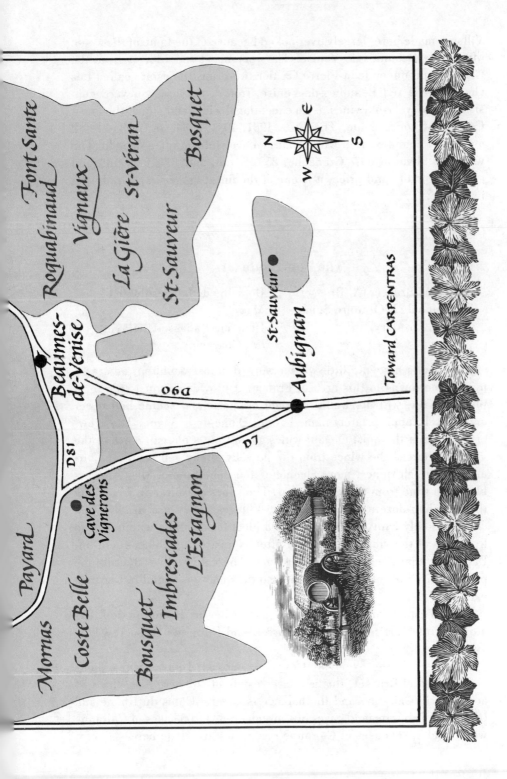

Payard
Mornas

Coste Belle

Cave des
Vignerons

D81

Beaumes-
de-Venise

D90

D7

Bousquet
Imbrescades
L'Estagnon

Font Sante
Roquabinaud

Vignaux

La Giēre   St-Véran

St-Sauveur

Bosquet

St-Sauveur
Aubignan

N
W   E
S

Toward CARPENTRAS

Villages made here, largely overlooked because of the fame of the sweet Muscat de Beaumes-de-Venise. The very finest red wine is from the Gigondas producer Jean-Pierre Cartier, who runs the estate called Les Goubert. His red Beaumes-de-Venise, from a ten-acre vineyard consisting of 65-year-old vines, is an exceptional wine, and one of the finest Côtes du Rhônes made. The 1979, 1981, 1983, 1984, and 1985 are all amazingly complex, rich wines that can evolve for up to a decade. The wine is a blend of 65% Grenache, 25% Syrah, and 10% Cinsault, and given its quality and price, it is one of the finest values in top red wine in France.

CAIRANNE

The Top Producers

Domaine Brusset (A. Brusset)
Domaine de L'Oratoire Saint-Martin (D. Alary)

Domaine de la Présidente (A. Max)
Domaine Rabasse-Charavin (M. Charavin)

Cairanne is a scenic little village spread across a hilltop, as are so many wine towns in this area of France. It provides a must stop for a photographer, with its well-preserved ramparts and scenic bell tower and church, appropriately named Notre Dame-de-la-Vigne. The growers claim that the most elegant wines come from a plateau north of the village, whereas the wines from the gravelly, stony soil south of Cairanne are much richer, more alcoholic, and more tannic. Most growers blend the wine from these two areas. The wines of Cairanne are among the best half-dozen Côtes du Rhône-Villages. They are usually well colored, richly fruity, full-bodied, and ideal for drinking within four to five years of the vintage. They are often compared to Châteauneuf-du-Pape, but that seems nonsense to me. The cooperative at Cairanne produces 75% of this village's wine and the quality is sound rather than exciting.

The top estates and best three wines are from the **Domaine de L'Oratoire Saint-Martin, Domaine Brusset,** and **Domaine Rabasse-Charavin.**

At the top is the excellent **Domaine Brusset.** Run with fastidious care by Daniel Brusset, this is a large estate of 151 acres, of which 74 acres are in Cairanne and the balance is generic Côtes du Rhône and Gigondas. Ten thousand cases of Cairanne red, 1,200 cases of Cairanne white, and 1,000 cases of Cairanne rosé wines are made here—all of it is of high quality. The red wine is rich in color and extract, full-bodied, sometimes smoky, and scented with aromas of Provençal herbs, quite long and clearly one of the best examples of a well-made Côtes du Rhône-Villages. It can age for four to five years. The 1985, 1982, and 1981 were particular successes at the Domaine Brusset.

Another excellent red wine is that from the **Domaine de L'Oratoire Saint-Martin.** The 79 acres of vineyards produce a big, intense, chocolatey, spicy wine that is called Réserve de Seigneurs.

The **Domaine Rabasse-Charavin,** with its 50 acres of vines planted with 65% Grenache, 15% Syrah, 10% Mourvèdre, and 10% assorted varieties, produces an opulently fruity, velvety wine that has great appeal young. They produce different cuvées, one called Cuvée d'Estevenas, another from 100% Syrah, but all of their wines are round and generously flavored with oodles of sweet, ripe fruit. Their 1985s are much more successful than their 1984s.

Lastly, the **Domaine de la Présidente** of Max Aubert, located in Sainte Cecile-les-Vignes, not Cairanne, produces full-bodied, rather tannic wine that benefits from two to four years of cellaring. Shrewd, value-conscious consumers should also look for Aubert's good generic Côtes du Rhône.

CHUSCLAN

On the right, or western bank of the Rhône, the village of Chusclan sits in the shadow of one of France's largest nuclear power plants. This 1,400-acre appellation has no estate-bottled wines, since the entire production of the 140-plus growers goes to one of the cooperatives in this small peasant village. The village was famed for its rosé and despite the fact that rosé sales are off, rosé is the best wine made here. The red wines of Chusclan are very rustic, quite alcoholic, and lacking for the most part in anything resembling finesse. The largest cooperative, the Caves des Vignerons de Chusclan, inexplicably calls its best cuvée of rosé Cuvée de Marcoule, Marcoule being the name of the nearby nuclear power plant.

LAUDUN

The Top Producer

Domaine Pelaquié

This hillside town's wine production is again dominated by its cooperative. Laudun is just a few kilometers south of Chusclan and there is quite a bit of history to this area—Julius Caesar had an encampment here for his soldiers. Red wine dominates the production figures and it is superior to that made at Chusclan, yet it also seems to possess a very rustic character and spicy bite to it. The best wine consistently comes from the **Domaine Pelaquié,** where a fresh (and not excessively alcoholic) white wine and deep, fruity, full-bodied red wine are made. This estate is sizable, with 117 acres under vine. They have also planted some Viognier, a grape that has shown much potential at the nearby estate in St.-Gervais of the Domaine Ste.-Anne.

RASTEAU

The Top Producers

Caves des Vignerons
Domaine Char-à-vin (M.
Charavin)

Robert Charavin (R.
Charavin)
Domaine de Grangeneuve
(Bressy-Masson)

Rasteau, another tiny village perched on a hill not far from Cairanne in the Vaucluse department, is better known as a Côtes du Rhône-Villages producer of dry white and rosé wine than for its full appellation status as a producer of sweet, fortified vin doux naturel. Even though this sweet, alcoholic wine has fallen from favor, several private domaines and the cooperative continue to produce it. Made from the Grenache grape, it has been optimistically compared to the fortified Grenache-based sweet wine of Banyuls. In truth, it in no way compares in stature to a fine Banyuls from a proprietor such as Dr. Parcé. Today this sweet Rasteau has become nothing more than a curiosity piece, and it is on that basis that any potential imbiber should consider it.

With respect to the dry table wines, four producers stand out. The cooperative of Rasteau, **Les Caves des Vignerons,** which produces 80% of the wine of this appellation, is one of the best co-ops in the southern Rhône. Both their red and rosé Côtes du Rhône-Villages offer delicious fruit and freshness and consistently good quality at a very low price.

Among the estates of Rasteau, the **Domaine de Grangeneuve, Domaine Char-à-vin,** and the **Domaine Robert Charavin** are the reliable producers of dry red Rasteau, which is quite similar in style and taste to the nearby wines of Cairanne.

ROAIX

Just north of the splendidly picturesque hill town of Séguret is another medieval village with immense photogenic interest. The **Cave Coopérative de Roaix-Séguret** produces the wine made here. It is not one of the better run cooperatives, and the wines reflect a lack of direction, little attention to detail, and not much commitment to quality. Visit Roaix for its scenic charm, not its wine.

ROCHEGUDE

Perhaps the only reason to make the eight-mile drive north of Orange is to stay at the luxurious hotel located here, the Château de Rochegude, a seventeenth-century edifice that dominates this tiny village. However, this is also an official Côtes du Rhône-Villages. It is said that Thomas Jefferson enjoyed the village wines. The **Cave Coopérative Vinicole de Rochegude** is the only producer of red wine; it turns out sound, chunky, foursquare wines that offer decent value for uncritical quaffing. They also produce run-of-the-mill, generic rosé and dull white Côtes du Rhônes.

SABLET

The Top Producers

Domaine de Boissan (H. Bonfils)

Jean-Pierre Cartier

Domaine Saint-Antoine (Caves St.-Pierre)

Château du Trignon (A. Roux)

Domaine de Verquière (L. Chamfort)

There are 988 acres under vine in Sablet and 95% of the wine produced here is red, the balance is white and rosé. This is a very good source for excellent Côtes du Rhône-Villages wines. The tiny village, 4.5 kilometers from Gigondas and 3 from Séguret, is very old, with many narrow, winding medieval alleys that offer much charm. In the late nineteenth century, the invention of a machine for grafting American root stock to French vines took place in Sablet, giving this tiny village a certain "réclame." As this village's name implies, the soil here is sandy. The overall quality of winemaking at Sablet is excellent, something that cannot be said of many of the Côtes du Rhône-Villages.

There are five leading producers of Sablet Côtes du Rhône-Villages. Hubert Bonfils runs the excellent 99-acre **Domaine de Boissan.** His red wine, a product of a blend that includes 88% Grenache, 10% Syrah, and 2% Mourvèdre, is a deep, richly colored, fruity wine best drunk within four to five years of the vintage.

Jean-Pierre Cartier lives in nearby Gigondas; he is an enormously talented winemaker. Cartier produces the finest white wine of Sablet from a blend of 50% Bourboulenc, 35% Roussanne, and 15% Clairette. Unfortunately, he makes only about 300 cases of it. He also produces a rich, lush, opulent red wine from Sablet that is a blend of 65% Grenache and 35% Syrah.

The **Domaine Saint-Antoine** sells its entire production each year to a large négociant, the **Caves St.-Pierre.** They bottle the wine with the domaine's name because of its consistently ripe, broad, fruity character and depth.

One of the most important estates of Sablet is **Château du Trignon.** Run with obvious enthusiasm by the amiable André Roux, Trignon produces a bevy of good Côtes du Rhônes, but their best wines are from Gigondas and Sablet. Roux has 126 acres. He is a disciple of the late Dr. Dufays, who believed fervently in the carbonic maceration method of vinification for red wine. Roux's red Sablet is a fruity, soft wine that drinks well young. He is augmenting his proportions of Mourvèdre and Syrah in his vineyard to give his wines more structure and complexity.

The finest domaine in Sablet is without doubt the **Domaine de Verquière.** Run by the Chamfort family, this 124-acre estate produces very traditionally made wines that incredibly spend (and sometimes survive) three to four years in wooden foudres. Their wines seem to benefit from this in vintages such as 1981, 1979, and 1978, but I thought the 1980 was dried out, and I would bet the 1984's meager fruit will not stand up to this period of oak aging. However, the top vintages of Verquière have more in common with a Gigondas than a Côtes du Rhône-Villages. This estate also produces a very fine generic Côtes du Rhône. This is a producer to search out.

Lastly, the local cooperative, called **Le Gravillas,** produces a pleasing, rather cheery white wine from Grenache Blanc, Bourboulenc, Clairette, and Ugni Blanc. Their red wine is also pleasant, cleanly made, light, but round and fruity.

ST.-GERVAIS

The Top Producer

Domaine Ste.-Anne (G. Steinmaier)

Above the town of St.-Gervais is one of the best estates in the entire Rhône Valley. The Domaine Ste.-Anne, the 64-acre estate of Guy Steinmaier, is superbly located on a hilltop with a vast view of the southern Rhône River basin. The thin, balding Steinmaier is an innovative as well as serious winemaker; his description of his wine as "an intermediary wine between Gigondas and Châteauneuf-du-Pape" hardly does it justice. He has impeccably high winemaking standards. Should you find a bottle of Ste.-Anne's Viognier (most recently the 1985), it is stunning, not only the most successful Viognier made in the southern Rhône, but similar to a very fine Condrieu. However, Ste.-Anne's bevy of red wine selections, while typical of the richly fruity, clean, modern style of winemaking, also possess plenty of personality. Steinmaier believes his 1985s are the best wines he has made since 1979. The 1985 Côtes du Rhône is ripe and fruity, with a good alcoholic clout to it. The 1985 Côtes du Rhône-Villages is similar, but with a more smoky, exotic character. The 1985 Cuvée Notre Dame des Cellettes, which always has a healthy dosage of Syrah in it, is a top-flight Rhône wine—plump, full-bodied, very spicy with intense aromas of peppery, raspberry fruit. It will keep for four to five years. The 1985 Cuvée Saint-Gervais is the most complex, no doubt because of the addition of 40% Mourvèdre. Complex aromas of berry fruit, saddle leather, and toast are very attractive. On the palate, the wine is quite concentrated, has some tannin to lose, and though accessible now can be kept for at least four to six years. The wines from 1983, 1982, and 1979 are all successful here. Steinmaier is intent on further increasing the amount of Mourvèdre and Syrah in his wines. A believer in naturally made, unmanipulated wines, Steinmaier, referring to the American and Canadian markets, says he will forsake them altogether rather than filter his wines so that "ignorant consumers" will not have to worry about sediment.

Domaine Ste.-Anne is one of the leading estates in the southern Rhône, its exciting wines offering both high quality and outstanding value.

The other wines of St.-Gervais are made by the cooperative, which seems to be led by a group of particularly uninspired individuals at the moment, and the wines have suffered as a result.

ST.-MAURICE-SUR-EYGUES

This is another questionable selection as a Côtes du Rhône-Villages. The local cooperative, **La Cave des Coteaux de St.-Maurice-sur-Eygues**, is the only producer of wine, and it is quite undistinguished. Even the village is uninteresting.

ST.-PANTALÉON-LES-VIGNES AND ROUSSET-LES-VIGNES

The drive up to the remote little village of St.-Pantaléon-les-Vignes is a great way of taking in some savage mountain scenery while traversing some of the least traveled roads in the otherwise overly visited southern Rhône. But go for the scenery, not the wine. The cooperative of St.-Pantaléon-les-Vignes is the only producer of wine here. The rosé is heavy, the white very bland and neutral, and the red rather charmless and insipid. However, should you arrive here, be sure to take route D538 through Rousset-les-Vignes; the drive is lovely. Rousset-les-Vignes is another official Côtes du Rhône-Villages, but the growers there use the same cooperative of St.-Pantaléon-les-Vignes. The cooperative offers two cuvées, one marked St.-Pantaléon-les-Vignes, the other Rousset-les-Vignes. As already indicated, neither wine merits interest.

SÉGURET

The Top Producers

Domaine de Cabasse   Paul Jaboulet Aîné

The windswept village of Séguret appears to be carved from the cliff that it sits on. If there is one view of the Rhône Valley not to be missed, it is from either the restaurant or bedrooms of Séguret's fine hotel and restaurant, La Table du Comtat. The vista westward, particularly at sunset, is magnificent. With a bottle of the Séguret produced by the Domaine de Cabasse at your side, the view and experience are sublime. Powerfully run by Nadine Latour, **Domaine de Cabasse** produces textbook red, white, and rosé Côtes du Rhône-Villages wines. They are meant to be drunk young, but are full of flavor, round, and if not complex, are always immensely satisfying.

Although the label does not indicate Séguret as the source, the **Paul Jaboulet Aîné** Côtes du Rhône-Villages is made entirely from wine produced by vineyards in the Séguret area. It is a very reasonably priced, plump wine that requires drinking within its first five to six years of life.

VACQUEYRAS

The Top Producers

Clos des Cazaux
(Archimbaud-Vache)
Domaine La Fourmone (Roger
Combe)
Paul Jaboulet Ainé
Domaine les Lambertins
(Lambert)

Château de Montmirail
(Archimbaud)
Château des Roques (Dusser-
Beraud)
Le Sang des Cailloux

If you are a gambler, you might want to lay odds on the hunch that Vacqueyras will be promoted to a full-fledged appellation within the next five to ten years. This old, somewhat dormant village, right on the main "Route du Vin" (D8), just north of Beaumes-de-Venise and south of Gigondas, has a number of good winemakers and important estates. Something to ponder is that if this Côtes du Rhône-Villages does get a promotion, one can expect its wine prices to jump by at least a third.

The taste, texture, and overall character of Vacqueyras is often compared to its neighbor, Gigondas. There is some truth to that observation, but the best Vacqueyras is not comparable in the least to a wine from Les Goubert, Domaine Raspail, St.-Gayan, or Les Pallières, the leading estates of Gigondas. However, it is a big, chewy, full-throttle wine with plenty of body and robustness.

One of the leading wines of Vacqueyras, perhaps the best, is produced by the estate called **Clos des Cazaux**, located just outside the town and right in the middle of a vineyard. Run by the Archimbaud-Vache family, this 50-acre property produces a good rosé, an adequate white, and excellent red wines. (Their Gigondas was mentioned in the section on that appellation.) They produce two separate wines from Vacqueyras. One is called the Cuvée des Templiers and is almost 100% Syrah. Not surprisingly, its black color and intense, smoky, plummy, rich cassis flavors suggest a Hermitage. The other wine, Cuvée Saint-Roch, is less exciting only in comparison with its stablemate. It is a delicious, broadly flavored Vacqueyras that has 75% Syrah and the balance Grenache.

Another excellent domaine is Roger Combe's **Domaine de la Fourmone.** They also produce a good Gigondas, but two-thirds of their production is from Vacqueyras. They offer two wines, one called Trésor du Poète and the other Sélection du Maitre du Chai. The wines receive identical vinifications, but the Trésor du Poète has less Syrah and more Grenache in its blend. The likable Combe owns 44 acres of vines on all the slopes of the nearby Dentelles Mountains. Combe refuses to fine or filter his wine, which no doubt contributes to its almost black color, intense, chewy fruit, and full-intensity bouquet of rich, roasted, ripe fruit.

The famous northern Rhône négociant **Paul Jaboulet Ainé** of Tain L'Hermitage produces a very good Vacqueyras from purchased wine from growers. Ironically, as this firm's heretofore excellent Gigondas has slipped in quality in the eighties their Vacqueyras has significantly improved. It relies almost exclusively on the Grenache grape, but delivers plenty of juicy, rich fruit and body. The 1985 is very good.

The 49-acre estate of the Lambert family, **Domaine des Lambertins**, is another good supplier of Vacqueyras. Their wine is produced by the carbonic maceration method and is light, fruity, less ageworthy than that of the other top growers, but seductive, and when drunk within four years of the vintage, full of life and freshness.

Château de Montmirail, the excellent maker of Gigondas, also has 62 acres of vineyards at Vacqueyras. The team of Monique Bouteiller and Maurice Archimbaud produces three cuvées of Vacqueyras. The most ageworthy of this trio is their 50% Grenache, 50% Syrah blend called Cuvée L'Ermite, named after the reclusive legendary crusader Gaspard de Stérimberg, who built the solitary chapel on the famous granite hill of Hermitage. This is a big, tannic wine that one can keep five to eight years without worry. The other two cuvées are identical wines, but one, the Cuvée Deux Frères, is bottled earlier and is grapy and fruity, whereas the other, the Cuvée Saints Papes, spends six to twelve months longer in wooden foudres. Château de Montmirail is a fine producer of Vacqueyras, and their wines are always deep in color, loaded with fruit, and filled with personality.

I am less familiar with the Vacqueyras made by the **Château des Roques** of Edouard Dusser, having tasted only the 1983, 1982, and 1981, but this large estate of 87 acres in the village of Sarrians produces rather big, spicy, very old-style wines that are marked by a long sojourn in wooden foudres.

Two other potential sources for very good Vacqueyras are **Le Sang des Cailloux** (the blood of the stones), a small domaine in Sarrians of 40 acres that produces 6,000 cases of deep, full-bodied, very traditional, interesting red wine, and the local cooperative, the **Cave des Vignerons Le Troubadour.** Their red Vacqueyras is named after this village's most famous citizen, the twelfth-century musician and singer Raimbaud (pronounced Rambo), who was the son of the village idiot. He became the legendary musical talent of his day, and the wine produced by the cooperative is named after him. It is a good, chunky, harmonious wine.

VALRÉAS

The Top Producers

Domaine des Grands Devers (René Sinard)

Le Val des Rois (Romain Bouchard)

Valréas, a hilltop village situated in rather forbidding countryside, resembles an undersized version of Avignon. With its castle and twelfth-century church, lively marketplace, and ideal location, Valréas makes a fine stop for the tourist in the region. But be warned, the drive there from Orange over narrow, circuitous roads seems much further than the 20 miles it covers. The two industries are the production of wine and the fabrication of cardboard boxes. Most of the wine is made by the **Cave Coopérative La Gaillarde** and though not bad, is not very distinguished, either.

Everyone seems to agree that the top private domaine is **Le Val des Rois**, run by Romain Bouchard of the famous Burgundy family of the same name. This area has one of the cooler microclimates of the southern Rhône, and not surprisingly the wines average a full degree lower in alcohol and in some cases taste more delicate. Bouchard purchased this 36-acre vineyard in 1964. It is planted with 46% Grenache, 26% Syrah, 15% Cinsault, and the balance Mourvèdre, Carignon, and Gamay.

His red wine is fruity, cleanly made, and is bottled after a 12-month stay in vats. I find it among the most elegant of the Côtes du Rhône-Villages wines. He also produces a small amount of very good, fresh, vibrant rosé wine.

VINSOBRES

The Top Producers

Domaine les Aussellons
Château de Deurre

Caves C. N. Jaume

South of Valréas, sheltered from the blast of the *mistral* winds, is the old Roman village of Vinsobres. The name of the village seems a contradiction in itself ("sober wine"), but the peasants who inhabit this typical Provençal village say that this name came from the Bishop of Vaison-la-Romaine in the seventeenth century. Whether folklore or historical fact, it has stuck with the local denizens.

The wine production of Vinsobres is dominated by two cooperatives, **La Cave du Prieuré** and **Cave Coopérative La Vinsobraise**. The former deals strictly in aging and marketing the wine. Neither cooperative merits much interest because the quality of their wines is at best quite mediocre, which is sad, because the potential for top wine at Vinsobres is readily apparent. Since the vineyards are more susceptible to spring freezes than elsewhere, the growers of Vinsobres have planted more Syrah—the date of its bud break is later than other grape varieties and it is rarely a victim of late spring frosts. With more Syrah in Vinsobres than in any other Côtes du Rhône-Villages, the wines (theoretically) should have more personality, richness, and complexity. However, the availability of fine raw materials has not yet been translated into excellent wine, except in the case of the following three wines.

The three leading private domaines are **Château de Deurre, Caves C. N. Jaume,** and the **Domaine les Aussellons.**

Jaume's wines are certainly the finest. Claude Jaume, an articulate man, also makes a good rosé, but it is his full-bodied, heady, intense red wine that has caused local experts to call it the Hermitage of Vinsobres. It sells for 18 francs at the property, an amazing value. His 1981, 1982, and 1983 were all very successful. It is a wine that one can cellar for five to seven years.

Another top producer of "sober wine" is **Château de Deurre**, run meticulously by Aymon de Saint-Priest. A fine rosé is also made here, but the red wine is complex, full-bodied, rich, and filled with scents of black pepper, coffee, thyme, and berry fruit. The 1985, 1984, and 1982 are excellent.

Lastly, the **Domaine les Aussellons** has been converting quite a few wine enthusiasts to its richly scented, ageworthy wine that has been racking up medals at the French wine fairs. The proprietor, M. Ezingeard, is a perfectionist, and his 1985, 1983, and 1981 impressed me greatly.

VISAN

The Top Producers

Domaine de la Cantharide
(J. Roux)

Clos du Père Clément (H.
Depeyre)

Southwest of Valréas and west of Vinsobres is another medieval village filled with winding passageways, endless photogenic charm, and Provençal peasants, many of whom look like the colorful *santons* for which the region is famous. The wines produced here are very full-bodied and quite alcoholic, yet when bottled early have an undeniable earthy charm and uncomplicated, robust nature. The **Cave Coopérative les Coteaux Visan** is one of the better cooperatives of the region, but it must take a back seat to the two private domaines of **Clos du Père Clément**, which has modern winemaking facilities and produces a round, effusively fruity, full-bodied wine, and the **Domaine de la Cantharide**, which makes a very serious, deeply colored wine that has depth, backbone, and plenty of character.

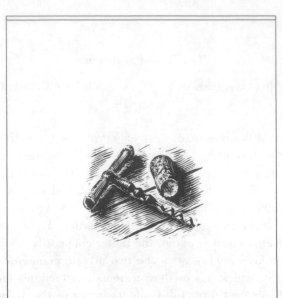

CÔTES DU RHÔNE

CÔTES DU RHÔNE AT A GLANCE

Type of wine produced:	Red wine accounts for 99% of this appellation's production, plus white and rosé wines
Grape varieties planted:	All legal varieties are permitted
Acres currently under vine:	100,754; 80% of the entire Rhône Valley wine production is generic Côtes du Rhône
Quality level:	At the cooperative level, which accounts for 70% of the generic Côtes du Rhône, it ranges from poor to adequate; at the domaine level, the quality ranges from average to exceptional

Aging potential:	3–6 years (except for Cru de Coudelet and Château Fonsalette)
General characteristics:	Enormous variability in quality and style, impossible to safely generalize (see text)
Greatest recent vintages:	1985, 1981, 1978
Price range:	$3–$6; a few top estates charge $8–$13

At the bottom level of the Rhône Valley's wine hierarchy is the generic Côtes du Rhône. These regional wines, which represent just over 80% of the entire area's production, range from shabbily made, oxidized, alcoholic wines to good, sound, fruity, generously flavored, satisfying wines, and even to a few stunningly rich, exceptional wines with a decade's worth of cellaring potential.

The cooperatives of the Rhône Valley dominate this region. Seventy percent of the wines at the generic Côtes du Rhône level comes from one of these cooperatives. Yet there are hundreds of estates, domaines, or more grandly named châteaux making straight Côtes du Rhônes. I have made an effort to visit those that are well publicized, as well as those with fine reputations. In researching this book, I made a commitment to visit and taste with every major grower of the Rhône appellation, but it would have taken several years to visit all of the Côtes du Rhône domaines, and I doubt I would have learned much more about the quality of these basic Rhône wines than I have gleaned from the extensive tastings of their wines. I am sure that there are some worthy domaines tucked away in the hillside villages, but I believe the following is an accurate guide to the best Côtes du Rhônes that are now available. There are over two dozen Côtes du Rhônes that I believe stand above the tide of mediocrity that typifies wines with the Côtes du Rhône appellation. They are listed in alphabetical order. (The town or village in which the domaine is located appears in parentheses, next to the estate's name.)

A Personal Rating of the Côtes du Rhône Producers

*****(OUTSTANDING PRODUCERS)*
Château de Fonsalette

****(EXCELLENT PRODUCERS)*
Cru de Coudelet

***(GOOD PRODUCERS)*

La Berthète	Domaine Mazurd
Château La Borie	Mont-Redon
Paul Coulon	Domaines Mousset
Château de Domazon	Domaine de la Reméjeanne
Château D'Estagnol	Château de Ruth
Les Gouberts	St.-Apollinaire
Château Gourdon	St.-Estève
Château Grand Moulas	St.-Gayan
E. Guigal	Domaine des Treilles
Paul Jaboulet Ainé	Vieux Chêne
Château Malijay	La Vieille Ferme

RECENT VINTAGES

1986—This is a variable vintage because of the rain at the end of the harvest that caught many growers. The quality will vary even more enormously than usual. Optimum maturity: 1988–1991.

1985—A huge crop of very well-colored, deeply fruity, alcoholic wines was produced. The wines are low in acidity, but will provide good drinking until 1990. Optimum maturity: now–1990.

LA BERTHÈTE (CAMARET)

This sound, fruity, round, and generous Côtes du Rhône is made by the Cohendy Gonnet family. The red wine is quite reliable.

CHÂTEAU LA BORIE (SUZE-LA-ROUSSE)

This property, like a number of estates in the southern Rhône, is owned by a French Algerian who left after France gave that country independence in 1961. Emile Bories, the proprietor of this beautiful property of 175 acres, produces very fruity, generally well-colored wines under the Château La Borie label. They are bottled early, aged only in tanks prior to bottling, and are marked by the Syrah grape since M. Bories feels this grape renders an extra dimension to his wines. They should be drunk up within three to four years of the vintage.

CRU DE COUDELET (CHÂTEAUNEUF-DU-PAPE)

This excellent estate is owned by the Perrin family, who produces one of the greatest Châteauneuf-du-Papes, Château Beaucastel. They also produce a very rich, intense, long-lived Côtes du Rhône from a 74-acre vineyard separated from the Châteauneuf appellation by only a two-lane road. The stony soil at Coudelet is virtually the same as at Beaucastel. I have cellared bottles of the 1978 Cru de Coudelet that are just now reaching their peak. The price of Coudelet, half that of Beaucastel (and Beaucastel is one of the greatest wine values in the world), makes it a super bargain. The recent vintages are all excellent; the 1980, 1981, 1983, 1984, and 1985 will last for another five to seven years, but now offer heaps of supple, smoky, peppery, raspberry fruit, very good length, body, and great personality. The 1983 and 1985 are more opulent and powerful; the 1984 is more elegant and not quite as full-bodied. These wines have all of the trademarks of the Perrin winemaking style. They are totally organic wines, unfined and unfiltered, and therefore will throw a heavy sediment. The blend used for them is 20% Syrah, 10% Cinsault, 30% Mourvèdre, and 40% Grenache. Keep an eye out especially for the 1985, which is a blockbuster Côtes du Rhône. Coudelet is as good as many Châteauneuf-du-Papes, and certainly as long-lived as all but a handful of them. It offers splendid value.

PAUL COULON (CHÂTEAUNEUF-DU-PAPE)

Coulon, who produces the very good Châteauneuf-du-Pape, Château Beaurenard, in 1980 purchased a hillside vineyard above the village of Rasteau. Planted with 70% Grenache, 10% Cinsault, 10% Syrah, and 10% Mourvèdre, the vinification Coulon uses for his Côtes du Rhônes is the same as for his Châteauneuf; 50% of the berries go into the fermentation tanks whole, the rest crushed. His Côtes du Rhônes, which must be drunk within its first five years of life, is round, well colored, and fruity. The 1985 is the top recent vintage, and according to Coulon the best wine he has yet made from this domaine.

CHÂTEAU DE DOMAZON (DOMAZON)

The 73-acre estate of Christian Chauderac provided 12,500 cases of good, reliable Côtes du Rhône that is produced from 50% Grenache, 25% Syrah, 20% Cinsault, and the balance is a field blend of other varieties. This is an intensely fruity wine oozing with aromas of jammy berry fruit in vintages such as 1985. The wine is vinified under very modern conditions, and should be drunk within four to five years of the vintage.

CHÂTEAU DE L'ESTAGNOL (SUZE-LA-ROUSSE)

Just east of Bollène is the Château L'Estagnol. Owned by the Chambovet family since 1936, both red and white Côtes du Rhônes are produced here. This is a large property of 180 acres, and the wine is made in a very modern cellar that the Chambovets built in 1966. If the wines

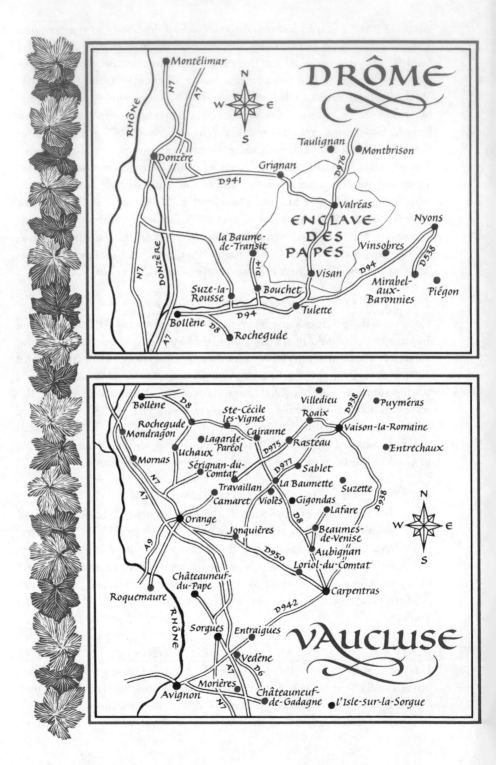

DRÔME

Montélimar

N7 · A7 · RHÔNE

Donzère

DONZÈRE

N7

Taulignan

D976

Montbrison

Grignan

D941

Valréas

Nyons

ENCLAVE DES PAPES

la Baume-de-Transit

D14

Vinsobres

Visan

D94

D538

Suze-la-Rousse

Bouchet

Mirabel-aux-Baronnies

Piégon

Tulette

Bollène D8

D94

Rochegude

A7

VAUCLUSE

Bollène

D8

Ste-Cécile-les-Vignes

Villedieu

Roaix

D938

Puyméras

Rochegude

Mondragon

Cairanne

Vaison-la-Romaine

Lagarde-Paréol

D975

Rasteau

Entrechaux

Uchaux

D977

Mornas

Sérignan-du-Comtat

Sablet

Travaillan

La Baumette

Suzette

N7

Camaret

Violès

Gigondas

Lafare

A7

Orange

D8

Beaumes-de-Venise

Jonquières

Aubignan

A9

D950

Loriol-du-Comtat

RHÔNE

Châteauneuf-du-Pape

Carpentras

Roquemaure

D942

Sorgues

Entraigues

Vedène

A7 D6

Morières

Avignon

Châteauneuf-de-Gadagne

l'Isle-sur-la-Sorgue

N7

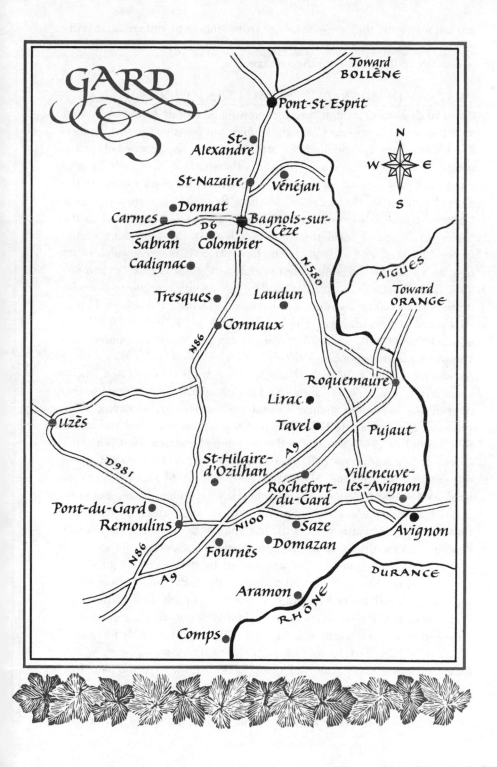

GARD

Toward BOLLÈNE

Pont-St-Esprit

N
W E
S

St-Alexandre

St-Nazaire
Vénéjan

Donnat
Carmes
Bagnols-sur-Cèze
D6
Sabran
Colombier
Cadignac

AIGUES

Toward ORANGE

Tresques
Laudun

N580

Connaux

N86

Roquemaure

Lirac

Uzès
Tavel
Pujaut

A9

St-Hilaire-d'Ozilhan

D981

Villeneuve-les-Avignon

Rochefort-du-Gard

Pont-du-Gard
Remoulins
N100
Saze
Avignon

N86
Fournès
Domazan

A9
DURANCE

Aramon
RHÔNE

Comps

are not inspiring, they are consistent from vintage to vintage, and fairly priced. Both the red and white wine must be drunk very early, normally within two to three years of the vintage.

CHÂTEAU DE FONSALETTE (LAGARDE PARÉOL)

Château de Fonsalette and the aforementioned Cru de Coudelet are not only the two best generic Côtes du Rhône, but are also the two longest-lived wines from the appellation Côtes du Rhône. Each can easily reach ten years of age without a problem. Curiously, both are made by producers who are famous for their sublime Châteauneuf-du-Papes. In the case of Fonsalette, the eccentric Jacques Reynaud, who runs the great Château Rayas, also owns and manages this 30-acre vineyard in the Côtes du Rhône. Fonsalette is unquestionably the best wine of the Côtes du Rhône and sells at the highest price. It is often worth every cent as it is an exhilarating wine to drink and better in quality than 80–90% of the Châteauneuf-du-Papes. Though a white Fonsalette is made, it tends to be heavy and dull, but the two red wine cuvées from Fonsalette merit serious interest. The regular cuvée is made from 50% Grenache, 30% Cinsault, and 20% Syrah. It can be stunningly opulent and voluptuous in years such as 1979 and 1982. Reynaud also makes a 100% Syrah cuvée that, believe it or not, is even more concentrated than a great Hermitage such as Jaboulet's La Chapelle. It is produced in tiny quantities. Unlike his regular Fonsalette, which can be drunk when released, the Fonsalette Cuvée de Syrah is so concentrated and tannic that it requires 10–15 years of cellaring—but oh, what a wine. The 1978 Cuvée de Syrah from my cellar needs another ten years, the 1983, about the same amount of time. My tasting notes on the 1983 Cuvée de Syrah read as follows: "Dense, opaque, black ruby color, huge, peppery, tarry, blackberry and olive scented bouquet, extraordinary concentration and body, sensational length, but gobs of tannin—a long-distance runner." As for the more accessible regular Fonsalettes, the 1979 is a classic. I suspect some buyers are put off by the price, but this is no ordinary wine. Approaching full maturity, the big, complex bouquet of toffee, toast, lush berry fruit, and pepper is first-rank. Full-bodied, rich and chocolatey, it has oodles of fruit. The 1982 contains a great deal of Rayas (Reynaud declassified Rayas in 1982) and will possibly be as good when it is fully mature in two or three years. Very opaque, with a bouquet rich in berry fruit and complex with hints of cedar and Provençal herbs, it is a big, powerful, yet harmonious wine. The 1981 and 1984 are a trifle less grand when tasted side by side with the 1979 and 1982, but they are very meritorious efforts. The 1985 out of cask also looked like a blockbuster, so there is a great deal here to get excited about. I cannot urge you enough to try these sumptuous wines.

DOMAINE LES GOUBERT (GIGONDAS)

The talented Jean-Pierre Cartier, who has received glowing reviews for his splendid Gigondas and Côtes du Rhône-Villages (Beaumes-de-Venise), also makes an excellent, full-bodied, very inexpensive red Côtes du Rhône from a blend of 65% Grenache, 15% Syrah, 14% Cinsault, and 1% Mourvèdre. Cartier, who believes in organically made wines, uses no fertilizers or insecticides in his vineyard. His Côtes du Rhônes last better than most producers', as a recent tasting of the 1981, 1982, 1983, 1984, and 1985 poignantly proved.

CHÂTEAU GOURDON (BOLLÈNE)

One of the more impressive wine châteaux in the Rhône region is that of Château Gourdon. Administered and owned by the Sanchez-Gauchet family, the 95-acre vineyard is dominated by the Grenache, and produces supple, easy to drink, quick-maturing red wine and small amounts of a decent, fresh rosé.

CHÂTEAU GRAND MOULAS (MORNAS)

In 1958, Marcel Ryckwaert immigrated from Algeria and founded this estate of 72 acres in the little village of Mornas. There are two red wines made, the Côtes du Rhône, with 25% Syrah in the blend, and the Côtes du Rhône-Villages, with 50% Syrah incorporated. The 1985 Côtes du Rhône is a spicy, chunky, fruity wine that has a pleasing, warm, mouth-filling generosity. The 1985 Côtes du Rhône-Villages is larger, deeper, has more tannin, and it can be drunk with pleasure when released, or kept. Seventy percent of the wine is made by the carbonic maceration method. The Ryckwaerts never crush the grapes, and they keep the fermentation temperature rather low, always preferring to bottle the wine within six to eight months of the vintage. The wines here are cleanly made, stylish, and consistent from vintage to vintage.

E. GUIGAL (AMPUIS)

The Ampuis-based, superb Rhône wine négociant E. Guigal purchases lots of wine from numerous growers to produce its white and red Côtes du Rhône. The white wine has tended to be rather dull, but certainly the 1985, a blend of Roussanne, Marsanne, and Clairette, showed better than past efforts. The bargain and star, however, is the red Côtes du Rhône, a wine that has gone from strength to strength over recent vintages. Marcel Guigal has embarked on a plan to use more Mourvèdre and Syrah in its composition and the result has been a series of excellent, rich, full-bodied, surprisingly complex wines in vintages such as 1981, 1982, and 1983. Unlike most Côtes du Rhônes, those of Guigal will last four to seven years in the bottle. This is a name to seek out for palate- and purse-pleasing wines.

PAUL JABOULET AINÉ (TAIN L'HERMITAGE)
Jaboulet's very well-known, very successful Parallèle 45 is that firm's generic Côtes du Rhône. It is certainly among the top two dozen or so Côtes du Rhônes. Always fruity, round, fairly alcoholic, and reasonably priced, the Jaboulets routinely use at least 80–85% Grenache in this wine. In most vintages, the Parallèle 45 will keep for four to six years.

CHÂTEAU MALIJAY (JONQUIÈRES)
This lavish château, reconstructed on the site of the original eleventh-century castle that stood on the property, produces an enormous amount of wine. The annual production approximates nearly 90,000 cases from nearly 500 acres, and the wine can be found easily in the world marketplace. It is a fruity but rather bland, one-dimensional wine. It should be drunk within one to three years of the vintage. Although I have found it pleasant enough, I prefer the soft, fruity rosé made here.

DOMAINE A. MAZURD (TULETTE)
The Domaine Mazurd produces one of the better carbonic maceration red wines among the generic Côtes du Rhône producers. Located in a hilly area almost 12 miles east of Bollène in the direction of the olive orchards of Nyons, 190 acres of vineyard of the Mazurd family is planted with 70% Grenache, 15% Syrah, 10% Cinsault, and 5% Carignan. A well-colored, broadly flavored, rich, fruity wine capable of lasting four to five years is produced here. Mazurd's top recent vintages have been 1985, 1982, and 1981.

MONT-REDON (CHÂTEAUNEUF-DU-PAPE)
The Abeille-Fabre families, owners of the famous Châteauneuf-du-Pape, Mont-Redon, in 1981 purchased a beautiful hillside Côtes du Rhône vineyard near Roquemaure. Fifty acres in size, it is located less than a kilometer from the Châteauneuf-du-Pape appellation. The cépage, or blend of grapes, is 70% Grenache, 20% Cinsault, and 10%

Syrah. The wine is vinified traditionally, but given less time macerating on the skins than the firm's famous Châteauneuf-du-Pape. Only four vintages were available to taste at the time of writing; the 1985 was excellent, followed by the 1983. The 1984 was quite mediocre. This, I am sure, will be a Côtes du Rhône to take seriously.

DOMAINES MOUSSET (CHÂTEAUNEUF-DU-PAPE)

The huge empire of the Domaines Mousset, located just outside the village of Châteauneuf-du-Pape, is noted for its four Châteauneufs, particularly Château des Fines-Roches, but they also produce large quantities of three Côtes du Rhônes. The lightest is from a vineyard called **Domaine de Tout Vent** (54 acres) where a fine rosé and effusively fruity, soft red wine are made. The **Château du Prieuré** (111 acres) is another Côtes du Rhône made here—a little fuller in body and usually more alcoholic. Their best Côtes du Rhône is the **Château du Bois de Garde** (148 acres), a vineyard composed of 35–40 year old vines. Recent vintages of this generic Côtes du Rhône have been rich, round, and deliciously fruity, with a good measure of flesh and character. The 1985 is particularly successful. The Moussets own another Côtes du Rhône vineyard called **Domaine du Grand-Vaucroze** (30 acres), but I have never seen or tasted that wine. These Mousset family estates are good sources for well-made Côtes du Rhône wine at very reasonable prices.

DOMAINE DE LA RÉMÉJEANNE (CADIGNAC)

François Klein, a transplanted Frenchman who left Morocco to settle in the Rhône, produces only red wine with a rather high percentage of Syrah (nearly 25%). The wine is a chunky, full-bodied, fruity wine that shows more class and personality than most of the rank and file Côtes du Rhônes.

CHÂTEAU DE RUTH (SAINTE-CECILE-LES-VIGNES)

The famous Meffre family, who live and produce wine at Château Raspail in Gigondas as well as own the Château Vaudieu at Châteauneuf-du-Pape, also own this large estate of 325 acres. The Meffres have other Côtes du Rhône properties (including more than 2,400 acres of Rhône vineyards), but their wine from Château de Ruth is their best generic Rhône wine. It is a full-bodied, somewhat overly manipulated and filtered wine, but has good body and clean, correct, narrowly focused flavors. It should be drunk within four to five years of the vintage.

ST.-APOLLINAIRE (PUYMÉRAS)

In the northern sector of the southern Rhône viticultural area, not far from the ancient Roman village of Vaison-la-Romaine, is the tiny, quaint village of Puyméras. The estate of St.-Apollinaire is an eccentric anachronism in the high-tech world of winemaking and production. The proprietor, Frédéric Daumas, believes in totally organically produced wines. No sulfur dioxide is used in any of this domaine's very densely colored, intense wines. A cuvée of 100% Syrah is also produced. The naturalness of these wines is refreshing, but there is a troublesome inconsistency from bottle to bottle that I suspect is the price one must sometimes pay for completely natural, living wines. Should you try a St.-Apollinaire red wine, decant it one to two hours prior to serving and stand it up well in advance because these wines will throw a heavy sediment.

ST.-ESTÈVE (UCHAUX)

North of the old Roman town of Orange is the lovely château of St.-Estève, run by the Français-Monier family. This sizable estate of 140 acres produces a very sound line of good Côtes du Rhône—a fresh, vibrant rosé as well as several very good red wines. The regular cuvée has good color, a deep bouquet of raspberry fruit, soft texture, modern winemaking, and a general impression of finesse. The Grande Réserve, which contains 50% Syrah in the blend, has a big, smoky, spicy, berry-scented bouquet, very fine color, full body, and a generous finish. Both wines are meant to be drunk upon release, but will keep up to three years. A tiny amount of Viognier is made here, but the young vines have not produced anything nearly as exciting as the Viognier made by the Domaine Ste.-Anne in St.-Gervais.

ST.-GAYAN (GIGONDAS)

Roger Meffre, the excellent producer of Gigondas, also owns a 38-acre Côtes du Rhône vineyard. The Grenache grape dominates his vineyard (80%), but there is also some Syrah, Mourvèdre, and Cinsault planted. His Côtes du Rhône is a broadly flavored wine with a jammy, berry bouquet and in vintages such as 1981, 1982, and 1985 there is a powerful alcoholic kick to it. It is best drunk within five to six years of the vintage.

DOMAINE DES TREILLES (MONTBRISON-SUR-LEZ)

This 57-acre vineyard produces a plump, richly fruity, very satisfying red wine. The vineyard is located in the cooler northern part of the southern Rhône Valley, but the excitable proprietor, M. Rey, says he generally achieves at least a hearty 13.5% alcohol in his wine. In his old and impressive underground cellars Rey ages his wine 10–12 months before bottling. Domaine des Treilles seems content to keep a low profile, but it is a name to search out for high-quality, generic Côtes du Rhône.

DOMAINE DU VIEUX CHÊNE (CAMARET)
Two energetic brothers, Jean-Claude and Dominique Bouche, run the very good Domaine du Vieux Chêne. Their 74-acre estate has always been one of my favorite sources for very good Côtes du Rhône. Their two cuvées represent different styles of wine. The Cuvée des Capucines is a deliciously fruity, round, berry-scented, plump wine that goes down very easily. It will drink well for one to three years. The Cuvée de la Haie aux Grives is excellent—black ruby in color with a rich, complex bouquet of pepper and cassis, full-bodied, broadly flavored, and quite long. It has more Syrah in the blend and can, in vintages such as 1985 or 1986, take cellaring of two to four years.

LA VIEILLE FERME (ORANGE)
Jean-Pierre Perrin, of the famous family that owns and manages the two outstanding estates, Château de Beaucastel in Châteauneuf-du-Pape and Cru de Coudelet in the Côtes du Rhône, has a négociant business called La Vieille Ferme. He produces a good Côtes du Ventoux, but since 1983 has been making delicious red and white generic Côtes du Rhônes from purchased grapes. Very reasonably priced, his red Côtes du Rhône is full-bodied, deeply fruity, and capable of lasting four to six years. The white is crisp, fresh, and well above the pack of neutral-tasting, bland, white Côtes du Rhônes. These wines offer notable values, even for the very modestly priced Côtes du Rhônes. Perrin plans to add a Vacqueyras Côtes du Rhone-Villages and Gigondas to his stable of offerings.

Other Meritorious Generic Côtes du Rhônes
Château d'Aigueville (Arène); marketed by the Caves St.-Pierre in Châteauneuf-du-Pape
Domaine de L'Amandier (U. Pages), Carmes
Domaine des Amoureuses (A. Grangaud), Bourg St.-Andéol
Cave Coopérative (Venéjan), Bagnols-sur-Cèze
Cave Coopérative Vinicole (Comtadine Dauphinoise), Puymèras
Château de Farel (Pierre Silvestre), Comps

Domaine de la Girardière (L. Giraud), Rasteau

Domaine le Haut Castel (A. Arène), Bagnols-sur-Cèze

Le Mas des Collines (Jean Gorecki), Gigondas

Domaine Mitan (Frédéric Mitan), Vedène

Domaine de L'Olivet (Rodolphe Goossens), Bourg St.-Andéol

Domaine du Petit Barbaras (R. Feschet), Bouchet

Domaine des Riots (F. Riot), Saint-Michel d'Etuzet

Domaine de la Taurelle (Roux), Mirabel-aux-Baronnies

Château du Trignon (A. Roux), Sablet

Domaine de la Vieille Julienne (Arnaud-Daumen), Châteauneuf-du-Pape

ESOTERIC RHÔNE WINES

Clairette de Die,
Côtes du Vivarais,
Coteaux du Tricastin,
Côtes du Ventoux

CLAIRETTE DE DIE AT A GLANCE

Types of wine produced:	Dry and sweet white sparkling wine, and dry still white wine
Grape varieties planted:	Muscat and Clairette
Acres currently under vine:	2,200
Quality level:	Mediocre to good
Aging potential:	1–4 years
General characteristics:	The best sparkling wines, because of the high quantity of Muscat in the blend, can be fragrant and tasty; most, however, are bland
Price range:	$7.00–$10.50
Best producers:	Union de Producteurs, Claude Achard, Achard-Vincent, Buffardel Frères, and Jean-Claude Vincent

Few wine enthusiasts seem to claim any experience or even knowledge of Clairette de Die, an area that has been making sparkling wine longer than Champagne. There are historical references to the wine of this region as far back as 77 A.D., but it is not an easy area with which to become familiar.

The Die vineyards are an appendage of the main Rhône viticultural district, stuck out in the mountain countryside east of Valence. The tortuous drive from Valence, over 40 miles of labyrinthine roads, seems to take half a day. As one begins to encounter more and more forbidding mountains, a patchwork carpet of vines and walnut tree orchards announces to the visitor that Clairette de Die, the least-known Rhône wine appellation, has been reached. There are three types of white wine made here. The still wine, usually a rather bland, innocuous drink, is made from 100% Clairette. The second type of wine is a sparkling wine simply called Clairette de Die Brut. It must be made from 100% Clairette also. It, too, is a bit dull. The best wine of this appellation is the Clairette de Die Tradition, a sparkling wine made from a blend of Muscat (usually 50–75%) and Clairette. The Clairette de Die Tradition is an exuberant, quite delightful wine that has a particularly perfumed character to its bouquet. It comes in both the dry brut style or the sweeter demi-sec style. Given its broad commercial appeal, I am surprised that the wine has not become better known.

The appellation's production is dominated by the huge, extremely modern **Union de Producteurs** that has high sparkling wine standards. Their Clairette de Die Tradition Cuvée Impériale is a wonderfully perfumed, delicious wine that is well marked by the Muscat grape. Their Brut Cuvée Impériale, which contains no Muscat, is somewhat one-dimensional.

Among the growers, the sparkling Clairette de Die of **Claude Achard, Achard-Vincent, Buffardel Frères,** and **Jean-Claude Vincent,** especially their cuvées of Tradition with their high percentage of Muscat grapes, offer surprisingly good drinking.

CÔTES DU VIVARAIS AT A GLANCE

Type of wine produced:	Red, white, and rosé
Grape varieties planted:	Both vinifera and hybrid grapes, but largely Grenache, Syrah, Cinsault, Mourvèdre, and Picpoul
Acres currently under vine:	1,825 acres (of a potential vineyard area of 20,000 acres)
Quality level:	Mediocre to good
Aging potential:	1–4 years
General characteristics:	Dull white and rosé wines; increasingly good, well-made, fruity, solid red wines
Price range:	$3–$6
Best producers:	Domaine Belvezet, Domaine Gallety, Domaine de Vigier, Caves Coopératives Vignerons de Saint-Montan

On the right or western bank of the Rhône, between the noisy little half-horse town of Viviers in the north and Pont St.-Esprit to the south, is the emerging viticultural region of the Côtes de Vivarais.

Over a decade ago my wife and I spent a week in this area, enjoying its primitive wilderness and splendid landscape studded with gorges. Until just recently, we had never realized that this is a promising region for good red wine. It has not yet been granted appellation contrôlée status and the wines are sold under the VDQS (or Vins délimité de qualité supérieure) designation. My experience with the white and rosé wines has been disappointing. However, the red wines from the best three estates are certainly as good as the better Côtes du Rhône-Villages and Côtes du Rhône wines. The soil (much of it limestone) and climate are ideal, and I predict increasing interest in the good red Côtes de Vivarais wines; they are quite inexpensive.

Certainly the area's best producer has done nothing to date to dampen one's enthusiasm. Léon Brunel's **Domaine de Belvezet** has 106 acres planted with 40% Grenache, 40% Syrah, and the rest Cinsault, Cabernet Sauvignon, Merlot, and Gamay. It is a big, beefy wine with considerable flavor, body, and four to five years' aging potential. For the low price this wine fetches, it is a great bargain.

For a red wine made with the carbonic maceration method, the light, agreeable, fruity red wine of the **Domaine Gallety** fills the need. Proprietor Caroline Gallety has 25 acres planted with 50% Grenache, 30% Cinsault, and 10% each of Syrah and Carignan. Her wine is less profound than that of the Domaine de Belvezet, but still very fruity and satisfying.

Two other reliable sources for solid red Côtes du Vivarais are François Dupré's **Domaine de Vigier** and **Caves Coopératives Vignerons de Saint-Montan.** Dupré's wine is rustic and chunky in style, although the 1985 shows some finesse. The Coopératives produce various lots that vary enormously in style and quality. Their Cuvée Syrah, however, is very good.

COTEAUX DU TRICASTIN AT A GLANCE

Types of wine produced:	Red wine (95%); some white and rosé is also produced
Grape varieties planted:	Red wine: Grenache, Cinsault, Mourvèdre, Syrah, Picpoul, Carignan White wine: Grenache Blanc, Clairette, Picpoul Blanc, Bourboulenc, Ugni Blanc
Acres currently under vine:	4,940
Quality level:	Mediocre to very good for the red wines
Aging potential:	1–4 years
General characteristics:	The white wine is heavy; the rosé fruity and decent; the red wine richly scented, supple, and potentially very good, but it must be drunk young
Price range:	$5–$8
Best producers:	Domaine de la Tour d'Elyssas, Domaine de Grangeneuve, Château des Estubiers

Tricastin is the fastest-growing viticultural region of the Rhône Valley. A quarter of a century ago this area, beaten by the *mistral* wind more severely than the rest of the southern Rhône, was known only for its barren, moonlike landscape and fall truffle harvest. Many French natives of Tunisia, Algeria, and Morocco, uncertain of their future after the granting of independence to these former French possessions, came to the southern Rhône and began to establish vineyards. Several of them made Tricastin their home, and in the last 25 years have elevated this vast area from a *vin de pays* to a VDQS, and finally to a full-fledged appellation contrôlée wine.

The Tricastin viticultural area is located between Bollène and Montélimar, and takes its name from a tribe of warriors called the Tricastini, who battled unsuccessfully with the Romans during their conquest of Gaul. As mentioned, the area is famous for its truffles as well as tomato, melon, and asparagus crops.

The producers have wisely not attempted to compete with nearby Châteauneuf-du-Pape and Gigondas, and aim for large-scaled, full-bodied wines of power and depth. The style of red wine that has emerged from Tricastin is one in which the intense, supple aromas and flavors of berry fruit are emphasized. These are deliciously round, fresh wines that might well become the Rhône Valley's alternative to the hedonistic appeal offered by the wines of Beaujolais.

The best estate of Tricastin has recently had a great deal of financial difficulties and its future is unclear. However, the best Tricastin red wine continues to be made at the **Domaine de la Tour d'Elyssas**, run with great visionary zeal by Pierre LaBeye. LaBeye has 346 acres and produces two vineyard-designated Tricastins called Le Devroy and Les Echirousses. He also makes a 100% Syrah cuvée that is even deeper and more concentrated, but still in full possession of its wonderful fruitiness and supple, generous texture. LaBeye's rosé is also the best of the appellation. With quality like this available at such low prices, one hopes this dynamic estate can solve its current financial woes.

The other well-known estate in Tricastin is the **Domaine de Grangeneuve.** Run by Odette Bours and her lovely daughter, this property of 247 acres produces a very fruity, soft, easy to drink, understated wine that offers immediate gratification. A decent, dry fruity rosé is also made here.

The other top grower in Tricastin is **Château des Estubiers.** A 227-acre property run by Hector Roth and Léopold Morel, Estubiers applies the same winemaking philosophy as the other domaines mentioned above. It eschews wood aging and bottles its wines early to preserve all of their fruit and charm. Their vineyards are planted with 55% Grenache, 18% Syrah, 9% Mourvèdre, 9% Cinsault, and 9% Carignan.

COTES DU VENTOUX AT A GLANCE

Type of wine produced:	Light, fruity red, white, and rosé
Grape varieties planted:	Primarily Grenache, Carignan, Cinsault and Syrah for the red wine; Clairette and Bourboulenc for the white wine
Acres currently under vine:	16,000 (of a potential 25,000 acres)
Quality level:	Good
Aging potential:	1–3 years
General characteristics:	Soft, light, fruity wines meant for very early consumption
Price range:	$5–$7
Best producers:	La Vieille Ferme, Vieux Lazaret, Domaine Ste.-Sauveur, Domaine des Anges

This giant appellation has nearly 16,000 acres of vineyards spread out over an enormous area. There are over 4,000 growers producing wine from this region that fills the eastern areas from Vaison-la-Romaine in the north, south through Carpentras to L'Isle-sur-la-Sorgue, all in the shadow of the Ventoux mountain range that forms the backdrop for these vineyards. Cooperatives again dominate the area, but there are four producers who stand above the others. **La Vieille Ferme,** run by Jean-Pierre Perrin, produces a very good red and white Côtes du Ventoux, as does Jérome Quiot of the **Domaine Vieux Lazaret.** Like Perrin, he also makes wine at Châteauneuf-du-Pape. Both styles of wine emphasize fresh berry fruit. Their wines, like any Côtes du Ventoux, must be drunk within two to three years of the vintage.

The **Domaine St.-Sauveur** has been mentioned previously for producing a good, sweet Muscat de Beaumes-de-Venise. They also produce a very flowery, fruity Côtes du Ventoux.

Lastly, an Englishman, Malcolm Swan, has settled in France and makes one of the best Côtes du Ventoux at his property called **Domaine des Anges.** Recent vintages of this wine have exhibited exceptional charm and delicious fruit.

VISITING, STAYING,
AND DINING
IN THE RHÔNE VALLEY

In addition to the obvious attraction of the wines of the Rhône, this area is loaded with wonderful restaurants, hotels, and inns that do justice to the spectacular natural scenery. Since the Rhône Valley is one of the most traveled regions of western Europe, reservations are a must during the peak travel season of May through September. My hotel and restaurant recommendations are arranged by viticultural areas, beginning in the north at Vienne and concluding in the south at Avignon. As a general guide, the price of a meal for two people with one bottle of good wine, taking into account the current exchange rates, is as follows:

What a meal for two will cost	
Very expensive	$100–$150
Expensive	$ 75–$100
Moderately expensive	$ 50–$ 75
Moderate	$ 25–$ 50
Inexpensive	$ 15–$ 25

Visiting Côte Rôtie and Condrieu

For visiting the most northern of the Rhône Valley's vineyards, Condrieu is the best place to use as a base. It is a quiet riverside town only five minutes from Côte Rôtie. If you prefer a noisier, more urban base, Vienne is only ten to fifteen minutes away by car.

Condrieu: Beau Rivage (74.59.52.24)—This lovely inn right on the river offers very comfortable rooms, classic cuisine, a superb wine list and an excellent sincere reception from Madame Castaing, the generous and friendly owner and chef. The cuisine no longer merits two stars from the Michelin Guide, but it is surely of one-star quality, and it is unlikely ever to be disappointing. Moderately expensive.

Les Roches de Condrieu: Bellvue (74.56.41.42)—Located across the river from Condrieu on a noisy street, the splendidly situated Les Roches de Condrieu has adequate rooms but delicious cuisine, particularly fish. The wine list is excellent. Moderate.

Vienne: La Résidence de la Pyramide (74.53.16.46)—This is the hotel everyone stays at when dining at the historic Pyramide only one block away. Moderate.

Vienne: Pyramide (74.53.01.96)—Both the legendary Fernand Point and his wife have passed away, yet this remains one of the great temples of cuisine in France. Its high Michelin rating is very questionable, but much of the modern cuisine of France owes a great measure of its success to the genius of Fernand Point and his beloved La Pyramide. The wine list is filled with treasures. Very expensive.

Visiting Hermitage, Cornas, Crozes-Hermitage, or St.-Joseph

For visiting the southern part of the northern Rhône viticultural region, the distance from Vienne or Côte Rôtie is only 40–45 miles. However, it makes sense to make your base for this area in and around the large commercial city of Valence, which puts you within a five-minute drive of St.-Péray and Cornas, and only 11 miles from the heart of Hermitage. This area is filled with some marvelous restaurants and hotels.

Valence: Pic (75.44.15.32)—This is the finest restaurant in the Rhône Valley, and fully merits its Michelin three-star rating. There are five small, modest hotel rooms above the dining room. Chef Pic, unlike many of his peers, stays in the kitchen, having decided not to promote himself or become a traveling salesman. Consequently, the food is imaginative, consistently superb, and the wine list loaded with the riches of the Rhône Valley. Very expensive.

Pont de l'Isère: Chabran (75.84.60.09)—There is little reason to stop in Pont de l'Isère, a tiny, dull village six miles north of Valence, except to eat and/or stay at the restaurant and hotel Chabran. The young, handsome Chabran is a great talent, and his restaurant is fully capable of turning out three-star cuisine even though the Michelin people only recently gave him a two-star rating. The wine list is one of the best in France, and the small, modern rooms comfortable and air conditioned, a luxury that is appreciated in this area in the summer. Expensive.

Saint-Romain-de-Lerps: Château du Besset (75.58.52.22)—For a romantic, idyllic getaway when price has no relevance, this sumptuous retreat tucked away up and behind the hills around St.-Péray has everything. There are only six rooms in this enormous castle, but they are the finest rooms this author has ever seen. The grounds are splendidly maintained, the pool is large, and the cuisine good, but too precious and overworked. Nevertheless, this is a spectacular spot to go when money is no consideration, but tranquillity is. Very expensive.

Rive-de-Gier: La Renaissance (77.75.04.31)—An emerging star among the great restaurants of France, the pilgrimage to La Renaissance will take about 45 minutes from Vienne. The food and service are highly inspired, and I predict Chef Laurent is on the threshold of stardom. Expensive.

Montmeyran: La Vieille Ferme (75.59.31.64)—For a rustic country setting and excellent cuisine served without pretension at modest prices, this restaurant nine miles from Valence offers the rich and bountiful cuisine of the countryside. Inexpensive.

Charmes-sur-Rhône: La Vieille Auberge (75.60.80.10)—Six miles south of Valence is this extremely popular country restaurant that serves excellent country cuisine at astonishingly low prices. Inexpensive.

Château Bourg: Hostellerie du Château (75.40.33.28)—On the western bank of the Rhône, six miles north of Valence, the Reynaud family turn out a splendid local cuisine that is complemented by a very complete, very reasonably priced wine list. Moderate.

St.-Hilaire-du-Rosier: Bouvarel (76.36.50.87)—This attractive restaurant northeast of Valence is given one star in the Michelin Guide, but the food is much closer to two-star quality. It remains a surprisingly well-kept secret, but I predict a promising future. There are 14 nice rooms available at this inn. Moderately expensive.

Granges-lès-Valence: Auberge des Trois Canards (75.44.43.24)— Just west of Valence, but before passing into St.-Péray on the west bank of the Rhône, is the little town of Granges-lès-Valence. This inexpensive, always packed, smoky bistro serves generous portions of very good food from the former chef of the famous Paris restaurant Dodin Bouffant. It is an ideal spot for lunch. Moderate.

Visiting Châteauneuf-du-Pape

If you are not a great admirer of bright sun or gusty winds, then you may well want to pass quickly through this area, which has plenty of both. Châteauneuf-du-Pape is, however, among the easiest places to visit as virtually all of the châteaux or domaines are used to the hordes of summertime tourists who descend on this tiny village. Therefore, there are free tasting rooms set up by many of the châteaux right in the town. Châteauneuf-du-Pape has only two good hotels, the Hostellerie des Fines Roches and Logis d'Arnavel, but the fascination of the walled city of Avignon is only ten miles away, and this can also make an ideal base for exploring the southern Rhône.

Châteauneuf-du-Pape: Hostellerie des Fines Roches (90.83.70.23)— This is a quiet place in the middle of the vineyards, just south of the village. The food is very good, the rooms spacious and comfortable, and the prices moderately expensive.

Châteauneuf-du-Pape: Logis d'Arnavel (90.83.73.22)—Run by Jérome Quiot, the proprietor of Vieux Lazaret, a Châteauneuf-du-Pape estate, this modern hotel has clean, spartan rooms, a cheery, decent restaurant, and a pool. Inexpensive.

Châteauneuf-du-Pape: La Mule des Papes (90.83.73.30)—This second floor restaurant does plenty of business since it is located in the middle of the village, but the wine list is inexcusably limited to only the wines produced by the négociant Père Anselme. The generous portions of food are good and cheap. Moderate.

Châteauneuf-du-Pape: Le Pistou (90.81.83.75)—This tiny hole-in-the-wall right in the village offers many Provençal specialties at remarkably low prices. The food and service have flair and personality. Inexpensive.

Avignon: Hiely-Lucullus (90.86.17.07)—This famous restaurant's look and cuisine have remained unchanged since my wife and I first ate there in 1971. For a Michelin two-star restaurant, it has no pretentiousness at all. The rotund, matronly waitresses perform flawlessly, the cuisine, though never adventurous, is always immensely satisfying, and the wine list chock full of treasures. For its pedigree, the prices are very reasonable. Moderately expensive.

Avignon: Brunel (90.85.24.83)—This is the most exciting restaurant in Avignon. The young staff and chef turn out imaginative meals that offer thrilling juxtapositions. Small and intimate, this one-star restaurant has both two-star cuisine and prices. Expensive.

Avignon: Auberge de France (90.82.58.86)—This noisy, commercial restaurant looks like it lives off the frequent tourists to the region. However, forgetting the crowds and loud rooms, the food is generous and faithful to the region. The wine list is inexpensive. Moderate.

Avignon: La Fourchette II (90.85.20.93)—This simple, crowded bistro offers excellent regional specialties, a noisy, packed atmosphere, and good wines by the carafe. Inexpensive.

Montfavet: Hotel les Frênes (90.31.17.93)—Located in a quiet park, ten minutes outside Avignon, this splendid hotel complex has a superb pool, very fine rooms, and a good kitchen. The wine list is excellent and reasonably priced. This is a top spot to stay in the Avignon area when silence and an absence of street traffic are desired. Expensive.

Pontet: Auberge de Cassagne (90.31.04.18)—Located just outside Avignon, this is another good place to stay and dine, as well as escape the noise and heat of Avignon. Located in a calm and quiet spot, this family auberge offers excellent rooms, has beautiful gardens, and good food. Expensive.

Villeneuve-lès-Avignon: Le Prieuré (90.25.18.20)—Splendidly located at the back of an alley, this gorgeously furnished hotel and restaurant offers good food and warm service in a marvelous medieval, vaulted stone priory. The setting is hard to beat. Expensive.

Les Angles: Ermitage-Meissonnier (90.25.41.68)—This restaurant and hotel has led a roller-coaster life over recent years. Michelin dropped one of its two stars in 1986, and the elderly Meissonnier went into retirement, leaving the kitchen in the very capable hands of his son. My wife and I had several splendid meals here in the summer of 1986, but later in October were sadly disappointed by what we ate. Frankly, it seems that the meals and service can range from mediocre to exceptional. The talent is obvious, but this is a hard place to figure out. Expensive.

Visiting Tavel and Lirac

Tavel and Lirac are to the west of Avignon and one could easily remain in the city of the popes since neither Tavel nor Lirac are more than 30 minutes away by car. But if you want to bed down in the countryside, the following spots are recommended.

Tavel: Auberge de Tavel (66.50.03.41)—The food is good, not excellent enough to merit its one star, but regional in orientation and well presented. The rooms are adequate. Moderate.

Tavel: Hostellerie du Seigneur (66.50.04.26)—Less renowned than the above Auberge de Tavel, this charming bistro has excellent cooking and very attractive prices, plus a lovely array of Tavels on the wine list. Moderate.

Castillon du Gard: Le Vieux Castillon (66.37.00.77)—This spare-no-expense establishment near the stunning Roman aqueduct, the Pont du Gard, has only one star from the Michelin Guide, but seems certain to get two in the immediate future. It is one of the most luxurious hotels and restaurants in this part of France. The cuisine is inspired, the wine list outstanding, the views over the valley memorable, and the eleven rooms fit for the rich and famous. Take plenty of money to Le Vieux Castillon. Very expensive.

Visiting Gigondas and the Côtes du Rhône-Villages

The eastern flank of the Rhône Valley is studded with medieval hill towns, tiny, charming, rustic restaurants and red-faced vignerons offering a free taste of their wines. One could spend weeks traveling through this area and not see all it has to offer. Travel in these parts is slow going. The circuitous mountain roads, hilly terrain, and spectacular vistas all contribute to a snail's pace. One could make Avignon a base for exploration of these areas, but I highly recommend staying at one of the inns in the villages. Some of the favorite restaurants and hotels my wife and I have enjoyed are those that follow.

Mondragon: La Beaugravière (90.30.13.40)—This simple, family restaurant in the small village of Mondragon has France's best wine list for Rhône wines and some of the finest regional cuisine money can buy. The spectacular omelette with truffle and leg of lamb are so good that the omission of this restaurant from the Michelin Guide is a sacrilege. This is a must stop for Rhône wine enthusiasts as well as gourmets. Moderate.

Séguret: La Table du Comtat (90.46.91.49)—Another fabulous place to stay and dine, La Table du Comtat, which sits in the tiny hilltop village of Séguret, is a required stop, if only to have a meal while looking over the endless miles of Côtes du Rhône vineyards during a radiant Provençal sunset. The rooms are lovely and the pool refreshing. Moderate.

Séguret: Domaine de la Cabasse (90.46.91.12)—There is no menu, only Madame Nadine Latour's excellent daily fare to keep you contented. Her wines are served directly from the tanks in carafes, and her cooking is excellent, but you must take whatever it is she is cooking that day. It is well worth the risk. Inexpensive.

Gordes: Domaine de L'Enclos (90.72.08.22)—This spectacular retreat is off the beaten path, but the hill town of Gordes is so stunning and this hotel and restaurant complex so relaxing and beautifully situated that the 45-minute drive to Avignon or Gigondas seems worth the tranquillity and fine cuisine this spot offers. Very expensive.

Gordes: Les Bories (90.72.00.51)—There are only four attractive rooms, but the real reason to come here is the cuisine. It merits one star from Michelin, but frequently seems closer to two. Expensive.

Joucas: Mas des Herbes Blanches (90.72.00.74)—A meal here overlooking the Lubéron Mountains on the open-air deck is memorable by any standards. This luxury resort is hidden away on a hillside. The food is excellent and clearly merits the one star it has earned from the Michelin people. The view over the valley below and the mountains at sunset are unforgettable. Very expensive.

Gigondas: Les Florets (90.65.85.01)—This family-run restaurant in Gigondas serves up big portions of skillfully prepared regional cuisine, and has a wine list composed, of course, of Gigondas wines that is staggering in its depth. The prices are unbelievably low. Inexpensive.

Food Specialties of the Rhône Valley

Brandade de morue—It may sound terrible, but this delicious treat is composed of salt cod reduced to a paste and blended with olive oil and garlic.

Quenelles de brochet, sauce Nantua—Pike fish dumplings with a sauce made from freshwater crayfish sounds terrible in English, but just try them.

Tapenade—A paste made from black olives, garlic, herbs, and olive oil.

Ratatouille—A concoction of sliced or chopped eggplant, onions, tomatoes, and zucchini, cooked in olive oil.

Soup à l'ail—Garlic soup.

Pistou—A hearty vegetable soup loaded with aromatic herbs and garlic.

Gigot d'agneau d'Alpilles (or Sisteron)—A remarkably tasty leg of lamb from the two most desired areas for raising this animal, the Alpilles south of Avignon and the Sisteron region in the mountainous gorge-laden area east of the Côtes du Ventoux.

Aioli—A garlic-based, very spicy mayonnaise that is used as a garnish for soups and vegetables.

Anchoïade—A pasty anchovy and garlic vinaigrette.

Bourride—A hearty fish chowder that comes in endless variations.

Picodon—Very fashionable at the moment, this soft goat cheese is made in small discs and has a pronounced fresh, nutty flavor.

St.-Marcellin—One of the region's most famous cheeses, it is made from cow's milk in the Isère area, and has a creamy texture and mild flavor.

Tomme—A mountain cheese made from either goat's or sheep's milk, it has a distinctive flavor.

Rigotte de Condrieu—As the name implies, this cheese is regularly encountered in the northern Rhône. Made from cow's milk, it is a firm, creamy cheese.

Truffles—Black truffles from Tricastin are not as famous as those from Périgord, but they taste every bit as good. They are in season during the fall, but most restaurants preserve enough of them to last for six to eight months.

III

PROVENCE

Bandol, Bellet, Cassis, Coteaux d'Aix-
en-Provence, Côtes du Provence, Côtes du
Lubéron, Palette

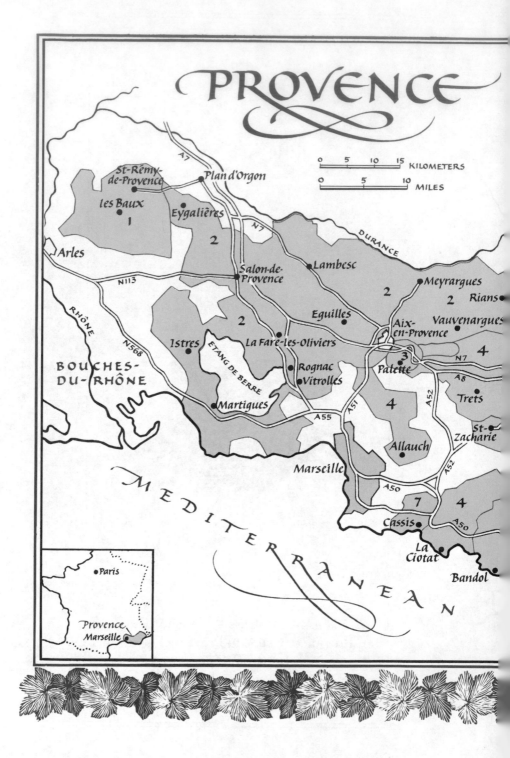

PROVENCE

KILOMETERS
0 5 10 15

MILES
0 5 10

St-Rémy-
de-Provence
Plan d'Orgon
les Baux
1
Eygalières
2
Arles
N113
Salon-de-
Provence
DURANCE
Lambesc
Meyrargues
2
Rians
N7
RHÔNE
2
Eguilles
Vauvenargues
N7
N568
Istres
La Fare-les-Oliviers
Aix-
en-Provence
4
BOUCHES-
DU-RHÔNE
ÉTANG DE BERRE
Rognac
Palette
3
A8
Vitrolles
A52
Trets
A55
A51
4
St-
Zacharie
Martigues
Allauch
A52
Marseille
7
4
A50
Cassis
A50
La
Ciotat
Bandol

MEDITERRANEAN

Paris

Provence
Marseille

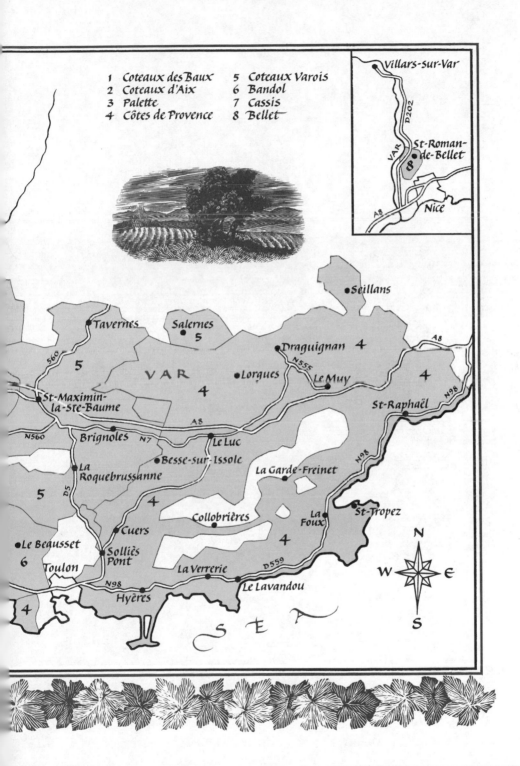

1 Coteaux des Baux   5 Coteaux Varois
2 Coteaux d'Aix   6 Bandol
3 Palette   7 Cassis
4 Côtes de Provence   8 Bellet

Villars-sur-Var

D202

VAR

St-Roman-
de-Bellet

8

A8

Nice

Seillans

Tavernes

Salernes

5

Draguignan

4

A8

V A R

Lorgues

Le Muy

4

N555

St-Raphaël

560

5

St-Maximin-
la-Ste-Baume

N98

4

N560

Brignoles

N7

A8

Le Luc

La
Roquebrussanne

Besse-sur-Issole

La Garde-Freinet

N98

5

D5

4

Collobrières

La
Foux

St-Tropez

Cuers

4

Le Beausset

Solliès
Pont

6

Toulon

La Verrerie

D559

N

N98

Hyères

Le Lavandou

W   E

4

S E A

S

INTRODUCTION

The name Provence conjures up thoughts of vacations, of an aromatic and rich cuisine, of the sun and sea, and, of course, of the glamorous playground for the rich and famous from all over the world. Geographically, Provence encompasses virtually all the famous southern Rhône appellations since Provence as an area begins at Montélimar. It is here that the landscape begins to offer up the garrigues, the Provençal name referring to the low limestone hills that are studded with outcroppings of calcareous rock and sparse clumps of wind-beaten vegetation. While the famous southern Rhône appellations of Châteauneuf-du-Pape, Gigondas, Lirac, Tavel, and Beaumes de Venise all fall within the physical parameters of Provence, the viticultural regions of this sun-drenched area do not begin until below Avignon. South of Avignon is a vast area that stretches due south and east, including the entire Mediterranean coastline as well as inland areas. Within this mammoth area are seven specific viticultural areas that comprise the winemaking regions of Provence. They are:

Bandol—Named after the quaint seaside village and port of the same name, Bandol, only 30 miles east of Marseille, is potentially the finest appellation of Provence. The red wine is the most famous, but some unexciting white wine and an excellent rosé are also made there.

Bellet—Chances are that unless you have spent a holiday on France's famed Côte d'Azur, particularly Nice, you have never seen the wines from this micro-appellation situated in the hills behind Nice. One of Provence's best white wines is made there, but good rosé as well as decent red wine are also produced.

Cassis—Five miles west of Bandol, the heavily visited, charming fishing village of Cassis serves as the hometown for the wines of this tiny appellation. While red and rosé wines are made there, Cassis is famous for its white wine, which seems to possess the aromas of wild Provençal herbs. In my opinion, it is one of the few white wines that can stand up to the great but rarely well-made Provençal culinary classic, the fish soup called bouillabaisse.

Coteaux d'Aix-en-Provence—A vast area that runs from Aix-en-Provence northwest and west toward Avignon and Arles is the newest appellation of Provence. Previously, this consisted of two VDQS areas, the Coteaux d'Aix-en-Provence and another smaller viticultural area located in the moonscape-like, hauntingly forbidding landscape near Les Baux called Coteaux des Baux-de-Provence. Two of Provence's greatest red wines are made here, the Domaine Trévallon and Château Vignelaure. The potential for superb red wines in this area is enormous.

Côtes du Lubéron—In the northern, mountainous portion of Provence east and southeast of Avignon is another emerging viticultural region called the Côtes du Lubéron. Rarely serious, these wines offer great commercial appeal and value.

Côtes de Provence—This enormous area that stretches across the entire Mediterranean coastline of France from Marseille to St.-Raphael and inland as far as Aix-en-Provence and Draguignan offers an incredible array of wines of varying price and quality. Everything exists here, from vibrant, delicious rosés to heavy, dull reds, but the potential is obvious.

Palette—One of France's tiniest appellations, Palette, in the shadow of Cézanne's famed Mont Ste.-Victoire near Aix-en-Provence, has only two wineries producing good red, white, and rosé wines.

There are several other minor viticultural regions in Provence. The **Coteaux de Pierrevert,** which sits far inland, just east of the Côtes du Lubéron, and the **Coteaux Varois,** a larger area running from the seaside port of Toulon inland and due north to Rians, are just two of them. Neither area has appellation contrôlée status, nor have they yet shown the potential of the other Provence winemaking regions.

In researching this book, I began with a naïve wine prejudice that Provence was synonymous with good, stylish rosés, but not much else. After extensive visits, tastings, and discussions, it was very apparent that not only are deliciously crisp and flavorful rosés made here, but there are some magnificent, undervalued red wines being made as well, and some surprisingly good white wines. The word "potential" kept coming up in my notes, and that word perhaps more than any other summarizes this scenic, diverse region that is, from a climatic and geographical sense, one of the most fortunate on the face of the earth. Provence is indeed an area that is surging forward. There are new winemaking estates sprouting up over the entire area. State-of-the-art wine cellars are being installed at numerous domaines, and there is significant expansion of the existing vineyard areas. Prices for some wines seem unreasonably as well as unjustifiably high (much like the hotel and restaurant prices in this sunny, exquisite paradise), but for most of the wines of Provence the prices are moderate, and fine bargains can be found.

In short, Provence, so exhilarating and pleasure-giving because of its staggering natural beauty, climate, and cuisine, is also emerging as a serious supplier of top-quality red and rosé wines, as well as a handful of white wines.

BANDOL

The Most Privileged of Provence's
Appellations

BANDOL AT A GLANCE

Types of wine produced:	Red, rosé, and white wines; the great majority of the wine is red
Grape varieties planted:	Red wine: Mourvèdre content must be at least 50%; other varieties planted at Bandol include Syrah, Grenache, Cinsault, Carignan White wine: Clairette, Ugni Blanc, Sauvignon, and Bourboulenc
Acres currently under vine:	2,223 (of a potential vineyard area of 5,000 acres)
Quality level:	Mediocre to exceptional; there is tremendous diversity in quality and winemaking styles

Aging potential:	Red wines: 4–15 years
	Rosé and white wines: 1–3 years
General characteristics:	Red wines: very long-lived, rich, fragrant, tannic, with scents of berry fruit, tree bark, truffles, and wild herbs
	Rosé wines: crisp, fresh, yet full-bodied and among the finest in the world
	White wines: dry, medium-bodied, bland, neutral-tasting
Greatest recent vintages:	1985, 1982, 1979, 1975, 1971, 1970
Price range:	$8–$15

Bandol is often called the most fortunate appellation of France. For pure scenic beauty, only the storybook viticultural area of Alsace offers any competition. Bandol, a lovely little seaside port and village perched right next to the Mediterranean, has an azure-colored sea as its backdrop. However, the vineyards are spread out over a number of hillsides as well as the valley floor behind the seaside town. Two gorgeously located medieval hilltop villages, La Cadière and Le Castellet, serve as the home base for many of the producers and are must stops for any tourist to this region.

There are 50 independent estates or domaines producing wine in Bandol, and several cooperatives that buy the grapes from their members. As of 1987, there were 220 small growers who sold their entire crop to the cooperatives.

While the wines of Bandol are very fashionable in France, they are rarely seen outside that country. Certainly, the area's viticultural history is among the oldest in France; the Romans found the vineyards of Bandol flourishing in 125 B.C. According to marine archeologists, there is evidence that the Romans used the port of Bandol to ship wine back to Rome. Louis XV, when asked about the source of his youthful appearance and fitness, is quoted as responding that it came from "the wine of Bandol; it gives me all the vital sap and wits I need."

While Bandol produces the three basic types of wine (red, white, and rosé), it is the red wine that has made this region famous. It is produced under strictly controlled laws that were adopted when Bandol received appellation contrôlée status in 1941. Required to be made from at least 50% Mourvèdre (the only red wine in the world with this distinction),

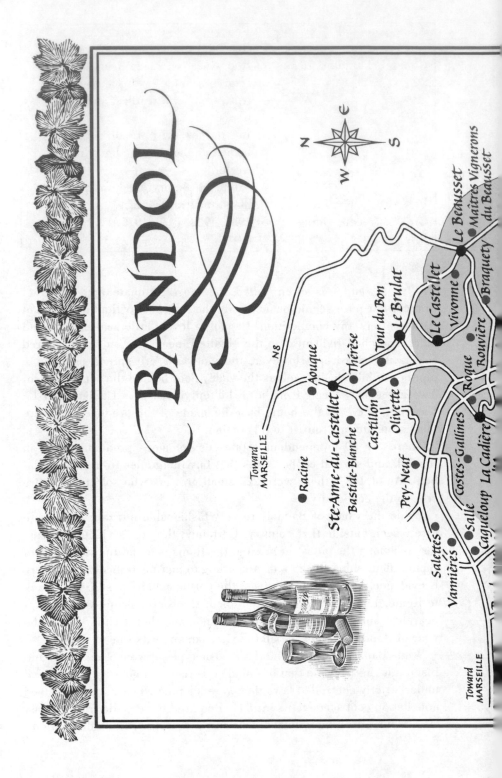

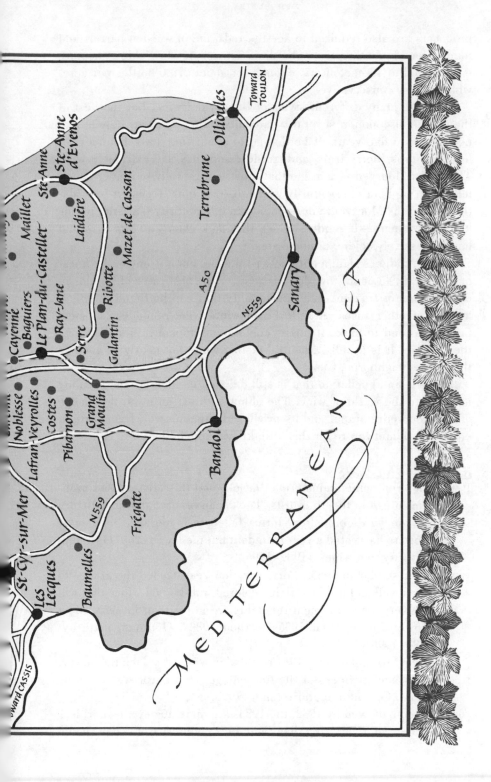

Toward Toulon

Ollioules

Ste-Anne d'Evenos

Ste-Anne

Maillet

Cayenne

Baguiers

Le Plan-du-Castellet

Laidière

Mazet de Cassan

Terrebrune

Ray-Jane

Serre

Rivotte

Galantin

A50

Sanary

N559

Noblesse

Lafran-Veyrolles

Costes

Pibarnon

Grand Moulin

Bandol

St-Cyr-sur-Mer

N559

Frégate

Les Lecques

Baumelles

Toward Cassis

MEDITERRANEAN SEA

producers are also required to age the red wine in wooden barrels and foudres for 18 months prior to bottling. The maximum yield per hectare is restricted to 40 hectoliters, enough for about 2,100 bottles per acre, which is very conservative.

There are many different styles of Bandol red wine, but the best of them have in common several personality traits. They are tannic and need three to five years of bottle age to open; they have bouquets of leather, herbs, berry fruit, and truffles; and they age extremely well. The use of Mourvèdre, a grape that must mature fully to render excellent wine, produces very sturdy wines that are quite resistant to oxidation. When the Mourvèdre does not attain full maturity—a rarity in this hot, arid climate—it renders wines that lack color and ripeness and have excessively acidic, tannic tastes.

Bandol produces significantly less rosé wine, but it is one of the finest in the world. No doubt the Mourvèdre gives the best rosés of Bandol an extra degree of fragrance and personality that can be found in only a handful of other rosés. A little bit of white wine is made, but most producers tend to make it for its commercial appeal rather than aesthetic value. It is usually a neutral-tasting wine, not nearly as good as that of the neighboring Cassis.

Bandol is an appellation that is still defining its identity and learning its place in the world of wine. The climate, the strict laws, the choice of the Mourvèdre grape, and its privileged situation will, I am certain, ensure a brilliant future for this little-known appellation.

RECENT VINTAGES

1986—The September rainstorms that plagued this area caused problems of rot in the vineyards. The ocean breezes that usually dry the vineyards out after storms failed to materialize, and most growers harvested a very abundant but mediocre crop. Optimum maturity (red wines): 1989–1996.

1985—Very similar to 1983, a dry, very hot year caused the grapes to ripen well and produce richly colored, full-bodied wines that will age very well, although the acids are lower than in 1983. Most growers prefer their 1985s to their 1983s. Optimum maturity: 1988–1998.

1984—A very irregular year, 1984 resulted in wines that lack the power, body, and richness of the top vintages, but surprises are to be found. Optimum maturity: now–1993.

1983—Overshadowed by 1982, the 1983s are more austere, leaner, less opulent and flattering than their 1982 counterparts. They should age well after their tough tannins have been shed. Optimum maturity: 1989–1998.

1982—A great year in Bandol, 1982 is ranked by most growers as the finest vintage since 1970, and one of the best in the last three decades. The wines arc powerful, very concentrated, tannic, and loaded with layers of ripe fruit. Optimum maturity: 1988–2000.

OLDER VINTAGES

The best older vintages include the splendid years of 1979, 1975, 1971, and 1970.

A Personal Rating of the Bandol Producers
*****(OUTSTANDING PRODUCERS)
Domaine Tempier

****(EXCELLENT PRODUCERS)

Domaine le Gallantin	Château Pradeaux
Domaine de l'Hermitage	Domaine Ray-Jane
Moulin des Costes/Mas de la	Château Romassan
Rouvière	Château Vannières
Domaine de Pibarnon	

***(GOOD PRODUCERS)

La Bastide Blanche	Château Sainte-Anne
Domaine Cagueloup	Domaine de Frégate
Domaine de la Laidière	Domaine des Salettes
Domaine de la Loubière	Domaine de Terrebrune
Château de la Noblesse	

LA BASTIDE BLANCHE (M. BRONZO)***

The large-framed, smiling Monsieur Bronzo uses the required 50% Mourvèdre in his red wine, but also a high percentage of Grenache. His red wine, therefore, has more of a Rhône Valley style and texture than that of a Bandol. He does produce one of the very best white wines of the appellation. Bronzo now has 55 acres of vines in production.

VINTAGES

1985—*Bandol Blanc de Blancs*—Typically chunky and leaning toward
·   being heavy, the 1985 white Bandol is still lively, quite fruity,
82   and well made. Drink it over the next 18 months. Last tasted
        10/86.

1984—*Bandol (red)*—Well colored, the 1984 has a big, ripe, fruity
·   Grenache bouquet, austere, tannic flavors, and a dry finish. An-
77   ticipated maturity: now–1992. Last tasted 10/86.
1982—*Bandol (red)*—A rich, powerful wine that is still young and
·   tannic, the 1982 has excellent color, a full-bodied palate impres-
87   sion, and plenty of alcohol. This is one of the best wines of the
       vintage. Anticipated maturity: 1988–1996. Last tasted 10/86.
1979—*Bandol (red)*—Bandol wines age extremely well, and the 1979 is
·   still very much alive, very fruity, more elegant than the 1982,
83   spicy, and fully mature. Last tasted 6/86.

DOMAINE CAGUELOUP (GASTON PREBOST)***

This 69-acre estate near St.-Cyr-sur-Mer produces white, red, and rosé
Bandol. The 1985 rosé was disappointing, the 1985 white, chunky,
fleshy, and flavorful enough to stand up to the garlic-scented, robust
soupe de poissons typical of the region. The red wines are this house's
specialty.

VINTAGES

1983—*Bandol (red)*—Many 1983s are presently very tannic and hard.
·   For example, Cagueloup's offering from this vintage is austere,
78   tannic, and closed. Anticipated maturity: 1990–1993. Last
       tasted 10/86.
1982—*Bandol (red)*—The 1982 is deep in color with a moderately in-
·   tense berry fruit bouquet, fleshy, broad flavors, and good depth.
84   Anticipated maturity: now–1992. Last tasted 10/86.
1981—*Bandol (red)*—A deliciously fruity wine, the 1981 is fully mature,
·   has a good ruby color, and soft, supple texture. Drink over the
83   next 3–4 years. Last tasted 10/86.
1978—*Bandol (red)*—A full-intensity bouquet of tobacco, herbs, cedar,
·   and roasted fruit is quite complex. On the palate, the wine is
85   quite spicy and complex, but should be drunk up since it tails
       off in the mouth. Last tasted 10/86.

DOMAINE DE FRÉGATE (COMTE DE PISSY)***

One of the prettiest domaines, Frégate is situated next to a lovely
seaside cove, and has spectacular wine cellars carved out of the rocky
hillside. Its 50 acres of vines produce all three wines, but most of it is
red. Their wines are certainly above average in quality; my notes show
an excellent 1975 red Bandol. However, this estate is not in the top tier
of Bandol producers. The white wine is dull, the rosé sound but lacking

in excitement, and the red wine variable in quality. It was certainly good in 1975, 1979, and 1983, but the 1985 and 1982, probably the two best recent vintages for Bandol, are much less successful.

DOMAINE LE GALLANTIN (ACHILLE PASCAL)****

This is one of Bandol's smallest estates, only 35 acres. Run by the ruddy-faced, black-haired Achille Pascal, it produces one of the best red wines, a good white wine, and an adequate rosé. Le Gallantin's cellars are in Le Plan du Castellet, and Pascal's approach to vinification is very traditional. The grapes are crushed, fermented at hot temperatures, and given a long sojourn in oak barrels. The proprietor's first love is clearly red wine, which is easy to detect in tasting—Pascal's is one of the deepest and richest red wines of the appellation.

VINTAGES

1985—*Bandol Rosé*—For Bandol rosé, this is a light, bland style with-
·   out much flavor authority or personality. Last tasted 10/86.
73

1985—*Bandol Blanc de Blancs*—A light, fresh, vibrant, fruity style,
·   the 1985 should be drunk before the end of 1988. Last tasted
78   10/86.

1985—*Bandol (red)*—Very dense color with a richly scented, tarlike,
·   smoky, herbaceous nose, powerful, deep flavors and quite a
87   long, tannic finish characterize the 1985 red Bandol from Le
     Gallantin. Anticipated maturity: 1990–2000. Last tasted 10/86.

1984—*Bandol (red)*—A lovely, fragrant bouquet of ripe fruit and spices
·   is followed by a wine that is supple and attractive, yet short in
81   the finish. Drink this wine over the next 3–4 years. Last tasted
     10/86.

1982—*Bandol (red)*—Quite opaque ruby/purple, this is a very une-
·   volved, broodingly deep, full-bodied, tannic wine that is excep-
86   tionally concentrated and very impressive, but needs cellaring.
     Anticipated maturity: 1990–2000. Last tasted 10/86.

1978—*Bandol (red)*—Another serious effort, the 1978 has still not
·   reached its apogee. Deep ruby/purple to the edge, this full-
88   throttle, intense, still aggressive young wine should last out this
     century. The Hermitage of Bandol? Anticipated maturity: 1990–
     2000. Last tasted 10/86.

DOMAINE DE L'HERMITAGE (GÉRARD DUFFORT)****

In an average year this 90-acre domaine produces 8,000 cases of Bandol red wine, 6,500 cases of rosé, and about 650 cases of white wine.

Proprietor Gérard Duffort purchased this abandoned property in Le Beausset in 1973 and has completely resurrected it. All the wines here merit attention, particularly the red and the rosé.

VINTAGES

1985—*Bandol Rosé*—An attractive, very dry, austere style of rosé, the
·   1985 makes an ideal wine to have as an apéritif. Drink it over
82   the next two years. Last tasted 10/86.

1985—*Bandol (red)*—Very dense ruby/purple in color, the 1985 is very
·   rich and full-bodied, not showing much complexity or finesse,
84   but if all the component parts come together, this wine will merit
    a higher rating. Anticipated maturity: 1990–1998. Last tasted
    10/86.

1984—*Bandol (red)*—Very deeply colored, the 1984 is tannic and tight,
·   but exhibits plenty of rich fruit beneath the veneer of tannin. It
84   is surprisingly intense and rich for a 1984. Anticipated maturity:
    1989–1996. Last tasted 10/86.

1983—*Bandol (red)*—Not a very successful 1983, this wine has hard,
·   narrowly focused flavors, a one-dimensional character, and little
76   charm. Anticipated maturity: now–1992. Last tasted 10/86.

1982—*Bandol (red)*—Wines of this caliber demonstrate the potential
·   for excellence in the Bandol appellation. Approachable now, it
87   has a broad creamy richness, full body, a lot of power and tan-
    nin, but heaps of fruit. Quite impressive. Drink it over the next
    3–6 years. Last tasted 10/86.

DOMAINE DE LAFRAN-VEYROLLES (MME. JOUVE-FEREC)**

This is a tiny estate of 20 acres run by the exceptionally friendly Madame Jouve-Ferec. Her wines have a good reputation, but with the exception of her 1978, I found the recent vintages to be very light and simple.

VINTAGES

1985—*Bandol (red)*—Extremely shallow and light-bodied, this wine
·   seems fully mature and meagerly endowed. Last tasted 10/86.
68

1984—*Bandol (red)*—A trace more fruit can be found here, but again,
·   this is a diluted, watery version of a Bandol wine. Last tasted
70   10/86.

1982—*Bandol (red)*—The 1982 is thin and very acidic. Something
·   seems to have gone awry here. Last tasted 10/86.
60

1978—*Bandol (red)*—A big, powerful bouquet of olives and herbs is
· top-rank. On the palate, the wine is spicy, round, fruity, and
83 fully mature. Last tasted 10/86.

DOMAINE DE LA LAIDIÈRE (GAEC ESTIENNE)***

This is a very well-run estate of 44.5 acres located in the tiny, quiet
town of Ste.-Anne d'Evenos. The white wine is among the best of the
appellation, since it avoids the heaviness typical of many and emphati-
cally offers oodles of crisp, fresh fruit in a medium-bodied, vibrant
style. The rosé is good, too. The red wine, which accounts for 3,300
cases a year (about 50% of the estate's production) is traditionally made
from a blend of 60% Mourvèdre, 20% Grenache, and 20% Cinsault.
Founded in 1941, Domaine de la Laidière is owned and managed by
Freddy Estienne.

VINTAGES

1985—*Bandol (white)*—A modern-styled, fresh, perfumed, crisp white
· wine that offers a great deal of straightforward fruit and zesty
81 acidity. Anticipated maturity: now–1989. Last tasted 10/86.
1985—*Bandol (red)*—Very full-bodied, deep in color, and chunky, this
· wine shows no finesse or complexity at the moment, but has
84 plenty of power and depth. Anticipated maturity: 1990–1998.
Last tasted 10/86.
1982—*Bandol (red)*—An impressive wine, rich in fruit, deep, chunky,
· and full-bodied, the 1982 Laidière is concentrated and not nearly
85 at its peak yet. Anticipated maturity: 1989–1996. Last tasted 10/
86.

MOULIN DES COSTES
AND MAS DE LA ROUVIÈRE (BUNAN)****

The Bunans, who own Moulin des Costes and Mas de la Rouvière, are
one of the leading families of Bandol. They own three important estates
in Bandol comprising 173 acres altogether. Paul Bunan, a serious, soft-
spoken man, purchased Moulin des Costes (a vineyard near La Cadière)
in 1961. His brother Pierre, a broad-faced, affable, gregarious man,
bought Mas de la Rouvière (near Le Castellet) in 1969. Subsequently,
they added another vineyard at Le Castellet called Bélouvé.

The wines are marketed under both the Moulin des Costes and Mas
de la Rouvière labels, but they are identical.

The Bunan family work as an enthusiastic, strong team, not only to
make their wines but to market them as well. Their hillside vineyards

are in impeccable condition, as is the wine cellar. They use a blend for their red wine of 65% Mourvèdre, 14% Grenache, 6% Syrah, and 15% Cinsault. The rosé is made from 70% Cinsault, 24% Mourvèdre, and 6% Grenache. For the white wine the blend is 45% Clairette, 45% Ugni Blanc, and 5% each of Sauvignon and Bourboulenc. The Bunans also produce a good Marc de Bandol from the skins of the grapes, a non-appellation Cabernet Sauvignon called Mont Caume, and about 2,000 bottles each year of a kosher Cabernet Sauvignon made in strict observance of the orthodox Jewish requirements. It is an excellent wine, and among the finest kosher wines I have ever tasted.

The Bunans are also the leaders of one of two growers' associations or syndicates in Bandol. (The other is headed by the irrepressible Lucien Peyraud of Domaine Tempier.) For whatever reason, there appears to be a lively rivalry between the Bunans and Peyrauds, not unlike that which existed for decades in Bordeaux between the owners of Haut-Brion and La Mission-Haut-Brion. It is difficult to comprehend what has caused them to become opponents, for both families own leading estates, produce fine wine, are great believers in the Bandol appellation, and are keenly competitive. Perhaps therein lies the answer.

The wines made by Bunan are the products of the modern school of winemaking. The red wines are put through the Kisselguhr filtration system after malolactic fermentation and are filtered again prior to bottling. There are two cuvées produced of red Bandol. Bottles marked "Cuvée Spéciale" have 75% rather than 65% Mourvèdre in their makeup, and are made to last ten years. The whites and rosés are centrifuged as part of the winemaking process. The quality level is very good, but perhaps a little less filtration would result in even more impressive wines. As a general rule, the white and rosé should be drunk within three years of the vintage, the red within five to eight years, except for the Cuvée Spéciale, which will last ten years.

VINTAGES

1985—*Bandol Blanc de Blancs*—Bunan's white Bandol is light, fruity,
· delicate, with good clean acidity, and a fresh, lively finish. It
83 requires drinking within 1–3 years of the vintage. It represents an intelligent style. Last tasted 10/86.

1985—*Bandol Rosé*—This is a fairly light style for a Bandol rosé, yet
· its delicious, well-delineated fruit and flowery, fruity bouquet
84 give it plenty of appeal. Last tasted 10/86.

1985—*Bandol (red)*—I was surprised this wine did not show more stuff-
·   ing and concentration given the vintage. Medium ruby, with a
83   moderately intense, plummy-scented bouquet, it is very forward
      and fruity. Anticipated maturity: 1988–1994. Last tasted 6/86.

1984—*Bandol (red)*—Quite ready to drink, with a moderately intense
·   bouquet of raspberry fruit, this medium-bodied, elegant wine
84   has a kinship to a lighter styled red burgundy. Drink it over the
      next 4–6 years. Last tasted 10/86.

1983—*Bandol (red)*—Round generous berry fruit aromas swell in the
·   glass. On the palate, the wine is rich in extract, medium- to full-
85   bodied with a broad, creamy texture. Drink it over the next 5–6
      years. Last tasted 10/86.

1982—*Bandol (red)*—Very similar to the fine 1983, the 1982 is, how-
·   ever, more tannic, has more delineated aromas of raspberry fruit
85   and spicy oak to it, and is slightly fuller-bodied. It is very bur-
      gundian. Drink it over the next 4–5 years. Last tasted 10/86.

1979—*Bandol (red)*—Fully mature with an elegant, spicy, oaky, richly
·   fruity bouquet, soft, well-balanced, clean flavors, and medium
84   body, this stylish wine has developed well and should be drunk
      up. Last tasted 10/86.

1976—*Bandol (red)*—Quite light in color yet very fruity and round on
·   the palate, the 1976 may be just beginning to decline ever so
83   slightly. Drink it up. Last tasted 10/86.

1975—*Bandol Cuvée Spéciale (red)*—Deep ruby color, the 1975 Cuvée
·   Spéciale is very concentrated, quite rich and full-bodied, and
87   though fully mature will keep another 5–6 years. It is made from
      75% Mourvèdre. Last tasted 10/86.

1974—*Bandol Cuvée Spéciale (red)*—Overwhelmed by the 1975, the
·   1974 Cuvée Spéciale is on the decline, tastes a trifle flat and
78   fading, and should be drunk up. Last tasted 10/86.

CHÂTEAU DE LA NOBLESSE (JEAN-PIERRE GAUSSEN)***

This 37-acre estate is run by Jean-Pierre Gaussen, a rather cynical, cold, reserved man. His cellars are in the hilltop village of La Cadière d'Azur. His red wine is good, his white ideal with soupe de poissons, and his rosé surprisingly bland.

VINTAGES

1985—*Bandol Rosé*—For a Bandol rosé, this wine is very simple and
·   lacking in character. Last tasted 10/86.
75

1985—*Bandol Blanc*—A big, chunky, sturdy wine with considerable
· body as well as a spicy personality, the 1985 Bandol white from
83 La Noblesse will stand up nicely to a rich fish soup. Last tasted
10/86.

1984—*Bandol (red)*—For a 1984, this wine has very dark color, a bou-
· quet of leather and ripe plums, medium to full body, and some
84 tannin to lose. Anticipated maturity: 1988–1993. Last tasted
10/86.

1983—*Bandol (red)*—The best of the La Noblesse red wines I tasted,
· the 1983 is a powerful, full-bodied, deeply concentrated, firm
85 wine with plenty of fruit and character. Anticipated maturity:
1988–1995. Last tasted 10/86.

1982—*Bandol (red)*—Despite the obvious weight and depth of this
· wine, it was brutally tannic and astringent with a sharpness in
74 the finish that kept the rating lower. Last tasted 10/86.

DOMAINE DE PIBARNON
(COMTE HENRI DE SAINT-VICTOR)****

The tall, handsome, aristocratic-looking Comte Henri de Saint-Victor
makes one of the most impressive red wines of Bandol. White and rosé
wines are also produced at his estate of 74 acres located near the old
hill town of La Cadière d'Azur. The Comte is one of the few producers
to use new oak barrels for his red wine, which is a blend of 80%
Mourvèdre, 10% Grenache, and 10% Cinsault. Consequently, it often
has the toasty, vanillin aromas of new oak intertwined with scents of
berry fruit and wild herbs. Of all the Bandol wines, the Domaine de
Pibarnon seems to receive the most medals and awards at the yearly
French wine competitions. The rosé here is good, though hardly the
best of the appellation, and the white wine simple, fresh, well made,
and pleasant.

VINTAGES

1985—*Bandol Rosé*—Lovely scents of strawberry fruit are fresh and
· lively. Spicy, fresh, and light, this is a good rosé. Last tasted
83 10/86.

1985—*Bandol (white)*—A very high-acid style with little fruit, there is
· a crispness and cleanliness to this wine, but little else to get
78 excited about. Last tasted 10/86.

1985—*Bandol (red)*—Deep in color, very spicy with scents of ripe berry
· fruit and toast, this full-bodied wine has plenty of extract and
85 should age well. Anticipated maturity: 1989–1996. Last tasted
10/86.

1983—*Bandol (red)*—Aromas of blackcurrants and other berry fruit
  · dominate the bouquet. On the palate, the wine is medium-
  85 bodied, tannic, and stylish. Anticipated maturity: 1988–1993.
  Last tasted 10/86.
1982—*Bandol (red)*—One of the finest Bandols I have tasted, the 1982,
  · which is pure Mourvèdre, has a toasty, rich, multidimensional
  90 bouquet, opaque color, a very rich, concentrated yet tannic palate impression, and smashing length. Anticipated maturity:
  1990–2000. Last tasted 10/86.

CHÂTEAU PRADEAUX (MLLE. DE PORTALIS)****

One of the more eccentric domaines of Bandol, Château Pradeaux is
run by the rather difficult Comtesse Arlette Portalis. She seems to have
a distaste for visitors, and is unwilling to offer an explanation of why
she ages her red Bandol a minimum of four full years in oak barrels.
Perhaps her keen interest in cats—the run-down château is filled with
cats of all types, sizes, and ages, all of which she adores—precludes
any attention to visitors. Her estate of 59 acres is near St.-Cyr-sur-Mer.
Her red wine, a blend of 95% Mourvèdre and 5% Grenache, boasts the
oldest vines in Bandol, and can be the most dramatic wine of the appellation in those vintages where the fruit is ripe and concentrated
enough to handle four to as many as eight years of oak. In the lighter
years, her inability to demonstrate flexibility often results in the wine
tasting oxidized, dried out, and of course excessively oaky. This inconsistency should not deter one from experiencing the wines of Pradeaux
in top years such as 1975, 1979, and presumably, 1982 and 1985.

VINTAGES

1981—*Bandol (red)*—Faded, washed-out flavors exhibit only the scents
  · and flavors of oak barrels since the fruit has dried out. Last
  64 tasted 10/86.
1979—*Bandol (red)*—A great wine that is deep in color and very spicy
  · with a bouquet of tobacco, ripe plums, fresh thyme, and roasted
  90 chestnuts. This intense, full-bodied wine has layers of fruit and
  extract, and while drinkable now, will keep 5–8 years. Very
  special. Last tasted 10/86.
1975—*Bandol (red)*—The full-intensity bouquet of oriental spices,
  · toasty oak, and ripe fruit is very captivating. On the palate, the
  87 wine is full-bodied, powerful, still tannic, but delicious. Drink
  over the next 5–6 years. Last tasted 10/86.

DOMAINE RAY JANE (R. CONSTANT) * * * *

This tiny estate of 27 acres is planted with 80% Mourvèdre and the balance Grenache and Cinsault. The vines are among the oldest of Bandol. The proprietor, the wrinkled, squeaky-voiced Raymond Constant, produces massive, backward, tannic wines that require (in the top vintages) at least a decade of cellaring. The wines here are made very traditionally, not destalked, nor fined or filtered. Therefore, they are the densest in color and flavor extract of all the Bandols.

VINTAGES

1985—*Bandol (red)*—Black/ruby in color, with a huge, gamelike,
· smoky blackberry bouquet, huge, massive tannic flavors and
90 body, this large-proportioned wine needs plenty of cellaring to reveal its potential. Anticipated maturity: 1995–2005. Last tasted 3/87.

1984—*Bandol (red)*—Less massive than the 1985, the 1984 is fruity,
· medium-bodied, quite deep in color, well balanced, but a bit
83 short in the finish. Anticipated maturity: 1989–1993. Last tasted 3/87.

1982—*Bandol (red)*—An intense bouquet of smoky, plummy, spicy
· fruit is followed by a wine that is dense, powerful, loaded with
86 extract, still very unevolved, but very promising. Anticipated maturity: 1992–2003. Last tasted 3/87.

CHÂTEAU ROMASSAN (OTT FRÈRES) * * * *

Probably no producer's name in Provence is better known than that of the Ott family. Originally from Alsace, the Ott family moved to Provence at the end of the nineteenth century, and has since introduced thousands, if not millions, of tourists visiting both Provence and the Côte d'Azur to this region's wines, particularly the Ott rosés, which are among the most thirst-satisfying in the world. Much of the credit for this must got to Marcel Ott, a handsome, distinguished, middle-aged man who can often be spotted flitting back and forth between his properties in Provence in what must be one of the most decrepit-looking Citroëns in France. His brother manages their domaine in Bandol, the lovely Château Romassan, a 25-acre property that produces 3,200 cases of red and rosé wine. Ott's wine is of very good quality, distinguished by the eccentric bottle they have chosen to commercialize the majority of their wines. Given the great popularity and unrelenting demand for Ott's wines, they rarely represent the bargains that other wines do; however, the quality level is consistently very high.

VINTAGES

1985—*Bandol Rosé*—This is about as good as rosé wine can be. Bright
· salmon in color with an intense bouquet of berry fruit and flow-
87 ers, what sets Ott's rosé apart is its surprising body and depth.
On a hot summer day, this would be my ideal beverage. Last
tasted 1/87.

1985—*Bandol (red)*—Very deeply colored with a ripe, roasted black
· cherry bouquet, Ott's red Bandol is plump, full-bodied, chewy,
85 and will mature nicely for 5–10 years. Anticipated maturity:
1989–1997. Last tasted 10/86.

1984—*Bandol (red)*—A lively, spicy bouquet is followed by a wine that
· is soft, fruity, not very deep, but fully mature and pleasurable.
82 Drink it over the next 3 years. Last tasted 10/86.

1983—*Bandol (red)*—The 1983 has more stuffing than the 1984. An
· interesting bouquet of cured olives and Provençal herbs jumps
84 from the glass. On the palate, the wine is soft and round. Drink
it up. Last tasted 10/86.

1982—*Bandol (red)*—A more powerful wine than the 1983 or 1985, the
· 1982 is still quite deep in color, loaded with berry fruit and the
85 scent of herbs, full-bodied and deep as well as balanced enough
to age well. Anticipated maturity: now–1993. Last tasted 10/86.

1961—*Bandol (red)*—This was shown to me by the Otts in order to
· display the aging potential of the red wines of Bandol. Orange at
75 the rim with an aroma of tea leaves and fading fruit, it still had
a good measure of character and fruit on the palate, and though
obviously very old, was still quite drinkable. Last tasted 10/86.

CHÂTEAU SAINTE-ANNE (DUTHEIL DE LA ROCHÈRE)***

The production of this 50-acre estate in Ste.-Anne d'Evenos is split
evenly between red and rosé Bandol wine. A tiny quantity of white wine
is made also. The Marquis Dutheil de la Rochère runs the property with
considerable enthusiasm. In tasting through the wines, I found the rosé
very good, the white quite flat and dull, and the red wine very inconsistent from vintage to vintage.

VINTAGES

1985—*Bandol Rosé*—One of the better rosés of the appellation, the
· 1985 rosé from Ste. Anne is very aromatic, dry, and loaded with
84 fruit and flavor. Last tasted 10/86.

1985—*Bandol (white)*—The 1985 white Bandol is very dull, low in acid-
·   ity, flat, and lacking in fruit. Last tasted 10/86.
70

1985—*Bandol (red)*—Quite full-bodied, aromatic, rich in fruit, and
·   deeply colored, the 1985 Ste.-Anne red is a very promising Ban-
86   dol. Anticipated maturity: 1989–1995. Last tasted 10/86.

1984—*Bandol (red)*—Very light in color with simple, thin, somewhat
·   diluted flavors, this meagerly endowed wine should be drunk up.
72   Last tasted 10/86.

1983—*Bandol (red)*—A soft, moderately intense bouquet of raspberry
·   fruit is pleasant. On the palate, the wine is medium-bodied and
78   round, but lacking depth and distinction. Last tasted 10/86.

1982—*Bandol (red)*—A delicious wine, the 1982 has a deep color, a
·   big, spicy, richly scented bouquet of raspberry fruit and licorice,
85   full body, a supple, creamy texture, and good follow-through.
        Anticipated maturity: now–1993. Last tasted 10/86.

DOMAINE DES SALETTES (JEAN-PIERRE BOYER)***

One of the oldest domaines in Bandol, the Domaine des Salettes was
founded in 1602. Now owned by Jean-Pierre Boyer, an outgoing,
friendly man, the estate consists of 151 acres, though only 52 are currently under vine. Boyer uses more Grenache in his Bandol than other
producers. The blend he prefers for his red wine is 50% Mourvèdre,
20% Grenache, 20% Cinsault, and 10% Carignan from very old vines.
In contrast to other Bandol estates, he makes more rosé (3,900 cases)
than red (3,500 cases). Thankfully, only 400 cases of a bland white wine
are produced. Domaine des Salettes is an emerging estate in Bandol. A
completely new cellar was installed in 1984, and a proportion of new
oak barrels is now being used. This is a property to watch.

VINTAGES

1985—*Bandol Rosé*—A fresh, floral, fruity nose is clean and charming.
·   Like all Bandol rosés, this wine should be drunk over the next
82   year. Last tasted 10/86.

1985—*Bandol (red)*—Extremely impressive, the 1985 from Salettes is
·   one of the best wines of this excellent vintage in Bandol. It is
88   full-bodied, opaque, deep in extract, and long on the palate.
        Proprietor Boyer thinks it is the finest wine he has made. Antic-
        ipated maturity: 1990–2000. Last tasted 10/86.

1984—*Bandol (red)*—Very Bordeaux-like with the smell of new oak
·   barrels, the 1984 has a ripe, spicy, oaky nose, deep color, and is
85   undoubtedly a top success for this mixed vintage. Anticipated
     maturity: 1988–1994. Last tasted 10/86.
1982—*Bandol (red)*—A flawed wine, the 1982 is very musty and dirty
·   in its aroma, which spoils both the bouquet and flavors. Last
55   tasted 10/86.

DOMAINE TEMPIER (L. PEYRAUD)*****

The most vivacious, outgoing, charming as well as colorful proprietor I
have ever met must be Lucien Peyraud, the owner of the Domaine
Tempier. The squeaky voiced, diminutive Peyraud has a *joie de vivre*
and presence far greater than his size would suggest. Together, Peyraud and his effervescent wife of over 50 years, Lulu, have done much
to resurrect the reputation of the wines of Bandol. President of one of
the two syndicates of Bandol for 35 years, Peyraud was instrumental in
setting the high minimum requirement of 50% Mourvèdre and for keeping the yield of juice per acre conservatively restricted. This did not sit
well with some of the growers who had large plantings of the prolific
and easier to grow Grenache in their vineyards, and it is therefore not
surprising to hear several of the other Bandol growers criticize Peyraud.
The other syndicate of Bandol growers is headed by the Bunan family,
who own Mas de la Rouvière and Moulin des Costes. There is an obvious philosophical difference of opinion between the Peyrauds and
Bunans regarding the production and marketing of Bandol wine, yet
Lucien Peyraud has prevailed, and does indeed produce the appellation's greatest and longest-lived red wine, as well as its finest rosé. He
makes no white wine, claiming that the soil and climate are unsuitable
for the production of an interesting white wine.

The Peyraud cellars are in La Plan du Castellet. Lucien is helped by
his two sons, Jean-Marie and François, as well as by many visiting
Americans who seem to make Domaine Tempier a required stop on
their trips to Provence. The famous chef Alice Waters of Berkeley's
celebrated Chez Panisse is a frequent visitor here and generously gives
credit to Lulu Peyraud, a fabulous cook, for having had a profound
influence on her own culinary approach. And the noted food and wine
author Richard Olney, who lives in Provence, is another frequent visitor. The Domaine Tempier seems to be a mecca for those wanting to
experience spectacular hospitality, superb wine, and the innovative
cuisine of Lulu Peyraud.

The Domaine Tempier is not large. There are 64 acres of vineyards spread about on the hillsides of this bucolic, privileged area. There are five grape varieties planted at Tempier, including Grenache, Cinsault, Syrah, and Carignan, but Mourvèdre accounts for 54% of their vineyards and represents at least 50% to 80% of their red Bandol.

There are two basic red wines made here, a regular cuvée and a Cuvée Spéciale, the latter having 10–20% more Mourvèdre in it. Much of the Cuvée Spéciale also contains a healthy dosage of wine from the Peyrauds' two prized hillside vineyards, La Tourtine and La Migoua. In some vintages, the Peyrauds offer limited quantities (usually about 1,100 cases each) of the single-vineyard Bandols called La Tourtine and La Migoua. This practice was started only in 1979. Both single-vineyard wines are well worth seeking out because of their quality and rarity, but even other Bandol producers acknowledge that La Tourtine, a especially steep vineyard of 46-year-old-vines, carved from the hillside below the medieval village of Le Castellet, is in all probability the best single spot for making wine in the appellation.

Domaine Tempier is a very naturally made wine that changes and evolves constantly in the bottle. While the delicious, fragrant, aromatic rosé must be drunk within two to three years of the vintage, the red Bandols made here, particularly the two vineyard-designated wines and the Cuvée Spéciale, can age easily for 10–15 years. They are the quintessential Bandols, and will be revelations to those who have not tried them.

VINTAGES

1985—*Bandol Rosé*—Medium salmon-colored, Tempier's rosé vies
· with several Tavels of the Rhône Valley as being the finest still
87 rosé in the world. It is full-bodied, very fragrant, distinctive, quite dry, and loaded with berry fruit. It goes down far too easily for its 12.5% alcohol. Last tasted 1/87.

1985—*Bandol Cuvée Spéciale*—Similar to the 1979, the 1985 has very
· good color, a lovely floral, spicy, berry-scented bouquet, me-
87 dium to full body, and a forward, lush charm. Anticipated maturity: 1989–1996. Last tasted 10/86.

1984—*Bandol Cuvée Spéciale*—The Cuvée Spéciale is 96% Mourvèdre
· and 4% Cinsault. Deeper-colored than the 1985, richly fruity yet
86 firm and tannic on the palate, medium-bodied, and in need of cellaring, this wine, when it blossoms, may merit a higher rating. Anticipated maturity: 1990–1997. Last tasted 10/86.

1983—*Bandol (red)*—Softer than the spéciale cuvées, with a deep color
· and a pronounced bouquet of berry fruit, herbs, leather, and
85 spices, this is a very elegantly wrought wine with 5–6 years of
evolution ahead of it. Anticipated maturity: 1988–1994. Last
tasted 10/86.

1983—*Bandol La Tourtine (red)*—The percentage of Mourvèdre is 80%
· in the 1983 La Tourtine. It is more tannic and less obvious than
87 the regular bottling. Spicy, olive-and-herb-scented, less opulent
and fruity, it is a thoroughbred in need of 5–7 years of cellaring.
Only 500 cases of La Tourtine were made in 1983, and since the
drought had so reduced the crop size, no vineyard-designated
La Migoua was produced. Anticipated maturity: 1990–2005.
Last tasted 2/87.

1983—*Bandol Cuvée Spéciale (red)*—Slightly less tannic than the La
· Tourtine, the 1983 Cuvée Spéciale is dark, quite rich and full-
88 bodied, but loaded with fruit, exotic spices, scents of licorice
and black cherries, and has a very long finish. For the moment,
I prefer it to the La Tourtine. Anticipated maturity: 1990–2000.
Last tasted 10/86.

1982—*Bandol (red)*—Nineteen eighty-two, according to the Peyrauds,
· is their finest vintage since 1970. The wines are much more
87 concentrated and powerful than normal, and have two decades
of aging potential. The regular cuvée, made from 50% Mourvèdre, 30% Grenache, and 20% Cinsault, is a big, chewy, rich
wine with long, creamy flavors. Anticipated maturity: 1988–
1998. Last tasted 10/86.

1982—*Bandol La Migoua (red)*—Very deeply colored with a super bou-
· quet of roasted cherries, herbs, flowers, licorice, and spicy oak,
90 this full-bodied wine has outstanding depth and a vast, exceptional finish. The 14.3% natural alcohol is well hidden behind a
cascade of fruit. Anticipated maturity: 1989–2002. Last tasted
10/86.

1982—*Bandol La Tourtine (red)*—In comparison with the Migoua, the
· Tourtine has 80% Mourvèdre (versus 55% for Migoua) and less
90 Grenache in its composition. With 14.5% natural alcohol, it is
the most powerful wine made at Tempier since the 1970. Extremely deep in color, very chewy, dense, and filled with fruit,
this is a stunning wine that will provide great enjoyment for a
long time. Anticipated maturity: 1990–2005. Last tasted 10/86.

1982—*Bandol Cuvée Spéciale (red)*—Made from 75% Mourvèdre, the
· 1982 Cuvée Spéciale is more developed than the two single-
88 vineyard wines, has a complex, intense, smoked-meat, tobacco-

and-roasted-nut-scented bouquet, a rather huge, delicious, lush level of opulent fruit, and quite a finish. Anticipated maturity: now–1998. Last tasted 10/86.

1981—*Bandol La Tourtine (red)*—The 1981 Tourtine is an understated, elegant, spicy, polite wine with medium body and a restrained richness, but it has charm, finesse, and immediate appeal. Anticipated maturity: now–1993. Last tasted 10/86.

· 86

1981—*Bandol Cuvée Spéciale (red)*—Somewhat more open and fruity than the Tourtine, the Cuvée Spéciale has oodles of berry fruit, medium to full body, and a round, generous, supple finish. Anticipated maturity: now–1993. Last tasted 10/86.

· 86

1979—*Bandol Cuvée Spéciale (red)*—A bouquet of thyme and smoked meat is quite interesting. On the palate, the wine is medium-bodied, quite fruity, and very different in style, flavor, and texture from the single-vineyard Migoua. Drink it over the next 3–4 years. Last tasted 10/86.

· 85

1979—*Bandol La Migoua (red)*—The deep ruby color is still very youthful looking. The jammy bouquet suggests raspberries and violets, and there are heaps of plump, lush fruit in this full-bodied, youthful, yet supple wine. Tannin in the fruit suggests further aging potential. Anticipated maturity: now–1996. Last tasted 10/86.

· 88

1975—*Bandol Cuvée Spéciale (red)*—The bouquet of wild herbs, cherry fruit, fennel, and sweet candied fruit develops nicely in the glass. In the mouth, the velvety, sweet, ripe flavors persist, finishing with a powerful alcoholic kick. Fully mature, this wine will keep for 5–8 more years. Last tasted 6/85.

· 87

1970—*Bandol Cuvée Spéciale (red)*—A magnificent Bandol, the deep color, broad, sweet, plummy fruit, full body, and opulent, even unctuous texture give this wine tremendous palate presence. Very long and quite well preserved, this beautiful wine should be drunk over the next 4–5 years. Last tasted 6/84.

· 90

1961—*Bandol Cuvée Spéciale (red)*—This wine is now beginning to fade. In 1961 the Peyrauds employed only 50% Mourvèdre and so Grenache was much more in evidence. A fat, succulent texture with a hefty dose of alcohol gives a sweet, broad impression. The bouquet of roasted nuts and fruitcake is showing some signs of cracking up. Drink it up. Last tasted 6/84.

· 86

DOMAINE DE TERREBRUNE (GEORGES DELILLE)***

This estate is a relatively new enterprise created after 20 years of land clearing and preparation by the Delille family. The 49-acre vineyard extends over a series of hillside terraces, and is planted with 60% Mourvèdre, 20% Grenache, and 20% Cinsault. The Delilles acquired this lovely property in 1960, producing their first wine in 1975. The cellars, hollowed out of sheer rock, are spotless; major efforts being made toward quality are sure to be rewarded with better and better wines as the young vineyard matures. No white wine is produced, and as of 1986, the 6,000-case production consisted of 5,000 cases of red wine and 1,000 cases of rosé. The red wine spends two years in oak barrels, and then another two years in bottle prior to being offered for sale. The Delille family appears to have the advantage of sufficient financial resources to give their wine plenty of aging rather than rushing it to the market.

VINTAGES

1985—*Bandol (red)*—Very rich, powerful, intense, and potentially the best wine made at this young estate yet, the proprietor does not intend to put this wine on the market until 1989. Anticipated maturity: 1990–2002. Last tasted 10/86.

86

1983—*Bandol (red)*—The rich, complex, smoky, spicy nose suggests that a hefty percentage of Mourvèdre went into the makeup of this wine. On the palate, however, the wine tails off and the flavors do not live up to the bouquet's impression. Last tasted 10/86.

81

1982—*Bandol (red)*—Again, a very good, complex, ripe, interesting bouquet is followed by a wine that is somewhat shallow and light on the palate. Last tasted 10/86.

78

1981—*Bandol (red)*—Until the 1985, this was the best example of Domaine Terrebrune's Bandol I had tasted. A rich, roasted, plummy, exotic nose is followed by round, delicious, broad, fruity flavors. Drink it over the next 4–5 years. Last tasted 10/86.

85

1979—*Bandol (red)*—Light in color, and very light and a little feeble on the palate, this soft, one-dimensional wine requires drinking up. Last tasted 10/86.

70

CHÂTEAU VANNIÈRES (M. BOISSEAUX)****

The Bandol red wine produced at the beautiful Château Vannières is one of the finest of the appellation. This magnificent property situated near La Cadière d'Azur produces, in a good year, 13,000 cases of wine, two-thirds of which are red. The vineyard area covers 79 acres and is managed meticulously by Colette Boisseaux and her son, Eric. Along with the red wine from the Domaine Tempier, those of Château Vannières are among the longest-lived of the appellation—capable of lasting 10–20 years in specific vintages. I have never tasted the white wine made here, but the rosé is good, although not nearly as exciting as the red wine. Curiously, the label used by Vannières has more than a casual resemblance to that employed at the famous Château Lafite-Rothschild in Bordeaux. Coincidentally, the red wine of Vannières surprisingly has the cedary fragrance one often associates with a fine Pauillac.

VINTAGES

1983—*Bandol (red)*—Medium to deep ruby with spicy, leathery,
· smoked meat, and cedary aromas, this fleshy, medium- to full-
86 bodied wine has open, juicy flavors, a very concentrated taste, and a soft, silky finish. Anticipated maturity: now–1994. Last tasted 10/86.

1982—*Bandol (red)*—Slightly deeper color than the 1983, with a rich
· berry and Provençal herb-scented bouquet, as well as a touch of
87 cedar, this full-bodied, concentrated wine shows considerable power and finesse, and should age quite well. Anticipated maturity: now–1996. Last tasted 10/86.

1979—*Bandol (red)*—An elegant, spicy, fruity bouquet exhibits good
· cedary, herbaceous aromas. On the palate, the wine is less deep
84 and complex when compared with the 1982 and 1983, but is open and fully mature. Drink it over the next 4–5 years. Last tasted 10/86.

1975—*Bandol (red)*—The big, cedary, spice box bouquet seems to sug-
· gest a fine Pauillac as much as the label does. Rich, supple, ripe
86 fruity flavors are still fresh and lively. This medium- to full-bodied wine has a broad, creamy finish, and should be drunk over the next 4–5 years. Last tasted 10/86.

Other Bandol Producers

Domaine de L'Aouque (Jeannot Gantelme), Sainte-Anne du Castellet
Domaine des Baguiers (Gaec Jourdan), Le Plan du Castellet
Château des Baumelles (Thierry Grand), Saint-Cyr-sur-Mer
Château Braquety (Comte J. F. de Régis), Le Castellet
Château de Castillon (René de Saqui de Sannes), Sainte-Anne du Castellet

Domaine de Cayenne (Pierre Ventre), Le Plan du Castellet

Domaine des Costes-Gallines (Maurice Hautemulle), La Cadière d'Azur

Domaine de la Garenne (Comte Jean de Balincourt), La Cadière d'Azur

Domaine de la Loubière (Emile Canolle), La Cadière d'Azur

Caves Maillet (Claude Maillet), Le Beausset

Les Maîtres Vignerons du Beausset, Le Beausset

Domaine Maubernard (Les Héritiers de Maître Vidal), Saint-Cyr-sur-Mer

Mazet de Cassan (Monique Barthes-Dray), Le Beausset

Le Grand Moulin (Louis Brian), La Cadière d'Azur

Moulin de la Salle (Denis Roussellier), Saint-Cyr-sur-Mer

Domaine du Moutin (Bruno Jaubert), La Cadière d'Azur

Domaine de L'Olivette (Mme. Dumoutier), Le Brulat du Castellet

Domaine du Pey Neuf (Roger Arnaud), La Cadière d'Azur

Domaine Racine (Vincent Racine), Le Camp du Castellet

Domaine de la Ribotte (Maurice Desblaches), Le Plan du Castellet

Cave de la Roque, La Cadière d'Azur

Domaine de la Serre (Albert Cordeil), La Cadière d'Azur

Mas Thérèse (Gantelme), Sainte-Anne du Castellet

Domaine de la Tour du Bon (Mme. Hocquard), Le Brulat du Castellet

Domaine de la Vivonne (William Gilpin), Le Castellet

BELLET

Nice's Best-Kept Secret

BELLET AT A GLANCE

Type of wine produced:	Red, white, and rosé
Grape varieties planted:	An unusual concoction of grapes is found there: for white wine, Chardonnay and the Rolle are the principal varieties; for red and rosé, Folle Noire, Fuella, and Braquet, also Cinsault
Acres currently under vine:	111
Quality level:	Above average to very good
Aging potential:	White and rosé wines: 1–3 years
	Red wines: 3–7 years
General characteristics:	White wine: fleshy, chunky, surprisingly tasty and good

	Rosé wine: rare, but delicate and fresh
	Red wine: variable, can be heavy and alcoholic, but also ageworthy and elegant
Greatest recent vintages:	1985, 1982
Price range:	$8–$12

Tucked up in the hills behind the fashionable international seaside playground of Nice is the micro-appellation of Bellet. It is rare to find any of this wine outside the restaurants of France's Côte d'Azur since the production is tiny and the local demand is more than sufficient to dry up all that is produced. The vineyards are among the oldest in France, and it is believed that they were originally cultivated by Phocaean Greeks who colonized this area in 500 B.C. The fact that they still exist is remarkable, for they cover some of the most cherished real estate in the world, with developers willing to pay a fortune to replace the vines with high-rise condominiums.

The wines themselves are surprisingly good; Bellet has not only a unique microclimate but some especially rare grape varieties planted here that exist in only a few appellations of France. The most unusual include the white varietal called Rolle and a curiosity seen in Piedmont, Italy, but rarely in France, the red grape **Braquet**. The microclimate of Bellet is cooler than other areas of Provence. During the day, the sea breezes provide a cooling effect to the area, and at night the nearby mountains provide another set of winds that funnel down cool air from the higher altitudes. The result is that the harvest at Bellet rarely occurs before the middle of October, a time when most other regions of France have completed the *vendange*.

Between the red, white, and rosé wines, I prefer the white and rosé, although the red wine from the Château de Crémat is very good.

CHÂTEAU DE BELLET (GHISLAIN DE CHARNACÉ)

This tiny estate of 25 acres produces a very good white wine from the Rolle grape (a little Chardonnay is added), and a surprisingly long-lived rosé and red wine. The confident Ghislain de Charnacé owns this wealthy-looking estate and boasts that all of his wine is sold locally. The 1985 white is one of the most impressive Provence white wines I have tasted, full-bodied with heaps of fruit, and a spicy, intense bouquet. It is easy to see why these wines are so popular with the local fish soups and seafood. In 1986, I tasted a string of rosés back to 1979 that were all in amazing condition, disproving the idea that all rosés must be drunk within several years of the vintage. Unfortunately, unless you are dining on the French Riviera, particularly in the environs of Nice, you are unlikely to come across these well-made wines.

CLOS SAINT-VINCENT (RENÉ GOMEZ)

This tiny gem of a property, only five acres, produces an excellent wine from 70% Rolle, 20% Roussanne, and 10% Chardonnay. The 1983 and 1985 were very spicy, full-bodied, distinctive wines oozing with fruit and personality. The wines are only available within the Nice area since proprietor René Gomez has insufficient quantities to export.

CHÂTEAU DE CRÉMAT (JEAN BAGNIS)

The finest wines of the Bellet appellation are made by the Bagnis family from their splendid property in the hills behind Nice. They have 49 acres of vineyards, but their yields are so small they produce only 6,000 cases of wine, divided equally between a very fragrant, dry, stylish rosé, a big, fleshy, intense white, and a surprisingly long-lived, elegant, refined red wine. This same family also produces over 300,000 cases of Côtes de Provence wines from their négociant business under the trade name L'Estandon.

The white wine here is made from the spicy Rolle (90%), and the balance Chardonnay and Clairette. The red and rosé are produced from 60% Folle Noire, 30% Cinsault, and 10% Braquet. (The white wine is also very good.) The 1985 is excellent and the 1983 was still drinking well in 1986. I highly recommend Château de Crémat's 1985 rosé, which can rival the exquisite rosé made by the Domaine Tempier in Bandol.

As for the red wines, they have an undeniable burgundy-like character, with broad, soft, cherry flavors and a harmonious elegance and balance. The best recent vintages have been 1985, 1983, 1981, 1979, and 1978. The latter two vintages are in wonderful condition, proving that these particular wines do indeed evolve much longer than many have thought.

Château de Crémat is a very reliable producer that does export, so the wines from this estate can be found. They are well worth trying.

DOMAINE DE LOU CLOT DE LA TOURÉ
(J. SCHNEIDER-QUINAT)

Another good but very tiny estate of 9.9 acres in Bellet, obtusely named the Domaine de Lou Clot de la Touré, produces all three wines permitted under the Bellet appellation laws. However, the white and rosé here are less vibrant and fresh than elsewhere; but the red, a blend of Grenache, Folle Noire, Braquet, and Cinsault, is quite round, spicy and well made. The 1983 and 1981 are the top recent successes.

CASSIS

White Wines of Undeniable Character

CASSIS AT A GLANCE

Type of wine produced:	Red and rosé, but primarily white wines (70% of the production)
Grape varieties planted:	Ugni Blanc is the preferred choice for white wine, but Clairette, Sauvignon, Bourboulenc, Pascal Blanc, and Marsanne are also planted
	For the red and rosé wines, Grenache, Mourvèdre, Cinsault, and Carignan are used
Acres currently under vine:	400
Quality level:	Red and rosé wines: mediocre
	White wines: good
Aging potential:	1–3 years

General characteristics:	Rosé and red wines are usually dull White wines are vividly scented with wild herbs and flowers, and are full-bodied—an ideal wine with the spicy fish soup called bouillabaisse
Greatest recent vintage:	1985
Price range:	$7–$9

The tiny fishing port of Cassis, the most westerly resort on France's Côte d'Azur, lies in a secluded bay dwarfed by the surrounding steep limestone cliffs. The charm of Cassis has somehow been maintained, although the area is congested with hordes of tourists during the summer. Cassis has a justifiable reputation as an artists' village —Matisse, Dufy, and Vlaminck have all made it a subject of their paintings. It is also well known for its white wine. Although reds and rosés are made here, it is the white wine that seems to magically enhance and complement the mounds of fresh fruits de mer and many renditions of soupe de poissons that the local bistros serve. The vineyards of Cassis almost abut the azure-colored sea, being encroached on from all sides by the housing boom in this area. Gradually the surface area under vine has declined from over 1,200 acres a hundred years ago to one-third of that today. Like the small appellation of Bellet, Cassis has most of its production gobbled up by the local seafood restaurants and those in nearby Marseille. At present, there are four very fine domaines making meritorious wines in Cassis. The white wine of each of them is a serious, aromatic, spicy, fleshy wine that seems to beg for seafood as an accompaniment.

DOMAINE DU BAGNOL (MARQUIS DE FESQUES)
This small but excellent domaine of 17.3 acres produces red, white, and rosé wines, but it is the latter two that merit the most attention. The white wine is one of the most robust and spicy of the appellation, and seems also to have more alcohol to it. The rosé is very fruity, dry, and quite full-bodied as well. This estate made the finest 1984 of the appellation, and followed that vintage with an excellent 1985.

CLOS STE.-MAGDELAINE (SACK-ZAFIROPULO)
Only 4,100 cases of wine are produced from the 25-acre vineyard called the Clos Ste.-Magdelaine. Set against the magnificent cliffs of Cap Canaille on one side and the sea on the other, few vineyards in the world

can lay claim to a more enchanting setting. I have never tasted the small quantity of rosé made here, but the white wine, usually a brilliant golden color and made from 35% Ugni Blanc, 30% Marsanne, 30% Clairette, and 5% Sauvignon, is one of the best white wines of Provence, and is full-bodied and flavorful enough to stand up against the hottest and most powerful soupe de poissons. It will keep three to four years, and 1985, 1983, and 1982 are the top recent vintages.

LA FERME BLANCHE (FRANÇOIS PARET)

One of the oldest estates in Cassis, La Ferme Blanche has been run by the Paret family since 1715. At present they own 74 acres and produce on average 13,200 cases of wine, 60% of it white. The white wine here is very fruity, somewhat lighter than the other wines of Cassis, very fragrant, and one of my favorites of the appellation. It is made from a blend of 40% Clairette, 25% Ugni Blanc, 15% Bourboulenc, 10% Marsanne, and 10% Sauvignon. Both the 1985 and 1984 produced here were delicious white wines. The red wine is rather heavy and bland, but the rosé in 1985 showed finesse as well as good freshness and fruit.

CHÂTEAU DE FONTCREUSE (J. MAFFEI)

This 49-acre estate is dedicated exclusively to making white wine from a blend of 40% Ugni Blanc, 25% Marsanne, 25% Clairette, and 10% Bourboulenc. Château de Fontcreuse is a true château, and its proprietor, Joseph Maffei, is one of this appellation's most ardent proponents. He produces two Cassis wines, a good, normal cuvée and a very limited edition wine from an elevated cliffside vineyard called Coteaux Cassidains. Many observers feel that the Cassis made here is the finest of the appellation. The 1983 and 1985 are both robust, full-flavored wines that are ideal with seafood.

DOMAINE DU PATERNEL (JEAN-PIERRE SANTINI)

The 30-acre Domaine du Paternel makes straightforward, fairly one-dimensional wines. The white wine is often rather dark yellow in color, clumsy and flat in taste, and seemingly lacking in acidity. Recent vintages, such as 1983, 1984, and 1985, continued this stylistic approach.

COTEAUX
D'AIX-EN-PROVENCE

Great Potential

COTEAUX D'AIX-EN-PROVENCE AT A GLANCE

Type of wine produced:	Primarily red wines, some rosés, a few white wines
Grape varieties planted:	Syrah, Mourvèdre, Grenache, Cabernet Sauvignon, and Cinsault are primarily used for the red wine and rosé; for white wine, the standard southern Rhône Valley varieties as well as Chardonnay
Acres currently under vine:	7,900, of which 7,400 are within the Coteaux d'Aix-en-Provence and 500 in the area known as the Coteaux des Baux-en-Provence
Quality level:	Mediocre to exceptional

Aging potential:	Normally, 3–6 years; a few properties produce wines that can last 10–15 years
General characteristics:	Tremendous variation in styles among the red wines, ranging from one-dimensional, fruity wines to serious, even profound, ageworthy classics from estates such as Trévallon and Vignelaure; the rosés can be excellent
Greatest recent vintages:	1985, 1983, 1982, 1978
Price range:	$6–$12

For years it was accepted doctrine that this large area, primarily north and west of Aix-en-Provence, could not produce fine wine. Yet a few courageous pioneers cast their fortunes with grape varieties such as Cabernet Sauvignon, Cinsault, Syrah, and Mourvèdre rather than the heretofore popular Grenache and Carignan. The results were promising, and together with the advent of modern technology, great advances in winemaking have been made in the overall quality level of the wines. This progress, most of it since the late seventies, has resulted in the area being upgraded from a VDQS wine region to full appellation contrôlée status. This occurred in 1984, and included within the Coteaux d'Aix-en-Provence appellation another VDQS area, the Coteaux des Baux-en-Provence, a small viticultural region south of Avignon and northeast of Arles. Despite the fact that it is within the Coteaux d'Aix appellation, the wines, the soils, and the microclimates are totally different, and I for one wonder why the Coteaux des Baux did not receive its own separate appellation.

Most of the best vineyards in these areas are planted in the clay/limestone soils of the hillsides that seem particularly favorable to the Cabernet Sauvignon and Syrah grapes. There are few old vineyards, since winemaking and viticulture are a relatively recent development. I suspect that in 20 years this area will be studded with new domaines, as the potential for excellent wine becomes more successfully realized. For now, this is a source of some wonderful, undervalued red wines, a mixed bag of rosés ranging from poor to excellent, and a handful of decent white wines. The future, however, looks exciting.

RECENT VINTAGES

1986—Most growers seem to have weathered the severe rainstorms that hit the area in mid-October. The late pickers continued to harvest until early November under ideal conditions, as the cool, inland temperatures and gusty winds permitted the soils to dry out. It will be a variable vintage, but most growers seem satisfied that they have had a good year. Optimum maturity: 1989–1996.

1985—An excellent year, although the intense heat and drought caused stress in certain young vineyards. Highly regarded, 1985 will produce many very fine, special wines, but it is far more inconsistent than many reports have indicated. Optimum maturity: 1989–1999.

1984—A tough vintage because of the cool, wet summer, many of the wines have turned out much better than expected, with less opulence but good, healthy bouquets and fine color. Optimum maturity: 1988–1994.

1983—An exceptional vintage and the best year in this area since 1975. The wines are rich, tannic, and well balanced, with excellent color and staying power. Both Château Vignelaure and Domaine Trévallon made stunning wines that will last for more than a decade. Optimum maturity: now–1996.

OLDER VINTAGES

The top older vintages have been 1982, 1979. 1975, 1971, and 1970.

A Personal Rating of the Coteaux d'Aix-en-Provence Producers

***** (OUTSTANDING PRODUCERS)
Domaine Trévallon

**** (EXCELLENT PRODUCERS)
Château Vignelaure

*** (GOOD PRODUCERS)

Château Bas	Domaine de La Grande
Domaine les Bastides	Séouve
Château Beaupré	Mas de La Dame
Château La Coste	Mas de Gourgonnier
Château de Fonscolombe	Mas Sainte-Berthe

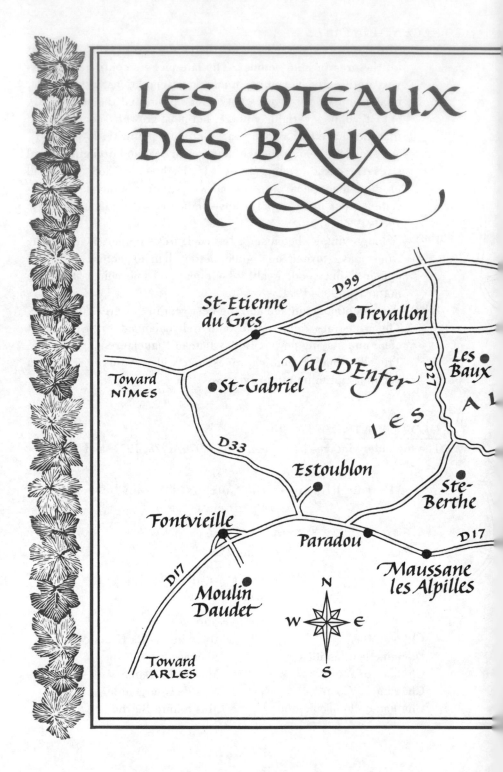

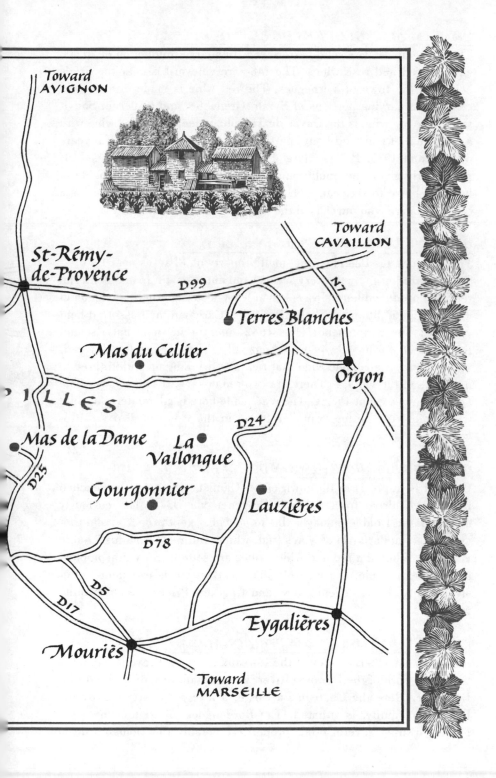

Toward
AVIGNON

Toward
CAVAILLON

St-Rémy-
de-Provence

D99

N7

Terres Blanches

Mas du Cellier

Orgon

ILLES

D24

Mas de la Dame

La
Vallongue

D25

Gourgonnier

Lauzières

D78

D5

D17

Eygalières

Mouriès

Toward
MARSEILLE

CHÂTEAU BAS (GEORGES DE BLANQUET) ***

The Château Bas is a solid performer with a large production of 20,000 cases of red and rosé wines. The 148-acre vineyard is near the firm's cellars in the town of Vernegues. The red wine is made in a modern cellar from varying portions of Syrah, Grenache, and Cabernet Sauvignon. The top wine is the Cuvée du Temple, a deeply colored wine with a good deal of fruit and body, particularly in the very successful years of 1983 and 1985. Prices charged for Château Bas are quite modest, particularly given the quality and the fact that the wine is capable of lasting for five to six years. The proprietor, Georges de Blanquet, is a German native who purchased the property only recently.

DOMAINE LES BASTIDES (JEAN SALEN) ***

The Domaine les Bastides is a small property of 12 acres near Le Puy-Ste.-Réparade run by the very serious and enthusiastic Jean Salen. The red wine produced here always has at least 40% Cabernet Sauvignon in its blend, in addition to Syrah, Grenache, Carignan, and assorted field varieties. The wine spends from 16–24 months in small barrels, and this accounts for its oaky taste. It is usually a herbaceous, full-flavored, soft, somewhat alcoholic wine that requires drinking up within three to five years of the vintage. There are two red cuvées, the Cuvée Spéciale and the Cuvée Saint-Pierre. The rosé made here is adequate, the white wine among the better examples found in the Coteaux d'Aix-en-Provence.

CHÂTEAU BEAUPRÉ (BARON DOUBLE) ***

Château Beaupré is in the town of St.-Cannat, which can be reached by a lovely drive from Salon-de-Provence via D572. The curiously named Baron Double manages this impeccably kept property, and produces the standard trio of wines (red, white, and rosé) from his 79-acre vineyard. While the red and white wines are sound, fruity, uncomplex, and properly made, the rosé of Château Beaupré is excellent—effusively fruity, light, delicate, dry, and fragrant. Prices are again quite modest.

CHÂTEAU LA COSTE (SICA BORDONADO) ***

In the very northern sector of the Coteaux d'Aix-en-Provence appellation, just south of the Durance River, is the small town of Le Puy-Ste.-Réparade. Here the Château La Coste, a lovely property run by the Bordonado family, is situated. The Bordonados are significant winemakers owning several other properties, notably the Domaine de la

Grande Séouve in Jouques. At La Coste, they produce all three Provence wines from their 198-acre vineyard. These modernly made wines are hardly prodigious efforts, but offer considerable value and an uncomplicated, clean, fresh, lively, fruity character. They are wines to drink when very young, usually within three to four years of the vintage. Their top wine is a special red wine called Cuvée Lisa.

CHÂTEAU DE FONSCOLOMBE (MARQUIS DE SAPORTA) ***
The Château de Fonscolombe is also located in the town of Le Puy-Ste.-Réparade. All three wines are normally quite successful here. This large estate covers 411 acres and produces close to 95,000 cases of wine. The white wine tends to be very fruity and full-bodied, with surprising character for a Coteaux d'Aix white. The rosé is good, and the red wines, particularly the top of the line Cuvée Spéciale made from 40% Carignan, 20% Cabernet Sauvignon, 30% Grenache, and 10% Cinsault, and aged in cask, is quite fruity, fleshy, and supple, and can hold in the bottle for four to five years. The prices for the Fonscolombe wines are shockingly low.

DOMAINE DE LA GRANDE SÉOUVE (GFA BORDONADO) **
Another property of the Bordonado family, this 80-acre estate in Jouques produces very fruity, smooth, easy to drink red and white wine.

DOMAINE DES LAUZIÈRES (J. BOYER) **
The Domaine des Lauzières in the distinctive viticultural area known as the Coteaux des Baux-en-Provence has 74 acres of vines from which a sound but unexciting tannic red wine is produced. The proprietor, Joseph Boyer, ages his wine in cask; it is made from a blend of Syrah, Grenache, Carignan, Cinsault, Mourvèdre, and Cabernet Sauvignon. The 1981 and 1982 tasted quite mediocre, the 1983 much better.

MAS DE LA DAME (R. FAYE) ***
The 123-acre estate of the Mas de La Dame is superbly situated beneath the forbidding, eerie, jagged rock outcroppings of Les Alpilles that form the setting for the remarkable hill village of Les Baux, one of France's top tourist attractions. Their vineyard, just east of the Val d'Enfer (Valley of Hell) is the oldest in the Coteaux des Baux, and is planted with 60% Grenache and the balance in Cinsault, Syrah, Cabernet Sauvignon, and Carignan. The owner, Robert Faye, an ardent proponent of the region's wines, was the principal reason why this viticultural region was recognized in the early thirties as being capable of producing fine

wine. A good, sound, fruity rosé is also made. The red wine, aged in cask, is round, full-bodied, sometimes a little watery, but in years such as 1982 and 1983 delicious if drunk within five to six years of the vintage. It appears under the name of two cuvées, Cuvée Réserve du Mas and Cuvée Gourmande.

MAS DE GOURGONNIER (NICOLAS CARTIER)***
One of the best estates in the Coteaux de Baux is Nicolas Cartier's Mas de Gourgonnier, located a few miles south of the aforementioned Mas de La Dame. Run by Cartier, this 99-acre vineyard produces totally organic wines. The red wine, made from 35% Grenache, 15% Cinsault, 10% Syrah, 10% Cabernet Sauvignon, 10% Mourvèdre, and 20% Carignan, comes in two styles, a fruity, supple, pleasant regular cuvée and a special lot called La Réserve de Mas that has more Cabernet and Syrah in it. The 1982 and 1985 were rich, smoky, deep, and impressive. The white wine, a blend of Sauvignon, Ugni Blanc, and Grenache Blanc, is well made, a bit chunky but serviceable, and the rosé, pleasant, clean, fruity, and full-bodied. Prices are extremely reasonable.

MAS SAINTE-BERTHE (MME H. DAVID)**
Madame Hélène David owns and manages this 74-acre estate in the Coteaux de Baux. She produces a simple rosé and extremely light red wine from the carbonic maceration method. The production of 16,000 cases seems to be pushing the maximum for a property of this size, and that may also account for the lack of depth in many of the wines from the Mas Sainte-Berthe.

DOMAINE DES TERRES BLANCHES (NOEL MICHELIN)***
Near Saint-Rémy-de-Provence, where the artist Vincent van Gogh painted some of his most moving works and also was institutionalized, the 111-acre Domaine des Terres Blanches in the Coteaux de Baux is located. Proprietor Noel Michelin believes in totally organic wines; no insecticides or herbicides are used. The red wine is made from a blend of 20% Grenache, 50% Mourvèdre, and 30% Syrah. If the wine lacks excitement, it is also consistent from year to year, a trifle hard, but deep in color, cleanly made, and capable of holding in the bottle for at least four to six years. The 1982 and 1983 are more successful than the 1981 and 1984. An agreeable rosé wine is also produced here.

DOMAINE DE TRÉVALLON (E. DURRBACH)*****
One of the greatest discoveries in my life has been the wine made at the Domaine de Trévallon. Only an exciting red wine is made here,

though there are plans to eventually produce a white wine. Virtually everything about this compelling wine is unique. Eloi Durrbach, a ruggedly handsome man in his early forties, gave up a promising career in architecture in Paris to create a vineyard out of the lunarlike landscape near the medieval ghost town of Les Baux and the phantomlike, weird Val d'Enfer, or Valley of Hell. These vineyards, planted with 60% Cabernet Sauvignon and 40% Syrah, have performed magically since Durrbach produced his first wine in 1978. Durrbach apprenticed under Georges Brunet of Château Vignelaure prior to starting his vineyard, to get, as he says, "some confidence"; he now has 37 acres of vines that seem to grow from the bauxite rock crags of this forbidding, desolate, windswept, surreal area of France. And he intends to expand onto the 101 acres of unplanted land he owns.

Although Durrbach plans to make a white wine from an interesting blend of Chardonnay and Roussanne, his love is his red wine, of which he now produces 5,000 cases. The wine here is made very organically, no herbicides are used, and Durrbach refuses to either fine or filter his wine for fear of removing some of its flavor and intensity. His wine spends 18 months in small wooden foudres after a fermentation/maceration period that lasts four to five weeks, an exceptionally long time that no doubt accounts for the wine's amazing flavor extract.

Durrbach's biggest fans are in England and Holland, and he is now developing an American following. In addition, he sells his wine to several Michelin three-star restaurants, especially the nearby L'Oustau de Baumanière, which has bought his wine from the start. He argues that the English know more about fine wine than the French, saying he sells 1,000 cases in England each year but only 40 in Paris.

To taste Durrbach's staggering wines is to see a progression from very good wines in 1978 (his first vintage), made from four-year-old vines, to something sublime in 1985, produced from eleven-year-old vines. They seem to show greater depth and dimension with each passing year, and the prospects here look to be exhilarating. This is a very special wine worth every effort to find since it belongs in any serious collector's cellar.

VINTAGES

1985—*Trévallon (red)*—Fabulously rich, deep, black ruby in color, the 1985 has a cascade of silky, very concentrated cassis and blackberry fruit intermingled with scents of wild thyme. Full-bodied with melted, soft tannins, this wine will provide very enjoyable

· 90

drinking early on, but will keep. Anticipated maturity: 1989–2000. Last tasted 10/86.

1984—*Trévallon (red)*—Deep in color, although noticeably less opaque
· than surrounding vintages (1985 and 1983), the 1984 is a firmer,
87 more austere style of Trévallon that is long and full-bodied on the palate, but tight, with higher acidity and more aggressive tannins. Anticipated maturity: 1989–1996. Last tasted 10/86.

1983—*Trévallon (red)*—The 1983 is not unlike a top vintage of Hermi-
· tage La Chapelle, except for the addition of scents of Provençal
90 herbs in the bouquet. The huge aroma of cassis, tobacco, and tar oozes from the glass. In the mouth, the wine is massive yet balanced, and well delineated. This is a sumptuous, very impressive wine. Anticipated maturity: now–2000. Last tasted 2/87.

1982—*Trévallon (red)*—The explosive richness this wine has and its
· breadth and depth on the palate are quite remarkable. The bou-
92 quet of roasted smoked nuts, plums, cedar, and herb scents is stunning. Seductively sweet and layered on the palate with a very long, full-bodied finish, this wine is exciting to drink. Anticipated maturity: now–1996. Last tasted 10/86.

1981—*Trévallon (red)*—Much lighter and not nearly as massive as 1982
· or 1983, this vintage offers Trévallon at its most elegant and
87 stylish. Ripe fruit, floral, and mineral scents dominate the expansive bouquet. On the palate, the wine is medium- to full-bodied, round, very fruity and complex, and should drink well for 5–7 more years. Last tasted 10/86.

1980—*Trévallon (red)*—Medium ruby, with quite a bit of orange at the
· rim, the 1980 shows full maturity, a very spicy, herbaceous,
81 peppery nose, soft, fruity flavors, but a little dilution in the finish. Drink it up. Last tasted 10/86.

1978—*Trévallon (red)*—made from 4-year-old vines, the 1978 has a
· deep ruby color with some signs of age at the rim, a full-bodied,
85 richly fruity palate and good length, but seems to lack the dimension and extra depth of the vintages in the eighties. Drink it over the next 4–5 years. Last tasted 10/86.

*CHÂTEAU VIGNELAURE (G. BRUNET)*****

The lovely Château Vignelaure, situated in the rolling terrain of the Coteaux d'Aix-en-Provence near the quiet tree-lined town of Rians, is the most famous vineyard in Provence. The property is owned by

Georges Brunet, an entrepreneur and visionary who formerly owned the classified-growth Bordeaux estate, Château La Lagune. Brunet, a bald man in his sixties with an uncanny resemblance to the super-villain Blowfeld of James Bond movie fame, sold La Lagune in 1966 after he had totally rejuvenated the wine cellars and vineyards. He acquired Vignelaure in Provence that same year and planted 134 of the estate's 250 acres with an intriguing selection—60% Cabernet Sauvignon, 30% Syrah, and 10% Grenache. The blended wine is fermented in stainless steel tanks at a surprisingly cool temperature, given a 12–18 day maceration, and then aged 16–26 months in large oak casks from Hungary. Brunet shows great flexibility in aging his wine, depending on the level of extract in the wine. The 1984, a light year, received 16 months, 1983, Brunet's favorite vintage, 30 months, and 1985, another excellent year, 26 months.

Château Vignelaure's wines are very good to excellent and have shown increasing quality as Brunet's vineyard has matured. His estate is one of the showpiece properties not only of Provence, but of France. It appears to be more of an art gallery than a winery, since modern masterpieces by Buffet, Arman, the sculptor César, and the photographers Cartier-Bresson and Brassaï hang everywhere. From such a setting comes 25,000 cases a year of red wine that can age up to a decade in the top vintages. In 1983, Brunet began to make a stricter selection, producing a secondary wine from young vines and designated lots. It is called Le Page de Vignelaure.

Vignelaure is a serious wine, made organically by a man who has remarkable passion and energy for life and wine. Its price is moderate, particularly in view of the quality. As Vignelaure's reputation has increased, the wine has become more and more popular in the export markets. I did notice, sadly, that Brunet has begun to filter his wines for export, and that bottles tasted outside France seem less intense than the unfiltered examples sold there. I hope he sees the harm that this can do. Ironically, this seems totally at odds with his basic philosophy of winemaking.

VINTAGES

1985—*Vignelaure (red)*—An excellent vintage for Vignelaure, the 1985,
· tasted from cask, is very dark in color, full-bodied with oodles
87 of jammy berry fruit. It will drink well young, but keep. Anticipated maturity: 1989–1997. Last tasted 10/86.

1984—*Vignelaure (red)*—A light year, Vignelaure's 1984 has good
· color, a herbaceous-scented bouquet, medium body, some tan-
80 nins, and good zesty acidity in the finish. Anticipated maturity:
1988–1993. Last tasted 10/86.

1983—*Vignelaure (red)*—This is certainly the finest Vignelaure I have
· tasted. Very deep ruby, even opaque, with a tantalizing bouquet
89 of weedy blackcurrants and spicy oak, this full-bodied fleshy
wine is extremely long, with all the power of the 1982 but more
finesse. Anticipated maturity: 1989–2000. Last tasted 10/86.

1982—*Vignelaure (red)*—I prefer (by at least 3–4 points) the 1982s I
· have drunk in France over what I have found in the American
87 market. Is this variation a result of filtration? At its best, it is a
young, exuberant, muscular, quite intense wine with a deep
color, full body, excellent length, and plenty of power. Anticipated maturity: 1988–1996. Last tasted 10/86.

1981—*Vignelaure (red)*—Less dark in color than either 1982 or 1983,
· this vintage of Vignelaure is characterized by soft, herb-influ-
83 enced flavors, medium body, good concentration, and a light,
adequate finish. Drink it over the next 3–4 years. Last tasted
10/86.

1979—*Vignelaure (red)*—A complex bouquet of ripe fruit and cedar is
· first-rate. On the palate, the wine is spicy, powerful, rich in
86 extract, but still tannic and rather long. It can be drunk now,
but promises to last and evolve for 6–10 more years. Last tasted
10/86.

1978—*Vignelaure (red)*—Fully mature, the 1978 has a moderately in-
· tense, herbaceous, toasted, ripe fruity nose, medium to full
84 body, soft, ample flavors, and a good finish. It is somewhat
similar to a good Cru Bourgeois. Drink it over the next 4–5 years.
Last tasted 10/86.

CÔTES
DE PROVENCE

Wines from France's Vacationland

CÔTES DE PROVENCE AT A GLANCE

Type of wine produced:	Sixty percent of the wine is made by the cooperatives of the region. Small quantities of white wine, an abundant amount of rosé wine, and increasing quantities of red wine are made
Grape varieties planted:	Primarily Grenache, Carignan, Mourvèdre, Syrah, Cinsault, and Cabernet Sauvignon for the red wine and rosé; Clairette, Rolle, Sémillon, and Ugni Blanc for the white wine
Acres currently under vine:	49,000
Quality level:	Rosé: good to excellent
White: mediocre to good
Red: poor to excellent

Aging potential:	White and rosé wines: 1–3 years
	Red wines: 3–10 years
General characteristics:	Rosé: textbook rosé wine—light, fresh, vivacious, fruity, but dry
	White: chunky, with a tendency toward heaviness
	Red: enormous variation in styles; quality is increasing by leaps and bounds
Greatest recent vintages:	1985, 1982
Price range:	$6–$9

The playground for the world's rich and famous is also the backdrop for a viticultural region that is at least 2,600 years old but has only begun to assert its potential in the last decade. It has always seemed paradoxical that such a chic and classy resort area did not produce very sophisticated wines. The Greeks were the first to cultivate the vine here, followed by the Romans. While the wines have always had a loyal local following, I suspect most foreigners have viewed Provence's wines as beginning and ending with the rosé wines that are gulped down with such thirst-quenching pleasure. I, like most visitors to this area, believed precisely the same thing for years. However, this is a hugely promising area for red wine, and I am certain that what I write here will be largely out of date in less than a decade as the explosion in interest continues and a number of new wineries become fully operational. In essence, a great deal of exciting things are going on in the Côtes de Provence. As potentially promising as the area is for red wines, the prospect for good white wines seems less encouraging.

The entire area that is entitled to appellation contrôlée status is vast, yet there are three distinct viticultural zones.

1. *The coastline zone*—This area stretches from Toulon (just east of Bandol) to just beyond the quiet, swimming resort of St.-Raphael, one of the least fashionable spots on the glitzy Riviera. The soil here consists of red sandstone and shale, and the vineyards are cooled by the sea breezes.
2. *The northern rocky, Mont Ste.-Victoire zone*—This area extends south and southeast of Aix-en-Provence. The soil is rocky, dominated by limestone deposits, and has a climate hotter than the coastal area.

3. *The foothills of the Alps zone*—In the northeastern part of the appellation, the vineyards are located primarily on clay-dominated soils, and the microclimate is much cooler than one would expect, largely because of the mountain air from higher altitudes that is forced south by the prevailing winds.

I have devoted my attention to the leading private estates in the Côtes de Provence rather than the cooperatives that produce in excess of 60% of the appellation's wine. It is the estates that produce the most interesting wine; they hold the key to the future success of this appellation. As everyone knows, plenty of lively, vibrant rosé wines are made in Provence, but there are also a surprising number of good red wines now being made there. Prices are extremely fair and values are to be had. The wines should only improve in quality, because many of these estates are working from very young vineyards.

RECENT VINTAGES
1986—For many growers, the harvest did not end until the very beginning of November, enabling them to let the vineyards dry out after the storms of mid-October. It will be a good quality crop everywhere in the Côtes de Provence. Optimum maturity: 1988–1992.
1985—An excellent year, the best since 1982 for the Côtes de Provence appellations. The intense heat that created problems elsewhere in France caused fewer problems in the cooler inland and coastal sections of Provence. The reds are delicious, fat, ripe, well colored, but a little low in acidity. The rosés are full-bodied and fresh, and the whites more powerful than usual, but lacking a little finesse. Optimum maturity: now–1991.
1984—In general, a mediocre year of rather short, austere wines that are clean and rot free but tend to lack fruit and flesh. Optimum maturity: now–1989.

OLDER VINTAGES
Certainly any rosé or white wine older than 1984 should be approached with a great deal of caution. The top red wines from the Côtes de Provence do not have a good reputation for aging, except for those from a half-dozen or so estates. However, specific wines can evolve for five to eight years, sometimes much longer. Nineteen eighty-three was a very good year for red wine, 1982 even better. After these two years,

1978 and especially 1975 were very fine vintages for Côtes de Provence red wine.

A Personal Rating of the Côtes de Provence Producers

**** (EXCELLENT PRODUCERS)

Domaine Gavoty
Domaine Ott
Commanderie de Peyrassol

Domaine Richeaume
Saint-André de Figuière

*** (GOOD PRODUCERS)

Domaine des Aspras
Château Barbeyrolles
Domaine de la Bernarde
Domaine de Bertaud
Domaine de Campouny
Château de Curebéasse
Domaine des Féraud
Château de Garcinières
Domaine Grand Boise
Domaine de Grand Pré

Domaine de L'Ile de
Porquerolles
Domaine Jas d'Esclans
Domaine de la Malherbe
Château Minuty
Domaine des Planes
Château Réal Martin
Domaine de Rimauresq
Château de Roux
Domaine Saint-Baillon
Château Sainte-Roseline

** (AVERAGE PRODUCERS)

L'Estandon
Mas de Cadenet

Domaine Source Sainte-
Marguerite
Château Saint-Pierre

DOMAINE DES ASPRAS (LISA LATZ)***

A tiny estate in the town of Correns, Domaine des Aspras produces fresh, modern-styled red, white, and rosé wines from 17 acres of vineyards. The wines are bottled very early, are quite cleanly made, and are inexpensive.

CHÂTEAU BARBEYROLLES (MLLE. RÉGINE SUMEIRE)***

The young, tan, very pretty Régine Sumeire runs the 31-acre vineyard of Château Barbeyrolles with a great deal of commitment and passion. She certainly has one of the best situated estates, located on hilly terrain within view of one of the Riviera's legendary spots, the fishing village and hangout for artists and high society, St.-Tropez. Sumeire, who has a doctorate in history, gave up a university career to make wine. Her rosé is of a very high standard, very fresh and lively, but she also makes a serious red wine from Grenache, Syrah, and Mourvèdre. It is aged 15–18 months in both foudre and barrel, and has five to seven years aging potential in top years such as 1985 and 1983. She also plans to make a white wine from Sémillon, Rolle, and Ugni Blanc. This is a good estate with high standards.

DOMAINE DE LA BERNARDE (MEULNART PÈRE ET FILS) ***

This decent-sized estate of 82 acres in the town of Le Luc, known for its mineral waters, is the home of the Domaine de la Bernarde. Sixteen thousand cases of red, white, and rosé wine are made here. The quality of the red wines has been inconsistent, the 1985 very promising, the 1979 drinking very well in 1986, but the 1982 and 1983 of only standard quality. Their Cuvée Saint-Germain is the top red wine, and contains much more Syrah and Cabernet Sauvignon in the blend. The rosés are well made, the whites somewhat heavy and neutral in taste.

DOMAINE DE BERTAUD (YVES LEMAÎTRE) ***

The 62-acre vineyard of the Domaine Bertaud is in Gassin, the old, pretty village perched on a rocky hilltop above the Gulf of St.-Tropez, with a splendid view of the tiny islands off the coast called L'Iles d'Hyères. The red wine is noteworthy here. Made from Cabernet Sauvignon, Mourvèdre, and Syrah, the wine is very deeply colored, full-bodied, tannic, and very ageworthy. The 1982, 1983, and 1985 all promise to last seven to ten years, a long time for a wine from this area. The rosé and white wine are adequate, but proprietor Yves Lemaître seems less interested in them than in his red wine. Prices are low.

COMMANDERIE DE PEYRASSOL
(YVES ET FRANÇOIS RIGORD) ****

The Commanderie de Peyrassol is one of the finest estates in the Côtes de Provence. Located near the town of Le Luc, it is managed with meticulous care by Yves and François Rigord. Their residence sits among 371 acres of forest. There are 161 acres of vineyards that produce 8,000 cases of red wine, 8,000 cases of rosé, and 2,000 cases of white wine. The rosé here is certainly among the top half-dozen of the Côtes de Provence. However, the red wine is even better. There are two cuvées. The Cuvée Eperon d'Or is made from 40% Cabernet Sauvignon and 20% each of Mourvèdre, Grenache, and Syrah. The wine is fruity, deep in color, and capable of lasting four to seven years. Their second red is a luxury cuvée. Called Cuvée Marie-Estelle, it is made only in top years such as 1982, 1983, and 1985, and is produced from

65% Cabernet Sauvignon, the rest being Grenache and Syrah. It is a deeper, very impressive Côtes de Provence red wine that can age for six to ten years. The 1982 and 1983 are excellent. A standard-quality white wine is also made here.

The Commanderie is a very serious property. With their expensive investment in new oak barrels for aging part of the red wine and their decision to declassify the entire red wine crop in 1984, the Rigords are aiming for the top level of quality among the Côtes de Provence producers.

DOMAINE DE CUREBÉASSE (JEAN PAQUETTE) ***

One of the most consistent winemaking estates in the Côtes de Provence, the Domaine de Curebéasse does an equally good job with red, white, and rosé wine. From the 44-acre estate, 7,600 cases of wine are produced. The white wine is surprisingly lively, floral, fruity, and fresh, and certainly one of the best of the region. The rosé is of high quality. The red wine is available in two styles: The primary cuvée is a fruity, well-colored, round wine for drinking within four to six years of the vintage. There is a special Cuvée Roches Noires made from Mourvèdre, Cabernet Sauvignon, and Syrah grown in dark volcanic soil; it is aged 18 months in oak casks (some of which are new) prior to being bottled, and will keep and evolve for six to ten years. Once again, the quality of the wines here is quite good, and the prices very fair. The Domaine de Curebéasse is located in Fréjus, a small city of significant historical interest, largely because of its fascinating Roman ruins (it was founded by Julius Caesar in 49 B.C.).

L'ESTANDON (J. BAGNIS) **

This branded wine is produced in gigantic quantities (300,000 cases) by the Bagnis family. They are also owners of the excellent Château Crémat in Bellet, but these wines are, at best, standard in quality—dull, straightforward, simple rosé, white, and red wines made for the masses, without much character.

DOMAINE DES FÉRAUD (BERNARD LAUDON) ***

One of the few delicious white Côtes de Provence wines made is from the 86-acre Domaine des Féraud. Situated in Vidauban, and managed by Bernard Laudon, a very interesting white wine, made from 50% Semillon and 50% Ugni Blanc is produced. It is a creamy, tropical fruit-scented wine with undeniable character. Like the good rosé wine made here, the white wine must also be drunk young. Domaine des Féraud also makes a robust, fruity, full-bodied red wine from 50% Cabernet Sauvignon and the rest Grenache, Syrah, and Mourvèdre. It is a wine that in vintages such as 1982, 1983, and 1985 can last for five to seven years.

CHÂTEAU DES GARCINIÈRES (VALENTIN)***

At this small- to moderate-sized estate of 40 acres in Cogolin approximately 6,200 cases of wine are made each year. The rosé and white wines are quite mediocre, but the red wine offers a charming, smooth fruitiness in one of the lightest styles in the Côtes de Provence. The 1985 and 1982 are the best two recent vintages for this property.

DOMAINES GAVOTY (PIERRE AND BERNARD GAVOTY)****

This large enterprise consists of several properties referred to as Le Grand Campduny and Le Petit Campduny. From the 136 acres of vineyards near Flassans, 25,000 cases of rosé, 2,500 cases of red wine, and 3,300 cases of white wine are made. The rosé tends to be rather deep in color, but loaded with fruit and very well made. The white wine, made from Rolle, Clairette, and Ugni Blanc, is not at all heavy or dull, but fresh and lively. Both are bottled as soon as possible to conserve their fruit and delicate aromas. The red wine, a product of various percentages of Syrah, Cabernet, Grenache, and Mourvèdre, is aged six to eight months in foudres and fermented partly by the crushed berry, classic method, partly by carbonic maceration. The 1985, 1983, and 1982 exhibited the potential to last for five to seven years, with aromas and flavors of framboise, spices, and toasty oak present. The 1981 is disappointing.

DOMAINE GRAND BOISE (THE GRUEY FAMILY)***

The Domaine Grand Boise is situated east of Aix-en-Provence, near a town called Trets. The hillside vineyard is composed of 106 acres. The normal trio of Provence wines is made there. The red wine, produced from Cabernet Sauvignon, Syrah, Cinsault, and Grenache, is a medium-bodied, straightforward style of wine without much distinction. Perhaps the 24 months it spends in oak foudres is excessive. The rosé is sound and the white wine is perhaps the most interesting of the three. It is made from the Rolle and Sémillon grapes. The production here is 13,800 cases. The best recent years have been 1985, 1983, and 1982.

DOMAINE DE GRAND-PRÉ (EMMANUEL PLAUCHET)***

A small 20-acre estate, the Domaine de Grand-Pré produces 4,800 cases of a fat, deeply colored, husky red wine, classy, fragrant, fruity rosé, and bland white wine. Prices are very low.

DOMAINE DE L'ILE DE PORQUEROLLES (MME. LE BER)***

The Ile de Porquerolles is an island just off the coast of the French Riviera. The closest city is the bustling tourist town of Hyères. The wine of the Domaine de L'Ile de Porquerolles is produced on the island, which itself is worth a visit, for its sandy coves, rugged coastline, and, I am told, nudist swimming resorts. There is also a serious wine made here by proprietor Madame Le Ber. The 49-acre vineyard is primarily dedicated to the production of red and rosé wines. The red wine is light, fruity, and not surprisingly, herb and pine tree scented. The rosé is explosively fruity, quite dry, medium- to full-bodied, a joy to drink within one or two years of the vintage.

DOMAINE JAS D'ESCLANS (R. LORGUES)***

A relatively large estate of 124 acres, the Domaine Jas d'Esclans in La Motte is run by M. Lorgues. The annual production of 14,500 cases is largely consumed within western Europe. The rosé seems to lack some freshness and charm when compared with its peers, and I have not been a great admirer of this property's white wine. That being said, the red wine, a blend of 50% Cinsault, 30% Grenache, 15% Mourvèdre, and 5% Syrah, is a richly fruity, rather powerful, spicy wine that exudes character. It is aged in oak foudres for 20 months, and seems capable —in vintages such as 1982 and 1985—of aging for five to seven years.

DOMAINE DE LA MALHERBE (S. FERRARI)***

One of the Riviera's most picturesque villages is Bormes-les-Mimosas, a tiny hill town several miles inland from the swimming resort of Le Lavandou. This village, which overflows in spring and summer with flowers, is the home of the Domaine de la Malherbe. The production of 4,200 cases is of white and rosé wines. The white wine, which has a large percentage of the Rolle grape in it, is chunky yet fresh and fruity. The rosé is quite dry, very exotic and flamboyant, and certainly one of the most distinctive rosés in Provence.

MAS DE CADENET (NEGRET)**

I had little luck tasting the wines from this estate. The production is 8,450 cases a year on the average, the majority being rosé (4,600 cases).

The vintages of red wine I tasted, 1983, 1982, and 1981, lacked flesh and fruit, and seemed excessively tannic. The white was one-dimensional, the rosé decent, but not among the better wines from the Côtes de Provence. The domaine's cellars are in Trets, 14 miles east of Aix-en-Provence.

CHÂTEAU MINUTY (MATTON-FARNET) ***

The lovely Château Minuty is in Gassin, four miles from the famed beach resort and fishing village of St.-Tropez. This is certainly one of the better Côtes de Provence estates. The white wine is especially good by Provence standards. It is made from the Rolle, Sémillon, Clairette, and Ugni Blanc grapes, and seems to always have a great measure of fruity charm. The rosé is good, not exceptional, but dry, salmon-colored, and meant to be drunk within 14–16 months of the vintage. The red wine impressed me in 1985 more than in the past. Quite fruity, rich, and supple, it was a fine example of the increased quality seen in this appellation. It is made from Cabernet Sauvignon, Mourvèdre, Cinsault, Grenache, and Tibourin. This large estate of 198 acres produces nearly 22,000 cases of wine per year.

DOMAINES OTT
(CLOS MIREILLE AND CHÂTEAU DE SELLE) ****

No one has done more to promote the wines of Provence than the Ott family of Antibes. Marcel and Oliver Ott have established an impeccable reputation with the quality of their Provence wines. They must also have good connections with the area's restaurants, because their wines are widely represented and promoted by most of the eating establishments of the area. The Otts have two domaines in the Côtes de Provence, the 99-acre Château de Selle and the 124-acre Clos Mireille. (They also own the Bandol estate Château Romassan.) The Clos Mireille produces 17,000 cases of white wine that the Otts have ingeniously marketed in a very heavy bottle that resembles that used for sparkling wine in Champagne. Made from Sémillon and Ugni Blanc, it is a dry, full-bodied wine that seems clumsy when drunk by itself, but curiously comes vividly alive with any of the spicy fish soups of the region. The Château de Selle produces very ripe, deeply colored, fruity red wines, a similarly chunky, intense white wine, and a lovely rosé. Ott also produces small quantities of a Château de Selle red wine that has at least 60% Cabernet Sauvignon in its composition. It is one of the finest red wines of Provence, and is recognizable because the gray label is marked "Cuvée Spéciale." It is made only in great years. Despite the obvious quality of the red and white wines made here, the Otts are largely known to foreigners for their delicious rosés, all of which are among the best dozen or so rosés of France. Crisp, full-flavored, authoritative rosés with surprising flavor dimension, they do indeed merit their reputation.

DOMAINE DES PLANES (CHRISTOPHE RIEDER)***
Approximately 10,000 cases of Côtes de Provence red, white, and rosé wines are produced each year by the Domaine des Planes in Roquebrune. The white wine is of average quality, the rosés satisfactory, but the red wine here is quite well made and somewhat similar to a Bandol. The excellent 1982 was made from a blend of 80% Cabernet Sauvignon and 20% Mourvèdre. The 1985 is another lush, rich, very attractive wine with four to six years' aging potential. The prices are low, so this is an estate to search out.

CHÂTEAU RÉAL MARTIN (JACQUES CLOTILDE)***
This 500-acre estate has only 79 acres planted in vines. The production averages 12,500 cases per year with 11,000 cases of that representing red and rosé wines. The red wine offers most of the interest here. The long maceration period, very late harvest, and two-year minimum aging in tank seems to ensure a rich, full-bodied, dense red wine with seven to ten years' aging potential. The infant 1985, very good 1983, and excellent 1982 tasted in 1986 were all very far from full maturity. M. Clotilde uses Syrah, Grenache, and Cinsault to produce his red wine, one of the best in the Côtes de Provence.

DOMAINE RICHEAUME (HENNING HOESCH)****
At the foot of the famous Mont Ste.-Victoire, outside Aix-en-Provence, is the single best estate in the Côtes de Provence for red wine. A German, Henning Hoesch, started this domaine of 60 acres in 1972. The vineyard is located between the two wine towns of Puyloubier and Rousset, and is in a sheltered area where the microclimate is quite hot and dry. Hoesch, who believes in the organic method of viticulture and winemaking, uses nothing but animal manure as a fertilizer, and employs no pesticides or herbicides. He produces 6,000 cases of wine, two-thirds of which are three separate cuvées of red wine. They are his Cuvée Tradition, a Cuvée Syrah (normally 60% Syrah and 40% Grenache), and Cuvée Cabernet Sauvignon (usually 85% Cabernet Sauvignon and 15% Grenache). The wines age 18 months in small oak barrels, and are given only a very coarse filtration prior to bottling. The

results from vintages such as 1978, 1982, 1983, and 1985 have been stunning. They are true *vins de garde*, serious, dense-colored wines loaded with heaps of fruit, power, and tannins. In vintages such as these, there is no doubt that the Domaine Richeaume's wines will evolve for a decade. My notes show greatest enthusiasm for the cuvées of Cabernet Sauvignon and Syrah. This is a relatively unknown estate committed to making world-class wines of the highest order. They provide surprising drinking.

DOMAINE DE RIMAURESQ (HUBERT ISNARD)***

This 64-acre property in Pignans produces 4,200 cases of a supple, fleshy, easy to drink red wine from the Grenache, Mourvèdre, Syrah, and Cinsault grapes. It spends two to three years in wooden foudres, which gives it an intense spicy character in vintages such as 1982 and 1983.

CHÂTEAU DE ROUX (ELISABETH GIRAUD)***

This estate produces 7,800 cases of sound Côtes de Provence wine. Located near Le Luc, the Château de Roux has 74 acres of vines. The red wines are one-dimensional, but cleanly made, fruity, and should be drunk within their first three or four years of life. Prices are very fair, but these are wines for uncomplicated quaffing.

SAINT-ANDRÉ DE FIGUIÈRE
(ANDRÉ AND DANIEL CONNESSON)****

This is one of the finest estates in the Côtes de Provence appellation. Approximately 6,800 cases of wine are produced from the 38 acres of vineyards near La Londre-des-Maures. The property is maintained in the organic manner that rules out insecticides and herbicides. I have never tasted the white wine, which has an excellent reputation. The rosé is quite good, full-bodied, fresh, and lively—if drunk within its first two years of life. There are three red wines offered here, a Cuvée du Marquis, with 30% Grenache in it, a Cuvée Grand Roy, with the amount of Grenache increased to 50%, and a Cuvée Spéciale, with 65% Mourvèdre in it. The other grapes used are the Cinsault and Carignan. Some of Connesson's vines average 75 years in age, and the wine from these vines always goes into the top of the line Cuvée Spéciale. The reds from Saint-André de Figuière age very well. The 1979 and 1980 Cuvée Spéciales drunk in 1986 were not unlike a very good Bandol. The 1982s are very good, the 1983s good, the 1984s surprisingly supple and fruity, and the 1985s promise to be the best wines yet made here. This is a very serious estate that produced its first wine only in 1979. The rapport in terms of price and quality is excellent.

*DOMAINE SOURCE SAINTE-MARGUERITE (J. R. FAYARD)***

A 25-acre property, the Source Sainte-Marguerite is located in La Londre-des-Maures. The red wine is fruity and one-dimensional, and not very distinguished.

*DOMAINE SAINT-BAILLON (HERVÉ GOUDARD)****

A small vineyard of 22 acres, the Domaine Saint-Baillon produces a fleshy, well-made white, a red wine, and a particularly good rosé from its cellars located well inland from the Mediterranean at Le Luc. The top red wine, Cuvée du Roudai, is quite good in years such as 1983 and 1985, mediocre in 1984 and 1981. It can be aged for four to six years.

*CHÂTEAU SAINT-PIERRE (VICTOR HOIRS)***

This is a very reliable source for good rosé wine, vinified at very cool temperatures, bottled early, and ideal for drinking within its first one or two years. The red wine is tough and one-dimensional, the white undistinguished and neutral-tasting. The vineyard of Château Saint-Pierre comprises 84 acres near the town of Les Arcs-sur-Argens.

CHÂTEAU STE.-ROSELINE
*(BARON LOUIS DE RASQUE DE LAVAL)****

Château Ste.-Roseline is one property well worth a visit in Provence. The ancient monastery here is classified as a historical monument and should be seen as well. The rosé wine made here is surprisingly heavy and flat, and I have never appreciated the dull white wine, either. However, the red wine, made from 60% Mourvèdre, 30% Cabernet Sauvignon, and 10% Syrah, is powerful, densely colored, rich, full-bodied, with a very complex aroma of coffee, chocolate, and jammy berry fruit. It will also age well, as a 1978 and 1980 tasted in 1986 proved. It is aged two years in wooden barrels. Château Ste.-Roseline is situated in Les Arcs-sur-Argens and its vineyard covers 128 acres.

CÔTES DE LUBÉRON

Soft, Fruity, Commercial Wines

CÔTES DU LUBÉRON AT A GLANCE

Type of wine produced:	Red, white, and rosé
Grape varieties planted:	Primarily Grenache, Syrah, Mourvèdre, Cinsault, and Carignan, but also Cabernet Sauvignon, Pinot Noir, Gamay, and Counoise for the red wine; for the white wine, Ugni Blanc, Clairette, and Bourboulenc dominate the plantings
Acres currently under vine:	5,600
Quality level:	95% of Côtes du Lubéron is made by one of the cooperatives, and the quality varies from below average to average. At the grower level, the wines are more interesting

Aging potential:	1–3 years
General characteristics:	Light, fruity, soft red wines; light, fragrant rosés; straightforward, somewhat dull white wines
Price range:	$4–$6
Best wines:	Château La Canorgue, Château de Mille, and Château Val-Joanis

Quite fruity, easy to drink and appreciate red, white, and rosé wines are made in the hilly terrain north of the Durance River in the Vaucluse Département. The mountains here are called the Côtes du Lubéron, from which the wine draws its name. The major vineyards lie between the northern village of Apt and Pertuis to the south. This is a tranquil, remote area of France where surreal "Bories" (dry stone huts), usually one or two stories high with conical roofs, bear witness to the past cultures that lived in this remote area. The altitude of the vineyards is high, and the area is much cooler than one might initially suspect. It is not unusual for the growers to begin and finish the harvest in mid to late October. The area is not yet entitled to full appellation contrôlée status, but only VDQS. At present, large cooperatives dominate the production, but three estates provide very fine wine at extremely reasonable prices. This backwoods area of Provence should not be overlooked.

CHÂTEAU DE LA CANORGUE (JEAN-PIERRE MARGAN)

The Château de La Canorgue is an estate of 37 acres that began to produce wine only in 1978. Run by the very serious, outspoken Jean-Pierre Margan, Canorgue produces a supple, effusively fruity red wine from 40% Syrah, 30% Grenache, 15% Cinsault, and 15% Mourvèdre. The 1985, 1983, and 1982 had heaps of fruit and charm, and were priced below most Beaujolais. Château de La Canorgue is located in Bonnieux, a fascinating hill town that has a collection of the stone Bories that are found in this region of France.

CHÂTEAU DE MILLE (CONRAD PINATEL)

In Apt, a bustling town in the northern part of the Côtes du Lubéron, is Château de Mille, one of the outstanding estates in Provence. Owned and run by Conrad Pinatel, Château de Mille produces the best and most expensive wines of Lubéron. Pinatel, an independent chap and something of a maverick, feels his wine is one of the best in southern France. Certainly the 1985, 1983, 1982, and 1979 red wines exhibited surprising richness, length and depth of fruit as well as showing five to seven years of aging potential. Château de Mille also makes a very dry, austere rosé that is not enjoyable by itself but seems to take on character when served with food.

CHÂTEAU VAL-JOANIS (JEAN-LOUIS CHANCEL)

The most promising estate in the Côtes du Lubéron is Château Val-Joanis. An entirely new property, Val-Joanis is the creation of the single-minded, former business tycoon Jean-Louis Chancel. A very wealthy man, he proudly boasts he could have bought Château Margaux in Bordeaux if he had so desired. Instead, in 1978 he chose to invest six million dollars in a 494-acre vineyard and château in Lubéron, just north of the dull town of Pertuis. His vineyards are very young, and his first vintage was only in 1982. But Chancel is a driven man. The estate is impeccable, with state-of-the-art technology in the winery and no expense spared in the château and grounds; it is clearly the showpiece property of the Côtes du Lubéron. Chancel and his son Jean are very personable, energetic individuals who seem convinced they have found the perfect spot for making wine. They are great believers in the Syrah grape, rather than Grenache, and proudly point to the perfect limestone soil of their vineyards as evidence that the Syrah will flourish in this area. Their red and rosé wines are made from 60% Syrah, 30% Grenache, and the remaining 10% from Cinsault and Mourvèdre. For the white wine, the Ugni Blanc is represented by 80% and the Chardonnay by 20%. Chancel, though opposed to the carbonic maceration method of vinification and the use of a high proportion of the Grenache grape, is in favor of mechanical harvesters, which he claims do a much better job than human harvesters. Their white wine shows surprising style, with good fruit and acidity. Their rosé is pleasant, but it resembles the majority of rank and file rosés found in Provence. Their red wine is promising and should get better with each vintage as the vineyard reaches maturity. The 1985, deep in color, round, fruity, and generous, is better than the 1983. The vineyards may be young, but the commitment to quality and the modest pricing policy implemented by the Chancel family are sure to propel the name of this domaine into the public's eye. Val-Joanis is one of the bright, new, bold, innovative vineyards of Provence.

PALETTE

A Serious Wine from one of France's
Smallest Appellations

PALETTE AT A GLANCE

Type of wine produced:	Red, white, and rosé
Grape varieties planted:	Grenache, Mourvèdre, Cinsault, and Syrah for the red and rosé wines; Ugni Blanc, Clairette, and Sémillon for the white
Acres currently under vine:	49.3
Quality level:	Only two estates make wine at Palette—Château Simone, which produces excellent wine, and Domaine Crémade, which produces standard quality wine
Aging potential:	Red wine: 5–10 years White wine: 3–10 years

General characteristics:	Elegant, stylish red and rosé wines; fresh, spicy, flavorful whites
Greatest recent vintages:	1985, 1982
Price range:	$7–$10

DOMAINE CRÉMADE (M. VIDALIN)

This tiny estate of 12.3 acres produces red wine only from a blend of 50% Grenache, 30% Mourvèdre, and 20% Cinsault. Though not very distinguished, it is usually simple, medium-bodied, technically sound, but uninteresting.

CHÂTEAU SIMONE (RENÉ ROUGIER)

I suspect few people realize that just south of Aix-en-Provence is one of the best kept winemaking secrets of Provence. The lovely, beautifully landscaped Château Simone of René Rougier, who bears a resemblance to the American actor William Shatner of "Star Trek" fame, is strategically placed on a shaded hillside. Rougier, whose family has run Château Simone for over 150 years, is a conservative winemaker. He has some vines that exceed 100 years in age, therefore preexisting the phylloxera scourge of the late nineteenth century. The average age of the entire vineyard is an amazing 70 years. He works from a small vineyard of 37 acres, and turns out white, rosé, and red wines.

The white wine is a curiosity to me. Produced from 80% Clairette and the balance Ugni Blanc, Sémillon, and Muscat, Rougier has always aged it a long time in small oak barrels. For that reason, though it smells too woody, it keeps and keeps. Bottles of the 1974 and 1978 were drunk with pleasure in 1986, and were impressively rich, deep wines that had thrown off the woody cloak that seems to dominate the wine when young, giving it a clumsy taste. To Rougier's credit, he has begun to offer an early bottling of his wine to the American market, and the 1985 is excellent, loaded with fruit, fresh, and exuberant, but full-bodied and muscular, as if it aspires to be a Chave white Hermitage.

Rougier's rosés are old-style, slightly oxidized, woody wines. They taste superb from the cask, but he does not bottle them soon enough; I wish he would.

Rougier's very traditional approach to making wine, while less successful with whites and rosés, works extremely well with the red wine of Château Simone. Given three years' aging in cask, it is made from an assemblage of 40% Grenache, 40% Mourvèdre, and the rest Cinsault and an old Provençal grape indigenous to the region called Manoscan.

It is an elegant, stylish wine with plenty of flavor, a bouquet of spicy oak, herbs, and ripe fruit, and ten to twelve years of aging potential. The top vintages for Château Simone's red wine have been 1985, 1982, 1979, 1978, and 1975.

Château Simone's white and red wines are among the most distinctive of France, as well as among the rarest, given the fact that Palette is the second smallest appellation of France (after Château Grillet). It is therefore surprising that the prices for Château Simone's wines are so reasonable.

VISITING, STAYING,
AND DINING
IN PROVENCE

I am sure no one needs to be persuaded to travel to Provence —this is among the top tourist attractions and vacation spots in the world. Most people, however, go there to enjoy the sun and sea, the towering hill towns perched precariously on the edge of limestone cliffs, the dramatic coastline, and the rich and varied cuisine. For the wine enthusiast, staying at a few well-chosen hotels can put you within striking distance of some of Provence's best wine producers. My hotel and restaurant recommendations are not exclusive, but rather ones my wife and I have found to merit their reputations and to offer hospitable service, or ones strategically located for an expedition into the nearby vineyards. Remember, Provence is a much vaster region than the Rhône Valley, and travel time from the westernmost area of the Coteaux Baux-en-Provence to Bellet near Nice can take up to three or four hours during the congested holiday season that starts in mid-June and ends in early September. Also, most hotels raise their rates by 30–50%

during these summer months. Because much of this area serves as the world's playground for the rich and famous, going in the off-season can minimize the high cost of visiting Provence. The restaurants and hotels are grouped under each viticultural region.

Visiting Bandol and Cassis

Cassis is only 15 miles east of Marseille, Bandol, 30 miles east. Cassis is the more scenic of the two seaside resorts, largely because it has maintained its tiny fishing village charm, and is set in a secluded, sheltered bay dwarfed by tall cliffs that are sprinkled with vineyards. Bandol is larger, seemingly much bigger than the local population of 6,500 attributed to it. Bandol is probably the better place to use as a base for exploring the wineries of this area. Just inland from Bandol are two lovely hilltop villages, La Cadière d'Azur and Le Castellet, that offer the usual Provençal fare, spectacular vistas, tiny shops filled with the work of local artisans, and art galleries. Both are a five to ten minute drive from Bandol, and are set among the vineyards of the area. From Bandol, the fjordlike Les Calangues of Cassis and the fishing village are easily reached by car in 20 minutes.

Bandol: Hôtel Ile Rousse (94.29.46.86)—The best choice for a hotel in Bandol, Ile Rousse is located on a tiny isthmus away from the noisy town center. There is a lovely sandy beach in front of Ile Rousse, and a large swimming pool. The bar is very fashionable, but the restaurant is pretentious and overpriced. Expensive.

Bandol: Auberge de Porte (94.29.42.63)—Right on the water; the choice of fine restaurants in Bandol is very limited, but for fresh seafood, including the heady saffron-and-garlic-scented fish soup, this is the place to go. Expensive.

Le Castellet: Castel Lumière (94.32.62.20)—This quaint, rather touristic restaurant is perched on a cliff in the medieval hilltop town of Le Castellet. The food is good, the wine list loaded with everybody's Bandols, and the views across the vineyards toward the sea on a clear evening stunning. Expensive.

La Cadière d'Azur: Hostellerie Bérard (94.90.11.43)—Many Bandol producers have their cellars in La Cadière d'Azur, another tiny hill town that looks out over the vineyards in the direction of the above-mentioned Le Castellet. The hotel and restaurant Bérard offers simple rooms, but also well-prepared regional cuisine that is faithful to its origins, very inexpensive and consistently delicious. This is a good place for lunch while spending the day in the vineyards. Inexpensive.

Cassis: Les Roches Blanches (42.01.09.30)—This stylish, well-situated hotel, with its terraced gardens and thrilling views of the sea and port, is run with great charm and care. Expensive.

Cassis: La Presqu'Ile (42.01.03.77)—This restaurant would merit a visit just for the view of the sharp, tall, limestone cliffs of Cap Canaille. However, in addition to the view, the food, especially the fish courses, are excellent, and the selection of the local wines of Cassis and Bandol quite extensive. Expensive.

Visiting Coteaux d'Aix-en-Provence
(Including the Coteaux Baux-en-Provence)

There is no simple advice for visiting the Coteaux d'Aix-en-Provence because it is so vast and the major estates are not close to each other. Consequently, there is no single town that might serve as a totally useful base. Should one want to visit the Coteaux Baux-en-Provence, where the exquisite Domaine Trévallon is located (as well as a number of other wine producers), one does, however, have several enticing possibilities. The most celebrated and most visited Provençal hill town of all, the mysterious Les Baux, is only a five-minute car drive away from Trévallon. In addition, the town of St.-Rémy-de-Provence, the birthplace of the astrologer Nostradamus and where the famed artist Vincent van Gogh was institutionalized in the mental hospital of St.-Paul-de-Mausole, is only ten minutes from Trévallon and the other estates in the Coteaux Baux-en-Provence.

Les Baux-de-Provence: Oustau de Baumanière (90.54.33.07)—If the cuisine itself rarely deserves more than two of the three stars the Michelin Guide awards Oustau de Baumanière, this enchanting restaurant/hotel at the foot of the village is still a magical spot. The cavernous dining room or the flowery terrace make ideal settings for fine dining. The food is classic, very good, not terribly innovative, but delicious and faithful to the local specialties. The wine list is excellent, even superb for Rhône and Bordeaux wines. The rooms are exceptional. Very expensive.

St.-Rémy-de-Provence: Château des Alpilles (90.92.03.33)—This restored château is in a splendid park and has all the amenities one could hope for. Domaine Trévallon is only 15 minutes away via the surreal route through the Val d'Enfer (Valley of Hell). Expensive.

St.-Rémy-de-Provence: Auberge du Grès (90.49.18.61)—This family-run bistro is six miles west of St.-Rémy, but offers skillfully prepared, regional cuisine in a relaxed setting at very fair prices. Moderate.

La Fuste: Hostellerie de la Fuste (92.72.05.95)—Located southeast of the town of Manosque, this superb restaurant and tranquil hotel is situated in a large park, and makes an ideal spot for dining and lodging while visiting the nearby Château Vignelaure. The food gets one star from Michelin and two toques from Gault-Millau, but our meals have been as close to three-star quality as one can expect. The service is remarkably warm, professional, and effective, and it is easy to sense that Chef Daniel Jourdan is looking forward to higher ranking by the critics. The wine list has Château Vignelaure's last ten vintages as well as many other gems at very reasonable prices. Expensive.

Visiting the Côtes de Provence and Palette

The seaside resort towns of Hyères, St.-Tropez, St.-Raphael, Antibes, or Nice are jammed with all types of hotels and fascinating restaurants and bistros that are covered in much greater detail in the guidebooks about this region. Given the difficult logistics of visiting so many domaines spread out over such an immense area, no one town can serve as a good base within striking distance of the best domaines. Staying in the environs of Nice is perhaps the most intelligent choice, for Antibes (the headquarters of the famous Ott firm) is only 12 miles away. In addition, the wines of Bellet, particularly the excellent Château de Crémat and Château de Bellet, are also only a ten-minute drive away.

For visiting some of the excellent Côtes de Provence estates that are well inland, as well as the micro-appellation of Palette, Aix-en-Provence would be a suitable base. For example, the Palette producer Château Simone is only 10–15 minutes by car from downtown Aix-en-Provence, as is the Côtes de Provence estate of Domaine Richeaume. Several worthy recommendations in Aix-en-Provence include the following.

Aix-en-Provence: Hôtel Le Pigonnet (42.59.02.90)—In midtown Aix, this old country house sits in a tree-filled park and seems miles away from the noise and bustle of the city. The rooms are spacious and well equipped. The only drawback is fighting the morning traffic while making your way to the wine country. Expensive.

Aix-en-Provence: Charvet (43.38.43.82)—Just off the most fashionable and famous street of Aix-en-Provence, the tree-lined Cours Mirabeau, Chef Charvet serves up an array of sumptuous courses that are generous, innovative, and delicious—can a diner ask for anything more? Expensive.

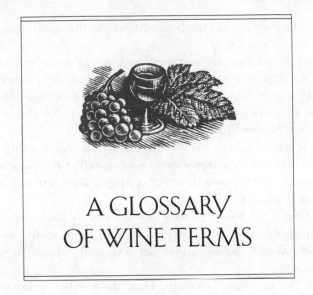

A GLOSSARY
OF WINE TERMS

acetic: Wines, no matter how well made, contain quantities of acetic acidity that have a vinegary smell. If there is an excessive amount of acetic acidity, the wine will have a vinegary smell and be a flawed, acetic wine.

acidic: Wines need natural acidity to taste fresh and lively, but an excess of acidity results in an acidic wine that is tart and sour.

acidity: The acidity level in a wine is critical to its enjoyment and livelihood. The natural acids that appear in wine are citric, tartaric, malic, and lactic. Wines from hot years tend to be lower in acidity, whereas wines from cool, rainy years tend to be high in acidity. Acidity in a wine preserves the wine's freshness and keeps the wine lively.

aftertaste: As the term suggests, the taste left in the mouth when one swallows is the aftertaste. This word is a synonym for length or finish. The longer the aftertaste lingers in the mouth (assuming it is a pleasant taste), the finer the quality of the wine.

aggressive: Aggressive is usually applied to wines that are either high in acidity or have harsh tannins, or both.

angular: Angular wines are wines that lack roundness, generosity, and depth. Wine from poor vintages or wines that are too acidic are often described as being angular.

aroma: Aroma is the smell of a young wine before it has had sufficient time to develop nuances of smell that are then called its bouquet.

The word aroma is commonly used to mean the smell of a relatively young, unevolved wine.

astringent: Wines that are astringent are not necessarily bad or good wines. Astringent wines are harsh and coarse to taste, either because they are too young and tannic and just need time to develop, or because they are not well made. The level of tannins (if it is harsh) in a wine contributes to its degree of astringence.

austere: Wines that are austere are generally not terribly pleasant wines to drink. An austere wine is a hard, rather dry wine that lacks richness and generosity. However, young Rhônes are not as austere as young Bordeaux.

balance: One of the most desired traits in a wine is good balance, where the concentration of fruit, level of tannins, and acidity are in total harmony. Well-balanced wines are symmetrical and tend to age gracefully.

barnyard: An unclean, farmyard, fecal aroma that is imparted to a wine because of unclean barrels or unsanitary winemaking facilities.

berrylike: As this descriptive term implies, most red wines have an intense berry fruit character that can suggest blackberries, raspberries, black cherries, mulberries, or even strawberries and cranberries.

big: A big wine is a large-framed, full-bodied wine with an intense and concentrated feel on the palate. Most red Rhône wines are big wines.

blackcurrant: A pronounced smell of blackcurrant fruit is commonly associated with certain Rhône wines. It can vary in intensity from faint to very deep and rich.

body: Body is the weight and fullness of a wine that can be sensed as it crosses the palate. Full-bodied wines tend to have a lot of alcohol, concentration, and glycerine.

Botrytis cinerea: The fungus that attacks the grape skins under specific climatic conditions (usually alternating periods of moisture and sunny weather). It causes the grape to become superconcentrated because it causes a natural dehydration. Botrytis cinerea is essential for the great sweet white wines of Barsac and Sauternes. It rarely occurs in either the Rhône Valley or Provence because of the dry, constant sunshine and gusty winds.

bouquet: As a wine's aroma becomes more developed from bottle aging, the aroma is transformed into a bouquet that is hopefully more than just the smell of the grape.

brawny: A hefty, muscular, full-bodied wine with plenty of weight and flavor, although not always the most elegant or refined sort of wine.

briary: I think of California Zinfandel when the term briary comes into play, denoting that the wine is aggressive and rather spicy.

brilliant: Brilliant relates to the color of the wine. A brilliant wine is one that is clear, with no haze or cloudiness to the color.

browning: As red wines age, their color changes from ruby/purple to dark ruby, to medium ruby, to ruby with an amber edge, to ruby with a brown edge. When a wine is browning it is usually fully mature and not likely to get better.

cedar: Rhône reds can have a bouquet that suggests either faintly or overtly the smell of cedarwood. It is a complex aspect of the bouquet.

chewy: If a wine has a rather dense, viscous texture from a high glycerine content, it is often referred to as being chewy. High-extract wines from great vintages can often be chewy.

closed: The term closed is used to denote that the wine is not showing its potential, which remains locked in because it is too young. Young wines often close up about 12–18 months after bottling, and depending on the vintage and storage conditions, remain in such a state for several years to more than a decade.

complex: One of the most subjective descriptive terms used, a complex wine is a wine that the taster never gets bored with and finds interesting to drink. Complex wines tend to have a variety of subtle scents and flavors that hold one's interest in the wine.

concentrated: Fine wines, whether they are light-, medium-, or full-bodied, should have concentrated flavors. Concentrated denotes that the wine has a depth and richness of fruit that gives it appeal and interest. Deep is a synonym for concentrated.

corked: A corked wine is a flawed wine that has taken on the smell of cork as a result of an unclean or faulty cork. It is perceptible in a bouquet that shows no fruit, only the smell of musty cork, which reminds me of wet cardboard.

cuvée: Many producers in the Rhône Valley and Provence produce special, deluxe lots of wine or a lot of wine from a specific grape variety that they bottle separately. These lots are often referred to as cuvées.

delicate: As this word implies, delicate wines are light, subtle, understated wines that are prized for their shyness rather than for an extroverted, robust character. White wines are usually more delicate than red wines. Few Rhône red wines can correctly be called delicate.

diffuse: Wines that smell and taste unstructured and unfocused are said to be diffuse. When red wines are served at too warm a temperature they often become diffuse.

dumb: A dumb wine is also a closed wine, but the term dumb is used more pejoratively. Closed wines may need only time to reveal their richness and intensity. Dumb wines may never get any better.

earthy: May be used in both a negative and a positive sense; however, I prefer to use earthy to denote a positive aroma of fresh, rich, clean soil. Earthy is a more intense smell than woody or truffle scents.

elegant: Although more white wines than red are described as being elegant, lighter-styled, graceful, well-balanced red wines can be elegant.

extract: This is everything in a wine besides water, sugar, alcohol, and acidity.

exuberant: Like extroverted, somewhat hyper people, wines too can be gushing with fruit and seem nervous and intensely vigorous.

fat: When the Rhône or Provence has an exceptionally hot year for its crop and the wines attain a super sort of maturity, they are often quite rich and concentrated, with low to average acidity. Often such wines are said to be fat, which is a prized commodity. If they become too fat, that is a flaw and they are then called flabby.

flabby: A wine that is too fat or obese is a flabby wine. Flabby wines lack structure and are heavy to taste.

fleshy: Fleshy is a synonym for chewy, meaty, or beefy. It denotes that the wine has a lot of body, alcohol, and extract, and usually a high glycerine content. Châteauneuf-du-Pape and Hermitage are particularly fleshy wines.

floral: Wines made from the Muscat or Viognier grape have a flowery component, and occasionally a red wine will have a floral scent.

forward: A wine is said to be forward when its charm and character are fully revealed. While it may not be fully mature yet, a forward wine is generally quite enjoyable and drinkable. Forward is the opposite of backward. Accessible is a synonym for forward.

focused: Both a fine wine's bouquet and flavor should be focused. Focused simply means that the scents, aromas, and flavors are precise and clearly delineated. If they are not, the wine is like an out-of-focus picture—diffuse, hazy, and possibly problematic.

foudre: Large, oak, sometimes chestnut barrels that vary in size but are significantly larger than the normal oak barrel used in Bordeaux or the *pièce* used in Burgundy. They are widely used in the Rhône and Provence.

fresh: Freshness in both young and old wines is a welcome and pleasing component. A wine is said to be fresh when it is lively and cleanly made. The opposite of fresh is stale.

fruity: A very good wine should have enough concentration of fruit so that it can be said to be fruity. Fortunately, the best wines will have more than just a fruity personality.

full-bodied: Wines rich in extract, alcohol, and glycerine are full-bodied wines. Most Rhône wines are full-bodied.

green: Green wines are wines made from underripe grapes; they lack richness and generosity as well as having a vegetal character. Green wines are infrequently made in the Rhône, although vintages such as 1977 were characterized by a lack of ripening.

hard: Wines with abrasive, astringent tannins or high acidity are said to be hard. Young vintages of Rhône wines can be hard, but they should never be harsh.

harsh: If a wine is too hard it is said to be harsh. Harshness in a wine, young or old, is a flaw.

herbaceous: Many wines have a distinctive herbal smell that is generally said to be herbaceous. Specific herbal smells can be of thyme, lavender, rosemary, oregano, fennel, or basil and are common in Rhône and Provence wines.

hollow: A synonym for shallow, hollow wines are diluted and lack depth and concentration.

honeyed: A common personality trait of specific white Rhône wines, a honeyed wine is one that has the smell and taste of bee's honey.

hot: Rather than mean that the temperature of the wine is too warm to drink, hot denotes that the wine is too high in alcohol and therefore leaves a burning sensation in the back of the throat when swallowed. Wines with alcohol levels in excess of 14.5% often taste hot if the requisite depth of fruit is not present.

jammy: When wines have a great intensity of fruit from excellent ripeness they can be jammy, which is a very concentrated, flavorful wine with superb extract. In great vintages such as 1961, 1978, 1983, and 1985 some of the wines are so concentrated that they are said to be jammy.

leafy: A leafy character in a wine is similar to a herbaceous character only in that it refers to the smell of leaves rather than herbs. A wine that is too leafy is a vegetal or green wine.

lean: Lean wines are slim, rather streamlined wines that lack generosity and fatness but can still be enjoyable and pleasant.

lively: A synonym for fresh or exuberant, a lively wine is usually a young wine with good acidity and a thirst-quenching personality.

long: A very desirable trait in any fine wine is that it be long in the mouth. Long (or length) relates to a wine's finish, meaning that after you swallow the wine, you sense its presence for a long time. (Thirty seconds to several minutes is great length.) In a young wine, the difference between something good and something great is the length of the wine.

lush: Lush wines are velvety, soft, richly fruity wines that are both concentrated and fat. A lush wine can never be an astringent or hard wine.

massive: In great vintages where there is a high degree of ripeness and superb concentration, some wines can turn out to be so big, full-bodied, and rich that they are called massive. A great wine such as the 1961 Hermitage La Chapelle is a textbook example of a massive wine.

meaty: A chewy, fleshy wine is also said to be meaty.

mouth-filling: Big, rich, concentrated wines that are filled with fruit extract and are high in alcohol and glycerine are wines that tend to texturally fill the mouth. A mouth-filling wine is also a chewy, fleshy, fat wine.

musty: Wines aged in dirty barrels or unkept cellars or exposed to a bad cork take on a damp, musty character that is a flaw.

nose: The general smell and aroma of a wine as sensed through one's nose and olfactory senses is often called the wine's nose.

oaky: Many Rhône wines are aged from 6 months to 30 months in various sizes of oak barrels. At some properties, a percentage of the oak barrels may be new, and these barrels impart a toasty, vanillin flavor and smell to the wine. If the wine is not rich and concentrated, the barrels can overwhelm the wine, making it taste overly oaky. Where the wine is rich and concentrated and the winemaker has made a judicious use of barrels, however, the results are a wonderful marriage of fruit and oak.

off: If a wine is not showing its true character, or is flawed or spoiled in some way, it is said to be "off."

overripe: An undesirable characteristic; grapes left too long on the vine become too ripe, lose their acidity, and produce wines that are heavy and unbalanced. This can happen frequently in the hot viticultural areas of the Rhône Valley and Provence if the growers harvest too late.

oxidized: If a wine has been excessively exposed to air during either its making or aging, the wine loses freshness and takes on a stale, old smell and taste. Such a wine is said to be oxidized.

peppery: A peppery quality to a wine is usually noticeable in many Rhône wines that have an aroma of black or white pepper and a pungent flavor.

perfumed: This term usually is more applicable to fragrant, aromatic white wines than to red wines. However, some of the dry white wines (particularly Condrieu) and sweet white wines can have a strong perfumed smell.

plummy: Rich, concentrated wines can often have the smell and taste of ripe plums. When they do, the term plummy is applicable.

ponderous: Ponderous is often used as a synonym for massive, but in my usage a massive wine is simply a big, rich, very concentrated wine with balance, whereas a ponderous wine is a wine that has become heavy and tiring to drink.

pruney: Wines produced from grapes that are overripe take on the character of prunes. Pruney wines are flawed wines.

raisiny: Late-harvest wines that are meant to be drunk at the end of a meal can often be slightly raisiny, which in some ports and sherries is desirable. However, a raisiny quality is a major flaw in a dinner wine.

rich: Wines that are high in extract, flavor, and intensity of fruit.

ripe: A wine is ripe when its grapes have reached the optimum level of maturity. Less than fully mature grapes produce wines that are underripe, and overly mature grapes produce wines that are overripe.

round: A very desirable character of wines, roundness occurs in fully mature wines that have lost their youthful, astringent tannins, and also in young wines that have soft tannins and low acidity.

savory: A general descriptive term that denotes that the wine is round, flavorful, and interesting to drink.

shallow: A weak, feeble, watery or diluted wine lacking concentration is said to be shallow.

sharp: An undesirable trait, sharp wines are bitter and unpleasant with hard, pointed edges.

silky: A synonym for velvety or lush, silky wines are soft, sometimes fat, but never hard or angular.

smoky: Some wines, either because of the soil or because of the barrels used to age the wine, have a distinctive smoky character. Côte Rôtie and Hermitage often have a roasted or smoky quality.

soft: A soft wine is one that is round and fruity, low in acidity, and has an absence of aggressive, hard tannins.

spicy: Wines often smell quite spicy with aromas of pepper, cinnamon, and other well-known spices. These pungent aromas are usually lumped together and called spicy.

stale: Dull, heavy wines that are oxidized or lack balancing acidity for freshness are called stale.

stalky: A synonym for vegetal, but used more frequently to denote that the wine has probably had too much contact with the stems, resulting in a green, vegetal, or stalky character to the wine.

supple: A supple wine is one that is soft, lush, velvety, and very attractively round and tasty. It is a highly desirable characteristic because it suggests that the wine is harmonious.

tannic: The tannins of a wine, which are extracted from the grape skins and stems, are, along with a wine's acidity and alcohol, its lifeline. Tannins give a wine firmness and some roughness when young, but gradually fall away and dissipate. A tannic wine is one that is young and unready to drink.

tart: Sharp, acidic, lean, unripe wines are called tart. In general, a wine that is tart is not pleasurable.

thick: Rich, ripe, concentrated wines that are low in acidity are often said to be thick.

thin: A synonym for shallow; it is an undesirable characteristic for a wine to be thin, meaning that it is watery, lacking in body, and just diluted.

tightly knit: Young wines that have good acidity levels, good tannin levels, and are well made are called tightly knit, meaning they have yet to open up and develop.

toasty: A smell of grilled toast can often be found in wines because the barrels the wines are aged in are charred or toasted on the inside.

tobacco: Some red wines have the scent of fresh tobacco. It is a distinctive and wonderful smell in wine.

unctuous: Rich, lush, intense wines with layers of concentrated, soft, velvety fruit are said to be unctuous.

vegetal: An undesirable characteristic, wines that smell and taste vegetal are usually made from unripe grapes. In some wines, a subtle vegetable garden smell is pleasant and adds complexity, but if it is the predominant character, it is a major flaw.

velvety: A textural description and synonym for lush or silky, a velvety wine is a rich, soft, smooth wine to taste. It is a very desirable characteristic.

viscous: Viscous wines tend to be relatively concentrated, fat, almost thick wines with a great density of fruit extract, plenty of glycerine, and high alcohol content. If they have balancing acidity, they can be tremendously flavorful and exciting wines. If they lack acidity, they are often flabby and heavy.

volatile: A volatile wine is one that smells of vinegar as a result of an excessive amount of acetic bacteria present. It is a seriously flawed wine.

woody: When a wine is overly oaky it is often said to be woody. Oakiness in a wine's bouquet and taste is good up to a point. Once past that point, the wine is woody and its fruity qualities are masked by excessive oak aging.

SELECTED
BIBLIOGRAPHY

Charnay, Pierre. *Vignobles et Vins des Côtes du Rhônes*, Paris: Aubanel, 1985.

Duyker, Hubrecht. *Grands Vins du Rhône et du Midi*. Paris: Editions Fernand, 1985.

Julien, A. *Topographie de Tous les Vignobles Connus*. 1832.

Lichine, Alexis. *Guide to the Wines and Vineyards of France*, New York: Alfred A. Knopf, 1985.

―――. *The New Encyclopedia of Wines and Spirits*. New York: Alfred A. Knopf, 1986.

Livingstone-Learmonth, John, and Melvyn C. Master. *The Wines of the Rhône*. London: Faber & Faber, 1978.

Robinson, Jancis. *Vines, Grapes and Wines*. New York: Alfred A. Knopf, 1986.

Spurrier, Steven. *Academie du Vin Wine Course*. London: Century Publishing, 1983.

INDEX

ABOUT THE AUTHOR

Robert M. Parker, Jr., is the author and publisher of *The Wine Advo-cate*, and the author of *Bordeaux: The Definitive Guide for the Wines Produced Since 1961* and *Parker's Wine Buyer's Guide*. He lives with his wife, Patricia, in Parkton, Maryland.

Much of the material in this book is based upon tastings and research done by Robert M. Parker In conjunction with the writing and publishing of *The Wine Advocate,* an independent consumer's guide to fine wine that is issued six times a year. A one-year subscription is $30.00 for delivery in the United States, $35.00 for delivery in Canada, and $55.00 for delivery via air mail anywhere in the world. Subscriptions or a sample copy may be obtained by writing to *The Wine Advocate,* P.O. Box 311, Monkton, MD 21111.